THE GUINNESS BOOK OF
RECORDED SOUND

THE GUINNESS BOOK OF RECORDED SOUND

ROBERT & CELIA DEARLING
with Brian Rust

GUINNESS BOOKS

ACKNOWLEDGEMENTS

The measure of interest in the subject of recorded sound and the history of the record industry may be gauged by the ready and enthusiastic assistance offered by many people whom the authors approached during the writing of this book. It is not possible to mention all these kind helpers by name, but our particular thanks go to Colin Biggs, BA, music and drama librarian, Lincoln, for much patience and co-operation; to Derek Lewis of the BBC Gramophone Library and Giancarlo Bongiovanni, present owner of the longest-established record shop, for helpful answers to correspondence queries; and to James Fleming (Marketing Manager, BBC Records), Miss Carol Fulton (PolyGram), and Peter Higgins (Production Manager, EMI Records), for willing assistance with illustrations. It is largely due to the authoritative co-operation of Peter Higgins that we were able to sort out the tangled history of the various companies that combined in 1931 to form EMI, and it was he who secured for us a copy of the new photograph of the HMV dog-and-trumpet trade mark painting which appears on the cover of this book. This, and the other EMI trade marks which occur in the text, are reproduced by kind permission of EMI Records Ltd.

Enthusiast Norman Stevens, who publishes the valuable bi-monthly magazine *Sounds Vintage*, also assisted with illustrations, as did Ray Tunnicliff, owner of the Rutland Cottage Music Museum, Whaplode St Catherines, Lincolnshire, which is the official museum of the Fairground Society and a fascinating repository of historical gramophones, phonographs, records, cylinders, and other memorabilia.

To these, to countless other friendly helpers, and to the editorial staff of Guinness Superlatives, goes the authors' warm gratitude.

EDITOR: Alex E Reid
DESIGN AND LAYOUT: Michael Morey
PICTURE RESEARCH: Sheila Goldsmith

First edition 1984
© Robert J & Celia A Dearling and Guinness Superlatives Ltd 1984

Published by
Guinness Superlatives Ltd
2 Cecil Court, London Road, Enfield, Middlesex

'Guinness' is a registered trade mark of Guinness Superlatives Ltd

British Library Cataloguing in Publication Data
Dearling, Robert
  The Guinness book of recorded sound.
  1. Sound – Recording and reproducing – History
  2. Music – History and criticism
  3. Sound recordings
  I. Title II. Dearling, Celia II. Rust, Brian
  621.389'32   TK7881.4
  ISBN 0–85112–274–4

Typeset by Fakenham Photosetting Ltd, Fakenham, Norfolk
Printed and bound in Yugoslavia by Mladinska Knjiga, Ljubljana

CONTENTS

INTRODUCTION

'I never look upon gramophone records as an extravagance but as a natural accessory to life.'

These words were spoken by actor, mimic and musician Peter Ustinov in a BBC programme as long ago as 1950. At the time, the long playing record was barely 2 years old in America, and was only just being introduced onto the British market, so most, if not all, of Mr Ustinov's experience of what he called the gramophone record had been restricted to noisy-surfaced, fracture-prone, short-playing-time 78s which gave a sound we would regard today at best as only a narrow approximation to concert-hall tone and at worst a grossly distorted parody of that sound. Yet this musician had accepted them in spite of all their faults. And he was not the first to express his appreciation of the invention in complimentary terms. Dr Percy A Scholes, a musical scholar best known for his *Oxford Companion to Music*, was an early champion of the gramophone as a 'populariser' of music and the writer of the notes accompanying the *Columbia History of Music* (1930–9). He had this to say in his *First Book of the Gramophone Record* (1927):

A very few years ago, fine music was the private preserve of a few people living in the largest cities. The gramophone, the Pianola, and Broadcasting have changed all that. The Pianola has certain advantages over the Gramophone; for instance it allows you a say in the interpretation, and it gives you genuine piano tone. But the Gramophone has these great advantages over the Pianola – that it is cheaper and that it can reproduce voices, words, and the tone-colours of stringed and wind and percussion instruments; and though it costs rather more than Broadcasting it triumphs over that in one or two ways, for it allows you to choose your own concert times, programmes, and performers, and to repeat any item as many times as you wish. By means of the Gramophone people everywhere can enjoy the Queen's Hall Orchestra, or Chaliapin, or the London String Quartet, or Sammons, or Samuel, or Busoni. No other agency of musical reproduction for years to come is likely to reduce the popularity of the Gramophone. At all events it is as popular now as it ever was, and I am told by Gramophone dealers that if Broadcasting is affecting the sales of records in any way, it is affecting them favourably, probably because it is spreading musical taste and awakening the desire to domesticate the most attractive of the works 'wirelessly' heard.

It is perhaps significant that this vote of approval for the gramophone record should have been written soon after the first electrical recordings came on sale. It demonstrates that this technical advance had brought the medium to a point of acceptability at which it was fit to be taken seriously by those who mattered in the musical world.

Other writers, and musicians in general, were not so impressed by the artistic possibilities of the gramophone. Who can blame them? Sir Arthur Sullivan expressed grave fears that the invention had brought with it the means by which countless musical items of low or zero value could be preserved for ever (an opinion which a century of enlightenment has not annihilated), while recording artists in those early days were forced to work in cramped studios without an audience, in conditions hardly designed to put them at their ease or draw from them their best efforts. Once made, the recordings were not marketed with the greatest delicacy; classical issues were particularly prone to inept handling, as the example of three early recordings of popular overtures will illustrate: Rossini's *William Tell* falls naturally into four parts: Andante; Allegro; Andante pastorale; and Storm. HMV issued the first three parts on three single-sided 12in (30·5cm) discs with the New Symphony Orchestra conducted by Sir Landon

Ronald. The fourth part, however, came out on one double-sided 10in (25·4cm) disc played by the Band of the Coldstream Guards under Capt Mackenzie Rogan – with Suppé's *Poet and Peasant* Overture on the other side! Tchaikovsky's *1812* Overture (abbreviated) appeared on three single-sided 12in HMV discs, non-consecutively numbered, the first two at 79rpm, the last at 78rpm. Similarly, Wagner's *Tannhäuser* Overture, again abbreviated, was issued on two single-sided 12in discs, non-consecutively numbered, the first side at 78rpm, the second at 80rpm.

Before World War I, the HMV catalogue contained two different recordings of the popular *Sextet* from Donizetti's opera *Lucia di Lammermoor*, both with Caruso and both at 30/– (£1.50) on single-sided discs. The standard price for such discs, however, was 6/– (30p), and in 1916 the same company issued the same music in an arrangement for violin (!) on a double-sided disc at 2/6 (12½p), coupled with Fauré's *Berceuse*. In

CELEBRITY RECORDS

SEXTETS

CARUSO, GALLI-CURCI, EGENER, JOURNET, DE LUCA and
    BADA
             12-inch record 30s.
   2—054067 Chi mi frena (" Lucia di Lammermoor ")   (*Donizetti*) (79)

CARUSO, SCOTTI, JOURNET, SEMBRICH, SEVERINA and
    DADDI
             12-inch record 30s.
   054205 Chi mi frena (" Lucia di Lammermoor ")   (*Donizetti*) (78)

QUINTET

CARUSO, HEMPEL, DUCHÊNE, ROTHIER and DE SEGUROLA
             12-inch record 25s.
   2—064050 È scherzo, od è folia (" Un Ballo in Maschera," Act I.)   (*Verdi*) (80)

QUARTETS

BATTISTINI, COLAZZA, SILLICH, E. CORSI and Chorus
             12-inch record 12s. 6d.
   054107 O sommo Carlo (" Ernani ")   (*Verdi*) (78)

CARUSO, ALDA, JACOBY and JOURNET
             12-inch records 20s.
   2—054031 Che vuol dir ciò (" Marta ")   (*Flotow*) (80)

CARUSO, FARRAR, GILIBERT and JOURNET
             12-inch records 20s.
   2—034003 " Seigneur Dieu " (" Faust "—Garden Scene, Part I.) (*Gounod*) (80)
   2—034004 " Eh quoi, toujours seule " (" Faust "—Garden Scene Part II.) (*Gounod*) (80)

CARUSO, GALLI-CURCI, PERINI and DE LUCA
             12-inch record 16s. 6d.
   2—054066 Un dì, se ben rammentomi (" Rigoletto ")   (*Verdi*) (79)

CARUSO, HEMPEL, ROTHIER, DE SEGUROLA and Chorus
             12-inch record 20s.
   2—054052 La rivedrà nell' estasi (" Un Ballo in Maschera," Act I.) (*Verdi*) (80)

These records should be played with " His Master's Voice " needles, sold only in boxes bearing our copyright picture, " His Master's Voice," on the lid

1

A listing of 'prestige' recordings from a 1914 HMV catalogue.

short, the whole scene was one of artistic and marketing chaos, and it is a wonder that the industry survived such abuse. Nevertheless, the appeal of recorded music bred a generation of enthusiasts and the industry grew and developed in a way not altogether to the liking of Thomas Edison, the real pioneer of recorded sound. (See Section II.)

In attempting to chart the achievements and problems of the industry we make no excuse for the fact that, of our nine Sections, by far the largest is VIII: Repertoire. Some authorities hold that the technical aspect of recorded sound – high fidelity – is the central pillar of the industry; that music is only a servant, to be tarted up and slicked down for immaculate presentation to the customer. There are few more depressing sounds in life than a brilliant, lifelike, technically impeccable, recording of relatively valueless music. What criminal waste of sophisticated recording techniques! Even worse, in some ways, are the glaringly artificial recordings of good music, made in a studio full of microphones by a tenth-rate ensemble. Every boring note is ruthlessly relayed to the listener in a grotesque misrepresentation of well-balanced sound. Somewhere between all these abuses lies true, lifelike, recorded sound, but central to everything is the music itself, without which there would never have been a record industry. Our Repertoire Section, including its sub-sections dealing with non-musical recordings, will illustrate the gradual growth and maturity of that industry. For the most part the arcane world of reproducing equipment is left to those better qualified to deal with it.

Numerous sources have been consulted in the preparation of the present study. Not infrequently, a 'fact' given in one authoritative source will be flatly contradicted in another, while a third may skate cleverly round the topic without coming down either way. We have made strenuous and sometimes fruitless efforts to track down the truth, but if the reader feels that we have misinterpreted any fact or simply taken as gospel a 'fact' that is simply wrong, the authors would be most grateful to receive a correction. Some of our references are deliberately approximate (see in particular Section VII, where reasons are given as to why disc sizes and speeds have to be rounded up or down), and in our category lists there has been no attempt at exhaustive data. In fact, during our research and preparation, we had decided to make a complete international listing of record labels, together with dates of introduction, demise, and brief description, but it quickly became clear that such a listing would not only be virtually impossible to compile in one lifetime, due to conflicting evidence from different sources, but if completed would take more space than has been allotted for the whole book. Therefore, 'completeness' has given way to what we feel is a more useful exercise: profiles of the major and most important companies.

It is likewise neither useful nor possible to give a list of the thousands of artists who have made records, but some of those artists stand out prominently by virtue of their popularity. These we have consigned to our 'halls of fame', their lives and achievements encapsulated for convenience.

In the ensuing Sections we examine the steps that led to the first viable sound reproducer; then we follow the history, fortunes and misfortunes, of the huge industry it created.

Before Edison

Bishop Albert Magnus (c 1200–80), the first man to store sound?

MARY EVANS PICTURE LIBRARY

In the year 1877 a patent was filed by an American inventor for a device that has changed and influenced the lives of an ever-increasing number of people. That invention preserved sound on a tin-foil-coated cylinder, and reproduced that sound at will. The inventor's name was Thomas Alva Edison and the patent was granted on 19 February, 1878. The first working phonograph had appeared.

However, although the first in a long line of inventions which translate sound to a mechanical format for storage purposes, the phonograph itself lay at the end of other experiments both practical and theoretical. This book is concerned with the *reproduction* of actual sound by mechanical (and/or electrical) means, and not with the mechanical *production* of sound. It is an important distinction.

The *production* of sound by machines has a long and complicated history. Strictly speaking, any musical instrument is a machine for producing music, and such machines were made by earliest man. Later, man's inventive ingenuity devised ways of generating sound by machinery second-hand, so to speak: by building devices that, when operated by the turn of a handle or by clockwork (invented about 1000 years ago), would make sounds without the direct intervention of the operator. The striking clock, invented in the late 13th century, comes into this category, but Plato's design for a water organ that played a tune every hour, once the flow of water into a container had brought that container to a weight sufficient to set off the mechanism, is very much earlier, dating from the fourth century BC.

A revolving barrel into which pins were fitted, to flex and release tuned wooden or metal tongues in a predetermined order, was invented soon after the appearance of the clockwork motor, ie around AD 1000, and this or some similar revolving device such as the pinned or holed disc, has been the fundamental design feature of countless musical machines of more recent date, including the musical box in most of its forms, the polyphon, mechanical carillons, organs, and the like. All are devices for producing sounds mechanically, and as such are outside the terms of reference of our present study.

The *reproducing* of sound waves is a much later and very much more sophisticated concept. It involves the capture of existing but invisible sound waves (or pulses) as they pass through the air, the storing of these pulses in some mechanical form, and, by some action upon this mechanical record, the *re*production of the original sound (or of an approximation to it) at will at a later time.

Were all the problems solved many centuries before Edison, the solutions lost again in a single moment of terror? According to Isaac D'Israeli in his *Curiosities of Literature* (1859):

> In the thirteenth century a certain Albert Magnus constructed a piece of mechanism which sent forth distinct vocal sounds, by which Thomas Aquinas was so greatly terrified that he struck at it with his staff, and to the mortification of Albert, annihilated the curious labour of thirty years.

Perhaps the good Albert's invention was merely a clockwork friction device, given added volume by a soundbox, or some gravity-operated gadget that gave forth a wail. In any event, it is unlikely that he would have approached the problem in the 13th century with all the scientific knowledge of the 19th.

In the wake of the Industrial Revolution the atmosphere was right for research and experimentation into the nature of things hitherto taken very much for granted. Electricity had been discovered and its effects (but not its nature) described, everyday natural phenomena such as light, sound, the workings of the human body, time and space, were being increasingly searchingly investigated, and ancient mechanical principles such as the lever and the Archimedes screw were being applied to ever more sophisticated inventions. Even so, the capture and reproduction of sound pulses required the patient and persistent endeavours of a number of men, each with his own original research, to bring it to a point at which it might be exploited commercially.

In 1857, Edouard Léon Scott de Martinville (1817–79), a typesetter of Irish descent but resident in France, built a machine which he called the Phonautograph. It consisted of a barrel-shaped cylinder with one end larger than the other, tilted about 25° from the horizontal. The narrow lower end was attached to a vertical membrane. From this membrane protruded a bristle. The wide opposite end of the barrel was open. When sound was fed into this open bell, the pressure of the sound pulses within the barrel caused the membrane to vibrate, this in turn causing the bristle to wag from side to side. This vibrating bristle traced a wavy line onto the smoke-blackened surface of a sheet of paper wrapped round a cylinder cranked by hand, leaving a visible record of the sound. The first complete winding was confused and partly obliterated by the second in the early model, so

Scott's associate, Koenig, introduced a threaded rod to move the cylinder laterally as it revolved, thus giving a helical trace. It was in this form that the Phonautograph was demonstrated in London in 1859. A later model substituted a disc for the cylinder, **the first time a disc was used as a sound storage medium**.

Twenty years earlier still, the French physicist J C M Duhamel, working on thermal stresses, produced on a strip of paper a trace of the vibrations of a tensioned cord. Yet earlier, in 1807, the English scientist Thomas Young (1773–1829) applied a vibrating tuning fork to the surface of a rotating cylinder and obtained a visual record of its deflections. **This was the first known occasion upon which sound waves had been converted to a visible pattern for sub-**

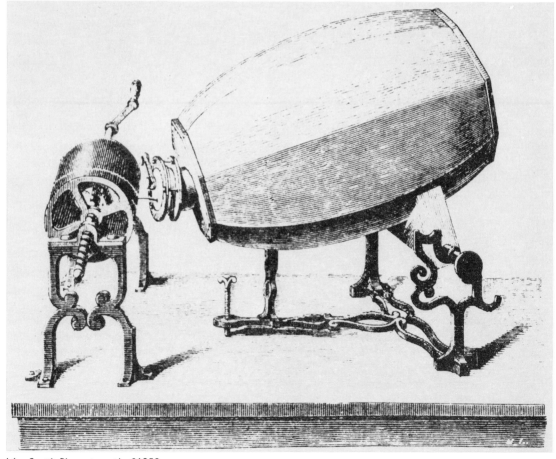

Léon Scott's Phonautograph of 1859.   ROYAL SCOTTISH MUSEUM

Alexander Graham Bell's first telephone, complete with 'sink-plunger' transmitter and receiver. MARY EVANS PICTURE LIBRARY

sequent analysis. Earlier experiments had shown that sound vibrations could be translated into mechanical movement by the use, for instance, of a mirror which, when fixed to a vibrating object, would trace light curves onto a screen, but these results were ephemeral; they could not be stored. Both Young's and Duhamel's experiments were purely mechanical in nature; the impulses behind Scott's researches, however, would seem to have been mainly medical but partially, perhaps, the result of curiosity. By the middle of the 19th century scientists had solved many of the puzzles posed by the observed nature of the everyday world, and advances were being made in the understanding of the various malfunctions of the human body. Speech therapists were turning to science for answers concerning the nature of vocal production: the way in which given sounds are produced by the vocal cords, the position and flexing of the tongue, the shape of the mouth cavity, and so on. They reasoned that an understanding of the hidden mechanics of the subject would help to solve the question of why these mechanisms bore or developed faults in some patients. This research led inevitably to investigations into the nature of sound itself, and Scott's Phonautograph showed by the curious wave formations on its paper-covered cylinder just how intricate are the sound waves produced by the human voice.

Léon Scott had succeeded in *transforming* sound into visual lines for subsequent examination, but the sound had become mute.

Alexander Melville Bell (1819–1905) was elocution teacher at Edinburgh University from 1843 to 1865 and at London's University College for the following 5 years. Two of his three sons had died from tuberculosis; when the third, Alexander Graham (1847–1922) also contracted this disease, at the age of 23, it was decided in 1870 to move the family from London's fogs to the healthier air of Canada, where there was a vacancy for a lecturer on philology and linguistics at Queen's College, Kingston, Ontario.

A M Bell's earlier work on the mechanics of speech production and an international phonetic alphabet resulted in his book *Visual Speech: the Science of Universal Alphabetics* in 1867. This dealt with how vocal sounds are made, and how to represent them unequivocally by written characters. It did not enter into the mechanical problem of engraving those sounds for permanent study, as had Léon Scott's Phonautograph.

Young Alexander Graham Bell had studied his father's activities with great interest, and, only 2 years after moving to Canada, he left for Boston, Mass., where he opened a school for training teachers of the deaf. Speech mechanics were the stuff of which his courses were made, and by 1876 he had developed a device that would transmit the human voice electrically over a distance. (This had been done mechanically with string stretched between two resonating boxes as early as 1667 by Robert Hooke in London.) Bell's device consisted of a strip of iron attached to a membrane which, when agitated by the sound waves of a voice, would vibrate before a battery-activated electromagnet. This sent an electric current along a wire, at the far end of which was a similar device used in reverse that reproduced the voice. **The first words spoken over the telephone** were from Bell to his assistant: 'Mr Watson, come here; I want you.' This 'telephone' (Gk: *tele* = far; + *phone* = sound – the first use of the word was for a megaphone in 1796) was submitted for patent on 14 February, 1876, and the American Telephone & Telegraph Company was formed later that year to market Bell's inventions.

Bell had *transmitted* sound electrically from one place to another (which, in theory, might be over an unlimited distance), but the sound was still ephemeral. It needed another step in the control of sound before it could be *stored* for later retrieval.

That step was very nearly taken by the Frenchman Charles Cros (1842–88) who, in April 1877, lodged with the French Academy of Sciences a sealed envelope containing a paper titled 'Procédé d'enregistrement et de reproduction des phénomènes perçus par l'ouïe' in which he described his invention of a glass disc, blackened with candle smoke, bearing an undulating spiral that had been traced on it by a stylus agitated by sound waves through the air. The spiral line would be made permanent in a metal matrix by the use of photoengraving, and the sound could then be *reproduced* simply by tracking the engraved spiral with another stylus. Unfortunately, although Cros published details of his invention in *La Semaine du Clergé* in October 1877, the device, which he called the Paléophone, was not successful, and it was left to another inventive genius, following rather different lines, actually to construct a working model.

The scene was set at last for the appearance of Thomas Alva Edison's phonograph.

Edison and the Cylinder

Thomas Alva Edison was the youngest of the seven children of Samuel Ogden Edison and Nancy Elliott Edison. He was born on 11 February, 1847, in the early morning, in the village of Milan, Ohio. His inquisitiveness as a child led him to ask questions constantly, and when the answers were in some way unsatisfactory to him he conducted his own experiments, sometimes with disastrous results. The story of the barn is well known. After it went up in smoke, fired deliberately by young Thomas 'just to see what it would do', his parents considered it wiser to answer his interminable questions more carefully.

His formal education was brief: three weeks at a grammar school at the age of 8. Thereafter, his mother attempted to fill the role of tutor, but Edison's mind was of the sort that learns for itself, following its own paths to knowledge untrammelled by timetables and curriculae and simply ignoring things it considered unimportant, like spelling. Fortunately his mother had sufficient intelligence to guide his questioning imagination profitably, leading him to the purchase of an elementary physics book, R G Parker's *School of Natural Philosophy*. Although this proved to be a turning point for young Thomas, it brought an unwelcome new dimension to the lives of his family, for experiments with chemicals, odd bits of wire, batteries, and the new-fangled electricity absorbed all his time and pocket money, and explosions of varying seriousness became a frequent part of everyday life. Within a short time he had produced his own telegraph system and was working on a Morse transmitter and receiver.

At the age of 12 he took his first job as a newsboy on the railway and was fascinated by the 'real' telegraph system and how it operated. Soon, he had built his own laboratory, right on the train. Later came a newspaper printing plant – probably the world's first mobile one. As the result of an accident at this time he became partially deaf, but characteristically he turned this to advantage: in the semi-isolation that deafness brought him he was able to concentrate on reading about things that most interested him in order to improve his education

(he taught himself French), and he found that the loud clicking of the telegraph would penetrate his impaired hearing while distracting sounds of less importance would not. This in turn fitted him well for a succession of posts as a telegrapher, but since he put his experiments before the requirements of these posts, he found himself dismissed from each one of them almost as soon as he had started.

Edison's first announced invention was for a 'mode of transmission both ways on a single wire'. It was described in an article by Milton F Adams (although Adams had been substantially guided by Edison in the matter of details), published in *The Journal of the Telegraph* dated June 1868. In it, Edison is described as being employed by the Western Union office in Boston, a post he had occupied only since arriving in that city in March. However, some of his earlier exploits at the Western Union office – such as his 'cockroach oxidizer', a typically unofficial, if useful, invention – had been noted already in the local papers. Working on nightshift, Edison began to set a pattern that eventually gave him the reputation of not needing any sleep at all, for by day he would continue with his inventions and his reading. Soon after taking the Western Union job he had purchased a second-hand copy of Faraday's *Experimental Researches in Electricity*, and this became of supreme importance to him since it dealt with research in a non-technical, not-too-mathematical, way, that Edison could follow empirically.

The onerous duties at Western Union eventually proved too oppressive for Edison's restless mind – or he became too restless for Western Union to handle – and he left shortly after Christmas 1868 to devote himself to full time inventing. **His first patent** had already been filed in Washington in October 1868: No 90 646. It was for a telegraphic vote-recording machine, and it was granted on 1 June, 1869. Unfortunately, this and other inventions failed to achieve the success he had hoped, and he found himself in debt. The experience taught him to concentrate only upon inventions for which an obvious need was evident; speculative experiments were to be left strictly alone.

Thomas Alva Edison with his first commercial phonograph in 1878.

Edison's sketch, from which the first phonograph was made.

Destitute, he made his way to New York in May 1869, a move that changed his luck and his life. He happened to be on hand when the Broad Street Gold Indicator seized up in the midst of a busy day's trading in stock, and Edison cured the fault. That earned him a position as a maintenance technician at an attractive wage. His dream of being a freelance inventor was thus delayed, but eventually he set up in business with some associates to market his inventions and various other electrical services in Jersey City. By keeping to his vow to invent only that for which he saw a real need, financial rewards for his efforts at last began to flow in, and he founded businesses at Newark, Menlo Park, and West Orange in New Jersey, at first mainly for the manufacture of appliances for the booming telegraphic industry, but later for research into a wide range of electromechanical inventions. After a hectic lifetime of brilliant inventions, many of which led him into prolonged, painful and expensive litigation, he died at West Orange on Sunday, 18 October, 1931, aged 84.

Edison's inventions ranged from the rat- and insect-exterminators of his early years, through developments in telephony, electric railways, dynamos, batteries, etc, to moving pictures, building construction and the motor tyre, and he filed altogether 1093 patents. The one of prime concern to us here is No 200 521, issued on 19 February, 1878, for the phonograph.

The first use of the word 'phonograph' occurred in 1835, when Egyptologists used it to describe a form of hieroglyphic writing. It appeared again in 1845 as a name for characters in a style of Pitman's phonetic shorthand. **Its first use as the description of a machine** was in 1863 for an electromagnetic Phonograph described by F B Fenby which was never built. **The first use of the word by Edison** appears in his notebook for 12 August, 1877.

Edison's attention had been absorbed for much of 1877 by the problems of storing and reproducing sound. His patent No 213 554, applied for on 3 February that year, was a design for a paper disc upon which could be stored telegraph messages for subsequent transmission at high speed, and at one time he considered the use of a disc of similar design for the storing of actual voices for later reproduction. He also turned to paper tape, thereby anticipating the principles of J A O'Neill's tape recorder of half a century later (see p. 99, Section V). In fact, Edison made notable progress in this field: **the first occasion upon which recorded sound was actually reproduced** is best told in Edison's own words, as quoted in *Edison and his Inventions* by J B McClure, which was published in 1870, close enough in time to the event for it to have a good chance of offering an authentic account.

I was singing . . . to the mouthpiece of a telephone, when the vibrations of the wire sent the fine steel point into my finger. That set me thinking. If I could record the actions of the point, and then send that point over the same surface afterwards, I saw no reason why the thing would not talk.

I tried the experiment, first on a strip of telegraph paper, and found that the point made an alphabet. I shouted the word 'halloo! halloo!' into the mouthpiece, ran the paper back over the steel point and heard a faint *'halloo! halloo!'* in return! I determined to make a machine that would work accurately, and gave my assistants instructions, telling them what I had discovered.

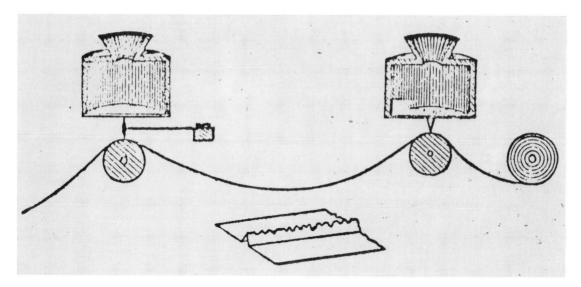

Above *The device using 'knife-edge' paper tape, Edison's first sound-storage medium.*

Right *The first tin-foil phonograph.*

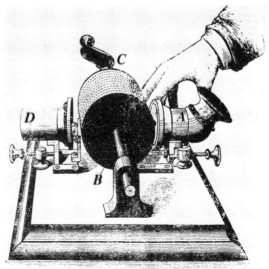

They laughed at me. I bet fifteen cigars with one of my assistants, Mr Adams, that the thing would work the first time without a break, and won them. That's the whole story. The discovery came through the pricking of a finger.

The paper tape was developed far enough for it to be described in some detail in an article in *Scientific American* dated 17 November, 1877. In simple terms, the paper strip was folded to form a central ridge along its length. The peak of this ridge (the 'knife-edge' Edison called it) was indented, via a diaphragm, by a stylus with a chisel-shaped point as the paper was driven across a revolving drum. The indentations were then reproduced by running the indented paper past a similar stylus attached via a flexible arm to another diaphragm.

By the time the description of this paper-tape machine had appeared in *Scientific American*, Edison had turned his attention to the revolving cylinder of Scott's Phonautograph. At the time he was interested in the commercial possibilities offered by a machine that would record and play back short messages. Playing time was of no

great importance: the theoretically endless duration of a roll of ridged paper was of less use than a self-contained cylinder offering about 2 minutes' playing time, certainly long enough for most of the messages that might need to be preserved in a busy office. The paper strip was discarded in favour of a piece of tin foil wrapped round a cylinder.

The first tin foil phonograph to be demonstrated outside Edison's workshops at Menlo Park was taken into the editor's office of *Scientific American*, and, in the words of the article

Some terms from Edison's British patent No 1644 of 24 April, 1878.

Edison's term	Meaning	Today's equivalent
'Phonograph'	The mouthpiece/diaphragm/stylus assembly that indents the surface of the 'phonogram' (and, by extension, the whole machine).	Cutting head
'Phonogram'	The object whose surface is modified by the 'phonograph', thus storing the information. (Later Edison described as a phonogram any recorded cylinder sent to a correspondent in lieu of a letter.)	Record
'Phonet'	The stylus/diaphragm assembly that traces the engravings on the phonogram and transmits them to the air.	Pick-up, or tone arm (which, however, now transmits the engravings to the amplifier).
'Indenting point'	A point made of 'diamond or other very hard substance' that directly engraves the phonogram.	Cutting stylus (the origin of the word 'stylus' goes back to the ancient Assyrians: it was an engraving or embossing implement for making pictographs and hieroglyphics).

published in the 22 December, 1877, issue of that journal, was displayed as follows:

Mr Thomas A Edison recently came into this office, placed a little machine on our desk, turned a crank, and the machine inquired as to our health, asked us how we liked the phonograph, informed us that *it* was very well, and bid us a cordial goodnight.

Two days later, on 24 December, 1877, Edison filed his invention at the Patent Office.

The machine with which Edison had made so memorable and dramatic an impact had been built by John Kruesi from Edison's sketches and verbal instructions, and had been completed on 6 December, 1877. It consisted of four components, keyed to an accompanying drawing:

A: the 'phonograph', a mouthpiece connected to a diaphragm, from the centre of which protruded a stylus;
B: a grooved brass cylinder about 4in (10cm) in diameter, mounted on a threaded shaft which was turned by a small handle, C. A sheet of tin foil coated the cylinder, and when indented with a recording this tin foil was known as a 'phonogram'.
D: the 'phonet', a reproducing unit comprising a metal point held against the tin foil by a spring and attached to a second diaphragm.

To make a record (or 'phonogram'), the operator shouted into the mouthpiece of the 'phonograph' while turning the crank, and the vibrations of his voice were conveyed via the diaphragm and the stylus to the tin foil, indenting it with a series of small marks. To reproduce the sound, the 'phonet's' stylus was placed in contact with the revolving cylinder and followed its indentations, these in turn vibrating its diaphragm. Playing time was $1\frac{1}{2}$–2 minutes, depending upon the speed of cranking.

The world's first phonograph company was the Edison Speaking Phonograph Company of 203 Broadway, New York, founded on 24 January, 1878. It leased out machines on a quarterly basis, together with a supply of tin foil blanks.

The first Edison-type phonograph to be built in England was made by Post Office employee Augustus Stroh (later to become the inventor of the amplifying horns applied to stringed instruments for use in early recordings of music) for the Chief Engineer of the General Post Office, William Preece, and demonstrated to the Royal Institution on 1 February, 1878.

The first commercial manufacture of phonographs in the UK was by the London Stereoscopic Company, founded later in 1878 in Cheapside and Regent Street.

In June the same year Edison put forward a prophetic list of ten uses which he felt the future would find for his phonograph and its successors. This is his list, together with commentaries as to how his predictions have come to pass.

1 Letter writing, and all kinds of dictation without the aid of a stenographer.

This avenue has been explored largely through the tape medium, as in the modern letter cassette and the Dictaphone, but Edison's phonograph *was* in a sense a 'dictaphone'; we have seen that he thought of it primarily as an office machine. Wax- and ferric-coated re-usable disc dictating machines have been used since World War II.

2 Phonographic books, which will speak to blind people without effort on their part.

Talking books for the blind first appeared in 1934, issued by the National Institute for the Blind on 24rpm discs. Other projects have been launched, usually utilising slow speeds and long playing times, but the greatest boon to the blind has been the tape cartridge and cassette, which may be operated with ease by the non-sighted. However, Edison was not the first to envisage talking books. **The first fictitious description of mechanical sound reproduction** occurs in Savinien Cyrano de Bergerac's (1619–55) *États et empires de la Lune* (published in 1657): 'A metal device full of strange springs and minute machinery. Really a book, but a wonderful book, lacking pages and characters, to be understood by the ears, not the eyes. To read, one merely winds up the machine to vitalise its nerves, and turns a pointer to a desired chapter, whereupon there emerges, as from the mouth of a man, the many and various sounds of language.'

3 The teaching of elocution.

Alexander Graham Bell, in the earliest days of the phonograph, considered its use in speech therapy, but largely the teaching of elocution is merely a by-product of sound recording, since the student will inevitably learn by imitation. Would-be orators find the instant play-back facility of tape to be of more use.

4 Music – the phonograph will undoubtedly be liberally devoted to music.

Undoubtedly! However, whereas Edison failed to appreciate the phonograph's full potential as a disseminator of fine music, only to be proved wrong, Sir Arthur Sullivan warned that the invention would perpetuate much musical rubbish. He has been proved right. **The first musical recording** was made in mid-1878 when Jules Levy, cornet, performed *Yankee Doodle* at a public demonstration of the phonograph in New York.

5 The family record; preserving the sayings, the voices, and the last words of the dying members of the family, as of great men. (See also No 8.)

This depends upon the home-recording facility, which faded with the production of hard-surfaced permanent cylinders and discs, returning again after World War II with the advent of the domestic tape recorder. It may be considered, in any case, that members of a family present at the deathbed of a loved one, may have too many things on their minds to allow for the setting up of a recording session.

6 Musical boxes, toys, etc. A doll which may speak, sing, cry, or laugh may be promised our children for the Christmas holidays ensuing.

The first talking dolls and phonographic musical boxes were developed in 1878 by Oliver D Russell, who worked separately from, but was answerable to, Edison.

7 Clocks that should announce in speech the hour of the day, call you to lunch, and send your lover home at ten.

In about 1911 the German company B Hiller made 300 talking clocks which announced the quarters for 12 hours per day.

8 Preservation of language by reproduction of our Washingtons, our Lincolns, our Gladstones.

The first politician to make a recording was President Rutherford B Hayes, in The White House during April 1878, but this cylinder has not survived. Of the three statesmen named by Edison, only Gladstone survived into the recording era – and was duly recorded. Many

Left *Audio-typing, c 1895, from a Bell and Tainter wax-cylinder Graphophone.* ANN RONAN PICTURE LIBRARY

Below *Children recording their lessons on an Edison phonograph, Chicago, 1893.* ANN RONAN PICTURE LIBRARY

Opposite top *Piano recording in the late 1880s, using an Edison phonograph.* ANN RONAN PICTURE LIBRARY

Opposite bottom right *A domestic tape recorder advert of the 1950s.*

Opposite bottom left *Pat Simmons, the face behind Britain's most widely-used recorded information service, the Speaking Clock.* BY COURTESY OF BRITISH TELECOM

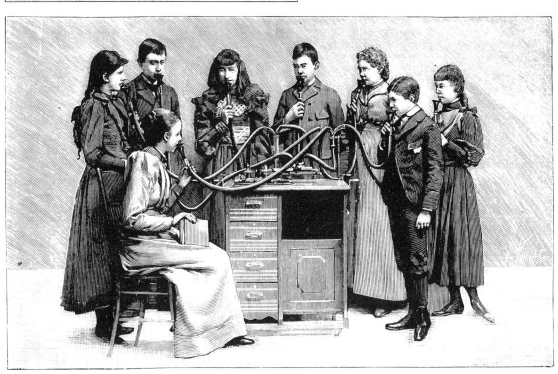

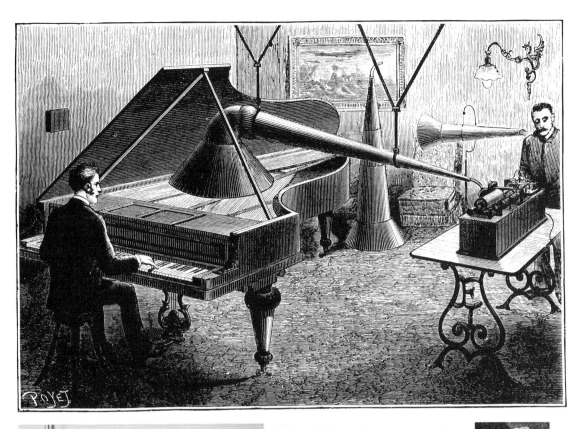

Making talking dolls fitted with Edison phonographs; a New York depot in 1890. The cylinders were recorded individually.

politicians have recorded since, **the largest repertoire being** that of Sir Winston S Churchill: apart from the large series and sets of records issued by HMV and Decca on LP in the 1960s (see Section VIII, Part Two: Statesmen), the Prime Minister had time during the war to record many HMV 78s titled *The Progress of the War* in multi-disc series. In 1965, both HMV and Decca issued commemorative recordings covering his State Funeral.

9 Educational purposes; such as preserving the instructions of a teacher so that the pupil can refer to them at any moment; or learn spelling lessons.

Again, this application relies upon being able to record and play back in domestic or academic surroundings, and is satisfied by tape. In a wider sense, records are used in many educational spheres:

Languages: **first** by the Academy of Languages, New York, in 1891; then a set of 50 cylinders with books by Dr Richard Rosenthal, made for Columbia in 1893; subsequently by Linguaphone, Assimil (ie Pitmans), EMI, Durium (a course directed by M E M Stephan), and by Visaphone on 33⅓rpm 7in (17·8cm) discs.

Histories of Music: **first**, the *Columbia History of Music* (UK and USA, edited by Dr Percy A Scholes, 1930–9); *Two Thousand Years of Music* (Parlophone, 1931–8); *L'Anthologie Sonore* (edited by Curt Sachs, 1934–9); *History of Music in Sound* (UK HMV, edited by Gerald Abraham, 1953–9).

Music Practice Records, with one part missing, **the earliest** being Tilophane (Austrian, 1935), Add-A-Part (US Columbia, 1942), Spiel Mit (DGG, 1948) and Music Minus One (US, 1949).

Educational Films. The **first** was made (with sound on disc) by Electrical Research Products Incorporated, in America in 1929. However, it would appear that motion pictures, with or without sound, and the still photograph have a greater appeal to educationalists in all fields except that of actual music training and appreciation. Educational motion pictures were well established by 1910 and were actively supported by Edison, who apparently failed to support his phonograph to the same extent, since no attempt was made by him to link sound to the picture.

10 The perfection or advancement of the telephone's art by the phonograph, making that instrument an auxiliary in the transmission of permanent records.

Edison's own Telescribe realised this ambition in 1914, and the telephone answering machine (using tape) has been widely developed since the end of World War II.

The immense widening of the musical repertoire, and the other uses to which the phonograph and the gramophone have been put, are outlined in Section VIII: Repertoire.

The first phonograph to be sold outright for home use was the Edison 'Parlor Speaking Phonograph', offered in 1878 for $10.

Edison's interest in things scientific took him with a party of other scientists to Wyoming in July 1878 to witness a total eclipse of the sun. During this expedition he talked of some old experiments he had made with electric lighting by the use of incandescent wires, and an offer to back further research with unlimited financial assistance was too great a temptation for him to ignore. It turned his attention away, at least temporarily, from continued development of the phonograph, and by October of 1878 all experiments with sound recording were laid aside.

Others, however, placed their faith in the phonograph. The *Illustrated London News* carried a report of a phonograph demonstration made by Colonel Gouraud, Edison's London agent, in August 1878, and **the first known advertisement offering speaking machines for sale** appeared in the UK in the very first edition of the *Boy's Own Paper* on 18 January, 1879.

The phonograph, then, had become nothing more than a sophisticated toy for the schoolboy or a means of making dolls talk, and even the novelty of these effects was quick to wear off. When office managers proved by their lack of interest that they could exist perfectly well without the help of the phonograph it looked as if the short and sensational life of Edison's amazing invention had come to an end.

Elsewhere, other minds were working almost furtively to improve the phonograph. Alexander Graham Bell, whose work with the blind and whose invention of the telephone are discussed in Section I, opened his Volta Laboratory in Washington, DC, in 1880, for the purpose of continuing these two lines of research. He brought from England his cousin Chichester Bell and an associate, Charles Sumner Tainter; between them, they could bring a unique inventive genius, expertise in chemical engineering, and the minute skills of the instrument maker to bear upon further developments. Yet it was to Edison's phonograph that they turned their attention. On 20 October, 1881, they deposited a sealed box with the Smithsonian Institution, Washington, containing what they called a 'Graphophone', and the description of a compressed-air amplifier. Although virtually identical to Edison's phonograph, the Bell and Tainter graphophone showed one important improvement: Edison's tin foil sheet was replaced by a wax-coated metal cylinder.

For nearly 4 years, work upon improving the graphophone continued at the Volta Laboratory. Then, on 27 June, 1885, the Bells and Tainter applied for a patent covering the following modifications: the wax-coated cylinder was replaced by a wax-coated cardboard tube of $1\frac{5}{16}$in (3·3cm) diameter, designed to fit over a spindle; the stylus assembly was flexible whereas Edison's had been rigid; and this assembly traversed the length of the 6in (15·2cm) long cylinder rather than the cylinder moving sideways under the stylus. The most important 'advance' over Edison's machine was not recognised as a real advance at all until subsequent litigation gave it a weight unsuspected by the inventors: whereas Edison's recording stylus 'indented' or 'embossed' tin foil, Bells' and Tainter's 'engraved' or 'cut' wax – a different process, it was argued, and one which, furthermore, produced a better sound.

The Bells and Tainter may have been surprised when their patent (No 341214, granted on 4 May, 1886) went through without a hitch. To be on the safe side they tried to head off

trouble by approaching Edison early in 1887 with very fair proposals to amalgamate their resources and work together harmoniously on the development and exploitation of the 'talking machine'. Not only did they concede Edison's priority in inventing the device but they were even ready to forget their name 'Graphophone', Spoonerised from Edison's 'Phonograph', in favour of the original. Edison was furious at the whole idea. Anyone who had the effrontery to patent a machine substantially similar to his own was not the sort with whom he wished to enter into partnership. Unceremoniously he rejected any consideration of a merger.

Rebuffed, the Bells and Tainter put their machine on view and sold it to a group of businessmen who formed The American Graphophone Company in Washington, DC, in June 1887, to market the machines as aids to office efficiency. Incidentally, the trade mark word 'Graphophone', conceived perhaps in a moment of wicked humour, continued to be used on LP sleeves of Columbia records in the UK at least until 1960.

Stung into action by his rivals' nerve, Edison, fresh from his success with electric lighting, bounced back with his 'Improved Phonograph', announcing it in October 1887, but there had been many problems to iron out and not enough time to solve them all. Chief amongst them was the establishment of a constant record/playback rotational speed. This was achieved by the use of a small battery-operated motor with a governor and flywheel, and the perfected machine, demonstrated to *Scientific American* in December 1887, was ready for the market by 16 June, 1888. It used the Bells' and Tainter's pliable play-back stylus assembly and solid wax cylinders with vertical groove indentations only one thousandth of an inch deep. A scraper was provided for wiping off a recording to make room for another, which meant that the $\frac{1}{4}$in (6mm) thick cylinder could be re-used many times. Edison's London agent, Colonel Gouraud, received a 'Perfected Phonograph' on 26 June, 1888; from that date his correspondence with Edison was conducted by cylinder, and he secured the voices of Florence Nightin-

Edison's Improved Phonograph recording the Handel Festival in the Crystal Palace, 1888.   MARY EVANS PICTURE LIBRARY

Two famous personalities who recorded for Edison in London in 1890. Left: *Alfred Lord Tennyson.* Right: *Florence Nightingale.*
NATIONAL PORTRAIT GALLERY

gale, Alfred Lord Tennyson, Robert Browning, and other famous personalities, operating from his house in Upper Norwood, London, which he turned into a recording studio and named – in honour of Edison's establishment – 'Little Menlo'.

In America, the Phonograph and Graphophone were now competing hotly in the same market, and so similar were they in design that

at his West Orange laboratory, for his assistant W K L Dickson had been busy combining two inventions. On 6 October, 1889, Edison witnessed **the first talking movie picture**. As he entered the room, the 'Kineto-phonograph', a lantern machine attached to a phonograph, showed a moving picture of Dickson saying: 'Good morning, Mr Edison, glad to see you back. I hope you are satisfied with the "Kineto-

Fascinated visitors at Edison's stand, Paris Exposition, 1889.
ANN RONAN PICTURE LIBRARY

suit and counter suit began to appear to prove priority of invention. The tycoon Jesse Lippincott (1842–94) realised the destructive action this rivalry would have on the promising future of the machine and, apparently by miracles of tact, diplomacy, persuasion and wheeler-dealing, plus the irresistible attraction of money available for investment, he brought the two sides together as the North American Phonograph Company, founded on 14 July, 1888. The commercial launch of the cylinder was made at the Paris Exposition of 1889. (On his return from Paris, Edison was greeted with a surprise

phonograph".' Perhaps Edison experienced some of the surprise felt by the editor of *Scientific American* at the first demonstration of the phonograph.)

Sadly, having laid the foundation of a potentially powerful business, Jesse Lippincott's health cracked under the strain of attempting to promote his product country-wide, and Edison was forced to take over, only to liquidate the company in 1894.

The first recordings of serious music were made in 1888: the 12-year-old pianist Josef

Edison's laboratory at West Orange.

Hofmann visited Edison's laboratory and made some 2-minute cylinders; while in England Colonel Gouraud set up a recorder in the press gallery of the Crystal Palace, London, to record parts of the Handel Festival's performance of *Israel in Egypt* on 29 June, 1888. This latter was **the world's first 'live' recording**.

The first serious composer to make a recording was Johannes Brahms. Edison's German agent, who had recorded Bismarck in 1888, visited Brahms the following year and recorded his performance of one of the Hungarian Dances. The cylinder was rediscovered in 1935: its atrocious quality may be due to the fact that the recording machine was placed out of sight – *under* the piano.

The first orchestral recordings, and **the first recording of a complete symphony**, were made when Edison set up two (some reports say four)

phonographs before the orchestra in the Metropolitan Opera House, New York, at a concert conducted by Hans von Bülow in 1889. The programme consisted of Wagner's *Meistersinger* Prelude, Haydn's B flat Symphony (No 102?), and Beethoven's *Eroica* Symphony (No 3). Apparently the whole concert was recorded but these experiments were never issued and the cylinders are lost.

Edison's first commercial recordings (1889–92)

Although Thomas Edison considered his 'favourite invention' principally useful as an aid to commerce, and as a means of preserving the voices of outstanding personalities of the time – the last two decades of the 19th century – the North American Phonograph Company, which had purchased the rights to the Edison Speaking Phonograph Company in 1888, began produc-

Johannes Brahms, the first 'serious' musician to record.
MARY EVANS PICTURE LIBRARY

ing commercial cylinders for the coin-in-the-slot trade the following year (see Section IV).

The first commercial cylinders of all date from 24 May, 1889, on which date one Frank Goede made in all 75 cylinders, comprising eight titles spread over 14 numbered records, starting with Gilmore's *22nd Regiment March* and *The Warbler*, both piccolo solos, continuing with four selections for the flute (a two-part selection from something described simply as *Marquis*, two waltzes – *Abandon* and *La Source* – and Scharwenka's *Polish Dance*). The session was completed by two 'takes' of *Liliput Polka*, some unidentified college songs described as 'Lanciers', and *Birds Festival Waltz*, all as further piccolo solos. No accompaniment is shown in the recording book, so presumably Mr Goede played alone. The following day, a violinist entered as Alf. Amrhein, also apparently solo, made 50 cylinders of 11 pieces, three of which were dittoed. These seem to suggest more

adventurous fare: they include the Overture to Auber's *Fra Diavolo*, something called *Offenbachiana*, and *Dreams On The Ocean*, presumably the concert waltz *Dream Of The Ocean* by Josef Gung'l. There was also a second version of the waltz *Abandon* that Mr Goede had already made the day before – evidently a top-of-the-pops favourite of the time!

Three days later still, 28 May, 1889, the enterprising company secured the services of a cornetist named John Mittauer, whose 14 recordings produced no fewer than 84 cylinders. As with the flute, piccolo and violin solos already recorded, there was in this programme a series of polkas, but there was also something identified as *Rigoletto* (probably as much of as many of the most popular arias as could be confined within the playing time of 2 minutes) and a series of what the files show as *Army Calls*, concluding with an item curiously identified simply as *Long Notes*.

The next day, 29 May, 1889, a group of three musicians assembled in the studio: clarinettist Henry Giese, flautist C August Joepl, and bassoonist John Helleberg. Between them they produced 141 actual cylinders comprising one untitled and 16 titled recordings. On the two parts of the opening number, *Volunteer March*, all three artists played together, with an unidentified pianist; the others are flute and clarinet duets, and Titl's famous *Serenade* for flute and bassoon duet, while *Ida Polka*, *Hash Galop*, and five figures of *University Lanciers* (sic) are evidently by the trio without the pianist. One title is a clarinet solo identified only as *Theme and Variat*. Over the next few days, Henry Giese returned apparently alone to record 16 more titles as clarinet solos, making 123 cylinders, and Frank Goede brought along his flute and piccolo again for some more waltzes, polkas, marches and galops. Between times, pianist Max Franklin played Schumann's *Spring Song* and nothing else; the file mentions a Miss Lankow, without saying what she contributed to the catalogue, but stating that four of one number, three of another, and eight of a third were made.

The first multiple, or 'ganged' recording was an isolated instance of 3 June, 1889, when

Frank Goede played apparently simultaneously into seven machines. The idea was taken up regularly from 23 August, 1890. Previously, all recordings had been made individually, but from then on, it seems that they were made by the method of having the artist or group face a battery of recording machines, as many as ten at a time, so that one performance would produce ten cylinders.

The most regular visitors to the Edison-North American studios during the next few weeks were Henry Giese and Max Franklin, but apparently separately rather than jointly. Their repertoire was on much the same lines as hitherto. On 26 June, Mr Giese was joined by a Mr Groeble, a trombonist, who aided the clarinettist in another recording of the *22nd Regiment March*, some more polkas and waltzes, and two 'songs for the trombone', one of which was *Am Meer* (by Schubert?). Comments in the form of asides make amusing reading: Henry Giese on 19 June, for example, had his work-sheet that day marked 'now dark wax and hard luck'. Several sessions following this are shown to have been 'short of cylinders', which suggests that they were being sold faster than they could be supplied.

It is noteworthy that in the first two months of this recording programme the entire repertoire consists of instrumental music, yet it has always been asserted that the human voice (along with the cornet, the banjo, and the xylophone) was the easiest of sounds to record in the earliest days. Cornet solos abound, not only from John Mittauer (who contributed *God Save the Queen* on 5 July, 1889) but also from Theodore Hoch; but not until 30 September do we find any banjo solos (there were 201 cylinders made that day and during the next 2), and those were by Will Lyle, who thus preceded Vess Ossman, 'The Banjo King', by some years. There are no xylophone pieces until 26 August, when A T van Winkle began 3 consecutive days' work, $2\frac{1}{2}$ hours each day, and making a total of 131 records.

The first evidence of a singer is on 9 July, 1891, when a Miss Stewart recorded *My Love and I, Pattison's Waltz Song* (whatever that was), and *Le Pré aux Clercs*, marked 'no record kept'. On 15 July it is noted that Mrs Lankow – Miss Lankow's mother? – arrived at noon, and apparently made two records each of '*Mignon* aria' (presumably *Connais-tu le pays*) and *Verlassen*. Here again, it is strange that no male voices were recorded, in view of the oft-repeated statement that they were easier to record and gave more satisfactory results. Four days later, 'Mr Fairlamb and Party arrived,' and the son of the house, Master L Fairlamb, recorded two duets with Miss Amy Murray, evidently one of the party: *Merry June* and *God Keep You Safe, My Little Love*. Once again the voices were female, or treble.

The earliest known recording of a male vocalist on these pioneer cylinders (apart from Master Fairlamb's contribution above) is on 10 January, 1890, when a Mr Handel made some experimental records of which no details were kept. The next male singer to record did so on 1 June, 1891, accompanied at the piano by Edward Issler, who by that time had had 2 years' recording experience. The soloist was the black laughing comedian George W Johnson, who whistled and sang for $2\frac{1}{2}$ hours, but of his efforts we know nothing – the files give no details. Two months later, on 3 August, the 'boy tenor' (who was a man approaching thirty), George J Gaskin, made 20 recordings, of much the same popular material as he was to make a few years later for Berliner: *Drill, Ye Tarriers, Drill*; *Katie Connor*; *Picture Turned To The Wall* and other Victoriana. Another stalwart of both the subsequent Victor and Columbia catalogues of 10 years and more later, Joseph Natus, visited the studios on 6 February, 1892, and made 15 numbers, again with Ed Issler accompanying.

The first duplicated recordings were made on 18 March, 1892 by a system in which as many as 150 copies could be obtained from each 'master' cylinder by a form of dubbing.

The first pre-recorded cylinders produced for use in private homes were made by the North American Phonograph Company on 1 April, 1892. They were used also by fairground stall-holders and shop keepers who would display them as an advertising gimmick. Sales to domestic users must have been very limited, however, since the machines cost anything from $150 upwards when purchased outright, as distinct from a leasing fee of $40 charged to public exhibitors.

To begin with, these cylinders cost $1.20 for each band recording, and 90¢ for each of any other kind. These prices were laid down in a letter dated 23 August, 1889; but by 19 June, 1890, band recordings had been reduced to $1 each, vocal quartets became the most expensive at $1.20, and instrumental solos – and presumably vocal solos also – were down to 75¢ each. Further fluctuations according to category continued through 1891.

The first commercial orchestral cylinder recordings were made by Ed Issler's Orchestra in late 1890, and the exact personnel is shown in the files. On 21 October, 1891, this unit features a vocalist, one B P Stout, whose repertoire included such titles as *Speak Easy* (30 years before Prohibition) and *The Wild Man of Borneo*. Another interesting entry under the name of Issler's Orchestra occurs on 6 December, 1890, when the above-mentioned van Winkle on xylophone, violinist von der Heide, D B Dana on cornet, and George Schweinfest on flute, with the leader at the piano, made 14 titles (including *New York at Night*, a march; selections from *The Mikado* and *Ermine*; various waltzes, and a polka called *From Vienna to Berlin*). Sixty-eight cylinders resulted – and the page notes, rather enigmatically, 'Emperor Germany'. Were these recorded for the pleasure of the All-Highest, Kaiser Wilhelm II, in the third year of his reign?

These earliest commercial cylinders were made of wax, of varying shades from off-white to dark brown. In length they measured $4\frac{3}{16}$in (10·7cm) and in diameter $2\frac{1}{8}$in (5·7cm). They were announced expeditiously with the title, the artist's identity, and the fact that the record was made by Edison.

Alas, that these wax impressions of the music that pleased ordinary folk nearly a century ago should have been so fragile, so easily worn out, so easily broken! In a few more years would come Emile Berliner and his more robust flat disc, and Edison himself with his gold-moulded cylinders that could be produced *en masse* from a single master ... and these valiant pioneers and their noble experiments would become no more than entries in a ledger. The mere handful of survivors in anything like reasonable condition show how much they must have filled their owners with a sense of awe at the achievements of science – even if it was only an unaccompanied flute or cornet playing a polka.

The first record catalogue was issued in 1891 by the Columbia Phonograph Company of Washington, DC. It consisted of 10 pages containing:

27	marches, including Sousa's *Semper Fidelis*
13	polkas
10	waltzes
34	miscellaneous, among them many national anthems
36	numbers by ('Whistling') John AtLee to the piano accompaniment of Fred Gaisberg
13	anonymous recordings for clarinet and piano
9	anonymous recordings for cornet and piano
32	miscellaneous songs (sentimental, comic, etc)
20	monologues

American Columbia at that time showed the most aggressive and successful marketing policy. Directed since 1889 by Edward D Easton, it was the most profitable of the many agencies which took out leases on the North American Phonograph Company's products in 1888. This lively sales activity is borne out by the printed evidence: by 1893 the Columbia catalogue had swollen from 10 to 32 pages. Furthermore, when the Lippincott-Edison enterprise failed in 1894, Columbia was the only former affiliate to survive, through good management and good luck, and in the same year – 1894 – it marketed the 'Graphophone Grand', **the world's first clockwork-powered cylinder player** invented by Thomas Hood Macdonald, retailing at $75.

The first known commercially made UK recordings were issued by the London Phonograph Company about 1892. Harry Bluff (possibly a pseudonym for a brilliant mimic) made a number of comic recordings on cylinder, accompanied on the piano by Edward Hesse. **The first French recording company** was begun in 1894 when the Pathé Brothers opened two factories. (See Company Profile: Pathé.)

Edison formed the National Phonograph Company in January 1896 and marketed the Edison Home Phonograph, a clockwork-motored machine for $40 in competition with Columbia's phonograph. This started a price war. Edison's 'Standard' model of 1897 retailed at $20; Columbia answered with the 'Eagle' model at $10 the same year, and the Edison

'Gem', the most popular of his machines, hit the market shortly before the turn of the century at $7.50. In the UK the 'Gem' cost 2 guineas (£2.10) from its appearance right up to World War I. This was the cheapest Edison cylinder player. Other makers sold machines for a mere 4 or 5 shillings (20–25p). On the other hand, **the world's most expensive cylinder player** was priced (in 1980!) at $5000 (ie: then £2150). It was made by Art Shifrin in New York in 1980 for the US National Archives: Motion Picture and Sound Recording Branches. Designed to reproduce all types and sizes of cylinder at, typi-

---

COMPANY PROFILE

Pathé

Early 1890s The brothers Charles and Emile Pathé, owners of a Paris *bistro*, entertained their customers with an Edison Phonograph, imported from England.

1894 The Pathé Brothers founded a small factory at Belleville to reproduce Phonographs (illegally?), and another at Chatou to make cylinder blanks. They sold their *bistro* and founded the French record industry, with their 'Le Coq' cylinder player.

1896 Recording studio opened at 98 rue de Richelieu, Paris, recording artists of the Paris Opéra and Opéra Comique. The cylinders were duplicated pantographically from large-diameter masters. The wax cylinders offered for sale were the 2-minute 'standard' and the 4-minute 'Celeste' extra large. **Pathé was the first to record Caruso** (three cylinders, made in either France or Belgium in 1898–1901).

c 1900–5 Around the turn of the century they opened factories also in London, Milan, Brussels, Amsterdam, St Petersburg, Moscow, Odessa, and Rostov, and studios in London, Milan, and Moscow.

1905 Puccini and Massenet sued Pathé Frères for recording royalties, but lost the case.

1906 October: First Pathé discs, copied pantographically until well into the 1920s. At first, the discs were label-less, centre-start, vertical-cut, to be played with a ball-tipped

permanent stylus at 90rpm. The sizes were 8½in, 11in, 14in and 20in approx. (respectively, 21·6cm, 28cm, 35·6cm, and 50·8cm, approx.).

1910 Russell Hunting opened the Pathé factory and studio in New York (which was to process the first Western Electric electrical records in 1924).

1920 Pathé *Actuelle* lateral-cut discs introduced in the UK and USA. (Victor and Columbia lateral-cut patents expired this year.)

1927 Converted to electrical recording.

1928 May: Columbia bought Pathé's UK branch; therefore, from 1931 Pathé was part of the EMI combine, continuing semi-autonomously into the stereo era. Pathé's French branch was the last company to produce vertical-cut discs: the final catalogue was published in 1932.

1931 American branch re-named Pathé Phonograph and Radio Corporation. Before World War II the success of Pathé lay in the fact that their prices in France were consistently lower than those of their rivals.

1948 The Englishman Peter De Jongh (1925–78) was sent to France to revitalise the company after the war. From 1953 he was instrumental in establishing artistic contact between Russian recording artists and the EMI group as a whole. (See Company Profile: EMI.)

cally, 120, 144, and 160rpm, it has many additional facilities for transfer to tape for further filtering and manipulation of these old recordings, including half-speed mastering. The price quoted above was for the standard model: custom-built examples for special projects and unusual requirements would obviously command a higher price. **The first machine in the 'renaissance' of cylinder playing** was developed in 1977 by David Dunmall and Joe Pengelly of BBC Plymouth.

In 1899, Edison sent Will Hayes of his West Orange staff to open branches for cylinder recording and manufacture in London, Paris, Berlin, Brussels, Vienna and Milan.

The first moulded cylinders were produced by the Lambert Company of Chicago early in 1900 (patent granted on 18 December, 1900). They were made of pink celluloid. Edison's 'gold-moulded' cylinders followed in 1901.

The cylinder achieved its peak of popularity in America in 1901 but the challenge of the disc, with its ease of handling and storage, was strong, and a number of improvements in cylinder manufacture, presentation and repertoire were to be attempted in the ensuing years to meet it. Edison correctly felt that cylinder reproduction was superior to that of the disc: the former's hill-and-dale groove was not distorted by being bent sideways round the central blank area, as on disc, and playing time was less limited. The ease with which flat discs could be mass-produced by the stamper method had meant that production costs were lower than with the pantographic and other cumbersome methods of making cylinder copies. Edison had been working on a viable method of moulding cylinders since 1888, but by the time that he and Lambert, working independently, had solved the major problems, the disc had already gained a strong commercial lead. It was the beginning of the end for the cylinder. The first disc-playing Graphophone had appeared in 1902, Columbia issued recordings in parallel cylinder and disc format in that year, and in 1903 that company offered its 'grand Opera' series in disc format *only*.

The Auxetophone compressed-air amplifier.

Before detailing the phase-out of cylinders, we should mention an important technical development which occurred at this time. Up to 1903, all recordings had been reproduced mechanically, with no artificial method of increasing their volume. In 1903 **the world's first amplifier** (called 'intensifier') was patented by Sir Charles Parsons (1854–1931). It was called the Auxetophone. Both this and the world's first amplifying valve owe their invention indirectly to Edison. The background to the invention of these devices is of considerable interest.

Thomas Edison's idea for an 'air relay' for amplifying sound dates from 1876. It was taken up by Horace L Short (one of the Short Brothers later renowned for building seaplanes), who had brought Paris to a standstill by operating a prototype at the top of the Eiffel Tower. The development was brought to workable stage by Parsons, who was granted the following patents for the use of the Auxetophone:

1903: 10468: Sound Reproducers or
            Intensifiers for Phonographs,
            Gramophones or Telephones;

1903: 10469: – for Musical Instruments
1904: 20892: – for Reproducers or Resonators

The rights were bought by The Gramophone & Typewriter Co (G & T) for $5000 in 1905, Parsons retaining them for musical instruments.

Sir Charles Parsons, who as early as c1890 made a bid 'to secure economy in the use of the World's resources of fuel' (Appleyard, see Bibliography, p. 218), is noted mainly as the perfector of the steam turbine and high-speed dynamo. It may be the influence of his marine activities that caused two huge fixtures resembling ocean liner ventilation inlets to be installed in the Queen's Hall, London, during the first week of October 1906, in time to be tried out on Promenade audiences. They were part of a contraption described by Parsons as 'a pneumatic device for increasing the volume and richness of tone of stringed instruments, (which) is worked by air supplied by a blower in the basement'. A comb-like aluminium valve was connected to the instrument near the bridge. 'This valve controls the exit of the air from a small box fed from a blower into a large spiral-shaped trumpet which emits sound-waves identical in quality and intonation but richer in tone and larger in volume than those produced by the instrument itself unaided by the Auxetophone.' Sir Henry Wood showed enthusiasm for the invention, especially for 'big Wagner items' and the Dragon's voice in *Siegfried.* In the event, the latter was played by a bass tuba into a large megaphone.

Meanwhile, G & T in the UK and Victor in the US were developing the Auxetophone for record amplification, and it was offered to the public in November 1906. Although pronounced successful as a means of amplifying records in large halls (too successful for those members of the audience at the first demonstration at Earl's Court, London, who, according to one of the organisers, 'quickly clapped their hands to their ears and made their way to the back of the building'), the Auxetophone was not suitable for domestic use because of the loud hissing noise to be heard in the vicinity of the instrument, a noise easily absorbed in large halls. Perhaps for this reason, too, the musical instrument version of the invention was never used in the recording studios to amplify sounds entering the recording horn.

Resistance from orchestral string players, fearing for the security of their jobs, also brought to an end the use of the Auxetophone in the concert hall due to Sir Henry Wood's vision that the invention 'will be able to reinforce five stringed instruments ... sufficiently to combat the complete wood-wind and brass of the Wagnerian orchestra.'

The first 'valve' (American: 'tube') was invented by Edison by mistake in 1883. He had been experimenting with his incandescent electric light bulb and noted a discoloration on the inner surface. This was caused by free electrons from the filament passing through the vacuum and impinging on the glass, although the existence of free electrons was not suspected at that time. Edison inserted a metal plate in the bulb to combat this effect (dubbed by Sir William H Preece 'the Edison effect' in 1885) and by so doing he commenced a trail of development that led to the thermionic valve (tube). The heated filament giving off electrons became known as the cathode, the cold receiver of the current as the anode, and both were termed electrodes. A third electrode, a controlling grid, was introduced between cathode and anode in 1905 by Lee De Forest, thereby enabling the flow of electrons to be amplified. This was the first amplifying tube, or valve.

The valve (or thermionic tube) has today entirely been replaced in normal usage by the semiconductor, although some reactionary enthusiasts still believe that true high fidelity can be achieved only with the use of valves, and a number of makers have catered for this small market. **The first transistor** was invented at the Bell Laboratories, New Jersey, in 1947 by John Bardeen and Walter Brattain, working under the guidance of William Shockley. The word 'transistor' (a contraction of 'transfer resistor') arose at the same time. Transistors were widely used by the end of 1960 in portable radios and some portable radiograms; their general hi-fi applications came somewhat later.

The challenge of the disc was making ever deeper inroads into cylinder sales in the first decade of the 20th century, but no-one can deny that the cylinder went down fighting.

1906 Edison launched his 'Grand Opera' cylinders, but these were unsuccessful, despite being cheaper than Columbia's rival discs, because of the limited playing time of only 2 minutes.

1906/7 **The first domestic automatic cylinder changer**, the 'Concertophone', marketed in America.

1908 (October) **The first narrow-groove cylinders** issued: Edison's wax Amberol series, with 200 windings to the inch (double the standard), running for 4 minutes. They were, however, brittle, and did not stand up well to rough handling. With the extended playing time, Edison returned to the operatic repertoire, and in time for Christmas the following year he had produced not only a new series of 4-minute operatic arias but also a resplendent new 'Amberola' Phonograph with an enclosed horn upon which to play them.

1909 Edison closed his European cylinder operation. Columbia made a final bid for the cylinder market with the 4-minute 'unbreakable'. The original patent for these metal-reinforced cylinders had belonged to the Indestructible Phonograph Record Co. of Albany, New York, in 1906.

1912 Edison replaced his Amberol series with the new and vastly improved 'Blue Amberols', made of hard-wearing, relatively silent-surfaced plastic which, when played on the Edison Diamond Reproducer, was said to give the best reproduction available and to survive 3000 playings without wear.

It was in this year that Edison made a historic decision and finally bowed to the advice that had been bombarding him for a decade. He produced **the first Edison discs**. They were extremely thick and unbreakable, and although of 10in (25·4cm) diameter, their fine hill-and-dale grooving gave 12in (30·5cm) playing time. Some even had a spoken commentary by Harry E Humphrey listing the music on the reverse side. The Edison Diamond Disc Phonograph

followed soon after. Its pick-up was driven across the disc by a rack-and-screw mechanism, it possessed a lifting/lowering device, and, as its name implies, it had a diamond stylus. It would not, however, play records larger than 10in in diameter.

1912 (July) Columbia finally abandoned all cylinder production, thereafter concentrating solely upon disc.

1919 (2 January) **The only recording made by Edison himself for commercial release** was 'Let Us Not Forget', being a tribute to the Allied Servicemen of World War I. The recording was issued on Amberol cylinder and on disc.

1926 Edison launched a 12in 'long playing' record. Unfortunately, the diamond styli of the day were too coarse for its narrow grooves and the LP discs were discontinued a few months later.

1927 Edison made his first electrical recordings, vertical cut at first, then lateral cut from 1929. But on 1 November, 1929, Edison gave personal instructions that all phonograph activity (cylinders, discs, and equipment manufacture) was to cease. The disc had emerged supreme, and the cylinder, apart from its continued use in some more remote areas, had lost its following. Nonetheless, Edison's prophesy of 1897 had been fulfilled and continues to have relevance even today:

'For the future it (the phonograph) has great possibilities, and the improvements that will continue to be made from time to time will in the end bring it to a perfection that will make the phonograph an important feature of every household.'

In 1961 the Thomas Alva Edison Foundation issued a recording titled 'The Sound of Fame' to commemorate 4 June, 1961, as the date upon which Edison was installed to the Hall of Fame for Great Americans at the New York University. The recording was of Edison's artists from 1888 to 1929, and included the voice of Sir Arthur Sullivan, recorded on 5 October, 1888.

Section III

Berliner and the Disc

Emile Berliner, the man on whose inventive genius a powerful 20th century industry was founded, was born in Hanover, Germany, in 1851. Little is known of his boyhood there, but he emigrated to the USA in 1870, arriving in New York a penniless wanderer, with no apparent idea of what he would eventually do in his adopted country. He secured a humble position as a clerk in a haberdashers in Washington, managed by a fellow-immigrant from Hanover, and for 3 years he kept himself alive in this capacity. In 1873 he decided he wanted to explore other possibilities offered by a new country, then still reconstructing after the Civil War a decade earlier. He tried various jobs, but one which seems to have inspired his scientific abilities was in the laboratory of the man who compounded saccharin some years earlier, Constantine Fahlberg.

Berliner's status in the Fahlberg laboratory was humble indeed; he washed bottles, but he was young and acutely perceptive, and he noted various aspects of laboratory procedure that were to stand him in good stead in the years to come. In 1876, however, he returned to his old job in the Washington haberdashery, but with improved prospects and position, with salary to match. He wasted no time, however, in setting up a small research laboratory of his own in his apartment, and by studying the sciences of electricity and acoustics, these being the areas which most interested him, he was soon able to carry out experiments in his own room.

Berliner applied for his first patent on 4 March, 1877. It was for a carbon button transmitter, an improvement to Alexander G Bell's telephone. The patent was eventually granted in 1891; meanwhile, Berliner interested the Bell Telephone Company in his improvement, and he sold it to them in 1878 for a large sum, which carried with it a retainer fee on a monthly basis to enable Berliner to proceed with further research.

In 1881, however, he returned to Hanover, and set up Telephon-Fabrik, Berliner, with his brother Joseph, to provide telephones for the German market. Two years later, he returned to America, richer than before, seceded from the

Emile Berliner.

Bell Telephone Company, built a house of his own in Washington, DC, and began addressing his energies and knowledge to the recording of sound, using the lateral tracing of sound vibrations as suggested by Léon Scott's Phonautograph. (See p. 12.)

Four years of determined experimentation eventually produced a means of engraving sound laterally on a lamp-blacked glass disc, revolved on a turntable and etched by a stylus mounted on a feed screw. On 26 September, 1887, Emile Berliner applied for a patent (granted in Germany – No 45048 – and England – No 15232 – on 8 November, 1887, and in America – No 7204 – on 15 May, 1888), thus registering in all three countries the proprietary name 'Gramophone', meaning a talking machine employing lateral cut discs, as opposed to the 'Phonograph' of Edison which employed vertically-cut cylinders. It was necessarily a crude and laborious affair, using photoengraving onto metal, but during the next 6 months, he devoted his attention to an improvement which involved tracing the laterally-cut groove in a thin film of fat on a zinc disc, then immersing the disc in an acid bath for about 20 minutes. The acid stabilised the groove by etching it into the zinc where the recording stylus had removed the fat; it had no effect on the fat itself, so a more or less permanent sound record was thus produced.

The first demonstration of disc recording and reproduction was on 16 May, 1888, before the members of the Franklin Institute, Philadelphia. Berliner envisaged the recording for posterity of any kind of sound, laying stress on the cultural value of such recording, for it would soon be possible to record and preserve the voices and instrumental abilities of many or all the great artists then or at any time later before the public. Unlike Edison, Berliner conceived that the use of his invention would be primarily in the home rather than in the office. Furthermore, limitless copies of each recording could be produced from one master, unlike the individually recorded Edison cylinder – and artists would consequently reap new fortunes in royalties.

Nevertheless, the sounds produced by these pioneer works of Berliner were not such as would encourage the established figures of the concert platform or opera stage to flock to his studio. Indeed, for some years after Berliner's records were launched as merchandise, in considerably improved form, this prejudice remained; so Berliner, in 1889, took another trip home to Germany, where he managed to interest a firm of toy manufacturers in selling his hand-wound gramophones. The turntable depended on the steadiness of the hand winding a small handle activating a thick rubber band slotted into the rims of two wheels attached to the spindle. Contemporary literature advises an even speed of some 70rpm, as anything faster or slower would produce diverting, but hardly lasting, entertainment from the results.

The toy merchants, Kämmerer und Reinhardt of Waltershausen, did some quite reasonable business in these rudimentary little

Recording in 1888. Note the electric motor (D) driven by the battery (E). ANN RONAN PICTURE LIBRARY

machines, which they sold as 'novelties' for each Christmas trade for the most part, but the appeal of the invention began to wear off until, by 1892 or 1893, demand had sunk to abysmal depths. Although many of the 'plates', as the just under 5in diameter (12·7cm) discs were then known, were designed for the German market, obviously, a considerable number seem to have been made with a wider trade in mind. The machines were imported and sold in England by Parkins and Gotto of 60, Oxford Street, London, and by Alfred Lomax (later Edison Bell's manager in Manchester) and James Lewis Young (Edison's agent who recorded Gladstone). Parkins and Gotto sold the gramophones for two guineas (£2.10) inclusive of six 'plates'; separately, the 'plates' cost one shilling (5p) each. **The world's first disc catalogue** was issued by this firm, probably in 1892. One of the best-selling titles was No 25, *The Lord's Prayer*. The catalogue consisted of a thin slip of paper, 8in (20cm) high by 5in

(12·7cm) wide, with a picture of the hand-wound machine on one side, surmounted by the words THE GRAMOPHONE or Speaking Machine, and with a quotation from *The Queen* magazine. Two sentences from this magazine will serve to illustrate the popular attitude of early '90s society towards Berliner's invention:

'One funny curiosity . . . should cause endless amusement to children of all ages . . . We had the pleasure of hearing one recite "Twinkle, twinkle, Little Star" in tones so absurd, that it was impossible not to laugh . . .'

The quotation further states that the gramophone was not claimed to be a scientific apparatus, although what else it was, if not this, is difficult to understand. But here we have the typical patronising view of the new wonder: it was an agreeable toy, and the delivery – by Berliner himself – of a well-known nursery rhyme in his thick German accent, was a matter for hilarity.

Which of the 54 'plates' listed on the obverse of this curious piece of advertising copy was actually recorded first will probably never be known. **The earliest number** is 17, on which Berliner quotes a random selection of proverbs; the record itself bears no recording date, although the majority of Berliner records of the latter '90s are dated exactly. One specimen of these earliest relics, however, does bear the number 14890, in addition to the usual copyright and catalogue numbers. The latter is 102, and the item is not amongst those in the Parkins and Gotto catalogue, but the possibility exists that the performance, an unidentified march (described simply as *March No 1*) played by four unaccompanied trumpets, may have been recorded on 14 August, 1890. Among those listed are 17 other spoken records, described as 'recitations', and although 11 of them are of nursery rhymes, the other six include the best-selling reading of *The Lord's Prayer*, again by Berliner – barely recognisable for what it is – and of Byron's poem *Manfred*. This must rank as **one of the first attempts to include anything that could be accepted as of cultural value** on a record. There are nine songs

in English, ranging from *Ta-Ra-Ra-Boom-De-Ay* and *Knocked 'Em In The Old Kent Road*, to *Rule, Britannia*; *We Don't Want To Fight*; and *Long, Long Ago*. Only two are sung in French, but there are six in German, including the National Anthem (*Deutschland Über Alles*) and other patriotic titles. There are 12 recordings by assorted brass instruments, some of them described in the vaguest of terms (*Concert Piece*; *Bugle Calls*; and *The Mikado*), and nowhere is there any indication as to who is playing.

In view of the apparent difficulty in recording the piano, even after 30 years of acoustic recording, it is strange that there are two piano solos on this first record list. It has always been maintained, too, that the banjo recorded best, along with the xylophone, but there is only one banjo record – a duet called simply *Boccacio* (sic) – and no xylophone records at all on the first known record catalogue. This banjo record is listed under 'Assorted Plates', the other four in this category being some incredibly inaccurate *Farmyard Imitations*; an unidentified 'clarionette' solo, with variations; an *Old-Fashioned Street Organ* and a *Roll of Drums*. It is worth noting that of all the earliest Berliners examined, whether vocal or instrumental, not one has any form of accompaniment. At one shilling (5p) each, and of a durability that must have been sorely tested by the very tough treatment they received, these 'toys' must have seemed quite expensive. It is hardly surprising that once their novelty had worn off with their surfaces, few who had invested in them initially felt inclined to continue to do so.

These earliest records, although anonymously performed, all bear the copyright No 45048, and in the case of record No 68 on which a gruff but not necessarily German voice recites *Tom He Was A Piper's Son*, the two patent numbers 15232 and 7204 (with their dates – see above) are etched on the central area. It is interesting to note that the words of recitations and songs are invariably given on printed stickers adhering to the reverse side of the disc.

Berliner's great invention languished for a year or two, then in the autumn of 1894, he and

Fred Gaisberg, the industry's first impresario.

records, if any, made between the formation of the United States Gramophone Company and the incorporation of the Berliner Gramophone Company, are at present unknown. While searching for backers through the 10 or 12 months between the launching of the parent company and the syndicate, no doubt Berliner and his associates relied largely on the records already marketed by Parkins and Gotto in London and Kämmerer und Reinhardt in Waltershausen. The story has often been told of how Berliner's erstwhile employers, the Bell Telephone Company, when invited to invest in his new project, received it with detached amusement as their directors listened to the record of Berliner himself reciting *Twinkle, Twinkle, Little Star*. They, and some others who were similarly solicited, wanted Berliner to produce a talking doll. This offended him, not unnaturally; he felt that for all its rudimentary crudeness, his Gramophone was not destined to be a toy forever, but to become a thing of beauty.

The first recording studio was opened by Fred Gaisberg in 1897 over a shoe shop on 12th Street, Philadelphia.

The first retail record shop was opened by Berliner in Chestnut Street, Philadelphia, in 1897; the manager was Alfred Clark.

Dance Records **The first records in America made for dancing** appeared in 1897, made by Sousa's Band ('this famous band has played for us during the summer', says the catalogue issued that autumn), along with the usual marches for which this conductor was famous. These records included two polkas, three waltzes, and some unspecified dances bearing such titles as *Happy Days In Dixie, Ma Angeline (Popular Negro Melody), Orange Blossoms (Arthur Pryor's New Negro Oddity)*, – probably an early form of ragtime-cakewalk – and *La Czarine*. Much the same kind of music was provided by Haley's Concert Band of Washington, DC, and by the Metropolitan Orchestra, which was a prolific contributor to Eldridge Johnson's Improved Gram-O-Phone Record catalogue 3 or 4 years later. (Several of this organisation's records in

some friends and relatives launched the United States Gramophone Company of 1410 Pennsylvania Avenue N W, Washington, DC. As already mentioned, the majority of the records in its catalogue (selling at 50¢ each or $5 a dozen) bear the date of recording etched into the central area along with the title, artist and catalogue number, and rarely any further information. Here again, it is impossible to determine by the numbers which is the earliest; but **the date that seems to be the furthest in times from our day** is 29 October, 1895, on which day a prolific recording artist, George J Gaskin, ('The Boy Tenor', so described in some of the announcements preceding his recordings, although he was a man in his thirties) sang *I Don't Want to Play in your Back-Yard*. This date is exactly three weeks *after* the incorporation of the Berliner Gramophone Company (8 October, 1895), a syndicate of Philadelphia investors initiated by B F Karns who were prepared to back the parent company to the tune of $25 000, and so launch Emile Berliner's Gramophone on the American Market. The

Respighi playing in Bongiovanni's shop.
COURTESY: BONGIOVANNI

Francesco Bongiovanni, founder of the oldest surviving record shop, established Bologna, 1905. COURTESY: BONGIOVANNI

the 1897 catalogue look very much like ragtime, but apparently only one – *Cotton Blossoms* – has yet to be found; it *is* ragtime.)

The first records by a dance band were made by the Hotel Cecil Orchestra, who recorded two polkas at its second session on 2 September, 1898, among the usual marches; there was also something called *Wild West Gallop* (spelt thus) made that day, and the Trocadero Orchestra made a number of sides evidently intended for dancing on 7, 8, 15, and 26 September that year. These were mostly Strauss waltzes, but they were dance records nonetheless. The Trocadero Orchestra made several similar records throughout 1899, but it was Herr Wilhelm Iff, conductor of a regular dance band, recording in Glasgow on or about 12 September, 1899, who provided a programme of recorded dance music that included waltzes other than those of Strauss. Herr Iff supplied polkas, but also a barn dance, reels, quadrilles, and lancers. They surely gave a much greater incentive to dance than the rather stilted efforts of a hotel orchestra!

Improvements and Expansions Before the Berliner Gramophone Company had been in business very long, the services of a young engineer named Eldridge R Johnson, who ran a small machine shop in Camden, NJ, had been acquired. He it was who had devised **the first gramophone to be powered with a clockwork motor**, in late 1895, developed from his sewing machine motor, which of course dispensed with the need for constant rotation of the handle. So popular was the $25 Berliner machine thus produced, and the 7in (17·8cm) vulcanite records to be played on it, that Berliner felt it was time to investigate the European market again. He sent William Barry Owen to London to sound out the position in 1897, but with little success until some interested businessmen were found who were prepared to invest in the European branch of the Berliner Gramophone Company. On 9 July, 1898, Fred Gaisberg and Sinkler Darby, two of Berliner's most valued staff, arrived in London.

Fred Gaisberg acted as talent scout, studio manager, accompanist, and general factotum. He had worked with Berliner since the beginning in 1894, after gaining experience with the Columbia Phonograph Company, and was only 25 when he began his work in London. The arrangements were that machines were to be made by Eldridge Johnson in Camden, shipped to England and assembled there, and master recordings made by the zinc-etching method in London would be sent to the factory in Hanover, pressings made there and imported into England – or anywhere else in Europe. As had been customary in America, almost every master record had its date included in the details etched into the central area. As Berliner had allocated blocks of numbers to each type of recording – bands, instrumental solos; popular vocals; concert-style vocals; etc – so the London recordings were also numbered according to type but with more emphasis on nationality, sex of singer, and in the case of instrumental solos, the kind of instrument used decided the block of numbers in which the record would appear.

London Recordings **The earliest known London recording session** took place in the rather dowdy

Johnson's machine shop in Camden, New Jersey, c 1895.

basement studio below the Company's headquarters at 31, Maiden Lane, at the back of the Strand. The archives of Berliner records held by EMI Ltd show no trace of any recording having been made before **Tuesday, 2 August, 1898**, when a young soprano named Syria Lamonte recorded *Comin' Thro' the Rye*. She made many other titles during the next 2 months, on at least five sessions, but six of her recordings bear no dates, which may mean that they all belong to that first session, or are spread over the others – or perhaps they were made even earlier than the

---

COMPANY PROFILE

HMV: the Early Years

1893 The US Gramophone Company was founded in Washington, DC (president: Emile Berliner), to manufacture and market disc records based on Berliner's patents. The first discs were actually marketed in the US in 1894.

1894 Emile Berliner formed the Berliner Gramophone Co in Washington, DC.

1896 28 October: The National Gramophone Co was formed by Frank Seaman and given exclusive rights to distribute Gramophone machines and disc records (except in the District of Columbia). Seaman's apparent liaison with the American Talking Machine Co led to the latter producing machines and discs which Berliner saw as infringing his patents. He sued, but some smart footwork by Seaman eventually turned Berliner's patents against him and he was prevented from marketing his own inventions in America. This forced him to look to Europe.

1897 William Barry Owen was sent to England by Berliner to sell Gramophone rights in Europe; instead, he arranged an agency to import Gramophone products from America.

1897 December: The Gramophone Co founded in the Cecil Hotel, London, by Owen, with Trevor Lloyd Williams.

1898 16 May: The Gramophone Co transferred to 31, Maiden Lane, London.

1898 Will and Fred Gaisberg were despatched to London by Berliner to run the recording studio. Joseph Berliner (Emile's brother) set up a disc pressing plant in Hanover, Germany.

1898 October: The 'Recording Angel' trade mark was devised by Theodor Birnbaum and first appeared on discs.

1898 January: Alfred Clark was sent by Berliner to London.

1899 25 August: The Gramophone Co became a limited company with Trevor Lloyd Williams, chairman, and William Barry Owen, managing director from 1 September. The 'Recording Angel' trade mark was registered in the UK in May.

1899 September: Owen purchased the picture of Nipper, which became the 'His Master's Voice' trade mark.

1899 Companies were formed in France, Italy (liquidated in 1909) and Germany to market Berliner's products, which were also represented in Russia, Spain, Austria and Hungary.

1900 July: Berliner registered the HMV trade mark with the US Patent Office. Eldridge R Johnson employed both picture and words as a trade mark in the US for his Consolidated Talking Machine Co.

1900 December: The Gramophone Co Ltd became The Gramophone and Typewriter Co (G & T), producing records in London, Paris, Moscow and St Petersburg, and possibly also in other centres.

1901 Spring: Johnson filed the name 'Victor' as a trade mark after a court decision was made to restrain his rival, the National Gramophone Co, from using the word 'Gramophone'. Perversely, Johnson himself then dropped the word and instead called his company the Victor Talking Machine Co. The word 'Gramophone' thereafter went out of use in America in favour of 'phonograph'. (The subsequent history of Victor is outlined in a separate Profile.)

1901 November: The first G & T catalogue was issued.

earliest known date. In 1949, Fred Gaisberg remembered Syria Lamonte and recalled playing her accompaniments; he seemed to think she had been an entertainer in Rule's, the hotel near the studio.

The first European gramophone catalogue

was issued on 16 November, 1898, when it reached dealers who were being beseiged by customers eager to acquire a Berliner machine and records. On that date, two separate pamphlets were issued: one covered the American recordings, the other the British. (A similar

1901–6 Branches and factories were opened by G & T in India, Russia, Denmark, Sweden and Persia. The company's head office was moved from Maiden Lane to 31 City Road, London, in February 1902. Ten-inch discs were introduced in 1901; 12in in 1903.

1903 G & T bought controlling shares in the International Zonophone Co and its American associates. The following year, British Zonophone was formed with Louis Sterling as managing director and Russell Hunting in charge of recording. (Both, however, left to form the Sterling Record Co in November 1904.)

1907 25 June: G & T and Victor signed a trading agreement dividing the world into two trading areas. (This was terminated in 1957.)

1907 1 November: The name was changed back to The Gramophone Co Ltd; head office was moved to the new factory at Hayes, Middlesex.

1908 The Hayes factory was opened to process and press discs. The plot had been purchased on 12 December, 1906, and the 'first sod' was cut by Edward Lloyd, the tenor, on 9 February, 1907, using a 'silver spade' costing £6 10s, plus 15s for engraving (total £7.25p). The foundation stone was laid on 13 May, 1907, by Dame Nellie Melba. The first discs were pressed in June, 1908; commercial pressing started the following month.

1909 The 'dog' trade mark was adopted for use in the UK at last. The following year the words 'His Master's Voice' were also adopted. The Recording Angel trade mark, although displaced, continued to be pressed into the label area of the 'wrong' sides of single-sided HMV celebrity discs up to 1924, and appeared on labels, in addition to the

dog, until the early 1950s, even on some LPs. The Angel trade mark re-emerged in America in 1953 and in the UK in 1963.

1912 By this year factories had been opened in Spain, India, France, Austria, Russia, Latvia and Poland, and there were branches and agencies throughout the world (outside America). Chaliapin opened the Hayes recording studios in June.

1914–18 The German branch was forced to become independent due to hostilities (see Company Profile – DGG).

1915–18 The Hayes factory was given over to munitions and aircraft parts manufacture.

1917 Deutsche Grammophon, the now separate German branch, began to use the trade mark of HMV, but with the words *Die Stimme seines Herrn.*

1920 9 June: Victor purchased a controlling interest in The Gramophone Co.

1921 20 July: HMV's world-famous Oxford Street shop in London was opened by Sir Edward Elgar.

1925 20 October: A new German branch was founded, using the trade mark 'Electrola'. It purchased a factory at Potsdam on 15 December and began trading in March 1926.

1929 March: The Gramophone Co bought Marconiphone Ltd and entered the radio business.

1931 21 April: The Gramophone Co and the Columbia Graphophone Co Ltd merged to form Electrical and Musical Industries (EMI), together with Parlophone, Regal and Zonophone; the last two themselves combined to form Regal Zonophone in 1933. This label ceased production in 1949.

For ensuing events, see Company Profile – EMI.

The Gramophone Company premises, 31, Maiden Lane, London, in 1898.

EMI

pair, much extended, was published on 22 February, 1899. Miss Lamonte's historic recording is included; it was omitted from the earlier edition.)

Some English recording 'firsts':

The first piano solo record was *Under the Double Eagle* (J F Wagner), played by Mr Castle (sic), on 8 August, 1898.

The first instrumental solo (other than piano) **record** was *Variations Brillantes* (Müller), clarinet solo by A A Umbach of the Trocadero Orchestra, on 8 August, 1898.

The first male vocal record was *They've All Gone in For 'Em*, comedy song by Ted Handy, recorded on 13 August, 1898.

The first spoken record was *Three Hard Questions*, humorous dialogue by Tom Birchmore (of the Moore and Burgess Minstrels) and John W Morton, recorded 15 August, 1898.

The first orchestral record was *Washington Post March* (by Sousa) by the Hotel Cecil Orchestra, recorded 18 August, 1898.

The first female vocal record after Syria Lamonte's *Comin' Thro' the Rye* referred to above was apparently her version of *A Geisha's Life* from *The Geisha*, recorded 28 August, 1898; she was the only female singer on Berliner records until the contralto Edith Clegg recorded *Still wie die Nacht* (Carl Böhm) on 4 October, 1898. By that date, Miss Lamonte had made all her 20 sides.

Opera It will be seen that none of the pioneers making these records, nor their immediate successors, was what might be termed a celebrity. Berliner may have talked hopefully to the Franklin Institute 10 years before about recording the voice of Adelina Patti (and by inference, those of other operatic celebrities of the time), but the only vocal operatic records of any kind in his American catalogue were those by a small-time tenor named Ferruccio Giannini. He recorded *La donna è mobile* from *Rigoletto* as early as 21 January, 1896, and on at least four other sessions that year, and a few more in 1897 and 1898, he made about 20 others; but it was Fred Gaisberg in London who captured a real coup for Berliner.

The first singer of international fame and importance to record on disc was Clara Butt, the world-famous British contralto, who visited Maiden Lane on 26 January, 1899 and sang Goring Thomas's *Night Hymn At Sea* in duet with her husband-to-be, the baritone Kennerley Rumford. **The first solo singer of comparable importance to record for Berliner** was the American soprano Ellen Beach Yaw, who made nine issued records in three sessions on 11, 13, and 18 March, 1899, beginning with *O dolce contento* from Mozart's *The Magic Flute* (which became *O dolce concento* on the record itself; this was by no means the only case of a mis-spelt title or artist name on early records. Some of them were quite hilariously funny).

Music Hall **The first artist whose name conveyed star-quality to record in London** was a member of the cast of *A Greek Slave*, which had opened with great success at Daly's Theatre on 8 June, 1898. He was Scott Russell, later to appear in *San Toy* (1899) and *The Beggar's Opera* (1920), and he made three titles on 19

August, 1898. But if few musical comedy and fewer opera stars were prepared to commit their art to the uncertain medium of the gramophone of 1898, at least the music-hall stars in the heyday of that very British form of art had no such inhibitions. George Lashwood of the precise diction recorded a parody on *I Want Yer, Ma Honey* on 22 September, following it 5 days later with *He Doesn't Know Any Different*; and on 19 October the French musical-comedy artist Maurice Farkoa made six titles. He, however, was something of a veteran, who had experienced Berliner's recording techniques as far back as 8 May, 1896, when he recorded in Washington his famous *Laughing Song* from *An Artist's Model*, in which he starred on both sides of the Atlantic.

Instrumental **The first instrumentalist of national repute to record** was the cellist W H Squire – despite the inherent difficulty in obtaining a reasonable facsimile of the sonorous tones of the instrument. He made *Simple Aveu* by Thomé on 2 November, 1898, and so began a long series of recordings that continued for 32 years, well into the electric era. Strangely, the same title was recorded only 9 days later as a viola solo by a lady identified as Miss F M Brooke-Adler; repetition was the rule even this early, for within 3 months of the opening of the Maiden Lane studios, we find duplicate recordings of *Under The Double Eagle* – the piano solo referred to above, and an orchestral version; we have Frank Lawton whistling *Il Bacio* and Syria Lamonte singing it – twice, both 'takes' being issued; while Burt Earl whistled *The Handicap March* and Messrs Mays and Hunter offered a banjo duet of it.

The American catalogue of 1897–8 lists hundreds of 'plates' then available: it has many records of military-type bands, chiefly Sousa's, whereas curiously, there are none on the British list. Nor was Sousa's Band as a body alone in brass representation; there were solos by his assistant conductor, trombonist Arthur Pryor; his euphonium soloist Simone Mantia; his principal cornetist Henry A Higgins, and even one of his other virtuosi, alto saxophonist Jean Moeremans. There were also records by Miss Alice Raymond, 'Famous Lady Cornetist', who is seen in her photographs dressed in the height of fashion, complete with piled-up hair surmounted by a towering hat with rich decoration, looking somehow rather incongruous as she holds her cornet in her right hand.

Perhaps a modest claim to a 'first' could be entered by Fräulein Eidner, soloist of the Graus Mountain Choir, which recorded several titles in 1896 and 1897. Her record of *Die Nachtigall* is commented on by the catalogue editor thus:

'The reproduction of this record gives a high C clear and full, with no blast or rattle. Have you ever heard this note in a soprano record?'

This seems to imply that soprano soloists up to that time were incapable of singing a pure high C, or that the machinery was unable to do justice to it, or perhaps both!

To both meet and stimulate America's demand for discs, the National Gramophone Company in 1898 began selling gramophones at $5 down and $3 per month for seven months, **the first hire-purchase agreement for disc players**. Now, famous voices would reach an even wider market.

Speech One of the first, if not *the* first, American public figures to record for Berliner was the militant freethinker Colonel Robert Ingersoll, who on the last day of 1897 made a well-balanced speech called *Hope*. Exactly a week later, business magnate Chauncey Depew made two speech records; but in the main, the European branch was more adventurous in securing the voices of celebrated people. Even the great actress Madge Kendal recorded two sides some time in December 1898 (they are not dated, strangely), and Charles Wyndham made three records of scenes from productions in which he had taken part, on 30 December, 1898, **the first recordings made in England by a front-rank actor**. The same day, the beloved Cockney character comedian Albert Chevalier recorded four of his best numbers, and autographed the central area.

The American end of the Berliner Company may have secured the services of Maurice Far-

Albert Chevalier, popular Cockney recording artist.

duologue from *The Jest*, with Mary Moore, a poem called *Two Kinds Of People*, and a speech from *David Garrick*. Sales must have been slow even of records by such eminent actors as these; a snatch of dialogue from *The Little Minister* by Winifred Emney and Cyril Maude on 3 February and something called *The Love Of A Woman And The Love Of A Girl* by Madge Kendal, on 4 March represented the total of Berliner's British excursions into the world of drama in the year 1899. Other semi-dramatic recordings made in that year and in the next two were done by far less stellar names.

The first factory solely devoted to record pressing was set up on the Kniestrasse, Hanover, in the autumn of 1898, four hydraulic presses shipped over from America being operated under a hastily erected tarpaulin. Joseph Berliner, brother of Emile, directed the project, and during 1899 the factory was completed and in full production. (In 1908 it was producing an annual total of 6·2 million discs.) It was to this factory that Fred Gaisberg and his busy recording team in London sent masters from which the 7in discs were made. The name of the company was Deutsche Grammophon AG, registered on 6 December, 1898, with headquarters originally in Berlin. Early branches were set up in Russia and Austria (1898), Paris (Compagnie Française du Gramophone, 1899), and Italy (1899). **The first UK pressing plant** was set up by Nicole Frères in 1903 (the Gramophone and Typewriter plant did not get under way until 1907).

The zinc-etching method of making a master was no doubt an ingenious one, but it occurred to Eldridge Johnson in his expanding workshop in Camden that part, if not most, of the criticism of the gramophone's rasping sound was based on the roughness by which the grooves were stabilised. He conducted experiments on his own, and devised the principle which remained unchanged as a means of producing gramophone records until half a century had passed. He recorded on a wax block, which was then covered with gold leaf, and a master could then be 'grown' from it. From this could come many

koa very swiftly after opening for business, but apart from a somewhat apocryphal record by Ada Rehan, the famous American actress and singer, little was done to preserve any account, however crude, of American theatre talent. There was a handful of sides by Alice Neilson singing with a chorus in *The Fortune Teller*, and her colleague Jessie Bartlett Davis, who died aged only 44 in 1905, made at least two sides in 1898. In England, however, on or about 10 December, 1898 – neither record appears dated – Madge Kendal delivered two dramatic recitations: *Love Up To Date And Love Out Of Date*, and *A Sermon To Children*. Then on 30 December, Charles Wyndham recorded a duplicate 'stampers', which were then used for pressing records of much superior, smoother, sound quality. These he called 'Improved Gram-O-Phone Records', which is nothing but the truth, and since there was no infringement of Berliner's patent, Johnson launched the Consolidated Talking Machine Company of Philadelphia. At this time, the picture of the dog 'Nipper' made its first appearance, on Johnson's products (see Hall of Fame: Nipper).

On 14 May, 1900, the comedian and impressionist George Graham made *The Colored Preacher* by the new mastering system, and in the following weeks all the old regulars, and some newcomers, spent many hours each day recording for the autumn season. When the records first appeared they made an immediate impression, and not only because of their tonal superiority. They had **the first paper labels**, black and glossy, with neat gold printing that was at once easy to read (which the hand written or die-stamped Berliners were not), and which had no superfluous fussy decoration. Johnson had been driven to this course by events involving the Berliner faction and their agent, Frank Seaman, who had secured an injunction in court to prevent Berliner from manufacturing his own product. (It was claimed by the rival cylinder-producing Graphophone Company that it infringed their patents; their lawyer brought suit against Seaman, who was already furious with the Berliner directors for not giving him a large enough share of the billowing profits. Seaman saw in the action a chance to get his revenge, and set up the National Gramophone Corporation of Yonkers, NY, making Zon-O-Phone records and machines. He admitted in court that Graphophone were right, and went into a kind of unholy alliance with that company, thereby gaining control of all patents covering the sound-recording process.)

This left Johnson with machines and records he could not sell to Berliner, because Seaman had secured the issue of a court injunction to restrain the Berliner company from selling any gramophones or records. By devising a new method of recording, and a much improved means of reproduction, Johnson knew he had come across the only way of making lastingly satisfactory results. Seaman again went to court against Johnson, claiming his product was an infringement of the Zon-O-Phone-Graphophone patents; but the decision went against Seaman; and Johnson, in his hour of triumph and victory, decided on a new name for his company and its products: Victor. The Gramophone Company in London bought the rights for $15 000 for the use of the wax process for its European recordings, and soon after this, adopted a paper label also – black, glossy, gold-lettered.

Meanwhile, Seaman had sent Joseph W Jones to London in 1900 to widen the Zon-O-Phone activity, and this was further extended when F M Prescott opened a German branch in 1901. The aim was partly to compete with The Gramophone Company in the prestigious concert hall repertoire, but in 1903 Seaman sold out his European rights to Gramophone and Typewriter Ltd, and, ironically, his American rights went to Victor.

Hitherto, all Berliner records since 1895, and all Johnson's Improved records, were about 7in in diameter. Even before he won his case in court on 1 March, 1901, however, Johnson was looking forward to something bigger and better than that which he had already achieved. He saw no reason why a larger turntable, a more powerful motor to drive it, and bigger records containing longer pieces of music, should not be offered. **The first 10in disc** was recorded on 3 January, 1901 when Johnson invited S H Dudley, one of the principal singers (and manager) of the Haydn Quartet, already well-established as recording artists, to visit his studio and record some titles on a 10in master. The first of these was *When Reuben Comes To Town*, a popular light comedy song of the time. It went on sale under the new Victor Monarch label immediately after the court decision, and by the end of the year, had sold nearly 2000 copies. By today's standards, that may seem paltry indeed, but in 1901, it was the equivalent of a gold disc! *Red Labels* In the UK, in December 1900, The Gramophone Company became Gramophone and Typewriter Ltd, set up by Barry Owen, with its scope widened to include Lambert office equipment and electric clocks as buffers should the 'luxury' gramophone side of the business suffer a decline. With the new title and organisation came a larger disc. Fred Gaisberg was soon primed in the art of making satisfactory 10in records, and began experimenting with these in London; his first reference to them in his famous diaries is on 8 April 1901, immediately after one of his many journeys to Russia for the purpose of recording all kinds of Russian music, from the stars of the Imperial Opera in Moscow

HALL OF FAME

Nipper

Like Gelert, Lassie, Rin-Tin-Tin and Toby, Nipper occupies an honoured place in the canine Elysium, yet firm information about him is sparse. His dates and final resting place have been given in respected books but are, in fact, not known for certain, and some details of his personal history are based upon circumstantial evidence and assumption. What is certain is that Nipper figures in **the most famous trade mark of all**: HMV, or 'His Master's Voice'.

Nipper, a bull-terrier cross, was born in ?1884, probably in Bristol, in which city his first owner, the scenery painter Mark Henry Barraud, lived. When Barraud died in 1887, Nipper was taken under the protection of Francis Barraud (1856–1924), Mark's brother, an artist who lived in Liverpool and who owned a cylinder-playing phonograph upon which he would on occasion record his own voice. Nipper's quizzical attention upon hearing his master's voice emerging from the black horn prompted Barraud to create a well-proportioned water-colour which was exhibited in London.

It is assumed that Barraud painted Nipper from life: since the family remembers that Nipper died at the age of 11 in about 1895, the date of the original painting must be put at not later than that. Barraud tried to interest Edison's London agent in his work, but meanwhile William Barry Owen had taken a liking to the picture and agreed on 21 September, 1899, to purchase it for The Gramophone Company, provided two changes could be made: the black enamel horn should be replaced by a more visually attractive brass one, and the cylinder machine should become a disc-player.

Barraud delivered the duly amended

Francis Barraud in his studio.

painting to Owen on 17 October, 1899. He received £50 for the painting and £50 for its copyright. Emile Berliner registered the painting as a trade mark at the US Patent Office in July 1900; **it first appeared on a record supplement sheet** in January 1900, and was **first used in an advertisement** later that year in America by Eldridge Johnson's Consolidated Talking Machine Company. That firm's successor, The Victor Talking Machine Company, registered in March 1901, first used the picture on its labels in 1902.

The first use of the trade mark in Nipper's own country was in February 1909 on black-label discs, some 14 years after his death (it had been registered in the UK on 22

to Cossack tribesmen and typical peasants in the south. It was Gaisberg's Russian contact Rappaport in St Petersburg who suggested a distinctive label for the opera celebrities, to set their records apart from the ordinary black labels. He thought they should have a red label.

The first red-label records were the 10in discs by Fedor Chaliapin and others, issued during the latter part of 1901. After an extremely buoyant beginning, the Russian market underwent a number of changes, the history of which may justify a short digression.

December, 1900); the title of the picture, 'His Master's Voice', was taken up as part of the trade mark on 22 July, 1910, and the picture appeared on the rest of HMV's series that same year, replacing the sign of the Recording Angel: a cherub with a quill pen, sitting on a disc and drawing a groove round himself.

Animal-loving Britain and America enthusiastically took to Nipper. Not so certain other territories. 'To sing like a dog' is an expression the Italian branch did not wish to suggest to their opera customers, while in Egypt the dog is regarded as 'impure' despite its being amongst the many animals worshipped by the Ancient Egyptians.

Mark Barraud, son of Nipper's first owner and nephew of the painter of 'His Master's Voice', owned a photographic and printing studio in Eden Street, Kingston-upon-Thames. He took Nipper to work with him each day and, when the dog died, Mark remembers burying him in his favourite blanket near a mulberry tree in the small garden behind the studio. The date was about 1895. Counter-claims for the burial site at Clarence Street, Kingston-upon-Thames, and at Melina Place, St John's Wood, London (Francis Barraud's studio) appear to be unfounded; as is the story that in 1949 EMI erected a plaque in Eden Street commemorating Nipper.

However, in August 1950 EMI mounted an expedition to try to find the spot. Bones were indeed found buried near an old mulberry stump in a garage yard in Eden Street, but there is no proof that they, or any other relics, are the mortal remains of the most frequently reproduced dog in history.

Nipper could not escape the disruptions of

war, even posthumously. During World War I, in 1917, HMV's German subsidiary was sold into German hands and the use of the Nipper trade mark in that country was out of the control of The Gramophone Co. Nipper appeared on German Gramophone Co records, together with the words *Die Stimme seines Herrn* until 1949. Meanwhile, The Gramophone Co formed a German branch called Electrola (1926) which, of course, was not able to use Nipper on its home market products but was permitted to do so for goods sold outside Germany. The German Gramophone Co, on the other hand, while proudly displaying Nipper on goods sold in Germany, was prevented from using him abroad, so they developed the trade mark 'Polydor' for export use.

In 1949 The Gramophone Co (EMI) regained control of the Nipper trade mark in Germany, but he did not reappear on record labels until Electrola's German long playing launch in 1953. The German Gramophone Co (Deutsche Grammophon Gesellschaft) meanwhile established the tulip-motif trade mark now familiar world-wide on its classical products, and retained the Polydor trade mark for issues of lighter music.

It seems to have escaped notice that one of the changes Barraud was asked to make to the picture made a nonsense of it: a domestic animal hearing his master's voice emerging from a *disc-playing* machine, capable of playing-back only (and of a design already long out of date by the time the trade mark was adopted in its country of origin) would occur only in the rarest of circumstances, ie: when an artist prominent enough to make commercial recordings was yet not affluent enough to invest in a modern gramophone!

The 1917 Revolution in Russia brought to an end the healthy existing industry, the State seizing all its assets but maintaining production under the aegis of the State Music Trust. Discs continued to be pressed in the factory at Aprelevka, about 45 miles south-west of Moscow. In 1931 the Trust asked the new EMI combine in England to tender for the construction of a factory to make 15 million records and $1\frac{1}{4}$ million portable players per year, but the tender was never taken up. The Soviet market has been virtually closed to the West for many decades, with the exception of a few barter deals. Russian recorded material was almost unknown outside that country until UK Decca and Columbia each secured rights to a few recordings during World War II. Since then some reciprocal deals have been made, notably with Ariola/Eurodisc in Germany, DG in Germany and for international distribution, Capitol in America, and EMI in the UK. The State Music Trust's trading logo MK (Mezhdunarodnaya Kniga) was changed to Melodiya in 1965.

The Russian red-label idea of 1901 was quickly extended to the principal branches of the company in Western Europe. The world-famous records made in Milan on 18 March, 1902, by the 29-year-old Neapolitan tenor Enrico Caruso – who first recorded on cylinder

---

COMPANY PROFILE

Victor (later RCA Victor)

The early history of Victor is that also of The Gramophone Co – see Company Profile: HMV, the Early Years. The name of Eldridge R Johnson is closely involved with both histories; his activities have been incorporated in the chronology below, but see also Personalia.

1895 Eldridge R Johnson, the owner of a small machine shop in Camden, New Jersey, was approached by Berliner to make clockwork gramophone motors.

1896 The first spring-wound motors were incorporated in Berliner's machines.

1896 September: Johnson invented the copper-plating process for wax negatives.

1897 Johnson supplied Berliner with complete gramophones, including his invention of an improved soundbox.

1899 Legal complexities surrounding the word 'gramophone' effectively brought the American disc trade to a halt, but Johnson merely suppressed the word on his own products and continued in business.

1900 July–August: Johnson formed the Consolidated Talking Machine Co in Camden, marketing his machines and 'improved' disc records using the famous 'dog' trade mark. He employed Leon F Douglass to promote his products, used paper labels for the first time, and sold his secret disc processing and paper labels ideas to The Gramophone Co of London.

1901 3 October: Johnson formed the Victor Talking Machine Co in Camden, with stock shared between himself and Berliner.

1903 Johnson started an aggressive promotion campaign, including full-page advertisements in widely-read magazines and newspapers. He opened a Red Seal recording studio in Carnegie Hall on 30 April.

1904 Victor Red Seal series was inaugurated in America, using stars of the Metropolitan Opera, following the popularity of Red Seal celebrity imports of 10in discs from G & T, England, since 1902. 12in Victor discs were introduced; also 14in to special order only (1904–5).

1905 Victor took over the Universal Talking Machine Co and the 'Zon-O-Phone' trade mark.

1906 Johnson introduced his internal horn 'Victrola', the design of which may have been suggested by a German machine of *c* 1905 called the 'Hymnophone', in which the horn emerged from underneath the turntable.

1907 25 June: Victor and G & T signed a trading agreement dividing the world into two trading areas; this remained in force for 50 years.

for Pathé (see p. 33, Company Profile: Pathé) and the Anglo-Italian Commerce Company (AICC) of Genoa, with offices in Milan – were issued in this category. These were soon joined by examples of the repertoire of most of the great names in opera appearing in London that Coronation summer: Antonio Scotti, Pol Plançon, Suzanne Adams, Emma Calvé, Maurice Renaud, and David Bispham. At 10/– (50p) a single-sided record, their work must have represented the very peak of luxury in records but as the material they sang was the kind normally only appreciated by the wealthy – or those who had risen up the rigid social scale by dint of hard work in business, and who looked on such red-

VICTOR  RCA

1908 Victor issued their first double-sided discs.
1920 9 June: Victor purchased a controlling interest in The Gramophone Co of England.
1925 Victor concluded an agreement with Western Electric and incorporated the Orthophonic recording process into its new electrical recordings. An arrangement was made with the Radio Corporation of America for radios to be included for the first time in Victrola machines.
1926 15 December: Victor sold to a banking syndicate, Seligman & Co and Speyer & Co, who therefore became the owners of both Victor and The Gramophone Co.
1929 4 January: Victor Talking Machine Co purchased by RCA, operating from 5 March. (RCA itself had been formed just under a decade earlier, on 17 October, 1919.)
1945 Eldridge R Johnson died.
1957 May: The RCA–HMV link was severed. HMV had set up its own distribution company in March 1953, while RCA's UK pressing and distribution was to be handled by Decca from September.
1968 RCA opened an independent distribution, recording, and (later) manufacturing operation in the UK as RCA Great Britain Ltd.

Emma Calvé, c 1892, an early red-label recording artist.
BBC HULTON PICTURE LIBRARY

labelled discs as status symbols, to be displayed rather than played – the sales, especially of the Caruso records, were satisfactory indeed. For the less moneyed, there were the regular 10in black-labels at 5/– (25p) each, and the 7in at 2/6 (12½p).

The first catalogue of red-label discs in the UK was published in September 1902 in London by G & T. It carried photographs of the company's impressive roster of artists. In the same year Victor's first cumulative catalogue appeared in America, coincidentally with their first 'Red Seal' records licensed from G & T.

In autumn 1902, Fred Gaisberg headed a team of recording experts to the Far East, where they spent nearly a year travelling and recording local music by the stars of India, China and Japan. He left his younger brother William in the London studios and in charge of recording any other celebrity who could be induced into facing the recording horn. During that year, some remarkable captures were made by G & T. The most impressive was that of the *tenore robusto* Francesco Tamagno, for whom Verdi had written the title-role of *Otello*. Tamagno was not an easy catch by any means. He insisted that each record should bear an individual number on its label so that the exact amount of royalties due could be assessed. He further refused to record unless the sessions took place in his own home. This was to obviate the strain on his already weak heart. In fact, he died of heart trouble on 31 August, 1905, slightly over $2\frac{1}{2}$ years after the momentous sessions in his home *Ospedaletti* in the Italian Alps.

Tamagno was **the first recording artist to receive royalties on his work**. The rate was 10% of the retail price of each record sold, with an advance of £2000. Composers, however, did not receive royalties for recordings of their music until as late as 1911.

The first 12in records appeared in April 1903. Five of the titles recorded by Tamagno earlier that year were issued on this size. A few months later Tamagno again faced the recording horn in his home, and recorded, prophetically enough, the famous closing aria from *Otello*: *Niun mi tema* ('Otello's Death'). Even at £1 per copy, it became something of a best-seller; the vivid drama is captured with astonishing fidelity, and the aria fills the 12in side admirably. Tamagno was probably **the first operatic celebrity to record his speaking voice**. One of the sides made in the opening days of 1903 (but not issued until 5 years after his death) is prefaced with the words: 'Dedico alla memoria di mio padre' ('I dedicate (this) to the memory of my father').

Incidentally, some of Caruso's early records have spoken announcements, but these were not made until some months after the Tamagno disc, which is the aria *Deserto sulla terra* from Verdi's *Il Trovatore*. Although the select group of Metropolitan singers who made some generally rather indifferent records for Columbia in New York had spoken announcements by the artists themselves, these, too, were not made until the spring of 1903.

Pianists That spring also saw the first recordings of two major personalities in the world of instrumental concert music. To be sure, Landon Ronald, composer and conductor, and impresario to G & T, had made some necessarily edited and truncated piano recordings for Berliner in 1900, soon after his appointment as musical director; but in Paris, at the end of April and early May 1903, within a few days of each other, the composers Raoul Pugno and Edvard Grieg each recorded a number of piano solos. Pugno left the studio and went on to accompany no less a singer than Tamagno himself; a few days later he returned and made further recordings. (See also Section VIII.) It should also be mentioned that Alfred Cortôt, one of the greatest French pianists of his age, made *his* début about that time in the Paris studios – as accompanist to the great Russian diva Felia Litvinne, and a year later in 1904, the impressionist composer Claude Debussy provided the accompaniment in the same studios to Mary Garden singing part of the Tower Scene: *Mes Longs Cheveux* from his *Pelléas et Mélisande*, and three of his *Ariettes*. (In her autobiography, *Mary Garden's Story*, the singer gives incorrect details concerning these sessions; the above information is taken from company recording sheets.)

The quality of the Pugno and Grieg recordings leaves something to be desired; rare they may be as records, but it is easy to understand how the thin, tinny sound of the piano, not always recorded at an absolutely steady pitch, would fail to attract those to whom the names of Pugno and Grieg meant something, still less to those to whom they have no appeal. However, in the closing weeks of that year, in London,

Giuseppe Verdi conducting Aïda *in Paris in 1880.*
MARY EVANS PICTURE LIBRARY

Fred Gaisberg recorded several sides by a young pupil of Brahms, Ilona Eibenschütz, which reveal a considerable improvement in the technique of recording that most obstinate of instruments, the piano. Listening to these exquisitely rare recordings today under ideal conditions, one can only wonder at the beauty of the playing, secured so accurately as early as 1903.

The first recording of a complete opera was also made by G & T in 1903: the Italian branch recorded Verdi's *Ernani* on 40 single-sided 10in discs.

As the only one of the subsidiaries of the North American Phonograph combine to prosper in the early 90s, the Columbia Phonograph Company had established itself as a major power in the recording business by the end of the decade. It had shaken loose from Edison, and was indeed conducting good business in cylinder manufacture. A trade announcement on 6 November, 1901, notified the world that Col-

umbia had already begun to challenge Berliner and Johnson by producing lateral-cut discs in addition to cylinders. Having purchased a patent for wax recording devised in 1897 by a teen-age member of Berliner's staff, Columbia now had a legal weapon with which to beat Victor at its own new game; but their disc Graphophones were themselves a violation of the Victor gramophone patent. Sensibly, the two giants pooled their patents, and began the mutually respectful rivalry that dominated the American recording industry for the next 50 or more years.

The first Columbia discs appeared early in 1902, in 10in and 7in sizes. Assuming their numbering to be an indication of the sequence of recording (like Victor but unlike Berliner), the record bearing the number 1 is a strange nonentity with which to launch a vast enterprise – except, of course, that at the time no-one could accurately foresee how vast that enterprise would become. So Columbia 1 was nothing more epoch-making than a record of a group of musicians modestly described on the smart black and silver label as 'Columbia Orchestra', playing Orth's *In A Clock Store*. No documentary evidence appears to exist now as to when exactly this and the next 5000 Columbia records were made, but the appearance and general sound of the many surviving specimens prove that here was a quality product, well able to stand in the market place and challenge all comers.

There were several physical differences between Johnson's Victor records and Columbia's. Victor's were pressed in solid stock shellac compound; most Berliners had been made of the same material, but Columbia's were produced by laminating a thin outer coating of plastic on a stout core of fibrous composition, itself enclosed between two sheets of thinnest paper. This made for a much more durable product; it did not mean that the records were unbreakable, but it ensured that a blow that would disintegrate a Victor or Berliner would do no more than cause an inaudible crack in the outer surface of the Columbia.

Grand Opera Series To Columbia must go the

COMPANY PROFILE

Columbia

1888 The Columbia Phonograph Co was set up in Washington, DC, as the local agency of Lippincott's North American Phonograph Co to market Edison Phonographs and Bell/Tainter Graphophones on a 'let-on-hire' basis in the District of Columbia, West Virginia and Delaware.

1889 January: The Columbia Phonograph Co was incorporated as a subsidiary of the North American Phonograph Co; Edward D Easton was appointed as Columbia's first director. Frank Dorian was sent to open an office in Paris. This became the European headquarters in 1897.

1891 Columbia issued their first catalogue of cylinder recordings, and took over control of the North American Bell and Tainter patents.

1894 North American Phonograph Co was liquidated and its territorial rights passed to Columbia, which joined with the American Graphophone Co to form the Columbia Phonograph Co, General.

c 1896 The trade mark 'Columbia' was first applied to playing machines.

1897 May: Columbia Graphophones and cylinders were licensed in the UK through the London Phonograph Co.

1898 Columbia made their first wax vertical cut disc records. Although made in America, these were sold only in the UK.

1899 Columbia opened a depot in Berlin (Columbia Phonograph Co mbH from 1902).

1900 European head office transferred from Paris to Wells Street, London (then Oxford Street from 1901); English recordings were made in quantity but the majority of sales were of imported American recordings.

1901 The first Columbia disc records were issued in America in 7in and 10in sizes, with black and silver labels. Their name of 'Climax' was changed to 'Columbia Disc Record' in September 1902.

1903 Launch of the Columbia 'Grand Opera' series. The London premises were moved to Great Eastern Street. Cylinders were made for the UK and export markets.

1904 The first Columbia double-sided discs were issued in America but were quickly withdrawn due to patent infringement. The first Odeon Records were issued in Germany in February.

1905 Branches were opened in Warsaw and in Sydney. The 'Wandsworth Factory' was opened at Earlsfield, Surrey.

1906 Columbia and the American Graphophone Co were merged and were re-organised as the Columbia Graphophone Co. Columbia-Marconi 'Velvet-Tone' discs were introduced: they were made of thin plastic with a paper core.

1908 Operatic recordings were issued by arrangement with the Fonotipia and Odeon companies. Columbia leased selected disc titles to Rena for re-coupling and issue as 'Rena Double Face Records'.

1909 December: Louis Sterling was appointed sales manager of the Columbia Phonograph Co in London. Sterling's Rena company was absorbed by Columbia.

1910 Columbia recorded their own operatic issues, dispensing with those of Fonotipia and Odeon. The 'Columbia Grand Opera' series was launched in the UK in April 1911. Rena Double Face Records became Columbia-Rena records. The 'twin note' trade mark was registered (the associated words 'Magic Notes' came later).

1911 August: The London office was moved to 81 City Road and a recording studio was opened there.

1912 American Columbia ceased manufacture of cylinder records.

1913 28 January: The American and UK branches standardised their name as the Columbia Graphophone Co. The London headquarters and studio were moved to Clerkenwell Road.

1913 March: Columbia-Rena 10in opera discs were introduced at a 'popular price'.

1913 September: The 'Phoenix' label was introduced at 1s 1d (5p).

1914 January: The mid-price 'Regal' label was introduced at 1s 6d (7½p).

1915 The 'Rena' component of the Columbia-Rena name was dropped.

1915 14 September: The 'Grafonola' gramophone was introduced.

1917 February: Columbia Graphophone Co registered in England (under American control) with Louis Sterling as manager and Sir George Croydon Marks as chairman.

1922 A new quiet-surfaced 'scratchless' disc was developed by Columbia for USA and UK sales.

1923 26 April: An English syndicate purchased UK Columbia from the American owners.

1924 American Columbia (called Columbia Phonograph Co Inc from February) issued its first album sets: *Columbia Fine Arts Series of Musical Masterworks*. The 'Masterworks' series survives to this day worldwide on the CBS label.

1925 The American Columbia companies were bankrupted, but rescued by money raised by Louis Sterling. American Columbia therefore became British-owned on 31 March, and, by 1927, British-controlled under Sterling as managing director, with Sir George Croydon Marks (later Lord Marks) as chairman. UK Columbia acquired control of Carl Lindström (see Personalia) and its Dutch associate Transoceanic; their Parlophone trade mark thus passed into Columbia control (2 September).

1927 UK Columbia mark Beethoven's centenary with an ambitious series of recordings. The following year Schubert's centenary was similarly marked (see Section IV).

1927 4 September: Columbia Phonograph Corp Inc formed the Columbia Broadcasting System (CBS).

1929 Columbia began to produce radios, and by November were installing them in record players, calling them 'combination instruments'.

1930 The British company had by now purchased The OKeh Phonograph Co of America (formerly the General Phonograph Corp, acquired in November 1926), Nipponophone of Japan (formed in October 1910 and acquired in May 1927), Pathé of France (acquired May 1928), Lindström of Germany (acquired September 1925) and other companies, giving it a firm international basis with numerous factories round the world.

1931 January: Columbia GmbH formed in Germany.

1931 UK Columbia was merged with The Gramophone Co to form Electrical and Musical Industries (see Company Profile – EMI).

The American Columbia Phonograph Co Inc became completely independent of the UK company and was therefore not involved in the formation of EMI. For the subsequent history of the non-American branches, see Company Profile – EMI.

1932 In America, the Columbia Phonograph Co Inc was purchased by Grigsby-Grunow Inc, makers of radios; then purchased in 1934 by Sacro Enterprises; and in 1938 by CBS, together with the American Record Co, and re-named Columbia Recording Co, president Edward Wallerstein.

1939 CBS purchased the Brunswick Radio Corp (founded in 1920 as Brunswick Balke Collender Co, then as Brunswick Radio Corp in 1927, the year in which they made their first British recordings. Warner Brothers had bought Brunswick in 1929).

1948 American Columbia introduced the world's first successful long playing record (see Section IX).

1952 December: A reciprocal releasing agreement with EMI in the UK was terminated.

1955 American Columbia material began to be issued in the UK by Philips.

1965 American Columbia material launched independently in the UK (marketed at first by Oriole) on the CBS label. Because of the still-current use of the trade mark 'Columbia' outside America by EMI, all American Columbia recordings were exported under the CBS logo.

1980 The trade mark 'Columbia', a respected and historic name, was at last phased out in the US after 91 years, all issues worldwide henceforth of the Columbia Broadcasting System to bear the trade mark CBS.

credit for taking the initiative and being **the first to record artists of celebrity status in the United States**. Victor could draw on the stockpile of masters that Fred and Will Gaisberg and their colleagues were making in all the cultural centres of Europe, and thus the Victor catalogue was beginning to feature records by Enrico Caruso, Maurice Renaud, and Emma Calvé and the other red-label stars, and in advance of some of them making their American débuts. (In the case of the Russian soprano, Maria Michailova, her records were best-sellers on Victor from the first issue of them, but the singer herself never left Russia.) Columbia's European market was centred on cylinders and a handful of discs by the same sort of qualified but hardly stellar artists as were making much the same type of records in New York. Then in

HALL OF FAME

Enrico Caruso, tenor

1873 27 February: Born Naples.
1894 16 November: Début in *L'amico Francesco* by Morelli at the Teatro Nuovo, Naples.
1897–1903 First great success in *La Gioconda* by Ponchielli in Palermo in May 1897. Appeared in Buenos Aires (1899), Rome (1899), Milan (1900), Covent Garden, London (1902), Metropolitan Opera House, New York (1903).
1898–1903 **Made first recordings** 1898–1901: three titles for Pathé Frères (cylinders); then seven titles for the Anglo-Italian Commerce Co (AICC) in Genoa, early 1902 (cylinders). **First disc records** made on 18 March, 1902, in Milan for Gramophone & Typewriter Ltd. For the ten titles (listed below) he was paid £100. **The first known instance of a disc being used to promote an artist** was when Heinrich Conried of the New York Metropolitan Opera Co heard a 10in Caruso recording made in 1902 and engaged the singer the following year. Caruso made his début there on 23 November, 1903, and appeared regularly until a year before his death.
1902–21 Caruso is considered to be **the first serious musician to appreciate the value of the gramophone**, partly because the quality and tone of his voice recorded so well. During these years he received some $2 million in royalties from G & T (later HMV) in the UK and Victor in the US, and re-issues of his recordings continue to be popular. Sales of his *Vesti la giubba* from Leoncavallo's *I Pagliacci* (recorded first in November 1902) total over one million copies.
1920 16 September: Made his last recording: *Crucifixus* from *Petite Messe Solonelle* by Rossini.
1921 2 August: Died Naples, aged 48.

Some early Caruso recordings were 'cleaned-up' in the mid-1970s by Dr T G Stockham of Utah University, using computer enhancement. These were issued commercially by RCA.

The first ten recordings Caruso made for G & T in Milan in March 1902.

Record No	Composer	Opera	Aria	Remarks
52344	Verdi	*Rigoletto*	*Questa o Quella*	Re-recorded with orch., 1908
52345	Massenet	*Manon*	*O dolce incanto*	Re-recorded 1904
52346	Donizetti	*L'Elisir d'amore*	*Una furtiva lagrima*	Re-recorded 1904
52347	Boïto	*Mefistofele*	*Guinto sul passo estremo*	
52348	Boïto	*Mefistofele*	*Dai campi, dai prati*	Re-recorded November 1902
52349	Puccini	*Tosca*	*E lucevan le stelle*	
52368	Mascagni	*Iris*	*Serenata*	
52369	Verdi	*Aïda*	*Celeste Aïda*	Re-recorded November 1902
52370	Franchetti	*Germania*	*No non chiuder gli occhi vaghi*	
52378	Franchetti	*Germania*	*Studenti, uditi*	

All the above were recorded at *c* 73–74rpm.

February 1903, four eminent singers visited the Columbia studio within a few days of each other, and recorded 16 titles between them, initiating the Grand Opera Series, offered on discs but not cylinders. These were baritones Giuseppe Campanari and Antonio Scotti; soprano Suzanne Adams, and – at least from the point of view of recording a voice with a famous name – the bass Edouard de Reszke. Scotti and

Adams had recorded for G & T in London the previous summer, but the three sides made by de Reszke are the only commercial records he ever made. Certain early Victor records contain expeditious announcements concerning the music about to be played; Columbia's cylinders were announced similarly, and the discs also were prefaced by an announcement of title and artist, with the assurance that the product was a Columbia record (Victor modestly made no reference to this aspect of its performances). Usually the Columbia announcer provided this identification, but in some of the operatic celebrity records, the artists themselves did so: one exceptionally interesting example is de Reszke's record of Tchaikovsky's *Sérénade de Don Juan*, announced by the singer. These, the first celebrity vocal records to have been recorded in the United States, were not notable for their technical quality, however. They were not good sellers in the way that Victor's imported recordings were. They had cost Columbia a considerable sum of money in recording fees, and were slow at producing returns.

Red Seal Victor seized the initiative, and on 30 April, 1903, recorded **the first Red Seal** (as the red label celebrity issues were known) **record made in America**. It was by Ada Crossley, an Australian contralto. A few weeks later, one of the greatest interpreters of *Carmen* visited Victor's studios in Carnegie Hall to make some superbly natural-sounding records: Zélie de Lussan. She made no other Victors, few other records at all, which is as incredible as it is lamentable, as her work that Sunday morning, 17 May, 1903, is richly satisfactory.

Johnson realised that his Red Seal issues had got the Columbia Grand Opera Series on the run. To back his new American recordings and the valuable material he had leased from Europe, he took full-page advertisements in *Harper's Weekly* and many other luxury magazines in 1903. In April the following year he announced the exclusive contract he had just signed with Caruso across the whole back page of the *Saturday Evening Post*. This was **the first time the talking machine**, considered a toy not long before, **had been supported by such**

powerful and widely-read advertising. Caruso had recorded ten sides, some of 12in size, for which he was guaranteed $2000 per annum for 5 years. With his capital thus tied up, Johnson was determined to bring his Red Seal Series firmly before the public eye, and he aimed at the luxury end of a rapidly-expanding market.

The highest priced records at that time were Melba's first records for G & T, issued in July 1904 with special mauve labels at 1 guinea each (£1.05p). (Melba made her last recordings during her Covent Garden Farewell performance on 8 June, 1926.)

The first record company to issue serious music only was the Milan-based Societa Italiana di Fonotipia, formed in October 1904. Records were made at the Odeon factory at Weissensee, Germany, and were not on sale until 1905 (January 1906 in the UK). Fonotipia Ltd was formed in the UK on 24 April 1906, taking over the Milan company.

Consequent upon the demise in 1903 of International Zonophone, originally set up in 1901 by Frank Seaman, its erstwhile managing director F M Prescott formed a new company in Berlin that produced finely-recorded music by as many singers as were not contracted to G & T. The label was Odeon, and it made an impact on the infant industry by offering music on both sides of the disc. **These were the first double-sided records**. Columbia attempted a similar device, but Odeon threatened legal action, and Columbia's hasty coupling of fairly similar existing single-sided records as double-siders was as hastily withdrawn – for the moment. Four years later, Victor and Columbia in America, Zonophone (Twin), and Rena (later to be known as Columbia-Rena and then Columbia) in England, all launched double-sided records in competition with Odeon.

The first decade of the 20th century saw the flowering of Emile Berliner's recorded disc as a prime means of home entertainment. For reasonable outlay, even those of modest means could bring the voices of adequate singers performing the popular songs of the day into their homes; they might even choose to invite established stars of music-hall and – more rarely – the theatre to sing for them by means of their records. In the case of W H Berry, who made the first English Columbia disc record in 1901, or Billy Williams, an Australian music-hall singer billed as 'The Man in the Velvet Suit', who recorded prolifically for many labels between 1906 and his death at 38 in 1915, their diction and recording techniques were faultless. Those with deeper pockets suitably filled would patronise the operatic section of the catalogues, and one might even run to the $200 'Victrola' machine introduced by Victor in 1906, **the first instrument whose unsightly flared horn was enclosed entirely within the cabinet**. Whatever their financial status, however, few indeed were the owners of gramophones who had no military band records in their collections, for those occupied pride of position in all the catalogues once the immediate teething troubles of the industry were over. Prominent among these military recordings on Gramophone Concert (10in) or Gramophone Monarch (12in) – or simply Gramophone (7in, which disappeared from the market in February 1906) was the Band of H M Coldstream Guards; this worthy unit provided every kind of music from operatic selections and musical comedies to wedding and funeral marches, from arrangements of ballads – often featuring a solo cornetist – to dance music, meaning Viennese-type waltzes, lancers, polkas, military two-steps, and schottisches, and of course, marches. One looks in vain in any catalogue dated earlier than 1911 for anything remotely suggesting a symphony, a concerto, or any form of chamber music, unless it be an arrangement for solo violin with piano accompaniment of some well-known *morceau* from a ballet suite, hardly a satisfactory substitute for any of these! Orchestral records there were, indeed – a few stringed instruments adapted for acoustic recording by the addition of a small horn to amplify the sound supplemented the conventional brass and woodwind of the military band – but their records consisted of very much the same material as those by the bands themselves. Even the orchestral accompaniments to the great singers, replacing the usual piano from about 1906, sounded more like concert bands than anything to be heard accompanying those same singers in an opera house or concert hall. Earlier attempts to use wind instruments instead of piano accompaniments were hilariously disastrous; the porcine efforts of the 'orchestra' accompanying the Finnish soprano Aïno Ackté singing 'The Jewel Song' from *Faust* in 1905 have been known to reduce even stern-faced music-lovers to helpless mirth.

Orchestral Then, in the Columbia supplement for July 1911, there appeared a 12in record of what was called the Court Symphony Orchestra, playing Schubert's famous 'Unfinished' Symphony No 8 in B minor, one movement on each side. It had been recorded in New York by the 'house' orchestra under the baton of Charles A Prince, who conducted every kind of music. This recording was seized on avidly by enthusiasts who longed for instrumental music other than that provided by violinists, however strong the drawing-power of their names (Fritz Kreisler, Joska Szigeti, Jan Kubelík, Mischa Elman). The fact that a piece of music that in later years would occupy six 12in 78rpm sides had been ruthlessly pared down to make its quart fit the pint-pot of one 12in record troubled none. The issue by The Gramophone Company of Beethoven's Symphony No 5 in C minor played by the Berlin Philharmonic Orchestra conducted by Arthur Nikisch, on eight single-sided records in dribs and drabs from May to August 1914 must have seemed almost anti-climatical, even though they represented **the first more-or-less complete reading of a symphonic score** by a world-famous orchestra under a world-famous conductor. The recording had been made in Berlin in 1909. That the score had to be 'altered' to enable certain of the instruments to be accommodated in the studio (tuba for double-bass, for example), and that the manpower of each section of the orchestra had to be reduced almost to cadre, seems to have meant little to the public at which they were aimed. The Beethoven Fifth had been immediately preceded by the same orchestra playing Wagner's *Parsifal* music under Dr Alfred Hertz, with the same reservations. Other symphony orchestra records followed, in America from the Chicago,

Philadelphia and Boston Symphony Orchestras, and in England from the Royal Albert Hall Orchestra conducted by Landon Ronald, on 'His Master's Voice', and from Sir Henry J Wood and Sir Thomas Beecham conducting their own orchestras on Columbia.

The first orchestra formed especially for recording purposes was the Meister Orchestra in 1911, under the sponsorship of the German Beka Company. The best-known recording orchestra is the Philharmonia, formed in 1945 by Walter Legge of EMI Records. It became a self-governing body in 1964 as the New Philharmonia Orchestra, but dropped the 'New' in 1977. This orchestra gave concerts as well as undertaking a busy recording schedule; other orchestras have made records under pseudonyms for contractual reasons, eg: the Royal Philharmonic Orchestra recorded under the name Philharmonic Promenade Orchestra in the 1950s.

Chamber Music What, though, of chamber music? Was there no place in any of the rapidly-expanding catalogues for examples of the most sublime music of all? It might have been claimed justifiably in the earliest days, when a solo violin could barely be reproduced with any degree of similitude, that chamber music, specifically string quartets, could not be accommodated comfortably on a Berliner or early Victor-Gramophone record; but by the beginning of the second decade of the century, most of the problems surrounding such an enterprise had been overcome. Indeed, Victor had formed its own String Quartet but it had to play an arrangement of Stephen Foster's *Come Where My Love Lies Dreaming*, and, surprisingly, the Gavotte from Gluck's *Paris and Helena*. In England in 1905 the Renard Trio and Quartette had made **the first chamber music records** of such items as the *Adagio* from Beethoven's Trio No 4, Op 2 (sic), three short pieces by Schumann, and some readily-assimilable, well-known items by Tchaikovsky, Dvořák, von Blon, and Mendelssohn. So far, no attack had been made on the enormous string quartet repertoire. The famous string quartet, the Flonzalay, did make two attempts at recording the

Minuet from Beethoven's Quartet in C minor, Op 18, No 4, but neither the first, on 22 December, 1913, nor the second, on 16 March, 1914 (nor, for that matter, the *Molto Lento* movement from Rubinstein's Quartet Op. 17, No 2, also recorded at the second session and again at the third), were successful for reasons that have never been explained. The third session, on 26 May, 1914, also recorded one take each of a *Courante* by Glazunov, a Scherzo (no other identification) by Tchaikovsky, and the *Andante* from Mozart's Quartet in D, K 575, without success, although the latter was re-made nearly 4 years later and the result issued all over the world. Meanwhile, on 17 February, 1917, another noted chamber group, the Elman String Quartet, comprising the great Russian violinist Mischa Elman, with Adolf Bak, Karl Rissland, and Rudolf Nagel of the Boston Symphony Orchestra, had recorded for Victor, and the only take of the first recording they made was accepted for issue in America and Britain. It too was an *Andante*, from Dittersdorf's Quartet in G, but although the first to be recorded, the first from that session to be issued – in May 1917 – was yet another *Andante* movement, from Haydn's Quartet in C, Op 76, No 4 ('The Emperor').

The first string quartet recordings made in England other than arrangements of potboilers, were by the London String Quartet for Columbia, in late 1913, and a number of titles were successfully issued. They included *Andante* movements from quartets by Tchaikovsky (in D, Op 11) and Debussy (in G minor), and ante-dated the American Victor recordings by nearly 4 years.

Jazz **The first announcement of a jazz recording** appeared in the same Victor supplement of 1917 that listed the Elman String Quartet record mentioned above. It was the Original Dixieland Jazz Band, and it gave notice that the manners and modes of Western dancing and popular music were ready for a change. That first issue, comprising *Dixieland Jass Band One-Step*, with *Livery Stable Blues*, sold over a million copies in the ensuing 8 years, setting the popular music scene for the next four decades,

until the coming of rock 'n' roll. Once again, Columbia had beaten Victor – and lost the advantage, just as they had with American-recorded opera singers 14 years earlier. For the Original Dixieland Jazz Band, or 'Jass Band', as their first records spelt their name, had already recorded for Columbia about a month prior to the Victor date (26 February, 1917) that produced the million-seller. Columbia had no idea how to record a quintet of cornet, trombone, clarinet, piano and drums, nor did their musical director realise they were at their best playing the numbers they had worked out between them. Columbia insisted on their recording two popular dance tunes of the time, *Darktown Strutters' Ball*, and *Indiana*, but on hearing the results, decided against issue. Victor stepped in with superior recording and better understanding of what exactly was setting New York nightlife on fire, and though Columbia reversed the rejection decision, it was too late. Try as they might to find a similar band to pit against the Dixieland Jazz Band, they failed. As early as 1917–18 in the history of jazz, the talent simply was not there. The musicians of both races who tried to jump on the Dixieland band-wagon and make more million-copy sellers for the most part fell very flat. Columbia had to wait until 1919, when they recorded the Synco Jazz Band (one title issued), Gorman's Novelty Syncopators (one title issued), and the Louisiana Five (six titles issued), before they could find any jazz band to match the ODJB, who were by then creating a comparable sensation in post-war London.

Jazz had come from New Orleans, a delightful mixture of European march music and songs – even hymns – played with an exhilarating new beat that owed something to ragtime. Ragtime had been more successful in its pristine form in its own country than in Europe, although Fred Gaisberg had recorded a march from *Rice's Ragtime Opera*, played on guitar and mandolin by the Musical Avolos, a music-hall act, in London, on 4 May, 1899. This is without doubt **the first disc record made in Europe to bear any reference to ragtime.** In the purest sense that the music of Scott Joplin and his followers is the only true ragtime, then this is not a ragtime performance at all; it is more of a cake-walk, a strutting, parade-march tune, as the title infers, with a few touches of rather elementary syncopation. Even so, its recording date is 4½ months prior to the earliest American Berliner known to have an allusion to ragtime in its title (*You Got To Play Ragtime*, recorded 18 September, 1899, by, of all groups, the United States Marine Band), and over 7 months before ban-

The first jazz recording to be issued:

Titles:	Dixieland Jass Band One-Step		Tony Sbarbaro (later:
	Livery Stable Blues		'Spargo'), drums
Artists:	Original Dixieland Jass Band		Larry Shields, clarinet
Personnel:	Edwin ('Eddie') Edwards,	*Location:*	Victor's New York Studios
	trombone	*Date:*	Monday, 26 February, 1917
	Dominick James ('Nick')	*Engineer:*	Charles Sooy
	LaRocca, cornet	*Number:*	Victor 18255
	Henry Ragas, piano	*Release date:*	Wednesday, 7 March, 1917

Left to right: Eddie Edwards, Larry Shields, Tony Sbarbaro, J Russell Robinson (who replaced Henry Ragas), and Nick LaRocca.   COURTESY: MAX JONES

joist Richard L Weaver made what the details etched into the central area describe as *Ragtime Dance* on 14 December, 1899. This ante-dates Scott Joplin's work of the same title by just over 2 years; his masterpiece, *Maple Leaf Rag*, does not seem to have been recorded on disc until 1906, when again the Marines came to the rescue with a rather stilted reading of it.

Big Band Few jazz records, and no ragtime, actual or alleged, reached the dizzying heights of million-sales enjoyed by the first Victor issue of the ODJB; but such was the impact on the public of this vigorous, exciting new style of music that modifications and transformations were bound to follow. The leader of the dance band in the St Francis Hotel in San Francisco set the next scene in the dramatic story of popular music. Art Hickman and his Orchestra, which included a team of saxophones blending with the brass and rhythm to produce a new, rich sound, crossed the nation to New York to play an engagement there, and record a number of popular tunes of the time, September 1919, for Columbia. **This is the first 'Big Band' recording.** Saxophone teams were themselves no novelty; before the outbreak of World War I there had been a unit known as the Six Brown Brothers, which consisted of soprano, two alto, tenor, baritone, and bass saxophones played by unrelated musicians under the direction of Tom Brown, the lead alto. They had recorded for Victor and Columbia a considerable number of titles of commendable variety, from *La Paloma* to *That Moaning Saxophone Rag*, one of their own compositions. This is a genuine rag, and it sold steadily in England for 11 years, itself something of a record. Both the Victor and HMV issues of it are backed by a curious number called *The Original Fox Trot*, played by the banjoist Fred van Eps and his pianist, Felix Arndt, with drums by Eddie King.

Dance Despite its title, this is not the *original* fox trot (it would be quite suitable for marching, in fact); **the first Victor record to bear the designation 'Fox Trot'** that was to launch tens of thousands similarly described was recorded on 6 August, 1914, just two days after Britain and Germany went to war. The title was *Sweetie*

Dear, composed by the black rag composer Joe Jordan, and it was played by Patrick Conway's Band, one of Sousa's rivals. In England, despite wartime conditions, the fox trot also took a hold on the public fancy, and **the first English fox trot recording** was made by the great American comedienne Elsie Janis, released in May 1915. It was *Ballin' The Jack*, another number by a black composer, Chris Smith, and in it the singer gave instructions to her very British (and, for the purpose of the scene, rather witless) partner, Basil Hallam on how to dance the fox trot. On the same supplement, two 12in sides by Murray's Ragtime Trio, accompanied by the Mayfair Orchestra (HMV's 'house' band) provided practical assistance in the form of two fox trots that musically were some years ahead of their time – *Beets And Turnips*, and *Hors d'oeuvres*.

In none of these early fox trot records can a saxophone be heard, however; and while Art Hickman's 1919 records that featured a saxophone section were very popular, it was another band from California that secured the 'Oscar' of being **the first dance band to sell over a million records**. This was Paul Whiteman's Band playing *The Japanese Sandman* and *Whispering*, recorded August 1920 and issued that November. The band played from arranged scores, as distinct from jazz bands that worked from memorised arrangements. Rarely had success come so abruptly: this was Paul Whiteman's first recording. The sales figures in the United States alone reached 1 302 923 in the 5 years it was in the Victor catalogue, and it sold proportionately well in England.

War Songs It was said that jazz reflected the understandable desire of millions of young people who had survived the war to escape from the nightmare of those years. War songs were nevertheless top sellers on record, not only in that conflict, but in the Boer War of 1899–1902, and in America, at the time of the brief Spanish–American War of 1898, there were several recordings of jingoistic songs that mirrored the popular taste of the time. Many of the American recordings were of songs that had already seen active service in the Civil War over 30 years

HALL OF FAME

Paul Whiteman, bandleader

1890 28 March: Born Denver, Colorado, USA. His father was music supervisor to Denver schools. Paul studied violin and viola.

1907 He became lead viola in the Denver Symphony Orchestra and played also in the San Francisco Symphony.

1914–17 Bandleader in the US Navy at Bear Island, California.

1919 **Formed his first orchestra** in San Francisco.

1920 August: **Made his first recording**: *Whispering* and *The Japanese Sandman*, for Victor, issued in November, which sold over $1\frac{1}{4}$ million copies in 5 years.

1924 24 February: Gave his first concert at the Aeolian Hall, New York. The programme included the première of Gershwin's *Rhapsody in Blue* with the composer at the piano. (This was recorded shortly afterwards but met with little success; the re-make of 1927 was a best seller.)

1930 Starred in the film *King of Jazz* (dedicated to him, and including also Bing Crosby), all six titles of which became best sellers. This was the first of his many films.

1943 Appointed musical director of the American Broadcasting Co, New York, which post claimed much of his time at the expense of his orchestra. He attempted to re-form his band several times in the 1950s.

1967 29 December: Died at Doylestown, Pennsylvania.

In its heyday the Whiteman Band included many later famous names such as both the Dorseys, Bix Beiderbecke, Red Norvo and Joe Venuti, and The Rhythm Boys included Bing Crosby before he went solo. Whiteman's arranger Ferde Grofé scored Gershwin's *Rhapsody in Blue* and went on to become a successful composer in his own right.

Amongst Whiteman's best sellers, in addition to those mentioned above, were *The Parade of the Wooden Soldiers* (recorded 1922 and 1928), *Three O'Clock in The Morning* (1923), *Linger a While* (1923, featuring Mike Pingatore, banjo), *Side by Side* (1927), *Ramona* (1928), and *Slaughter on Tenth Avenue* (1936).

BBC HULTON PICTURE LIBRARY

earlier, but two sides were also made by Emil Cassi, billed as Chief Trumpeter of (Theodore) Roosevelt's Rough Riders. One of these was a selection of five US Army bugle calls, but the other gave the calls actually sounded by Mr Cassi at San Juan Hill, Santiago, Cuba, on 1 July, 1898, the Rough Riders' day of glory.

The first records of songs about a war then actually raging were those made for Berliner in the South African War. These were sung by a Scot named Ian Colquohoun, whose ringing baritone voice was admirably suited to projecting these songs from the stage of a music hall, and into the recording horn in the basement of 31, Maiden Lane, London. Although hostilities commenced on 11 October, 1899, Ian Colquohoun was ready to record the defiant songs *We're Not Going to Stand It* and *Take The Lion's Muzzle Off* on 15 November. **The first recording to occupy more than one disc** (in the

sense that one half was dependent upon the other for completeness) was made in the same month by the same artist. It was Rudyard Kipling's poem to Sir Arthur Sullivan's music, *The Absent-Minded Beggar*. (Record A exists in four different takes, record B in five; it must be one of the best-sellers of all on the Berliner catalogue.) Other songs in belligerent style followed: *Volunteers*, *Private Tommy Atkins*, *Bravo! Dublin Fusiliers*, and even *The Boers Have Got My Daddy*. The relief of Mafeking on 18 May, 1900, was celebrated by *Song Of Mafeking*, recorded by the Darnley Brothers on 4 September, and wishful-thinking was personified in several recordings made in 1900 of something called *Marching To Pretoria*.

Even wars in which neither America nor Britain were involved had their songs reflecting popular feeling on the conflict. Songs such as *We Don't Want To Fight* that gave the language the

The last two pages of HMV's September 1914 Supplement. Even Nipper was mobilised for the war effort.

word 'jingoism' and its derivatives were popular at the time of the Russo–Turkish War in 1878, too early to be recorded; but in the Russo–Japanese War of 1904–5, there were such songs as *Good Luck, Japan* (19 April, 1904, barely two months after hostilities had begun) and *Little Brown Man of Japan* (13 September, 1905, 3 weeks after peace was restored), both firmly biased towards Japan, both recorded by the Australian singer, Hamilton Hill.

At the outbreak of World War I, all the recording companies leapt to record as many jingoistic songs as possible, for home consumption; these made little or no appeal to the members of the British Expeditionary Force, who sang through the obscenity of Flanders, Passchendaele, the Dardanelles, and Mesopotamia with their own favourites. **The first record to deal with World War I**, other than those made by politicians or other national figures, was a simple message from Sgt Dwyer, VC, recorded in November 1915 for Regal, Columbia's recent inexpensive subsidiary label. The gallant sergeant was killed in action soon after his return to the front from the leave in which he recorded his eye-witness account of conditions in the trenches. A month before the war ended, as the Royal Garrison Artillery was bombarding the enemy position outside Lille with gas shells, HMV set up its recording gear in a ruined farmhouse near the front line, and actually succeeded in recording the sounds of command and firing of shells, as they whistled and crashed into the almost-defeated enemy. **This is the first on-the-spot recording of an actual event in world history**. (A recording in the Columbia studios in London on 13 June, 1917, by the London String Quartet actually took place during a daylight air-raid, but despite the explosion of several bombs in the vicinity of the Clerkenwell Road studios, nothing marred the recording. Similarly unaffected by the sounds of war was the concentration of Wanda Landowska as she recorded Scarlatti's Sonata in D, Kk 490, in Paris in March 1940. Anti-aircraft guns may clearly be heard as the French defenders fought vainly to stop the Nazi advance on their capital,

but Miss Landowska, according to an eye-witness, 'merely concentrated all the harder on the music'.) Further recordings connected with war are noted in Section VIII.

The earliest known recording of a 'live' performance on disc was a curious occasion in the Arcadia Ballroom, Detroit, on the night of 28 January, 1925, when the mobile recording equipment of the General Phonograph Corporation was set up on the bandstand, and Howard Steed directed Finzel's Arcadia Orchestra playing *Laff It Off*, in the presence of (allegedly) thousands of dancers. A photograph of the proceedings published in a trade journal a few weeks later certainly shows a vast multitude enjoying themselves, and the recording apparatus, horn, turntable and so on, can be seen on the stand, with the band huddled together round it. Attempts to locate a copy of this OKeh record, even in Detroit itself, have so far failed.

The recording, in August 1920, of a genuine Negro blues by a popular black artist named Mamie Smith, on the newly-established Okeh label, caused a sensation that sold 75 000 copies in a few weeks. This began a boom in records by black artists, many of whom were indeed 'discovered' by the talent scouts on their tours of the Deep South, the mid-West and South West, most of them on Victor or Columbia. These two companies had each been given a licence for recording by the new Western Electric sound system early in 1925, and at once set out to comb the country for further talent they hoped was hidden away in rural areas, which could be recorded and sold to country folk in those parts. White country-style artists were also 'discovered' in this manner, and one in particular made such a hit with his first record that the sales of this and his many subsequent records made in widely-separated cities such as New Orleans, New York, Atlanta, Louisville, Hollywood, and Dallas, made him a millionaire. He was a railroad worker named Jimmie Rodgers, who sang and yodelled songs based firmly on the Negro blues form to his own guitar accompaniment, often with others. Rodgers, who suffered from tuberculosis, was recording from August 1927 to May 1933, slightly less than 6 years, and died 2 days after his last session. He was 36.

With the advent of electrical recording, Berliner's acoustic era came to a close. He lived to see his son continue in the recording business (in Canada), producing the Ajax record into the mid-20s. He and Eldridge Johnson also lived to see the Victor Talking Machine Co being sold outright to two Wall Street banking houses, Speyer & Co, and J W Seligman & Co, at the end of 1926, and the absorption of the company by Radio Corporation of America, on 4 January, 1929. Seven months later, Emile Berliner died, and the end of October saw the Wall Street collapse, a turning point for gramophones and records since they at once became expendable luxuries. It had been an exciting era of progress and 'firsts', of unscheduled and unrehearsed moments which added colour to the history of the early disc, and we may pause to recall some of these moments before going on to discuss the new electrical age.

Facts and Oddities of the Acoustic Age

Noises 'Off' In the earliest days of disc recording some of the most curious comments were recorded. Less frequently on Berliner and Victor, but quite often on Gramophone Company and HMV records (and the subsidiary Zonophone) a recording would start or close with conversation which was apparently unnoticed at the time of recording or of testing. Modern hi-fi equipment reveals what the contemporary machines could not. Emma Calvé, for example, during her recording of *Séguidille* from *Carmen* in London in June 1902, comments excitedly in French on her own vocal ability, and towards the end of *Magali*, as she approaches the indescribably lovely, sustained final note, she murmurs, 'Ecoutez, maintenant!' In contrast to the volatile French soprano's self-admiration is the quiet approval given by Charles Santley at the end of his very rare and much sought-after recording of *Non più andrai*,

from Mozart's *Nozze di Figaro*, **the first 12in disc sung in Italian**. Having sung the aria impeccably, at the age of 69, the great baritone comments as Landon Ronald plays the concluding phrase, 'I think that's all right!' It was one of five sides made in the studios at 21, City Road, London, by this artist, whose career reached back to the second decade of the Victorian era, and on all of them, he can be heard saying something at the end. The 10in *To Anthea* has the shortest playing-time; but after a flourish from Landon Ronald, there ensues a three-way conversation:

1st voice: 'Just a minute, don't touch the grille ... (unintelligible)!'
2nd voice (probably Santley's): 'What?'
3rd voice: 'Mr Richardson says don't touch the grille.'
2nd voice (affably): 'All right.'

There follows some more conversation and subdued laughter, but the speakers had evidently moved away from the recording horn, and the speech is no longer intelligible. Fred Gaisberg remembered a Mr Richardson as an assistant engineer of the time. The grille was a device for controlling the input of sound, attached to the horn and operated like Venetian blinds.

After playing his *Shepherd's Hey*, HMV E 147 (1914), Percy Grainger remarks 'I think we'd better do that again'; evidently no-one agreed.

One of the most prolific, and most popular, of all recording artists, and probably a strong contender for the one with the longest recording career, at least among singers, was the Australian bass-baritone Peter Dawson (see p. 69, Hall of Fame), who began recording in City Road for G & T on single-sided discs in 1904 and who made his last record 53 years later, when he made an extended-play microgroove issue, pressed in vinylite. At the end of his 1920 recording of the *Toreador's Song* from *Carmen* he makes some unintelligible comments, but at the beginning of a duet with the tenor Ernest Pike, recorded on 30 April, 1914, and issued 6 months later, as soon as the stylus meets the groove of *I Arise From Dreams Of Thee*, Dawson can be heard saying quite clearly, 'Wars and the rumour of wars, civil wars.' We might well speculate on what conversation had been going on, right up to the moment when the cutting stylus was lowered onto the wax block and the signal given to the piano accompanist to play the brief introduction to the song.

A less ominous comment occurs on the locked groove after the last part of the sound track of Violet Essex's record of *Poor Wand'ring One* in the HMV album of *The Pirates Of Penzance*, recorded in 1920. Miss Essex was a regular member of all the complete Gilbert and Sullivan recordings by the company between 1917 and 1922, singing the principal

soprano parts impeccably; but on this record, she can be heard indignantly exclaiming, 'I just told him!' with every turn of the disc.

Poor Basil Hallam, star of *The Passing Show* at the Palace Theatre in 1914, when called on to record the song *Gilbert The Filbert*, takes rather longer than he should over his patter towards the end of the record, fairly gabbles the last sentence, catches up with the accompanying orchestra and concludes his performance somewhat breathlessly; five seconds afterwards, he comments, a trifle dubiously, 'That will do – I think.' Facing the recording horn for the first time must have seemed quite a daunting proposition, even for professionals like Basil Hallam, and for those accustomed to public

HALL OF FAME

Peter Dawson, bass-baritone

1882 31 January: Born Adelaide, South Australia.
1890 First public appearance as a singer at College Park Congregational Church, Adelaide.
1901 October: Won bass solo competition at Ballarat, 50 miles west of Melbourne, Victoria, South Australia.
1902 May: Arrived in Britain to study under Frank L Bamford and Sir Charles Santley.
1904 June or July: **Made his first commercial cylinder recording** for Edison Bell under the name Leonard Dawson: *To My First Love*.
1904 15 August: **Made his first recording under his own name** for G & T: *Navajo*, issued October 1904.
1904–50 Recorded for virtually every current company under various names. His sales exceeded 21 million by the start of World War II and possibly over 25 million before the LP era.
1906 January: Made his first Edison cylinder as Hector Grant: *For the Noo*.
1906 Signed exclusive disc recording contract with G & T, but continued to record for Edison, including 4-minute Amberol cylinders.
1928 **Made his first film**: *Chips*; he also starred in *The Winding Road*, made the same year.

1955 4 May: Made his last EMI recording in London (in stereo).
1958 April: Made his last surviving recording for Australian radio.
1961 27 September: Died at 12.30 in the morning.

In a recording career that lasted for 54 years he recorded about 1300 titles. Amongst his best loved were *The Floral Dance* (which he recorded several times, the first in 1912 for Zonophone/HMV), *The Cobbler's Song* from *Chu Chin Chow*, and *Keep the Home Fires Burning* (Ivor Novello's first big hit).

Peter Dawson recorded and composed under many pseudonyms, including:

Peter Allison	Mr Miles
Geoffrey Baxter	Alison Miller
Evelyn Byrd	Gilbert Munday
Will Danby	James Osborne
Fred Davies	David Peters
Dick Denton	Charles Stander
Arnold Flint	Will Strong
Victor Graham	Denton Toms
Hector Grant	Arthur Walpole
Charley Handy	Charles Webber
J P McColl	George Welsh
	Walter Wentworth

His most popular composition was *Boots*.

speaking, such as the Prime Minister from 1908 to 1916, the Rt Hon Herbert Asquith. He made only one record, a sturdy talk about the budget of 1909 which he recorded on 20 July that year: having wound up his 3-minute speech, he announces his name, waits a few seconds, then enquires nervously, 'There – will that do?'

Labelling Errors Some rather strange human errors crept into the labelling of certain Berliner records. For example, on two selections by the Royal Artillery Band, undated but made in October 1899, the Gilbert and Sullivan opera from which the numbers come is shown as *Patience* instead of *Pirates Of Penzance*; and on R T Mahood's record of *On the Banks of Allan Water*, the name is spelt 'Allen', and the title *The Flight of Ages* is visible, partially expunged, with the matrix number 1627 in addition to the correct number 1628. (1627 is untraced; it is probably the same artist singing *The Flight of Ages*!) Burt Shepard (also known on Berliner as Charles Foster) is the victim of a double labelling curiosity on his record of *I Guess I'll Have to Telegraph My Baby*. It is a song with a strangely forward-looking title; the use of 'baby' to denote 'girl-friend' is more commonly associated with the 20s or later. The date is shown as 15 January, 1901, when 15 February is correct, and the central area bears the odd legend, 'Glass Poll'. It was Burt Shepard who recorded, on 6 December, 1900, another song with a title that seems most out of place in the Victorian era, albeit the last month of that era. It was called *The Hootchee Kootchee Dance*, and can hardly have been popular in straitlaced British households at the time; nor, it would seem, would a title by what was termed the Municipal Band – *Boer National Anthem*.

Composers Among the earliest Berliner records made in London are several upon which the composers of the songs provide the accompaniments. Leslie Stuart and Paul Rubens are two of the more celebrated, and when we consider that the artists they accompanied are still known for the stars they were, the records become even more important as documents of value. Leslie Stuart accompanied Eugene Stratton and Albert Christian jointly or severally on five

titles made on 7 April, 1899; Stratton sings *Little Dolly Daydream*, *Is Yer Mammy Always Wid Yer?* and *The Cake-Walk*, Christian sings *The Soldiers Of The Queen*, and joins Stratton in *The Dandy Fifth*. Leslie Stuart returned to Maiden Lane on 3 October, 1900, to accompany Louis Bradfield, Florence St John, and the chorus of the Lyric Theatre in songs from his latest success, *Floradora*, and on 20 October Paul Rubens followed him to accompany the star of that show, Ada Reeve, in seven numbers, not all of them from the production, and Huntley Wright, the comedian, in *Chinee Soje' Man*, from *San Toy*. In view of the very few recordings made by either composer, these must rank as historical documents of great importance.

Long Careers **The longest recording career to date** must be that of the operetta composer and conductor Robert Elisabeth Stolz, who made his first recording in 1904 and his last 70 years later, a year or so before his death in July 1975. Other long recording careers are those of George Baker, colleague of Peter Dawson mentioned above, who, although not starting until 1909 (for Pathé records), was still recording Gilbert and Sullivan operas on LP records in the mid-60s, when he was in his 80s; pianist Alfred Cortôt and Wilhelm Backhaus, who both recorded over a half-century span, and violinist Mischa Elman, beginning on Gramophone Concert and Monarch records in London in 1906, made some LP Decca records in 1956, having recorded fairly constantly for Decca and HMV in various parts of the world in the intervening years. **The longest living artist** must be Eubie Blake, black ragtime pianist and composer who, although he did not record until 1917, was still doing so on his own label 60 years later, with the same expertise and artistry in his 90s that he showed in his 30s; but there were many years between, from the early 30s to the late 60s, when he made no records at all. He died on 12 February 1983, aged 100.

Short Careers One of Berliner's London artists holds the melancholy distinction of being **the first recording performer to die**. He was the baritone William Paull, who made a large number of songs and arias, from Gilbert and

Sullivan to Wagner via Pinsuti, Mendelssohn and Fauré in 1900 and 1901. He recorded for the early Zon-O-Phone label in New York in 1903, not long before its affairs were taken over by Victor, but a few weeks later, in the course of his tour in the US, he died suddenly in St Louis.

The youngest recording artist to depart this life is probably black pianist Hersal Thomas, who recorded two piano solos and a number of accompaniments to blues singers for the Okeh label when he was 16, in 1925. He was taken ill with food-poisoning when only 17, and died on 3 July, 1926.

Youngsters Some of **the youngest artists to record** did so for Berliner before the turn of the century, and thus could just possibly be still living in the 1980s. Master Birmy Burnside, described as 'Boy tenor' for whatever that may be worth, made just one record in Washington, DC, or possibly Philadelphia, in 1895 or 1896, of a song called *Grace O' Moore*, and in London, on 18 August, 1898, Master John Buffery, a boy soprano, recorded *Two Little Eyes Of Blue*. Neither of these youngsters seems to have made any further recordings.

Most Recordings **The artist who made the most recordings** in the acoustic era is band-leader Ben Selvin (1898–1980), who made his first records in 1917 (with his Novelty Orchestra) and made about 9000 recordings altogether under 39 different names. His total was exceeded, however, by Indian singer Lata Mangeshker (*b* 1928), who made at least 25 000 solo, duet, and chorus-backed records between 1948 and 1974.

Novelties Novelty records such as those by Masters Burnside and Buffery must have had a certain appeal, and no doubt even that early in the history of recording Emile Berliner realised their sales potential. As it happened, neither the American nor the British lads' work sold well. The 'novelty' record that sold best, apart from the obvious impressions of farm and other animals, auction sales of all kinds of articles, and of 'street pianos', which the Berliner catalogues assured its patrons were 'the real thing', was a London-recorded 'Puzzle Plate', which had three separate tracks cut in exact step with each

other, so that upon lowering the sound box it was anyone's guess as to which track it would pick up. Several different takes of this were made early in 1901, and the disc itself gives no clue as to who gave the (necessarily very brief) performances.

In 1911, perhaps by way of celebrating the tenth anniversary of the original puzzle plate, HMV issued a 12in variation on the same theme. This was called *The Conundrum*, and being that much larger, it could accommodate four separate tracks. Says the label: 'I'll make you languish, or I'll make you laugh, I'll stir your blood or I'll make you dance. WHAT AM I? Let the Needle decide'. The languishing was provided by a tenor singing part of Guy d'Hardelot's *Because*; the laughtermaker was Wilkie Bard singing *I Want To Sing In Opera*; the blood-stirring was done by baritone Robert Radford singing *Ho! Jolly Jenkin*, and the impetus to dance came from the 'house' band playing two strains of *Grizzly Bear Rag*. *Because* lasts 51 seconds, *Ho! Jolly Jenkin* a full minute, *I Want To Sing In Opera* slightly less than a minute, and the ragtime excerpt 55 seconds.

Miscellaneous Berliner's catalogue in 1897 shows his apparent determination to appeal to as wide a section of the American public as possible. Amid the plethora of marches, brass and banjo soloists, 'heart' ballads and comic songs, there is a small section headed simply 'Miscellaneous'. Under this heading we find such delights as *Reading of the 23rd Psalm and Lord's Prayer* (no artist shown, but with the parenthetic comment 'very impressive'); *A Day In A Country School*; the four impressions of auction sales already referred to; three clarinet solos by Sig Noritta of Sousa's Band, two by Sig F Jardelle; a piano solo of *Little Nell* by Noble McDonald; an anonymous cornet duet (despite there being a section for such things elsewhere); and *Two Little Bullfinches* ('Very loud and brilliant', but giving no indication as to who or what played it). One of the auction sales was set in a dime museum, with 'interruptions by an Australian Parrot', which must have been diverting to say the least, and just above, on the same page, there are shown ten sides in detail of the US Army and Navy Calls, given by A Samuels, instructor in United States Marine Corps, which are described as 'productive ... of pleasant reminiscences in the minds of those brave young men who have, in days past, responded to the call'.

Heads of State An important Berliner record was produced in the summer of 1902 to commemorate the Coronation of their Majesties King Edward VII and Queen Alexandra. It consisted of a 7in 'plate' whose rim was embossed with a statement of what it was, showing the date of the Coronation as 26 June, 1902. The central area depicted a cameo portrait in shellac of their Majesties and there was no spindle hole. The record was playable only by settling it in a wooden holder lined with green baize, the underside of the holder having a circular slot to accommodate the spindle of the machine. But when played, the disc simply offered an unnamed military band playing the National Anthem, which the Municipal Military Band (probably the same group of musicians) had already recorded on 27 February, 1901. It was perhaps not to be expected that the King and/or the Queen themselves would record at that early stage in the history of the gramophone, but for an occasion such as their Coronation, we might be forgiven for wondering why the Prime Minister or some other prominent public figure was not invited to record a speech of welcome. In the event, the date shown on the record was incorrect; at the last moment the King was stricken with appendicitis, a very serious complaint in 1902, and the Coronation was not held until 9 August, by which time the commemorative record in its neat little wooden tray had been on sale for some months. In view of its rarity today, it seems to have attracted far less custom than a record of, say, *Coronation Day* sung by Charles Foster, a pseudonym for Burt Shepard, who was an American remembered for the hundreds of records he made for Berliner, Victor, and other companies on both sides of the Atlantic between 1895 and 1905.

The first disc records made by a royal personage were the four recorded in 1903 in the Royal Palace, Bucharest, by 'Carmen Sylva', HM Queen Elisabeth of Romania, reading five of her own poems in English, French, and German. Her gentle voice and good diction make a pleasant contrast to the gruff tones of the aged Emperor Franz Josef of the old Austro–Hungarian Empire some years later.

The first British royal disc recording was made by King George V and Queen Mary in 1923. It carried a message for the Empire and was issued to coincide with Empire Day. HMV's royal-purple label was adorned with portraits of the King and Queen.

Other royal recordings are mentioned in Section VIII.

These early decades contained other interesting 'firsts': political speeches were made in quite amazing numbers between 1907 and 1910 by speakers such as the Prime Minister, the Rt Hon Herbert Asquith; the President of the Board of Trade, the Rt Hon Winston Churchill; and the Chancellor of the Exchequer, the Rt Hon David Lloyd George. There was also a series of highly amusing records made for the Conservative and Unionist Association by a comedian named Arthur Gilbert, who in monologue and song tore into the infant Socialist Party, lampooning its policies and beliefs and searingly attacking its upholders by name.

The first records of an ex-convict were made by Adolf Beck, in 1904–5. He had served several years in prison in England for a jewellery theft he was afterwards found not to have committed.

In 1905 some pygmies were brought to London from the Congo and, through an interpreter, recorded their impressions of the capital. The sales of oddities such as these must have been infinitesimal. The largest sales on the gramophone companies' books, in contrast, were of items that wrung the heartstrings, either by their sentimental impact (eg: the Australian comedian and character-actor Albert Whelan's account of *Darby And Joan's Christmas*), or by their artistic perfection (eg: the original 1902 recording of Enrico Caruso as Canio in Leoncavallo's opera *I Pagliacci*, singing *Vesti la giubba*).

PLATE 1 *Cylinder, four different types of disc (78rpm, 45rpm, 33⅓ LP and Compact Disc), and pre-recorded tape cassette*
COURTESY: RUTLAND COTTAGE MUSIC MUSEUM, PHOTO: LES PRUDDEN

PLATE 2 *A selection of cylinder boxes*
COURTESY: RUTLAND COTTAGE MUSIC MUSEUM, PHOTO: LES PRUDDEN

PLATE 3 78s came in various sizes and their paper labels gave designers the opportunity to practice eye-catching designs, sometimes of considerable intricacy
COURTESY: RUTLAND COTTAGE MUSIC MUSEUM, PHOTO: LES PRUDDEN

PLATE 4 Boxes that held gramophone needles were once heedlessly discarded. Today they can be collectors' items
COURTESY: RUTLAND COTTAGE MUSIC MUSEUM, PHOTO: LES PRUDDEN

PLATE 5 *The flimsy sleeves which housed 78s often spread the word of advertisers rather than protect their valuable contents*
COURTESY: RUTLAND COTTAGE MUSIC MUSEUM, PHOTO: LES PRUDDEN

PLATE 6 *Sir Charles Santley (1834–1922), English baritone who was world-renowned before making his first recordings*
MARY EVANS PICTURE LIBRARY

PLATE 7 *Edison's kinetographic theatre, c 1892. This combined the recording of sound and vision*
ANN RONAN PICTURE LIBRARY

Electrical Recording

The use of electricity in both recording and playback made its first tentative appearance in 1920. Up to that time, the sound relayed to the record surface was collected by a recording horn around which the artists were gathered in an uncomfortable crowd, making for cramped playing and singing conditions. A solo singer was more fortunate in that he was able to stand facing the horn and project his voice into it with little loss, but a group of singers had to either jostle amongst themselves as each in turn was called upon by the music to dominate, or to judge by guesswork how far away and at what angle each had to stand, and in what relation to each other, to get a proper balance. The recording engineer was there to advise, of course, but the end result was too often the product of pure luck, quite a lot of it bad. Meanwhile, the pianist had to be perched on a dais so that the sound of his instrument would not be physically too low to be caught by the recording horn. String players were compelled to play instruments to which a diaphragm and amplifying horn were attached to the bridge. The introduction of microphones changed everything.

The first microphone (ie: a device sensitive enough to detect very weak sounds: Gk *micros* = small + *phone* = sound) was the electromagnetic telephone transmitter of Alexander Graham Bell, invented in 1876 and further developed by Edison as a carbon telephone transmitter the following year. **The word 'microphone' was first used** by David E Hughes in 1878.

Since the microphone had been in increasing use for nearly half a century it is puzzling that none of the inventive geniuses involved with sound recording had thought to introduce it into that sphere of activity. Why, for example, had Edison himself not taken the step? **The first to do so** were two engineers, George William Guest and Horace Owen Merriman of The Gramophone Co who had been charged with the task of recording part of the burial service of the Unknown Warrior at Westminster Abbey on 11 November, 1920. No more graphic illustration of necessity being the mother of invention could be imagined. It was out of the

question that two technicians fussing over a bulky, ugly, noisy contraption would be allowed to mar the solemnity of the occasion, so Guest and Merriman rigged up a makeshift microphone, a silent and relatively inconspicuous object in the vastness of the great hall, and relayed the ceremony over GPO landlines to their mobile studio in a van parked in a nearby sidestreet. There, the signal was fed to the cutting stylus via an electromagnet. **This was the first electrical recording**, and **the first electrical location recording**. The double-sided disc sold for 7s 6d (37½p) from 17 December, 1920, either through *The Times* newspaper or direct from Westminster Abbey. The recording was badly distorted and ill-balanced, so that it was barely recognisable as a record of massed choirs and bands; but, as the first electric recording made in London, it presaged the coming of 'location' recordings in the 20s, when perfect results were obtained by exactly similar methods. Sometimes, however, due to a busy but imperfect telephone system, otherwise successful recordings were ruined by clicks and buzzes 'leaking' from other lines.

During the same year (1920) HMV built **the first record autochanger**. It was made from plans of Eldridge R Johnson by a Hayes engineer by the name of Tomsett. This was **the first electrical gramophone**. It played five discs in succession, rejecting each after it had been played. This experimental model was not offered to the public.

The acoustic recording process could capture sounds only within the range of 164 to 2088cps. (Cycles per second, previously abbreviated cps, are today abbreviated Hz, after Heinrich Hertz.) In theory, electrical recording could make a considerable improvement on this, but the earliest of them gave unsatisfactory results on the current acoustic players which were not able to meet the potential of the recordings. Perhaps realising this, the major companies involved in distributing the first electrical records agreed that the general public on both sides of the Atlantic should be kept in the dark about the nature of the advance for a year. The press, however, was given full details, but was

Harrison and Maxfield in the Bell Laboratories, 1925.

Sir Louis Sterling, the man who 'rescued' electrical recording.

asked only to say, if they wished, that the new recordings showed some technical advance. The word adopted for the new system by English Columbia – 'stereoscopic' – was apparently coined to confuse rather than enlighten. Obviously, the secrecy was meant to prevent faithful customers from thinking that their equipment and records had become obsolete overnight – which in fact they had.

Research into electrical recording first began at the Bell Telephone Laboratories, a division of American Telephone & Telegraph Company (A T & T) in New York late in 1915 and was developed by Joseph P Maxfield and Henry C Harrison who perfected a system by 1924. However, a rival in Chicago, Marsh Recording Laboratories, was **the first to actually put electrical recordings onto the American market**. They were made in the autumn of 1924 and issued soon afterwards on the Autograph label at $1.50 each. They contained performances by Jelly Roll Morton, King Oliver, Willard Robison, Merritt Brunies and his Friars Inn Orchestra, and Jesse Crawford playing the Wurlitzer organ. These records were not widely distributed and therefore failed to make the historic impact their priority merits.

In the spring of 1924, Bell Laboratories approached Victor, offering the rights to their new system in exchange for royalties, but Victor was unenthusiastic at first. Perhaps the Bell demonstration had been mishandled. Later that year, a disastrously poor sales season shook Victor into the realisation that the acoustic disc was losing its appeal in the market place and something was needed to stimulate interest. Another demonstration was arranged with Bell, and it was while preparations were being made for this that an apparently underhand trick (almost an act of espionage) brought the British record industry into the scene.

Bell Laboratories had sent their electrical masters for processing and pressing to the Pathé factory in Brooklyn, where manager Frank Capps became interested. As a friend and colleague of Louis Sterling, the manager of Columbia in the UK, Capps felt it his duty to press up extra copies of the Bell discs and send them to Sterling. He may have reported, too, the alarming intelligence that Western Electric, A T & T's licensing division, was planning to patent the invention, possibly with an exclusive licensing deal with the first comer – which looked as though it might be Victor.

With English Columbia's, and the rest of the industry's, interests at heart, Sterling sailed immediately for New York (26 December, 1924) and arrived in time to dissuade Western Electric from proceeding with its plans to patent electrical recording. That firm, however, did refuse to allow overseas companies to take up a licence unless it be through an American branch, so Sterling raised the money to purchase a controlling share in the ailing American Columbia company, thereby at a stroke rescuing that company from bankruptcy and securing for Columbia in the UK a licence to use the Western Electric electrical recording process. Victor, too, secured a licence. The race was on.

The first Victor electrical recordings were made in mid-March 1925. They were a location recording of Philadelphia University's 37th annual Mask and Wig Club production (10in black label disc no 19626), and *Let it Rain, Let it Pour*, played by Meyer Davis's Le Paradis Band. Both were issued in April in the US and in June in the UK on the HMV label.

The first Columbia electrical recording was a coupling of *John Peel* and *Adeste Fideles* sung by 15 glee clubs in New York's Metropolitan Opera House on 31 March, 1925; the latter number, according to Columbia, presented the unison singing of 4850 voices (12in disc no 50013-D). This was issued domestically in June and reached the UK in September.

The first electrical recording made by HMV in the UK was *Feelin' Kind o' Blue* by Jack Hylton and his Orchestra (with vocal refrain by Hylton himself), recorded at HMV's Hayes studio, Middlesex, on 24 June, 1925 (10in disc no B 2072). Immediately prior to this at the same session, Hylton recorded *Ah-Ha!*, but this was never issued.

At first, HMV electrical recordings were identified by a geometrical figure (usually a triangle; sometimes a square) pressed into the

Jack Hylton, singer/band leader, who made HMV's first electrical recording.   BBC HULTON PICTURE LIBRARY

wax after the matrix number (Columbia used 'W' or 'C' in a circle and Parlophone also used a circled letter or a '£' sign). This led to confusion when some Caruso recordings made in September 1919 and September 1920 were re-issued in the 1930s with the triangle mark. It was known that they could not be electrical re-makes since Caruso had died on 2 August, 1921. It transpired that these recordings had been merely reprocessed electrically from the acoustic masters. Some of Caruso's (and other artists') earlier recordings were also reprocessed electrically, new orchestral accompaniments conducted by Lawrence Collingwood being laid behind the voices. Yet more confusion was caused when a blues recording made by Ma Rainey for an American company was announced as having been electrically recorded when this was belied by its primitive quality. Enquiry on this occasion unearthed the truth that during the recording an electric light had been operating in the studio!

The first Victor Red Seal electrical recording

was made on 21 March, 1925, in America by Alfred Cortôt, who played Chopin's *Impromptu No 2* in F sharp, Op 36, and his own arrangement for piano of Schubert's *Litaney*, D343. This was released on 12in Victor 6502 in June that year.

The first of Victor's electric orchestral recordings was of Saint-Saëns's *Danse Macabre*, played by the Philadelphia Orchestra conducted by Leopold Stokowski and released on 12in Victor 6505 in July 1925. The same artists' Tchaikovsky *Marche Slave* (Victor 6513) followed that September.

The first real trade show coincided with the appearance of electrically recorded discs. It was The Gramophone Congress, which was opened in London by Sir Richard Terry in July 1925.

The first symphony to be electrically recorded was Tchaikovsky's No 4 with the Royal Albert Hall Orchestra conducted by Landon Ronald, recorded by HMV and released in the UK in December 1925; the second was Berlioz's *Symphonie Fantastique* with the London Symphony Orchestra under Felix Weingartner, released by Columbia in March 1926.

The advent of electrical recording came at a time when the industry was beginning to feel (and, according to Percy A Scholes's report quoted in the Introduction, benefit from) the competition from radio stations, which were flourishing by 1924. Domestic electric supply was by no means available everywhere, but those fortunate enough to possess it were able to enjoy virtually free entertainment at the adjustment of a cat's whisker or the throw of a switch. By introducing electric power into the cabinet, radio manufacturers had taken a step by which they had inadvertently assisted the record industry, and that industry was not slow to take advantage of it. 'Add-On' units began to appear, consisting of a small box upon which were perched a turntable and a pick-up, the wires of which led to the radio's amplifier. Then came a greater independence: **The first all-electric record reproducing instrument offered to the public** was Brunswick's 'Panatrope', which appeared in America in 1926 at $350 and up.

It is amazing that electricity (apart from a few battery-operated experiments) had not been introduced to record playing earlier than this, for the first electric motor had been made in 1829, nearly a century earlier, by Joseph Henry (1797–1878), who built a prototype which he called an 'oscillating machine with automatic pole changer'.

In 1927 **the first marketable auto-changer** was put on sale by Victor, developed from the experimental Johnson model of 1920 (see above). **The first UK auto-changer** was made by Garrard in 1932. **The first player able to track both sides of a disc without turning it over** was made in 1938, also by Garrard. In early 1981, however, Sharp announced the VZ 3000 model 'Dual-play disc Compo System', claiming it as the world's first disc player to do what the Garrard model had done 43 years earlier! Sharp's player held the disc vertically and tracked it with twin linear arms.

A number of other auto-change mechanisms have been offered, including one hair-raising model which tilted the spent disc and sent it hurtling into a padded slot under its own centrifugal force. Less clumsy was Thorens TD 224 of 1964, a transcription deck which automatically swung the played disc to one side. It was not capable of drawing the disc from its sleeve and returning it after playing, however, and thereby lay its great weakness: LPs had to be stacked naked one on top of the other, first on the supply pile, and then on the discard pile, where they gathered dust.

As we have seen, radio came as a benefit to the record industry and was soon to become an even greater ally since its broadcasting of recordings served as an effective advertisement. This brought a new phrase to the English language and a new employment opportunity to record enthusiasts with pleasing manners and voices. They became known as 'disc jockeys'. **The first DJ** was Christopher Stone (1882–1965) who, as a major during World War I, had relied upon a Decca portable record player for entertainment during the long hours spent in the trenches. As brother-in-law of (Sir) Compton Mackenzie, London Editor of *The Gramophone* magazine, Stone was well placed for access to the latest record releases for his programme, which began its long run in July 1927, broadcasting from Savoy Hill, London, every Friday lunchtime.

The centre-start disc was used quite extensively for transcription purposes until after World War II. It was said that this facility gave the operator a better chance of *seeing* when the needle reached the end of a side of music so that he might switch to the next side, on another turntable, with a minimum break in continuity. In theory, centre-start should result in less record wear since the pick-up tends to be driven outwards by centrifugal force, thus relieving the

groove walls of the strain of guiding it across the surface, but, although this may work with players designed with shorter arms specially for centre-start discs, in practice the standard arm has an overhang respective to the centre spindle that exerts an inward pull.

The only electrically recorded cylinders were a few Edison Blue Amberols dubbed in 1927 from Edison diamond electrical discs. They were on the market for only 2 years. Prior to their appearance, an Englishman named Adrian Sykes invented the 'Electrograph' for reproducing Blue Amberol cylinders electrically. Sykes, incidentally, was a prolific inventor, patenting

---

COMPANY PROFILE

EMI (Electrical and Musical Industries)
See also Personalia and the Company Profiles for HMV: the Early Years, Columbia, Deutsche Grammophon Gesellschaft, Victor and Pathé, and Hall of Fame – Nipper, for events prior to the formation of EMI.

1931 April: The Gramophone Co (ie: HMV and associated foreign trade marks) and the Columbia Graphophone Co merged to form Electrical and Musical Industries, together with Parlophone, Regal and Zonophone. This amalgamation created **the largest recording organisation in the world at that time**. Its capital stood at £6½m and it controlled 50 factories in 19 countries. Directors included Alfred Clark, Lord Marks and Louis Sterling. HMV, Columbia, and the other labels involved in the merger retained separate identities and repertoire for many years, often in apparent competition with one another. In the classical market, Regal and Zonophone were never serious contenders; in 1958 Parlophone was phased out, followed by Columbia in 1968, leaving HMV as the prime EMI classical label in the UK.
1931 October: The German Electrola factory was closed, manufacturing for that company being transferred to Lindström's factory.
1931 12 November: Sir Edward Elgar

opened HMV's Abbey Road studios in St John's Wood, North London, **the first studios in Britain to be built specially for recording purposes.**
1931 December: EMI engineer A D Blumlein took out a patent for stereophonic recording and disc cutting.
1932 April: The first 'Society' issues were released: Hugo Wolf *Lieder.*
1933 January: Regal and Zonophone merged, under the control of Columbia.
1936 EMI television sets marketed in the UK.
1937 26 December: HMV's famous record shop at 363, Oxford Street, London, was gutted by fire. The night-watchman lost his life. Temporary accommodation was found at 104, New Bond Street until the Oxford Street premises were reopened on 8 May, 1939.
1941 The two EMI Clerkenwell Road, London, premises (16–17 April and 10 May) and the Liverpool Depot (3–4 May) were severely damaged in air raids.
1944 7 July: A German flying bomb hit the EMI factory at Hayes, Middlesex.
1946 December: Trevor Williams (founder and chairman of The Gramophone Co – see HMV: the Early Years, 1897) died.
1948 January: EMI began distribution of the American MGM label in the UK.

no fewer than eleven devices for recording, reproducing, and duplicating sound electrically between November 1919 and June 1925.

Electrical recording brought about a profound change in the record industry, not only in quality but also in attitudes. It was as if a page had turned. Because of ill-health, Johnson was unable to continue as head of Victor and sold out to a syndicate in 1926; ironically, the company that had so feared and fought radio broadcasting came into the ownership of the Radio Corporation of America (RCA) in 1929 and henceforth carried the dual title RCA Victor. Similarly, after a series of deals, American Columbia was purchased by the Columbia Broad-

casting System in 1938 and retains the CBS logo to this day. Berliner died in 1929. In the same year Edison closed all recording operations, and he himself followed Berliner into history two years later. In the UK, as if squaring up to a depression that severely affected America but never brought the English market to an equally low state, the two old rivals, The Gramophone Co and the Columbia Graphophone Co, closed ranks in 1931 to form Electrical and Musical Industries (EMI). It was at that time **by far the largest record company in the world**, controlling 50 factories in 19 countries. (See panel, below.)

Other significant events were also occurring

1948 14 September: Capitol Records Distribution Corp formed in America out of five regional companies.

1951 October: **The first EMI long playing release** made by Pathé-Marconi in France.

1952 October: EMI's UK long playing launch on the HMV, Columbia, Parlophone and MGM labels; also the first UK issue of 45rpm discs on the HMV label.

1952 December: The reciprocal agreement with American Columbia was terminated, a 'sell-off' period to run until December 1956.

1953 March: Formation of EMI (US) Ltd.

1953 April: Termination of the HMV-RCA Victor exchange agreement announced to take effect in May 1957 after a 'sell-off' period.

1955 1 January: A mass EMI deletion of 78rpm discs.

1955 17 January: EMI took control of Capitol Records Inc. Capitol products, hitherto handled in the UK by Decca, were switched to EMI from January 1956.

1955 4 April: **The first UK demonstration of 'stereosonic' tapes** was given by EMI in London; the first release was made in October 1955.

1958 October: EMI began UK distribution of the American Mercury label. Some Mercury recordings had appeared previously on HMV and other labels in Britain.

1960 19 February: **EMI's last new coarse-groove 78rpm record** was issued: *Rule Britannia/Royal Event*, played by Russ Conway.

1961 29 February: All EMI 78rpm discs were deleted, with the exception of royal recordings and the History of Music in Sound series. These, too, disappeared on 23 March, 1962.

1961 **The first gold disc to be presented by EMI to a classical artist** was awarded to Yehudi Menuhin by Sir Joseph Lockwood to celebrate an unbroken association lasting over 30 years.

1962 October: EMI issued their first Beatles record.

1965 1 July: EMI Records Ltd and The Gramophone Co Ltd merged; trading to be continued under the name EMI Records.

1968 October: Reciprocal agreement signed between EMI and the Russian Melodiya company, selected recordings from the latter's catalogue to be released in the UK on the HMV label.

1979 November: Thorn-EMI formed.

1980 18 April: Thorn-EMI agreed to co-operate with JVC-Victor of Japan in the world-wide manufacture and marketing of JVC video and audio discs.

1983 July: EMI announced their first UK release of CD software for 'early 1984'.

at the turn of the new decade. Decca, the name on the portable gramophone introduced in 1914 (see above), was adopted in 1929 by a new 'software' producer, and under the inspired control of Mr (later Sir) Edward Lewis, the Decca Record Co launched a series of classical and popular recordings which offered top quality at a very competitive price. Amongst the earliest releases were some of Handel's *Concerti Grossi*, Op 6, played by a body known as the 'Decca String Orchestra' under Ernest Ansermet, and

several other important recordings. (See pp. 92/3.)

Then, in 1931, engineers at EMI in England and RCA in America were engaging themselves in technical experiments that, had it not been for other factors, might have brought other major advances in sound reproduction, and increased playing time. (See stereo and long playing in Section IX.) Instead, the 1930s became the decade of repertoire consolidation and expansion in classical recording, and of the universal

HALL OF FAME

Bing Crosby, crooner

1903 2 May: Born Harry Lillis Crosby at Tacoma, Washington. Played as drummer and singer as a boy in Spokane.

1923 Joined the 'Musicaladers', a band run by Al Rinker; stayed with Rinker after the band broke up in 1925.

1926 18 October: **Made first commercial recording** with Don Clark's Biltmore Hotel Orchestra: *I've Got The Girl* (US Columbia). From December sang with Paul Whiteman's Orchestra, often singing solo; his first engagement was at the Tivoli Theater, Chicago.

1927 Formed The Rhythm Boys with Al Rinker and Harry Barris, performing with Paul Whiteman until 1930.

1930 **Made first film**: *King of Jazz* (with Paul Whiteman), the success of which encouraged Crosby to launch his solo career in 1931.

1931 Signed with CBS for a series of radio programmes, the first going out on 2 September. Adopted *Where the Blue of the Night* as his signature tune, and recorded it on 23 November.

1932 **His first starring role in a feature film** was in *The Big Broadcast of 1932*.

1937 23 February: **Recorded his first million seller**: *Sweet Leilani*, with Lani McIntire and his Hawaiians (from the film *Waikiki Wedding*) which won an Academy Award for 'Best Song of the Year'.

1942 Made the film *Holiday Inn*, featuring Irving Berlin's *White Christmas*.

1944 Won Academy Award for 'Best Actor' in *Going My Way*: the song from the film,

Swinging on a Star, became a million seller.

1947 25 March: Made his only recording with Al Jolson: *Alexander's Ragtime Band/The Spaniard that Blighted My Life*. This became Crosby's 15th million seller.

1950 23 June: Recorded *Sam's Song* with his son Gary, their first duet and Bing's 21st million seller.

1956 Made film *High Society*. The duet *True Love* with Grace Kelly sold 1 million by the following year. The soundtrack LP also became a million seller.

1960 9 June: Presented with a platingum disc by the Hollywood Chamber of Commerce to commemorate the estimated sale of 200 million records (to that date he had recorded 2600 singles and 125 LP albums).

1970 15 September: Presented with a second platingum disc by Decca Records Inc to mark the claimed sale of 300 650 000 discs.

1977 September: Made his last recording (for Polydor).

1977 14 October: Died Madrid, Spain.

During the 1930s, Bing Crosby was so immensely popular that regular daily broadcasts, sometimes several, were devoted entirely to him. His recording of *White Christmas* made on 29 May, 1942 with the John Scott Trotter Orchestra (which he re-recorded in 1947) became **the best selling record of all time**: the latest available figure of over 25 million copies (plus more than 100 million in other versions) is put out of date at Christmas time every year.

popularity of dance music and jazz via the twin media of records and radio. Also of a new style of singer, intimately dependent upon the microphone: the crooner. Some of the earliest crooners on record were Gene Austin, Vaughan de Leath, and Nick Lucas; the greatest of all was Bing Crosby.

The technical advance provided by the electrical system encouraged the recording of music only sparsely and unsatisfactorily represented on acoustic records. In particular, instrumental and orchestral music benefited in tone from the use of the microphone. An American, Frederick N Sard, saw the opportunities offered by the new process and the approach of an important musical anniversary. In 1926 he suggested to American Columbia that a series of recordings be made to mark the centenary the following year of Beethoven's death. Since at that time the company was controlled by British Columbia, the suggestion was sent across the Atlantic. The result was **the most ambitious assault upon the repertoire of one composer** that the industry had attempted up to that time. Under the direction of Louis Sterling, Columbia embarked upon a massive programme of Beethoven recordings to be released in time for what they called 'Beethoven Week' (20–27 March, 1927), the extent of which may be judged by the panel on p. 82.

Its success, too, may be judged by the decision to mark Schubert's centenary in November 1928 by an international competition for composers to provide a suitable ending for Schubert's 'Unfinished' Symphony, or, for that matter, any 'Original orchestral work as an apotheosis of the lyrical genius of Schubert'. Prize money of £200 000 was put up, lure enough for many composers to submit entries. Another lure was the promise by Columbia to record the winning entries for commercial release. The whole scheme ran into serious criticism, however, from those who considered that Schubert was perfectly aware of what he was doing when he stopped at the end of his second movement and that any attempt to complete the work was nothing short of blasphemy. Incidentally, it has since been shown that Schubert sketched out a Scherzo and part of the Trio for this work, and probably went on to draft a Finale.

The Swedish composer Kurt Atterberg won first prize for his 6th Symphony (a work complete' in itself, not an attempt to round off Schubert's fragment), and this was duly recorded by Sir Thomas Beecham and the Royal Philharmonic Orchestra, but the criticism levelled against what was described as Columbia's inartistic lack of taste discouraged that company from further commemorative pro-

PICTORIAL PRESS LTD

The background to this project is discussed in the accompanying text.

Symphonies:
No 1 Royal Philharmonic Orchestra conducted by Sir George Henschel
No 2 London Symphony Orchestra conducted by Sir Thomas Beecham
No 3 New Queen's Hall Orchestra conducted by Sir Henry Wood
No 4 Hallé Orchestra conducted by Sir Hamilton Harty
Nos 5–8 Royal Philharmonic Orchestra conducted by Felix Weingartner
No 9 London Philharmonic Orchestra conducted by Felix Weingartner

String Quartets: recorded in London's Wigmore Hall by the Lener Quartet (all but Op 18/5, Op 74, Op 127, Op 131, and Op 132, some of which, however, were recorded later by the same group).

Piano Sonatas:
Pathétique, Op 13 William Murdoch
Moonlight, Op 27/2 Ignacy Friedman
Appassionata, Op 57 William Murdoch

Archduke Trio, Op 97 Albert Sammons, William H Squire and William Murdoch
Kreutzer Violin Sonata, Op 47 Albert Sammons and William Murdoch

Special matrices of these recordings, valued at £5000, were flown direct to New York in order to ensure that releases were made in time for 'Beethoven Week' in the country where the whole idea had originated, as well as in the UK.

grammes. Atterberg's Symphony has the distinction of being **the first work to be recorded and issued before being heard in concert**. (A number of other important recordings were *made* before their concert premières – see Composers Who Recorded their Own Music in Section VIII.)

The first use of 'montage' on a recording was in 1929 in an advertising disc called *Columbia on Parade*. It consisted of a series of re-recordings onto disc of a number of separate catalogue items by comedians, band-leaders, and other light artists.

The first 'run-in' grooves appeared in 1930 on a handful of American Columbia issues. Before this refinement which we now take for granted, the needle relied upon the inward pull mentioned above to bring it to the first music winding. The innovation caught on only slowly and was not generally adopted until 1936.

With the 1930s came a new idea in marketing classical music that falls outside the sphere of what was then regarded as standard repertoire. The scheme is credited to a 24-year-old HMV copywriter, Walter Legge. He persuaded HMV to establish a series of subscription societies in order to secure a guarantee that a given project would at least break even. Participants were obligated to buy the whole series, and records would not be available separately except as replacements for broken discs, and then only on the production of the pieces. In 1931, 500 subscriptions were invited for a six-disc volume of songs by Hugo Wolf. It aroused cautious interest, the requisite number was eventually achieved, and that **first society issue** appeared in 1932 in April. Meanwhile, a series of Beethoven piano music played by Artur Schnabel was mooted, and this brought the subscriptions rolling in. Legge was encouraged to expand the scheme, doing away (after the first two volumes) with the clumsy restrictions, and HMV's Society Series became **the most important repertoire-widening exercise of the inter-war years**.

The HMV/Columbia/Parlophone merger of 1931 did not affect Legge's plans; indeed, both sister labels joined in the scheme, although on a less ambitious scale.

The flow was halted by World War II, but the entire series (see associated chart) remained in the EMI catalogues until 31 January, 1955, when it was felled along with virtually all the rest of the 78 catalogue.

In 1961 the original subscribers were asked if they would be prepared to waive their 'rights' in the Beethoven piano sonatas society (originally issued between 1932 and 1939) so that the

Society Issues

The following list of Society issues notes by the abbreviation 'US' which of these volumes were taken up by EMI's American affiliates.

Repertoire	Prominent Artists	Company	Vol	No of Discs
BACH: Art of Fugue (US: Tovey's completion of No 20 was not included in the US issue)	Roth Quartet	Col	I	10
BACH: Cello Suites (US)	Casals	HMV	I	7
			II	6
			III	$6\frac{1}{2}$
BACH: Goldberg Variations	Landowska	HMV	I	6
BACH: Organ Music (US)	Schweitzer	Col	I	7
			II	7
			III	7
BACH: Das Wohltemperierte Klavier (US: part)	E Fischer	HMV	I	7
			II	7
			III	7
			IV	7
			V	4
BEETHOVEN: Piano Sonatas, etc (US: Vol X only: Hammerklavier Sonata)	Schnabel	HMV	I	7
			II	7
			III	7
			IV	7
			V	7
			VI	7
			VII	7
			VIII	7
			IX	6
			X	6
			XI	7
			XII	6
Diabelli Vars			XIII	7
Misc. works			XIV	7
Misc. works			XV	7
BEETHOVEN: Violin Sonatas	Kreisler; Rupp	HMV	I	7
			II	7
			III	7
			IV	6
BRAHMS: Lieder (US: Victor also issued a different set, of 8 discs, calling it Volume II)	Kipnis	HMV	I	6
COUPERIN: Keyboard works	Landowska	HMV	I	6
DELIUS: Works (US)	Beecham	Col	I	7
			II	7
			III	7
ENGLISH MUSIC (US)	Misc.			
Purcell		Col	I	5×12in
				3×10in
Bax		Col	I	7

Repertoire	Prominent Artists	Company	Vol	No of Discs
HANDEL: Suites (US)	Landowska	HMV	I	6
HAYDN: String Quartets	Pro Arte Quartet	HMV	I	7
			II	7
(US: all but the first two			III	7
volumes)			IV	7
			V	7
			VI	7
			VII	7
			VIII	7
HAYDN: Piano Trios (US: but later, on LP)	Kraus; Goldberg; Pini	Parlo	I	6
KILPINEN: Songs	Hüsch	HMV	I	5
MAHLER: Das Lied von der Erde (US)	Thorborg; Kullmann; B Walter (from a public performance, 24 May, 1936)	Col	I	7
MAHLER: Symphony No 9	B Walter	HMV	I	10
MEDTNER: Works	Composer; Ritchie; Slobodskaya	HMV	I	7
			II	7
			III	7
MOZART: Operas				
Così fan Tutte (US)	Glyndebourne/Busch	HMV	I–III	20
Don Giovanni (US)	Glyndebourne/Busch	HMV	I–III	23
Nozze di Figaro (US)	Glyndebourne/Busch	HMV	I–III	16½
Die Zauberflöte (US)	Berlin/Beecham	HMV	I–III	18½
MOZART: Piano/Violin Sonatas (US: but later, on LP)	Kraus; Goldberg	Parlo	I	7
			II	7
MUSSORGSKY: Songs (US)	Rosing	Parlo	I	6
SCARLATTI: Sonatas	Landowska	HMV	I	6
SCHUBERT: Die Schöne Müllerin	Hüsch	HMV	I	8
Winterreise	Hüsch	HMV	I	6×12in 3×10in
SIBELIUS: Orchestral Works	Kajanus; Koussevitzky; Schneevoigt; Beecham; Boult	HMV	I	7
			II	7
			III	7
(US: all but volume I;			IV	7
volume IV was issued as			V	7
two volumes)			VI	7
WOLF: Songs	Gerhardt; Kipnis; McCormack, and many others	HMV	I	6
			II	6
			III	6
			IV	6
			V	6
			VI	6

Repertoire	Prominent Artists	Company	Vol	No of Discs
The spirit of the Society issues was maintained in the following:				
DELIUS FELLOWSHIP: A Village Romeo and Juliet	Beecham	HMV	I–II	12
MONTEVERDI: Works (US)	Boulanger	HMV	I	5
SCARLATTI: Sonatas	Landowska	HMV	'II'	8

recordings might be re-issued on LP. Many owners agreed, and between September 1963 and June 1964 the British end of EMI followed its American and European associates by making these performances available on microgroove. So great an interest is shown in them still that these recordings have been transferred yet again more recently; other of the Society issues, too, have appeared on LP, among them works by Sibelius and Scarlatti as well as the original Hugo Wolf series, the shortcomings of the recorded sound doing little to diminish the value of these historic performances.

The first recording of a television picture onto disc was accomplished by the 1930s by John Logie Baird, using his 30-line system. The disc was a 78rpm shellac pressing, without sound; some were actually offered for sale in London, but there seems to have been no equipment generally available to play them on. Baird had demonstrated his 30-line TV for the first time to members of the Royal Institution in London on 27 January, 1926. In the early 1930s, A D Blumlein developed the 405-line system which would have been too intricate for the coarse-groove 78rpm disc to carry.

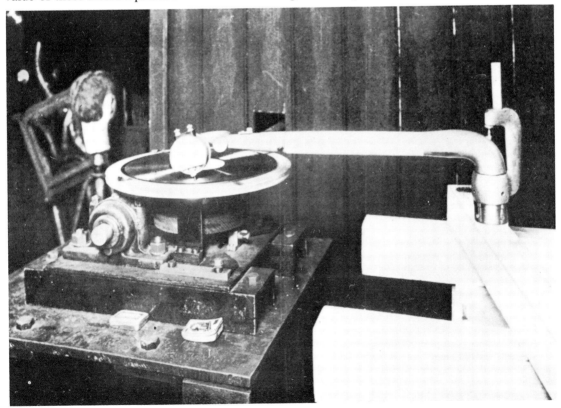

The 'Phonovision' process recording a dummy's head onto a disc, c 1930.

An early example of double-tracking appeared in December 1933 on a recording of the first movement of Grieg's Piano Concerto: Quentin Maclean performed the solo part on a piano and accompanied himself on an organ with a transcription of the orchestral part. Another technical trick was performed for a record released in 1938: John Bonner as a baritone dubbed an 'obligato' on his own recording made as a treble some years earlier of Tate's *Somewhere A Voice Is Calling* and Gounod's *Angels Guard Thee*.

The first record club was launched in 1934 by RCA Victor in America. Members were required to buy one disc per month for one year.

The first widespread use of the words 'high fidelity' occurred around 1934, used by radio stations in America, in particular WQXR in New York. The phrase had been invented by Harold A Hartley, an engineer working at English Electric in about 1926 as a description of the improved radios and electric gramophones.

After the far-reaching changes of the late 1920s and early 1930s, the record industry seemed set for a further period of consolidation, but all the estimates were confounded by the disastrous recession that hit America. As expected in such circumstances, the most expendable items in the average family's budget are luxuries such as gramophone records, and sales of the big companies' products sagged to perilous levels. As mentioned above, the dip was not so severe in the UK; a healthy export market kept British manufacturers relatively buoyant, and it was to America that much of

HALL OF FAME

Benny Goodman, 'The King of Swing'
1909 30 May: Born Benjamin David Goodman in Chicago.
From **1920** Studied music under James Sylvester and clarinet with Franz Schoepp of the Chicago Symphony Orchestra.
1921 First professional engagement at Central Park Theater, Chicago.
1925 After playing with various groups, he joined Ben Pollack's Band in Los Angeles with whom he made his **first solo recording**: *He's the Last Word* (1926).
1927 **First solos recorded under his own name**: *Clarinetitis*; *That's A Plenty*.
1928 Moved with Pollack to New York, playing there also with Sam Lanin, Nat Shilkret, Meyer Davies, Arnold Johnson, and Red Nichols; also as a freelance from 1929.
1934 Formed his own 12-man band, and hired Fletcher Henderson, the arranger who gave the Goodman Band its characteristic sound.
1935 21 August: Goodman's appearance at the Los Angeles Palomar Ballroom is said to have sparked off the 'swing era'. Gave first jazz concert at Congress Hall, Chicago on 6 November that year.
1937 Made first film: *The Big Broadcast of 1937*.

1938 16 January: Gave first-ever jazz concert at Carnegie Hall, New York. His recording made this year of Mozart's Clarinet Quintet with the Budapest String Quartet (Victor) started an active 'serious music' career that included commissioning, playing and recording many concert pieces.
1940 Re-formed his swing band with the composer/arranger Eddy Sauter.
1948 **Recorded his first million seller**: *On a Slow Boat to China* (Capitol).

From **1949** After disbanding his group, he concentrated on recording and on worldwide concert tours, appearing at the London Palladium in the early 1950s and in Leningrad in 1962.
At various times the Goodman Trio, Quartet, Sextet and Band included artists such as Count Basie, Gene Krupa, Lionel Hampton, Teddy Wilson, and many others who went on to great individual success.
The film *The Benny Goodman Story*, with Steve Allen in the title role, appeared in 1956.
Amongst Goodman's best record sellers were *King Porter Stomp* (1935), *Bach Goes to Town* (1938), *Why Don't You Do Right?* (1942).

their product went, filling shops left empty by panicking American producers.

The saviour of the record industry in America was undoubtedly the juke-box. Prohibition had been repealed on 5 December, 1933, and a new freedom was enjoyed in drug stores and places of entertainment, which offered escapism from the effects of the Depression. The juke-box, by no means a new invention, came back into its own, since those who were unable to afford mechanical music at home were nevertheless prepared to spend a nickel in the drug store juke-box. Conversely, records heard on the juke-box recommended themselves to their hearers, and somehow the money was found to purchase copies for home use. Slowly, sales began to pick up as artists such as Bing Crosby and Benny Goodman became increasingly popular.

Because of its importance, it is useful to look at the history of the juke-box.

The word 'juke' is derived from the African Negro verb 'jook' = to dance. Its first use is not known, but it was in general use for a box that played music for dancing to by the late 1930s. The concept of the juke-box dates, however, from much earlier. The first phonographs were rented out; they could not be bought outright until the North American Phonograph Co offered them for sale generally in 1892. (Edison's 'Parker' machine of 1878 was offered for sale to businessmen but these were for dictation, not for music.) The juke-box has always been an instrument for hire by proprietors of entertainment establishments and drinking houses, and remains so to this day.

The first juke-box was the result of an idea by Louis Glass, the general manager of the Pacific Phonograph Co who, in 1889, suffered a slump in his business. As an experiment, he fitted an Edison battery-operated phonograph with a coin-operated device and hired it out to the Palais Royal Saloon, San Francisco, on 23 November that year. A customer, by depositing a nickel (5¢) in the slot, released the listening tube and started the mechanism that played the cylinder. Other customers, attracted by the phenomenon, could make their own nickel con-

tribution and other listening tubes (there were four altogether) would be released.

The idea was an enormous success, and spread quickly to other companies and outlets. By 1891, drug stores offered the juke-box as a feature, and in 8 weeks during that year the Louisiana Phonograph Co took $1000 from one machine situated in a 'dive' in the city. By 1939 an estimated 300 000 juke-boxes were in use, absorbing 30 million discs per year.

The first selective automatic cylinder player was the 'Automatic Entertainer', designed by John Gabel and manufactured by the Automatic Machine and Tool Co of Chicago in 1906. It offered 24 selections. **The first juke-box to offer 100 selections** was the SICM (Seeking Industrial and Commercial Music) System of 1948. It both stored and played the records in the vertical position. **The first 200 selection juke-box**, playing both 45rpm 'singles' and 'EPs', was Seeburg's 'Select-O-Matic', of August 1955. Seeburg introduced the 45rpm 'singles' only 'Select-O-Matic' in October 1955.

All-electric coin-operated juke-boxes appeared soon after the introduction of electricity into the recording studios. Amongst the first was one made by the American company Automatic Music Instrument Inc in 1927.

The juke-box became so immensely popular that it was often used to excess in many establishments, to the distress of customers less than interested in the current popular music scene, and particularly the persistent rhythms of rock 'n' roll. One company even took advantage of this situation: Hush Records, offering a few minutes of silence, first appeared in the juke-boxes of Detroit University in January 1959; a nickel would buy some peace for frayed nerves.

It was the demands of the juke-box that led to many improvements in the manufacture of both software and hardware. Needles had to endure continuous hard wear, and the record surfaces were required to withstand repeated playings with needles changed only infrequently. Some machines automatically changed the needle for every new side, but cylinder and disc replenishment was left to the hirers, and their busy schedules inevitably meant that this duty was

A Wurlitzer juke-box.

LFI

sometimes neglected and the records would be left on the machines long after their surface quality had deteriorated. Probably the most durable of all records was a celluloid 'Everlasting' cylinder of *Peter Pan*, a xylophone solo played by Albert Benzler, which was played 40 444 times by a sapphire stylus in 7 months in 1910. The count was registered by an automatic numerator.

In addition to the interest generated by the juke-box, broadcasting had a strong influence, contrary to the fears expressed by record company executives upon its inception. Despite the disastrous world situation, a spirit of optimism was reflected in increased sales in America. This in turn was reflected in magazines devoted to music: **the first chart** of popular record sales was published in 1940 (see p. 144).

One of the leading musical influences in the early war years was the distinctive radio sound of the Glenn Miller Orchestra, which was also generating healthy record sales in America. With the entry of America into the war and the large-scale deployment of US service personnel in the UK and elsewhere, Miller's popularity was greatly widened. This was the beginning of the mass invasion of the UK market by the American dance and swing orchestras. Another American influence was felt in **the first public jam session recording**, which took place in the EMI studios, Abbey Road, St John's Wood, London, on the afternoon of Sunday 16 November, 1941, organised by the magazine *Melody Maker*. The four items issued from the considerable number played at this informal and spontaneous jazz session, in which anyone with a jazz instrument could join ('jam' in this instance being short for 'jamboree') were:

Tea For Two – HMV 10in B 9249
St Louis Blues – HMV 10in B 9250
Honeysuckle Rose/I've Found a New Baby – HMV 12in C 3269

These records were issued in January 1942.

In August 1942 the American Federation of Musicians decided that they wanted a bigger share of a constantly rising cake. They went on all-out strike in support of a demand that a flat rate be paid to the union on each record pressed. The industry held out for 27 months, during which recording of music involving instruments came to a virtual standstill. Even this misfortune was turned to advantage by American Columbia, wishing to satisfy the public thirst for new recordings and anxious to promote a new crooner who had just begun his solo career. During 1943, at the height of the strike, Frank Sinatra made a number of records lacking instrumental accompaniment, but with 'choir' backing. One of the most popular records from these unusual sessions was the coupling of *I Couldn't Sleep A Wink Last Night* and *This Is A Lovely Way To Spend An Evening*.

Eventually, though, with their reserve of instrumental recordings exhausted, Columbia, then RCA, capitulated. The rest of the industry followed suit, and the bitter struggle was over at last.

The United Kingdom was otherwise engaged, however. World War II was raging and the monthly release lists were seriously depleted due to shortages of both personnel and materials. As far as the record industry was concerned, the war proved in one way to be a stimulus to technological advancement. In 1940 the War Department asked Decca to develop a system of recording sensitive enough to reproduce the subtle differences between the sounds of British and German submarine engines. These recordings were required for the training of personnel operating listening devices.

Decca's engineers under the direction of Arthur Haddy tackled the problem. The requirement was for a recorded frequency range reaching reliably up to 12 000Hz. Eventually this target was achieved – and actually exceeded by some 2000Hz! Having thus widened the spectrum by an appreciable amount, what was more logical than to apply the knowledge thus gained to recordings of music? Consequently, the new recordings were marketed in 1944 with the advertising slogan 'full frequency range recording' – 'ffrr'.

The war adversely affected record manufacturers because of acute shortages of materials, particularly lac from India, a vital ingredient of

HALL OF FAME

Glenn Miller, bandleader

1904 1 March: Born Alton Glenn Miller at Clarinda, Iowa. In his early years he played in bands led by Boyd Senter, Ben Pollack, and Smith Ballew.

1934 Joined the Dorsey Brothers' Orchestra as trombonist and occasional singer.

From 1935 Studied orchestration with Joseph Shillinger.

1935 Joined Ray Noble's Band; formed a recording group for Columbia.

1937 Formed his own band; this was reformed in 1938 as The Glenn Miller Orchestra with the characteristic sound of one clarinet over four saxophones.

1939 10 April: **Recorded his first million seller**: *Little Brown Jug* (Victor).

1941 **Made his first film**: *Sun Valley Serenade*.

1942 10 February: For the sales of *Chattanooga Choo-Choo* (recorded 7 May, 1941) he was presented with **the very first gold sprayed disc** by RCA Victor.

1942 Made film: *Orchestra Wives*. Disbanded his orchestra to join the US Army, assembling a new band from Forces personnel. Recorded *American Patrol* on 2 April that year.

1944 ?15 December: Died ?English Channel. His service band continued under Ray McKinley (1956–65) and Buddy DeFranco (from 1966) and others.

The film *The Glenn Miller Story*, starring James Stewart, was made in 1954.

Sales of Glenn Miller's discs exceeded 60 million by 1970 and continue to sell healthily. Other best sellers, in addition to those mentioned above, were *Sunrise Serenade* (recorded 4 April, 1939), *Moonlight Serenade* (10 April, 1939), *In The Mood* (1 August, 1939), *Tuxedo Junction* (5 February, 1940), and *Pennsylvania 65000* (20 April, 1940). (All Victor.)

The Glenn Miller sound became the most imitated, the style being copied by Bob Chester (from 1940), Tex Beneke (from 1946), Ralph Flanagan (the 1950s), Jerry Gray (the 1950s), and Syd Lawrence (the 1970s).

Glenn Miller and his Orchestra.

POPPERFOTO

HALL OF FAME

Frank Sinatra, crooner

1915 12 December: Born Francis Albert Sinatra, Hoboken, New Jersey.

1937 Performed with three instrumentalists as the 'Hoboken Four'.

1938 Made his radio début.

1939 First sung with Harry James's Band.

1939 13 July: **Made his first recording**: *From the Bottom of My Heart* and *Melancholy Mood* with the Harry James Orchestra.

1939 17 September: Recorded *All or Nothing At All* (US Columbia) which, on its re-issue in 1943, became his **first million seller**.

1940–2 Sang with the Tommy Dorsey Orchestra.

1941 **Made film début in** *Las Vegas Nights* with Tommy Dorsey.

1942 Began solo career, becoming successful in records, radio and movies.

1943 **First starring film role** in *Higher and Higher.*

1953 Won an Academy Award for his performance in *From Here to Eternity.*

1961 Formed his own record company, Reprise, which he sold to Warner Brothers in 1963; became Vice President and Consultant to Warner Brothers Picture Group.

1966 His recording of *Strangers in the Night* (Reprise) won four Grammy Awards: Record of the Year; Best Male Vocal Performance; Best Arrangement; and Best Engineering Contribution.

1967 Recorded a duet with his daughter Nancy: *Something Stupid* (Reprise), which became a million seller.

1969 Recorded *My Way* (Reprise). This became the record to appear in the British best selling charts longer than any other: for a total of 122 weeks from 2 April, 1969 to 1972.

In the 1970s he made a number of international tours, despite having announced his 'retirement' in 1971. On 26 January, 1980, his appearance at the Maracaña Stadium, Rio de Janeiro, drew an estimated audience of 175 000.

Frank Sinatra, singer, and Dean Martin, conductor, discuss a point in the score.

shellac, the supplies of which were totally cut off. Furthermore, demand for records in the UK was significantly affected by the introduction in 1940 of the $33\frac{1}{3}$ per cent purchase tax. In America, manufacturers were reduced to grinding down slow moving records and recalling surplus stock from dealers at a few cents per disc in order to press even the few records not affected by the musicians' strike. The recycled material was mingled with the ever-diminishing supplies of raw lac, with progressively worsening results as regards surface noise. Clearly, an alternative material was needed, and experiments were carried out with some of the plastic substances that had been developed in attempts to make flexible and unbreakable records in earlier years. Ultimately, these experiments arrived at a plastic which could be moulded to the extremely delicate shapes demanded by a groove carrying a wide dynamic range.

The stage was set at last for another great advance: Decca, with ffrr, had widened the available frequency range, and the American makers, among them Columbia, had produced an almost ideal material: vinylite. A viable long playing, flexible disc was at last feasible; its story is told in Section IX.

Sound for Movies

It is usually considered that the coming of sound to films was a product of the electrical age of recording, and while it is true that electricity simplified the process and led to greater flexibility, the first experiments actually occurred early in the acoustic era.

There are two basic methods of producing talking movie pictures. The first synchronises the film with a cylinder or disc and is therefore dependent upon the inventions of Edison and Berliner respectively; this gave way eventually to the early sound-on-film method (eg: Phonofilm), which used a strip at the edge of the film negative to carry the sound in a modified light pattern, a system which is second cousin to that of Poulsen's 'Telegraphone'. This optical method in turn gave way to magnetic strips

which are simply coatings of iron oxide on both edges of the film; a coating identical to that on standard recording tape.

Once the first 'movie' had appeared in 1860 (this was simply a series of posed photographs mounted upon the blades of a revolving paddle-wheel; it was invented in Philadelphia by Coleman Sellers), the talkie had to wait until Edison had invented the means by which sound may be stored and retrieved. **The first motion-and-talking-picture device** was called the Kinesigraph, described by Wordsworth Donisthorpe; an Englishman, who immediately saw the possibilities inherent in Edison's newly-patented cylinder phonograph. Apparently the Kinesi-

---

COMPANY PROFILE

Decca
1914 The first Decca product was offered to the public in a front-page advertisement in the *Daily Mail* of 16 July, announcing the Decca 'Dulcephone' portable gramophone, retailing at £2 2s (£2.10). This was manufactured by the musical instrument makers Barnett Samuel and Sons Ltd, which had begun in 1869 on the shoulders of Henry Solomon and Co, which in turn had commenced trading in London in 1832 as the makers of pennibs. 'Decca', a word whose origins are lost, became widely known to soldiers during World War I as the name on the boxes of the portable gramophones so popular in the trenches. In the 1940s, its letters were equated with notes on a stave to form a distinctive 'classical' trade mark, along with a frowning bust of Beethoven, as the company's contributions to serious music recordings become telling competition for the EMI combine.
1929 Edward Lewis, a stockbroker, bought the Barnett Samuel company, which had been renamed the Decca Gramophone Co, and on 1 July he launched the Decca Record Company with a classical release including Delius's *Sea Drift*, Offenbach's Overture *Orpheus in the Underworld*, and Grainger's *Jutish Medley*, and a lighter selection featuring Billy Cotton, Ambrose and his Orchestra,

graph was a theoretical machine, never built, but Edison's attention may have been drawn to Donisthorpe's idea, which appeared in the magazine *Nature* in 1877. It took a further dozen years for the idea to become reality; the following chronology shows the chain of inventions that eventually brought *The Jazz Singer* and a new era to the cinema.

1889 6 October: Edison's 'Kineto-phonograph', later renamed 'Kinetoscope', demonstrated at the West Orange laboratory – see p. 28.

1894 14 April: **The first public demonstration of the 'Kinetoscope'** was given in New York.

1896 **The first public performance of a sound film** was given in Berlin in September, when Oskar Messter presented movie film synchronised with Berliner discs. Performers and titles are unknown; probably the filmplay was merely of actors miming to records. During the same year (or shortly after the beginning of 1897), scenes from an operetta (unnamed) were filmed by Giampetro and Fritzi Massary, again using synchronised records, probably cylinders.

1900 **The first operatic sound film** was of excerpts from works by Verdi and Gounod sung by Victor Maurel and Cossira, shown at the Phono-Cinéma-Théâtre at the Paris Exposition on 8 June. Also shown on the same occasion

DECCA

Gwen Farrer, and Billy Mayerl. There was also a recording conducted by Julian Clifford of the British National Anthem. Records were made at the old Duophone factory in New Malden, Surrey, recently purchased by Decca.

1930 British rights acquired to the German Polydor classical label.

1933 Decca buys the Edison Bell Company.

1934 The Decca Record Company (USA) formed; it purchased Warner Brothers' Brunswick record manufacturing plant. Jack Kapp, formerly of Brunswick, joined the new company, bringing with him many popular ex-Brunswick artists.

1937 March: UK Decca absorbed the Crystalate company.

1940 Arthur Haddy developed high frequency recording techniques for military purposes; this advance was eventually adapted to be marketed commercially as 'ffrr' (full frequency range recording) in December 1944. The first important ffrr release was of Ansermet conducting Stravinsky's *Petrushka* (1946).

1946 Decca institutes an ambitious programme of international classical recordings in many European centres.

1948 Decca perfects the 33⅓rpm long playing record, which is exported in quantity to

America to compete with the new Columbia LPs. British Decca were marketed in the USA, Canada, and South America under the 'London' trade mark, American Decca having become independent.

1950 June: Domestic launch of LP. Decca was the first to market LPs in Britain.

1955 Capitol, previously released by Decca in the UK, switched to EMI.

1957 September: Decca took over the UK distribution of RCA from EMI.

1958 Decca House, on the Albert Embankment, London, opened on 10 March by the Rt Hon Sir David Eccles, President of the Board of Trade.

1958 Decca launched stereo recordings with the slogan ffss (full frequency stereophonic sound).

(1974 The control of the independent American Decca Corporation was taken over by the Music Corporation of America (MCA), and EMI secured the British rights to MCA.)

1980 17 January: Decca merged with the Philips/DG group to become part of Poly-Gram.

1980 29 January: Decca chairman Sir Edward Lewis died.

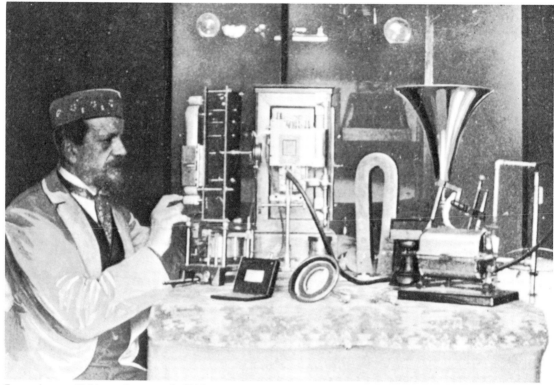

Eugene Lauste with his sound camera of c 1911.

were **the first talkies** (Sarah Bernhardt in a scene from *Hamlet*, and several other pieces mainly by French authors), and **the first ballet films** featuring the dancers Rosita Mauri and Zambelli. All these films used the synchronised record technique.

This system survived for many years and developed into the relatively sophisticated Vitaphone method of 1926 (see below). At first, sound and pictures were of necessity made separately because of the interference inevitably picked up from the noisy cameras; simultaneous filming and recording became possible only when the cameras were encased in heavy sound-proofing quilts or padded boxes.

1906 11 August: **The first sound-on-film machine** was patented by Eugene Lauste of London. His 'sound camera' did not successfully record sound until 1910 and did not pass its final tests until 1913, whereupon World War I intervened and his machine was never taken up commercially. It employed 'an electromagnetic

recorder and string galvanometer' (Robertson), so apparently relied for its soundtrack upon the principle used in Poulsen's 'Telegraphone'.

1911 **The first colour talkie** was *Vals ur Solstraten*, a short film using the Biophon synchronised disc system, made in Sweden and premièred in Malmö, Sweden, on 1 May.

1921 **The first full-length feature 'talkie'** was *Dream Street*, made this year by United Artists originally as a silent film. Sound was later added to two sections, using synchronised disc, and the film was shown in this part-sound form on 29 May, 1921.

1922 **Optical sound-on-film** introduced. This was of two types: variable area and variable density. Both converted amplified sound to light by, in the first case, feeding it to a galvanometer mirror upon which a light source is focused. The mirror, duly vibrated by the sound, directs the light through a system of lenses and onto the film negative, which records the vibrations in light and dark areas. In the second case, the

Landmarks in Talkie History

The First Talkie of All,
"The Jazz Singer"

First British Talkie,
"Blackmail"

1. The Jazz Singer *(1927)*. 2. *Alfred Hitchcock's* Blackmail *(1929)*. 3. Broadway Melody *(1929)*. 4. The Terror *(1928)*. 5. The Perfect Alibi *(1929)*. *Despite the contemporary claim made for* The Jazz Singer, *earlier 'talkies' had appeared. See text.*

sound is passed to a light valve which projects a strip of light of varying density onto the negative.

1922 9 June: **The first sound-on-film movie** was a monologue by Ellery Paine: *Lincoln's Gettysburg Address*, demonstrated privately by Prof Joseph Tykocinski-Tykociner in Illinois University.

1922 17 September: **The first public sound-on-film demonstration** was given at the Alhambra Kino, Berlin, using the 'Tri-Ergon' method. Both musical and dramatic films were shown.

1922 **The first feature sound film made outside the US** was *La Muchacha del Arrabal*, partly with sound, made in Argentina.

1923 15 April: At the Rialto Theater, New York, the main feature was the silent movie *Bella Donna*, with Pola Negri. It was supported by **the first demonstration before a paying audience of sound-on-film movies**: a series of brief musical shorts made by the Phonofilm system developed by Lee De Forest.

1923 14 June: **Phonofilm shorts were first demonstrated privately in the UK**, at the Finsbury Park Cinema.

1925 **The first Phonofilm musical feature film** was *Siegfried*, made in Germany by Fritz Lang.

1926 Vitaphone developed by Lee De Forest and others of Western Electric and taken up by Warner Bros. **The first commercial Vitaphone soundtrack with music** synchronised to a feature film was for *Don Juan*, premièred in New York on 19 February, 1927, and recorded by RCA on coarse-groove 16in (40·6cm) centre-start discs revolving at 33⅓rpm and synchronised to the film. The music was related only vaguely to the action. A spoken preface by Will H Hayes, Warren Harding's Postmaster General, introduced the new process.

1927 6 October: The première in New York of **the first real feature talkie**, in which dialogue *and* singing is heard in the body of the film (earlier examples had been music only) was *The Jazz Singer*, with Al Jolson, which was shown at the Warner Theatre, Broadway. It used the Vitaphone sound system. The dialogue passages were ad-libbed by Jolson and two other actors; if they had stuck strictly to their brief *The Jazz Singer* would have rated merely as one of the early feature films with part-music. **The first purpose-built film stage designed for sound** was opened in Hollywood in May by Warner Bros. Filming of *The Jazz Singer* commenced immediately.

1928 **The first all-talking feature film** was *Lights Of New York*, premièred in New York on 6 July, which dialogued ceaselessly from the first moment to the last. **The first feature-length sound film in colour** was *The Viking*, premièred in the US on 2 November with synchronised music and sound effects.

1929 **The first talkie feature film made in the UK** was Alfred Hitchcock's *Blackmail*, made at British International Pictures' studios at Elstree, and premièred in London on 21 June. Anny Ondra, the Czech actress, was unable to speak the English dialogue, so her part was dubbed by Joan Barry.

Apart from a Phonofilm documentary made in Cuba in 1926, the making of talkies did not become widespread until 1929, when sound films were premièred in France, Germany, Austria, Sweden, Canada, and Japan as well as in the UK. During 1930 the sound-on-film and synchronised disc systems had spread worldwide and continued to co-exist for several years.

1935 **The first film with stereophonic sound** was *Napoleon Bonaparte*, which was made in France in 1927. The stereophonic dialogue and sound effects were added in 1935, using a system patented in 1932.

1940 **The first American stereophonic sound films** were *Santa Fe Trail* and *Four Wives*, both of which used 'Vitasound'.

1941 **The first musical film with stereophonic sound** ('Fantasound', developed in conjunction with RCA) was Walt Disney's *Fantasia*.

1951 **The introduction of magnetic striping** (ie: a strip of iron oxide coating at the side(s) of the film.) This carries the soundtrack as in a tape recorder and was developed by Reeves Soundcraft, USA, using an RCA projector. It was distributed in this form in *This is Cinerama* in 1952. However, Warner recorded their soundtracks onto tape from 1949, converting them to optical tracks before distribution.

Section V

Tape Recording

Early wax cylinders were designed for home or office recording. One merely shaved off the previous recording, leaving a blank surface upon which to record the fresh message. In 1931, Victor put onto the American market a plastic disc with a blank groove which could be used for home recording by employing the pick-up needle as the indenting point, but this device, together with the Pye 'Record-Maker', a similar machine offered in England shortly after World War II, and HMV's model 2300 H of 1949, met with little success, and it was to wire and tape that the home recordist and the businessman turned.

The first wire recorder was the 'Telegraphone', invented by the Danish engineer Valdemar Poulsen (1869–1942) in 1898 and demonstrated by him the following year as a dictation and telephone message machine. It consisted of a brass cylinder, the surface of which was tooled with a helical groove into which fitted the recording wire. Despite the high linear speed of 7ft (2·15m) per second, reproduction from the wire was poor in comparison with later experiments with tape (and even with contemporary cylinders) and the only means of hearing the recording was via earphones. Poulsen and P O Pedersen set up the American Telegraphone Co in 1903. In 1948 Bang and Olufsen produced their 'Beocord' wire recorder, and as recently as 1952 Wirek wire recorders were being offered for sale by the London firm of Boosey and Hawkes at prices from £60 upwards.

In the early 1900s Poulsen experimented with recording onto metal discs about $\frac{1}{16}$in (2mm) thick and $4\frac{1}{2}$in (11·4cm) in diameter, but although he achieved some success the results were never marketed.

The first steel band recorder was the 'Blattnerphone', demonstrated on 11 October, 1929, by the Blattner Colour and Sound Studios of Elstree, Herts, UK. The electromagnetic recording was of a telephone conversation, a film soundtrack, and a direct voice recording; evidently Louis Blattner's company had in mind the potentialities of the machine in office, movies, and the recording studio. The flat steel

Poulsen's first magnetic recorder of 1900.   BASF

band was $\frac{1}{4}$in (6·5mm) wide by $\frac{1}{16}$in (2mm) thick, and one demonstration ran for half an hour without interruption. The extended, not to say unlimited, playing time potential of the 'Blattnerphone' was stressed at the demonstration. A highly-polished tungsten steel strip was used by the 'Marconi-Stille' machine of 1934. This strip was $\frac{1}{8}$in (3mm) wide by $\frac{1}{32}$in (0·08mm) thick, and a 3000 metre reel travelling at 90 metres per minute (ie: about 4ft 9in per second!) gave a playing time of just over $33\frac{1}{4}$ minutes.

A prophetic remark in Poulsen's Danish patent (applied for 1 December, 1898, see above) stated that 'a strip of some insulating material such as paper covered with a magnetisable metallic dust' would probably provide the best recording medium. The initial theory had been put forward earlier still, in an article written in 1888 by Oberlin Smith.

Both base and coating of modern tape have to fulfil a number of exacting requirements. The base must be flexible and durable, magnetically impermeable and of even thickness. It must also be smooth enough to glide noiselessly through the guides and pressure pads, but not slippery enough to allow adjacent windings to slide and buckle against the inside of the spool if wound too loosely. Coating requirements are even more critical. This, too, must remain flexible and durable in use and in storage at fairly wide temperature variations without losing its signal, it must adhere strongly to the base but not to the next winding, and it must be a faultlessly continuous coating of even density and thickness.

The first use of a non-magnetic base for recording tape was by J A O'Neill in America in 1927. He used coated paper, as did Fritz Pfleumer in a German patent of 1928. This format was adopted by the cinema from 1951. By 1935 the German company AEG had built the 'Magnetophon', the first machine to use a plastic base tape coated with iron oxide, as developed by BASF in 1934. It was demonstrated at the Berlin Radio Fair in 1935. The earliest surviving musical recording made on plastic base tape was a live recording of the Minuet from Mozart's Symphony No 39, made in the Feirabenhaus, Ludwigshafen, Germany, on 19 November, 1936.

The first commercially-marketed tape recorder was the 'Magnetophon' made by AEG/Telefunken in Germany in about 1937. In that year the American Brush Development Company put on sale its 'Soundmirror' tape recorder, but the more advanced German models were used during World War II by German radio stations for propaganda broadcasts and other spoken-word transmissions. When the Allies liberated Luxembourg in the autumn of 1944 they discovered these sophisticated machines and shipped them back home for examination. Technicians in the UK and America were able to benefit from the techniques that had been built into the machines by the German inventors.

Shortly after World War II recording studios switched over to tape for their master recordings. Artists now found themselves in the position of those pianists who, years earlier, had made piano rolls: performances once transferred to the paper roll were played back for artistic approval and, if necessary, parts could be re-made and slotted into the master roll for publication. Tape offered the same facility, and in the hands of a skilful tape editor the joins would be absolutely undetectable. Even difficult joins could be 'smoothed' over with a suggestion of echo, judiciously placed. Eventually there was an outcry from some customers who felt that what they were listening to was not a performance but a conflation of many performances, cobbled together to make a per-

fect and, to them, artificial whole. Some companies responded by announcing that their recordings were composed of complete and unedited 'takes' of complete movements or whole works, but by then the tape editors were so proficient at their job that even the most critical listener found it impossible to disprove the claim.

The first professional tape deck to be offered in the UK was the Wright and Weaire model of 1948. Open spool tape recorders were first offered to the general public in 1950 (America) and 1951 (UK), and in mid-1952 the Southampton firm of Thermionic Products offered for sale a 'Soundmirror' machine, probably a descendant of the Brush model mentioned above.

The first recording of a TV programme onto tape (black/white, and colour) was made by the RCA Laboratories in America in November 1953.

The first pre-recorded tapes, on 7in (18cm) spools at 7½ips, were marketed by Victor in America in June 1954 and by EMI in the UK on 3 September, 1954.

The first hybrid tape recorder/record player was the 'Selectophon', marketed in mid-1957. To the conventional disc player was added a device to play a tape in a 'book-type cassette' with several tracks giving a playing time of up to six hours. In 1959 the 'Gramdeck' appeared: a 'skeleton' tape deck designed to fit onto a standard record player's turntable. With the turntable running at 78rpm, a tape speed of 7½ips was achieved, but fast wind and re-wind were slow and cumbersome operations.

Although the amateur use of tape achieved a certain popularity, partly due to the facility with which the user could record his own programme and the voices of himself and others, and partly because quality was potentially higher than with commercial discs, many users found the fiddly job of threading the tape through the head block and onto the take-up spool both irritating and time-consuming. So much easier to put a disc onto the turntable and lower the pick-up. For handicapped users, especially the blind, while preparing to play a record was difficult, threading a tape was often impossible. Consequently, manufacturers urgently sought ways to reduce the problem, and talking books for the blind were sold in cartridge form as early as 1953. These, however, used conventional tape of ¼in (6mm) width running at 3¾ips, and in order not to make the cases too bulky the running time was not great. Real convenience, it seemed, lay in miniaturisation.

special equipment to play them on, and had offered licences to any other manufacturers who cared to take them up. A similar cartridge, or 'magazine', was offered in the UK in November 1959 by Garrard of Swindon. It consisted of a plastic case containing two 4in (10cm) spools of ½in (12mm) wide long play tape which slotted over a newly-designed deck playing at 3¾ips. This gave about 23 minutes of mono playing

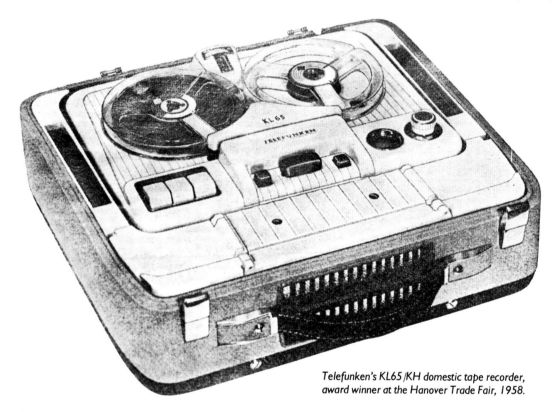

Telefunken's KL65/KH domestic tape recorder, award winner at the Hanover Trade Fair, 1958.

The first tape cartridge containing pre-recorded music was announced by RCA Victor in May 1958. It was a development of the talking book system with the same tape width and playing speed and it measured 7in × 5in × ½in (17·8cm × 12·7cm × 12mm). However, the recordings were four-track stereo, which meant that two twin-channel programmes were accommodated, one in each direction, the channels being interleaved with each other so that the first and third contained the programme of 'side one', the fourth and second that of 'side two'. Within a month RCA had produced

time for the home recordist; no pre-recorded tapes were issued in this format.

Once again, standardisation seemed doomed and another 'battle of the speeds' (see Section IX) threatened when American Columbia spurned their old rival RCA's licensing offer and produced their own totally different and incompatible design. Dr Peter Goldmark, of long playing fame, was once again the driving force. At the CBS Laboratories in Connecticut, he developed a cassette containing a three-track tape of half the standard width carrying a pre-recorded stereo programme in one direction only and running for 64 minutes at $1\frac{7}{8}$ips. The cassette casing was very much smaller than RCA's cartridge and Garrard's magazine, being only $\frac{5}{16}$in (8mm) thick and $3\frac{1}{2}$in (9cm) square (today's standard compact cassette measures $\frac{5}{16}$in $\times$4in $\times$ $2\frac{1}{2}$in, ie: 8mm $\times$ 10cm $\times$ 6·4cm), but a disadvantage was that there was no 're-cord' facility. The machine CBS designed for playing these cassettes was **the first cassette autochanger**: it would automatically play five cassettes consecutively, giving over five hours of virtually continuous music. The announcement of these cassettes and players was made in June 1960; they were marketed the next year.

Meanwhile, the American firms of Viking and Cousino, and RCA Victor, redesigned *their* cartridges, and a new format designed primarily for in-car entertainment was launched in the early summer of 1961. These cartridges gave a stereo signal, but a major disadvantage was that there was no fast-wind or re-wind facility. **The first re-windable tape cartridge** was developed by KRS Magnetics Inc of California in 1979.

The Philips cassette, at first called 'cartridge' but later known and marketed industry-wide as '**compact cassette**', was invented by engineers at Philips Gloeilampenfabrieken, Holland, and launched at the Berlin Radio Show in 1963. It

---

COMPANY PROFILE

PHILIPS

Philips

1933 Record shop owner H van Zoelen, director of Decca Dutch Supplies, started a pressing shop in Amsterdam.

1942 The company was sold to Fred Philips, a banker.

1946 Shares sold to Philips' Gloeilampen-fabrieken of Eindhoven.

1950 Recording activities begun by P Dijksterhuis and E B W Schuitema. The first Philips classical recording was made in June: Tchaikovsky's Symphony No 4, with Willem van Otterloo conducting the Hague Philharmonic Orchestra. Recording activities also begun in Germany, Austria, Belgium and (through the purchase of French Polydor) France.

1951 Pressing plant opened in Baarn. A reciprocal agreement was signed with American Columbia. Philips material appeared on the Epic label in the US from 1955.

1952 Branches opened in Italy, Norway, Finland and the UK. Disc configurations were established at:

25·4cm and 30·5cm	78rpm coarse groove
20·3cm	78rpm 'minigroove'
25·4cm and 30·5cm	$33\frac{1}{3}$rpm 'minigroove'

1953 Philips took over European distribution of American Columbia from EMI. Phonogram founded in Baarn to sell Philips and Decca records in the Netherlands.

Phonogram moved to Amsterdam. Australian branch formed.

1954 July: First classical releases made in the UK. Spanish branch formed.

1961 September: Philips signed a contract for exchange of repertoire with American Mercury.

1962 June: Philips Phonographic Industries (PPI) and Deutsche Grammophon Gesellschaft (DGG) merged in a 50/50 exchange of shares, combining their music activities but retaining label identity.

1964 Philips introduced the musicassette (compact cassette).

1972 3 January: PPI renamed Phonogram International as a subsidiary of the new combine PolyGram (ie: Philips and DG). PolyGram acquired MGM Records in the US.

1978 PolyGram became **the world's first recording organisation to exceed one billion dollars in turnover**.

1978 17 May: Philips announced a Compact Disc, using digital recording and replay systems, to be launched 'in the early 1980s'.

1980 17 January: PolyGram acquired the UK Decca Record Co.

1982 October: The Philips Compact Disc launched in Japan by CBS/Sony.

1983 March: European launch of CD in the UK, West Germany, France and the Netherlands.

was first advertised in the UK in June 1964. It gave 30 minutes' playing time per side and was offered originally in blank form; later, pre-recorded cassettes appeared. A certain amount of confusion arose at first over standards, but by mid-1966 the Philips standard had been generally adopted: tape width 3·8mm, recording speed 4·75cm per second (1⅞ips); stereo/mono compatibility to be attained by positioning the two stereo tracks adjacent to each other on the tape so that both may be read simultaneously by monaural players. An agreed and standardised norm had at last been established, thanks to Philips's generosity in offering royalty-free licences world-wide to any company agreeing to follow the basic design, and the compact cassette became ripe for mechanical sophistication and quality improvements, now that the two alternative cassette formats (the DC International Cassette System favoured by Telefunken and Grundig in Germany used a playing speed of 2ips, while another German firm, Saba, retained the standard open-spool tape width of ¼in, ie: twice the width of the tape in Philips's compact cassette) had been quietly buried.

The cassette's playing time of 30 minutes per side (known as 'C60' – the *total* playing time) is retained today, but the use of thinner tape allows 45 minutes per side ('C90', the optimum tape thickness), and 60 minutes per side ('C120', but achieved with extra-thin tape that requires care in handling if it is not to crease or break). The Japanese firm TDK offered blank cassettes giving 90 minutes per side ('C180'), but these were on the market for only a short time in the mid-1970s; one assumes that returns due to breakage were unacceptably high.

The mechanical improvements that have brought the compact cassette to its current reliability include plastic guides (known as 'tusks') within the shell to ensure that the tape is wound evenly in both 'play' and 'fast wind' modes, and smooth surfaces and free-running guide and tension wheels to prevent snagging or jamming. A further requirement of a good cassette is that the two halves of the shell should be screwed together (to facilitate easy examination

Dr Raymond M Dolby, who revolutionised cassette recording quality.　DOLBY LABORATORIES

in the event of jamming) rather than heat-welded. Heat-welded cassettes have to be prized apart like an oyster, quite often resulting in damage to the moulding, and even if opening is accomplished successfully, secure closing after repair may be managed only with the use of glue or sticky tape – substances which should not be let loose anywhere near the delicate recording tape. (Incidentally, it is wise to remember, while we are on the subject of cassette care, that the valuable music or messages on your cassettes is stored magnetically in the tape coating. The presence of a magnet anywhere near a cassette will interfere with that signal – so never place your cassettes near or on a speaker cabinet! Heat can also adversely affect the minutely thin plastic tape base, so never leave tapes by a fire or radiator, or where the sun can get at them.)

With the use of ever more sophisticated coatings, from cobalt, ferric oxide and black oxide to chrome dioxide and metal particles, cassette quality has been improved dramatically since the earliest Philips 'cartridge', which was adequate for speech but barely so for music. **The earliest experiments with chromium dioxide** date from 1966 and developments were brought to marketable form by du Pont in 1970. **Metal particle tape was first introduced in 1979** (eg: 3M's 'Metafine IV') after extensive laboratory tests. 'Metal' cassettes are considerably more expensive than those conventionally coated, but they offer incredibly high frequency range for the slow linear speed of $1\frac{7}{8}$ips. A good compromise is the cheaper 'ferri-chrome' formulation, with both ferric oxide and chromium dioxide coatings.

By far the most important advance in cassette quality was made when the Dolby process brought about a great reduction in surface hiss. The American inventor Raymond M Dolby opened a laboratory in London in 1966 to produce his noise reduction system for tape recordings. His was an idea of simple genius: during recording, one merely enhances artificially the amplitude of the music that lies in the range most affected by the tape hiss; then, on playback, the boosted sections are restored to their correct levels. The tape hiss is thus taken down with them and so disappears below the level of audibility. In a crude form, the same idea had been used by Paul G A H Voigt, who had given a treble pre-emphasis to Edison-Bell recordings in the early days of electrical recording, resulting in a noticeable reduction in surface noise on playback.

The Dolby 'A' system used in professional recording studios was modified to become Dolby 'B' for domestic cassette players, whereupon pre-recorded cassette manufacturers began processing their cassettes using Dolby. This simple development was immediately reflected in the retail shop. According to a Philips survey of 1971, 60 per cent of tape recorders sold in the UK in 1969 were of the open-spool type but only 40 per cent were cassette players. In the following year these figures had been reversed.

The first company to market pre-recorded Dolbyised cassettes was Decca in the UK: as

---

How Dolby noise-reduction works

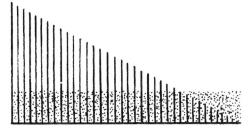

1 A diagrammatic representation of a musical sequence moving evenly from loud to soft. It will be seen that the shaded area, representing tape hiss, swallows up the quietest part of the music.

2 A Dolbyised recording emphasises the volume of that part of the music affected by the hiss, lifting it out of the shaded area.

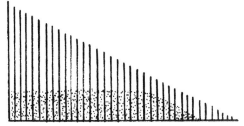

3 Upon playback, the volume is reduced to its former level, this action automatically taking down the hiss level with it.

---

from October 1970, all Decca cassettes were to be released in Dolbyised format only. This date is just 1 month after Decca first entered the cassette market: all tapes in that first Decca release in September 1970 were non-Dolby processed, but most were subsequently reissued in Dolbyised form. **The last major manufacturer to convert to Dolby-only pre-recorded**

cassettes was the Polydor/Phonogram Group (ie: DG and Philips) in mid-1974.

The compact cassette, as originally devised in 1964 and improved by countless developers since then, is **the most convenient and versatile form of recorded sound for the home user**. At first it had only convenience and compactness to recommend it, but the following changes have brought it to its present degree of sophistication:

Playing Time: at first a total of one hour, which equalled an exceptionally well-filled LP record. Now available in blank form in playing times up to 1 hour per side (C120), with alternatives of C96, C90, C66, C60, C46 and C30, which should satisfy most requirements for continuity.

Reliability: with improved tape base material, smoother internal surfaces, and gentler handling by modern tape decks, the early hazards of tape breakage and jamming are now virtually eliminated.

Sound Quality: without increasing the original running speed of $1\frac{7}{8}$ips, today's transfer techniques, vastly improved coatings and noise reduction systems can offer sound reproduction at least equal to modern discs. (The American BIC machine of 1979 gave the home recordist the option of using the standard cassette tape speed and the standard domestic open-spool speed of $3\frac{3}{4}$ips, the advertising copy pointing out the supposed increase in quality with music recording if the higher speed is used, but today's cassettes perform so well at the lower (standard) speed that few buyers took up BIC's option, with its hungrier consumption of tape, and the idea has been neither widely used nor copied by other makers.)

Compatibility: the twin track provides a stereo signal in each direction, but mono may be recorded on this twin track for replay as double-mono through a stereo reproducing chain; conversely, if a stereo tape is played on a mono machine a sum of the two tracks is heard, giving a balanced mono sound picture. Furthermore, even if the playback machine is a cheap portable or for some other reason omits the Dolby 'B' circuitry, Dolbyised cassettes may be played, the result being an increased brilliance in the upper range that tends to enhance the machine's reproduction.

Record Facility: home recordings may be made on blank cassettes (or on previously recorded cassettes, the old signal being 'wiped' automatically as the new one is laid down), and a tab at the rear of the cassette housing may be removed to prevent accidental erasure. Yet this tab may be replaced by sticky paper or tape, or by other materials, if it is subsequently decided to erase a previously preserved recording. Some machines automatically switch to an alternative circuit (chrome dioxide or metal) according to the instructions given by the other indentations on the rear of the cassette housing.

Pre-Recorded Cassettes: many record manufacturers issue pre-recorded cassettes, often in parallel with their disc releases, and while the cassette repertoire is not so wide as that of the disc, it is increasing constantly. Only rarely, however, do manufacturers take advantage of the larger and more flexible playing time which the cassette medium affords. Too often a cassette issue is a straight transfer of a disc, its limited side length and possibly disastrous turn-over point faithfully – and stupidly – preserved. There is some evidence that disc side lengths are being tailored for cassette issue: the disc sides are equalised as closely as possible so that there should not be an excess of blank tape on one side when the recording is issued on cassette. The tail, therefore; wags the dog. It is possible to produce pre-recorded cassettes to accommodate economically any piece of music lasting from, say, 10 minutes to about 43 minutes without breaks, and if a price structure geared to pence-per-minute were adopted the true music potential of the 'musicassette' would at last be realised. Much remains to be accomplished in this direction; attitudes, not the cassette format, need changing.

Compactness: if 24 hours of music on disc were to be stored, a shelf space of 4in (10cm) would be needed, assuming that the LP records had 30 minutes of music per side and were housed in standard sleeves. The same amount of music on C120 cassettes would take 8in (20cm),

A Philips cassette autochanger, marketed in 1970.   PHILIPS

against which have to be set the other dimensions: 12in square for records but a mere 2¾in deep by 4¼in high for cassettes (30cm for records but only 7cm × 10·8cm for cassettes). Furthermore, an LP disc in its sleeve weighs approximately 9oz (255g) while a cassette in its plastic container weighs only 3¾oz (106g) – a consideration for mail order firms.

Durability: tapes are much less prone to accidental damage through dust or mishandling than are discs. It is rare to find even a factory-fresh disc record absolutely free of blemish;

rarer still to find a pre-recorded cassette in less than perfect condition. Since such a tiny percentage of the playing surface of a cassette tape is exposed to dust and other atmosphere-borne pollution (whereas the whole of the playing surface of a disc is exposed all the time it is out of its cover), damage from this source is likely to be negligible over the life of the tape. On the other hand, print-through from one winding to the next – a perennial problem on tape – is liable to occur, especially on thinner tapes. This is another problem manufacturers need to tackle.

Against so many advantages in favour of cassettes, one serious disadvantage should be mentioned. On a disc surface, with the whole playing area exposed to view, all that is needed for the instantaneous selection of a desired track are a good eye and a steady hand. Should one require a track beginning elsewhere than at the beginning of a cassette, however, one may make a note of the register number and spool forward to approximately the correct position, which might take a considerable time. But it seems that no two makers' registers are identical (they can even differ between two examples of the same model), so if a subsequent updating of equipment involves a change of deck, one will need to re-number the selections in one's entire tape collection. A world-wide numerator standard is required, preferably one that in some way indicates elapsed playing time also. Some more expensive decks offer a 'search-and-find' mechanism (eg: Sharp's 'APLD' = 'Automatic Programme Location Device') which 'reads' the tape at fast-wind and can be programmed in advance to stop at a given track. The device simply counts the blank spaces between tracks and automatically starts to play at the one selected. Unfortunately, some serious music contains pauses of sufficient length to trigger the mechanism prematurely.

Further development is necessary, then, before the convenience of the cassette becomes overwhelming enough to conquer the strange fascination the disc has for collectors. It would be ironic if the new disc developments keep the cassette in second place just as it is poised to overcome all opposition and criticism.

The first autochanger for the Philips-type compact cassette was the Philips N2401 which was announced in April 1970. It was designed to play six stereo cassettes consecutively.

In 1976 four new types of tape cassette were announced: all were mutually incompatible, as well as being incompatible with the standard compact cassette. Both Philips and National Panasonic produced much smaller models for office use; and in attempts to improve quality by doubling the playing speed, BASF's 'Unisette' and Matsushita's 'Elcaset' once again utilised the once-standard $\frac{1}{4}$in (6mm) tape width.

The generally adopted tape speeds for commercial use are:

$1\frac{7}{8}$	inches per second			=	4·75cm per second	
$3\frac{3}{4}$	,,	,,	,,	=	9·5	,, ,, ,,
$7\frac{1}{2}$	,,	,,	,,	=	19	,, ,, ,,
15	,,	,,	,,	=	38	,, ,, ,,
30	,,	,,	,,	=	76	,, ,, ,,

The slowest practical tape speed for musical purposes is $1\frac{7}{8}$ips, but experiments have been carried out at $\frac{15}{16}$**ips** = **2·38cm/sec** for speech, and this speed is used in some dictating machines. At a reception on 27 November, 1978, the Foundation for Audio Research and Services for Blind People demonstrated a prototype cassette player which gives 12 hours from a standard C90 cassette. It has four mono channels running at $\frac{15}{32}$**ips** = **11·9mm/sec** and is recommended for talking books.

The fastest tape speed in general use is 240ips = 609·6cm/sec, which is the velocity of the master tape when used for the commercial dubbing of pre-recorded cassettes.

Literature

Record Publications

Catalogues

Collectors of recorded music and other sounds need printed information about their hobby, both to let them know what is, or was, available for purchase, and to keep them informed about the quality of recordings issued. They must also be kept abreast of current developments in record reproducing technology. Publishers have been busy in fulfilling this need, and a vast literature has accumulated since the invention of the phonograph.

The first catalogue of recordings offered for sale was a 10-page pamphlet issued by the Columbia Phonograph Co in 1891 (see p. 32, Section II). Since then, every company throughout the world has produced full or partial catalogues ranging in quality from the meanest scrap of paper to case-bound books. Many companies maintain a department solely to catalogue their products.

The first disc catalogue was issued by Parkins and Gotto in about 1892 and is discussed in Section III (see pp. 39/40). Other early catalogues are also mentioned there. **The first publication offering a complete world-wide coverage** of all makes of classical recordings was *The Gramophone Shop Encyclopædia of Recorded Music*, compiled by R D Darrell and Joseph Brogan and first published in New York in 1936. It had its origins in the second edition (1931) of the *Gramophone Shop Encyclopedia of the World's Best Recorded Music*, and itself ran to three editions (2nd: 1942; 3rd: 1948); supplements were published until February 1954.

In May 1952 appeared the *World's Encyclopædia of Recorded Music*, published in London by Sidgwick & Jackson Ltd in association with the Decca Record Co, Ltd, at a pre-publication price of £2·50 plus 5p postage and packing, an extraordinarily low price even in those days for a book of 904 pages (including the bound-in *First Supplement*) which endeavoured to list in great detail all the electrical recordings (ie: from 1925 to June 1951, plus

LIST OF PLATES NOW READY
FOR THE

"GRAMOPHONE."

RECITATIONS.	GERMAN.
17. Proverbs	52. Kühlengrund
18. Father William	53. Wacht am Rhein
20. Old King Cole	54. Rheinlied
23. Manfred *(Byron)*	61. Der Gute Kamerad
25. Lord's Prayer	64. Soldatenlied
26. Twinkle, Little Star	72. Deutschland über Alles
27. Thou knowest my pretty damsel	
28. Morning Hymn	BRASS INSTRUMENTS.
29. Jack and Jill	75. Quintet (March)—Gruss aus Kiel
30. Mary had a Little Lamb	77. Quintet—Hohenfriedberger
31. A Healthy Boy was Alfred Jones	78. „ Gasparone
32. Tom, he was a Piper	81. „ Zu Augsburg
33. Simple Simon	88. „ God save the Queen
34. My name is the 'Gramophone'	111. Piston Solo—Deutschland
35. Cock Robin	112. „ „ The Mail
36. Sing a Song of Sixpence	606. Concert Piece
37. Old Mother Hubbard	609. Mikado
38. Nursery Rhymes	113. Bugle Calls
	116. Trombone Solo—Drinking
SONGS.—ENGLISH.	376. Quintet—Alte Dessauer
40. We don't want to fight	
41. For you, for you, my Darling	PIANO.
42. Auld Lang Syne	121. Bierwaltzer
44. My Grandfather's Clock	122. Prophet's March
48. Rule Britannia	
50. Blue Bells of Scotland	ASSORTED PLATES.
53. Ta ra ra Boom-de-Ay	45. Farmyard Imitations (Animal Voices, &c.
54. Knock'd 'em in the Old Kent Road	120. Banjo Duet—Boccacio
56. Long, long ago	130. Clarionette Solo, with variations
FRENCH.	600. Old-fashioned Street Organ
164. Père Victoire	650. Roll of Drums
165. La Boiteuse	

PRICE OF PLATES, 1/- EACH.

PARKINS & GOTTO, 60, OXFORD STREET, W.

The first English catalogue of discs, issued c 1892, listing 54 5in 'plates'.   VINTAGE SOUNDS

a few earlier non-electrical recordings of outstanding interest) of 'permanent' music issued world-wide. The compilers were F F Clough and G J Cuming. Further supplements were issued in 1953 and 1957, bringing the coverage up to the end of 1955. Since then, files have been maintained of all notified issues at the British Institute of Recorded Sound in London. A complete reprint of the *World Encyclopædia* was announced in November 1966 by Sidgwick & Jackson, London, and distribution was arranged for the New World by Ambassador Books, Canada. There have been various plans to publish the contents of the immense files held by the BIRS, but so far none has been successful.

Multi-company catalogues have largely supplanted house catalogues today for both trade and customer use. **The first and best-known** is the *Schwann* cumulative catalogue of American issues, published monthly since October 1949 (now called *Schwann Record and Tape Guide*). Also worthy of note are the *Gramophone Classical Catalogue* (London, quarterly under various names since 1953) and the *Gramophone Popular Catalogue* (London, quarterly since 1954), and *Bielefelder Katalog* (twice a year since 1960 and preceded by *Der Grosse Schallplatten Katalog* from 1953), listing all classical records available in Germany. Similar multi-company catalogues have appeared in France (*Diapason*) and Italy (*Santandrea*), both of which started in 1953.

The most ambitious and exhaustive single-nation multi-company catalogue to appear so far is *Der Grosseschall Platten Katalog*, edited by Carl v d Linnepe for the German record trade.

The first issue appeared in 1966 and was dated 1967. It listed not only composers, artists and their works and performances, cross-indexed exhaustively, but also gave complete numerical listings of the available output of ten companies, covering 112 labels. It was a formidable document, measuring 12in tall, 9in wide, and $3\frac{1}{4}$in thick, and it weighed 8lb 9oz (30·5cm × 22·9cm × 8·3cm, and 3·9kg).

Selective discographies, listing recordings of a given artist, or type of music, or some other particular facet of recorded sound, appear from time to time in journals, magazines and, sometimes, independently. **The first discography appeared in America in 1919.** It was called *Phonobretto*, and it listed more than 700 recordings of songs and spoken word issues. **The first**

TCHAIKOVSKY / Chamber Music — WORLD'S ENCYCLOPÆDIA OF RECORDED MUSIC

Souvenir d'un lieu cher, Op. 42 *(continued)*

No. 3, Melody

- J. Hassid & G. Moore — G.B 9074 (*Elgar: La Capricieuse*)
- E. B. Nielsen & C. Browald — G.DA 5351 (*None but the weary heart, arr.*)
- ▲ G. Dinicu — C.DV 61 : C.D 30701, d.c.
- H. Stanke — Pol. 47433
- J. A120 — Pol. 121175
- V. Selinsky — AmC. 35731; C.DO 2205
- ¶ M. Elman — G.DA 1143
- § B. Huberman — C.L 2338 ; AmC. 67729/D & Od. O-8740
- T. Spivakovsky — P. 28514
- — ARR. VLC. & PF.
- B. Mazzacurati & pf. — P.CC 2207 (*Brahms : Waltz, Op. 39, No. 15*)
- § G. Cassadó (C.LX 146: L 2117, d.c.; AmC. 52043X, d.c.)
- — ARR. ORCH.
- Robin Hood Dell—Kostelanetz — C.DX 1373 (*Nutcracker Suite, Valse*) (AmC. 12278D, set M 601 & LP: ML 4151)
- ▲ Bastian Quintet — C.DW 3075

Trio, A minor, Op. 50 pf., vln., vlc.
(To the memory of a great artist)

- L. Oborin, D. Oistrakh, S. Knushevitsky (12ss) — USSR. 015696/707
- H. & Y. Menuhin & M. Eisenberg — G.DB 2887/92S (11ss—last blank) (Vic. 14526/31S, set M 388)
- T. Saidenberg, L. Kaufman, R. Reher — AmVox. (LP) VLP 6530
- § W. Murdoch, A. Catterall, W. H. Squire (C.L 1942/7; O 4163/8; AmC. 67337/42D, set M 73)
- ... 2nd movt. excerpts
- § Amsterdam Trio (P.E 11168; Od.O-6824; AmD. 25554)

I. (C) ORCHESTRAL (inc. BALLET)

Aurora's Wedding—Sleeping Beauty excerpts, q.v.

BALLETS

(The) NUTCRACKER, Op. 71 (Original Ballet)

... No. 1, Intro. ; No. 2, March
No. 12, Divertissement (excerpts) :—
Chocolate ; Trepak ; Dances of the Doll, the Buffoon and the Negress ;
No. 15, Waltz and Finale
- Bolshoi Theatre—Fayer USSR. 9214/7 & 7522/3 (6ss) (Comp. set 102)

... No. 8, Winter Scene ; No. 9, Waltz of the Snowflakes ; No. 12 (a), Chocolate ; No. 14, Pas de deux ; No. 15, Waltz & Finale
- Boston Prom.—Fiedler — Vic. 11-9820/1 (4ss) (& LP : LM 1029) M 1164

(The) Nutcracker Suite, Op. 71a
[Nos. in brackets refer to Op. 71]

1. Ouverture miniature
2. Danses caractéristiques
   (a) March [2]; (b) Dance of the Sugar-plum fairy [14, Var 2]; (c) Danse russe, Trepak [12d]; (d) Danse arabe [12b]; (e) Danse chinoise [12c]; (f) Danse des mirlitons [12e];
3. Valse des fleurs [13]

- Philharmonia—Malko — G.C 3835/7 (6ss) (G.SL 113)
- N.Y. Phil. Sym.—Rodzinski — C.DX 1342 4 (6ss) (AmC 12383 5D, set M 627; & LP : ML 4048)
- L.P.O.—Celibidache — Vic. B 2148 50 (6ss) (Lon. set LA 86, & LP : LPS 171)

- Philadelphia Sym.—Ormandy — Vic. 11-8912/4 (6ss) (o.n. Vic. 11-8247/9, set M 915) (s.1 only on Vic. 11-9231 in set M 1063)
- L.P.O.—Goossens — G.C 2922/4 (6ss) (Vic. 36266/8, set G 5)
- National Sym.—S. Robinson — D.K 1142/4 (6ss) (AmD. set EDA 9)
- Dresden Phil.—van Kempen — D.LY 6178/80 (6ss) Pol. 67546/8
- Chicago Sym.—Stock — AmC. 69799/801D (6ss) set M 395
- ▲ A. Kostelanetz Orch. — AmC. 7585/7M, set MM 714, & LP : ML 4151
- Little Sym.—Barlow — B 7360/2 ;
- Anon. Orch. — M.App. set S 103, discs SR 39/41;
- Anon. Orch. — n.v., sides nod. X 124/9
- § Philadelphia—Stokowski — ¶G.DB 2540/2 ; Vic. 8662/4, set M 265; o.v. G.D 1214/6 ; W 848/50 ; Vic. 6615/7, set M 54
- Sym.—Heger — P.E 11269/71 ; Od. O-6961/3;
- Royal Phil.—Fried — AmD. 25182/4
- Berlin State Op.—Pitt — C. 9260/2; AmC. 50104/6D
- Berlin State Op.—Fried — D.CA 813/2/4; Pol. 95030/2 : 516656/8
- Berlin Phil.—Borchard T.A 1862/5 ; U.B 14242/5
- Berlin Phil.—Mörike — P.E 10516/9: 57145/8
- ... Nos. 2 (c) & 3 only
- Tivoli—Jensen — Tono. X 25060
- ... No. 2 (a) only
- ▲ Victor Orch. (Vic. 45-5004 in E 72 ; o.v. 22168)
- ... Nos. 2 (a), 2 (b), 2 (c) & 3
- Chicago Phil.—H. Weber — Sil. 63 ; & in Mer. (LP) MG 20013)
- ... No. 2 (b) only
- Sym.—Stokowski — Vic. 10-1487 (*Mozart : Deutscher Tanz, K 605, No. 3*)
- ▲ In Nights at the Ballet (G.C 2914; Vic. 36214)
- ... No. 2 (d) only
- Dresden Phil.—van Kempen — Pol. 68410 (*Dvořák : Slavonic Dance, Op. 72-2*) (from set above)
- ... No. 3, Valse des fleurs, only
- Robin Hood Dell—Kostelanetz — C.DX 1373 (*Melody*) (AmC. set M 601, d.c.)
- C.B. Sym.—Barlow — AmC. 71570D (*J. Strauss: G'schichten . . .*) in set X 240
- ▲ Los Angeles Orch.—Wallenstein — AmD. 29224 (& LP : DL 6007)
- A. Bernard Str. Orch. — Pat.PG 368
- § Paris Phil.—Cloëz — Od. 238342
- Royal Phil.—Fried, from set — Arg.C 264961
- — ARRANGEMENTS (*inter alia*)
- 2 pfs. (Omitting No. 2 (d))
- ▲ M. Rawicz & M. Landauer — C.DB 2154 & 2157 ; FB 2188
- ▲ (No. 3 only) V. Vronsky & V. Babin — AmC. 72593/4D in set MM 760 & LP : ML 2030
- 4 pfs. (No. 2 (f) only)
- ▲ First Piano Qtt. — Vic. 12-0945 in MO 1310
- Celeste ▲ (No. 2 (b) only)
- ▲ H. Greenslade — G.C 3619
- "For Children"—Narrator & 2 pfs.
- ▲ M. Cross, L. Brown & N. Dolin — Mus. set 74
- "For Dancing"
- ▲ F. Martin Orch. — Vic. 27899/902, set H 24
- With Effects
- ▲ Spike Jones Orch. — D.BD 1182/4; Vic. set P 143
- Organ
- ▲ (Nos. 2a, 2c, 2f, 3) H. Croudson — RZ.MR 2474
- ▲ (Nos. 2a, 2f) M. Cross — C.FB 1771 : DW 4513
- ▲ (Nos. 1 & 3) R. Foort — G.C 1386
- Vocal (No. 3 only)
- § E. Bettendorf (S) — P.R 1605; Od.O-25101

¹ Re-issued 1946 with fill-up, Sarasate : Caprice basque on Vic. 14531   ² The Waltz, DB2542, is ¶

WORLD'S ENCYCLOPÆDIA OF RECORDED MUSIC — TCHAIKOVSKY / Ballets

(The) SLEEPING BEAUTY, Op. 66

(Items numbered from pf. reduction)

SET —	A	B	C	D	E	F
Introduction ...	12-0190†	C 3081	C 2853	K 1524	—	D 1719
Prologue						
1. Marche	0190	C 3081	—	—	—	—
3a. Pas de six	0190	—	C 2853†	—	—	—
b. Six Variations and Coda	0191†	C 3081	C 2854†	—	—	—
4. Final (Fée des lilas sort)	0191†	C 3081	—	—	—	—
Act I						
6. Valse	0191	C 3082	—	K 1525	—	D 1719†
8. Intro.: Pas d'action						
a. Adagio	0192	C 3082	—	—	—	D 1719†
b. Danse des demoiselles d'honneur et des pages	0192	C 3082	—	—	DX 1281	D 1719
c. Variation d'Aurore	0192	C 3082	—	—	DX 1281	D 1719
d. Coda	0192	—	—	—	—	D 1719
9. Final (Fée des lilas paraît)	0192†	—	—	—	—	D 1720
Act II						
12e. Danse des baronnes	0193	—	—	—	—	—
13a. Tempo di Mazurka	0193†	—	—	—	DX 1282	—
15a. Pas d'action (" Vision ")	0193	—	—	K 1525	DX 1281	D 1720
17. Panorama	0193	—	—	—	DX 1282	—
Act III						
20. Marche	—	—	—	—	DX 1282	—
21. Polacca	0194	—	C 2853	—	—	—
22. Pas de quatre						
a. Valse	0194†	—	C 2853	—	—	—
b. Polka	0194	C 3083	—	—	—	—
c. Saphir (variations)	0194	C 3083	—	—	—	—
d. Diamant	0194	C 3083	—	—	—	D 1720
24. Pas de caractère (Puss in boots)	0195†	—	C 2854	K 1524	—	—
24. Pas de caractère et variations	0195	—	C 2854	—	DX 1282	—
27. Pas de deux	0195	—	C 2855†	—	—	—
28. Sarabande	0195	—	—	—	—	—
29. Final						
a. Mazurka	—	—	C 3083†	—	—	—
b. Andante	0195	—	C 2855†	—	—	—

(† = Seriously abbreviated)

THE RECORDINGS TABULATED ARE :—

Set A—Sym. Orch.—Stokowski Vic. 12-0190/5† (12ss) (Vic. 18-0118/23, set V6)
Set B—Sadlers Wells—Lambert G.C. 3081/3 (6ss) (Vic. 12765/7, set M 673)
Set C—L.P.O.—Kurtz² G.C. 2853/5 (6ss) (Vic. 11987/9, set M 326)
Set D—B.B.C. Theatre—S. Robinson D.K 1524/5 (4ss)
Set E—Covent Garden—Lambert C.DX 1281/2 (C.M 15064/5; AmC. 72675/6D, set MX 302 & LP: ML 4136)
Set F—§ Hollywood Bowl—Goossens (G.D 1718/9; Vic. 6871/2, set M 40)

OTHER RECORDINGS
Intro. & Nos. 6, 8a, 9 (or 29)
Bolshoi Theatre—Fayer (6ss) USSR. 9818/23 Comp. set 200
Nos. 24, 17, 8c, 23, Variations
Bolshoi Theatre—Fayer (6ss) USSR. 14459/64
No. 17, Panorama, only
Covent Garden Op.—Collingwood G.C 1469
Nos. 22 & 24, Variations (Divertissement)
Bolshoi Theatre—Fayer³ USSR. 15519/20
§ Sym.—Szyfer (C.DX 782: DFX¶176; AmC. 68934D)

No. 6, Waltz, only
Liverpool Phil.—Rignold C.DX 1621 (*Delius: Serenade & Serenade*)
Robin Hood Dell—Kostelanetz C.DX 1278 (*None but the weary heart, arr.*) (AmC. 12277D, set M 601; & LP: ML 4151)
Hallé—Sargent C.DX 1079 (*Borodin: Prince Igor Overture, s.3*)
Danish State Radio—Malko G.Z 340 (*Serenade, Op. 48—Valse*)
Boston Prom.—Fiedler G.C 2892 (*Chopin-Glazounov: Polonaise, A*)
Berlin State Op.—Melichar P.R 2536 (*Dvořák: Humoresque*) (Od.O-26128)
▲ Tivoli—Felumb Tono. X 25106
Los Angeles—Wallenstein AmD. 29223 (& LP: DL 6002)
Chicago Phil.—H. Weber Sil. 65 (& in Mer. (LP) MG 20013)
§ Covent Garden—Sargent G.C 1451; L 672
§ Cleveland Sym.—Sokoloff B. 15120
Berlin Phil.—Borchard T.A 1865; U.B 14245 etc.
— ARRANGEMENTS
Band ▲ Coldstream Guards G.C 3150, etc.
2 pfs. ▲ M. Rawicz & M. Landauer C.FB 2188
F. Hatzfeld & M. Strong Rex. 9993
Salon Orch. ▲ V. Selinsky Ens. AmC. 55549
¶ M. Weber Orch.—G.C 2948: EH 892: AF 534; Vic. 36312
Vocal "Love's own Waltz"
J. Dragonette (S) Vic. 4457

¹ Labelled *Aurora's Wedding.*   ² Recently issued in G.B. as G.DB 9097/504, auto. only ; but the Vic. manual nos. are retained in the table for clarity.   ³ Labelled "Dance and Variations"—not heard for identification.

A page from the World's Encyclopaedia of Recorded Music, *published in 1952.*   SIDGWICK & JACKSON

use of the word 'discography' in print seems to have been in the magazine *Melody Maker* in December 1953.

Magazines

The first magazine for collectors of recordings was the short-lived *The Phonograph Record*, published in Chicago in 1895 and 1896. *Phonoscope*, with Russell Hunting as editor, appeared in America in November 1896; it dealt primarily with recordings but also with movies. Later came *The Talking Machine World* (New York, 1905–34), and *The Phonograph* (New York, from 1916) which also concerned itself with radio from 1928 and changed to its present title of *Electronic Industry Weekly* in 1978. **The first British recording magazine** was *The Talking Machine News and Record Exchange* (London, 1903–35). *The Sound Wave and Talking Machine Record* began publication in London in 1904.

The most widely-read, respected and influential record magazines of today which are concerned mainly with recordings are, in order of longevity:

Gramophone, London, monthly since 1923. This has evolved from being a magazine for enthusiasts written by gentlemen, to an oracle written for intellectuals by intellectuals. It is the most complete source of news and information about software produced by the record industry in the UK. It also contains a small but authoritative section devoted to audio matters.

American Record Guide, New York, monthly from 1944 to 1973, then since 1976. (Original names: *The Phonograph Monthly Review*, Boston, 1926–32; *The Music Lovers' Guide*, New York, 1932–5; *The American Music Lover*, New York, 1935–44).

High Fidelity, Great Barrington, Mass, bi-monthly 1951–4; monthly since 1954.

Fono Forum, Cologne, 1956–7; Bielefeld, 1958 to date, monthly.

Fanfare, Tenafly, New Jersey, quarterly since 1977.

The fan of popular music has been catered for

well by such periodicals as *Melody Maker* (since January 1926), *Down Beat* (from 1934), *Record Mirror* (1954–61) and *Sounds* (from 1969), and the coming of Rock 'n' Roll brought new publications, some of the 'underground' type, to cater for this narrower taste. These have come to be known as 'fanzines'. *Rolling Stone* was amongst the first. It appeared in San Francisco in 1967. **The first music publication to call itself a 'fanzine'** was *Who Put the Bomp*, which surfaced on the West Coast of America about 1971. Great Britain also has its share of 'fanzines', some of them with easily-remembered titles: *Supersnazz*, *Fat Angel*, *Ripped and Torn*, and *Sniffin' Glue*. **Probably the first** and certainly amongst the most successful is *Zig Zag* (launched 1969; its name comes from the song *The Zig Zag Wanderer*, sung by the American Captain Beefheart), which has its own concert promoting organisation and record label.

The word 'fanzine' itself emanates from outside the music and record industries. In the 1930s it was used for science-fiction journals which published contributions from readers.

Periodicals have often shown an interest in the quality of recordings and performances, with the aim either of encouraging their artistic merits or charting their progress in the market place.

The first award made to a recording of serious music was the Grand Prix du Disque sponsored by the literary weekly journal *Candide* in France: Cocteau's *La Voix Humaine* received the first award in July 1932. **The first popular record chart** (ie: a list of best selling records) was published in America by the magazine *Billboard* on 20 July, 1940, when the No 1 top seller was given as *I'll Never Smile Again* by the Tommy Dorsey Orchestra. **The first album chart** was published by *Billboard* on 15 March, 1945, when the No 1 seller was the *King Cole Trio* disc set featuring Nat 'King' Cole. **The first singles chart published in the UK** appeared in *New Musical Express* on 14 November, 1952: the No 1 was *Here In My Heart* sung by Al Martino. The film soundtrack of *South Pacific* was No 1 in the **first UK albums chart** published on 8 November, 1958 by *Melody Maker*.

Educational Publications

The larger record companies have often felt obliged to make recordings of serious music, even though in the early days, when the gramophone was still considered to be only a toy, expected sales were likely to be negligible. The pressures to enter the 'serious' market came from within: a few executives realised the documentary value of recording great artists for posterity; others felt that the image of their companies would be improved by the appearance of a number of 'prestige' items in their catalogues. Having made the recordings, however, it was futile to leave them sitting in the catalogues whilst a public largely ignorant of serious music spent its money on the hits of the day. It became necessary, therefore, for the companies to go into the education business.

The first music appreciation book to be sponsored by a record company was *The Victor Book of Opera*, by Samuel H Rous, which was issued in America in 1912 at 75¢. It outlined the stories of 70 operas and gave details of the Victor recordings available of those operas.

Other similar projects have been launched on both sides of the Atlantic, notable amongst them being a set of 12 *Music Guides* (9d each, or 12/6 the set; ie 4p, or 62½p for 12) issued by Decca in the UK in 1952, which were edited versions of Decca LP sleevenotes; EMI Institutes' 'The Enjoyment of Music', consisting of an illustrated book by Sidney Harrison and seven 12in newly-recorded 78rpm discs of musical lectures, also by Sidney Harrison; and an ambitious series of leaflets called 'The Enjoyment and Appreciation of Music', written by Frederick Youens for the London-based Classics Club. One leaflet was sent out with each monthly notification of current mail order record releases, starting in February 1960, and slowly building into a collection of essays on the 'History of Music', 'The Men of Music', and 'Musical Instruments and the Orchestra'. These and other publications were meant to acquaint the newly-educated listener with the delights awaiting him in the respective companies' catalogues. Wider educational projects have involved specially recorded items linked closely with substantial publications and are discussed in Section II.

Record Archives

As a manifestation of the general interest in recordings and the realisation that they represent documents of permanent historical value, organisations have been set up to preserve them for posterity.

The first institution dedicated to the preservation of recorded sound was the Phonogramm-Archiv of the Akademie der Wissenschaften, founded in Vienna in 1899. A year or so later a Phonogramm-Archiv was set up in Berlin. This was followed by other national institutions:

1928 Discoteca di Stato, Rome
1937 Glinka Museum of Musical Culture, Moscow
1938 Phonothèque Nationale, Paris
1940 Library of Congress, Washington, DC
1951 (June) British Institute of Recorded Sound, London.

In 1974 the Association of Audio Archives was set up to amalgamate the listings of the holdings of the Library of Congress with four other important American holdings: the Rodgers and Hammerstein Archive, New York, and the Universities of Stanford, Syracuse and Yale.

The BBC Record Library in London, started in 1931 by the British Broadcasting Corporation, today contains over 750 000 records, 5250 of them lacking a known matrix number. In reply to an enquiry as to the oldest recordings held there, Derek Lewis, the Gramophone Librarian, made the following interesting comments:

The position regarding the oldest recordings is not straightforward. We have been doing a little more research on our white wax cylinders, and have come to the conclusion that most of them are not 'originals' but copies made by Colonel Gouraud before he sent the originals

One of the biggest and most famous record libraries, the BBC Gramophone Library.   SANDY PORTER/RADIO 3 MAGAZINE

back to Edison in America. This would explain the very inferior sound quality of most of them. We do have one dated 16 June, 1888, which is a message from Edison in America to Gouraud, but the sound quality is very bad, and we suspect that that too may be a copy. The next in date order are Gladstone, 22 November (very poor) and we know that the original is in America and produces very passable results; followed by the Speaker of the House of Commons on 6 December, 1888. We have very good ones of Isaac Pitman on 20 October, 1891, and Cardinal Manning on 29 October, 1891. As regards discs, I think our oldest must be George Gaskin on Berliner 158, recorded some time in 1895. He sings a song called *Sweet Marie* ... With records of this vintage it is very difficult to be too precise.

Record Libraries

The first public record lending library was opened in Detroit, Michigan, in 1921; however, in 1913 a collection of records was donated to a library in St Paul's, Minnesota, but it is not known whether they were lent out for hire.

The first public record lending library in the UK was opened in 1940 in the Hereford County Library. In 1935, the Middlesex County Council began a system of lending records to societies and schools in the area.

The Record Number

With the exception of some early examples, discs have always carried catalogue numbers. Cylinders generally did not, but with the rise in popularity of the disc and the proliferation of titles and manufacturing companies, some kind of code became necessary so that a given record might be recognised unmistakably without the need for writing down the title and artist details. The record number became the shorthand symbol by which it was known in the trade, and quite often by enthusiasts outside it. It is, or should be, absolutely unique, although there have been instances of inadvertent duplication.

The record number for most of the history of recorded sound between the extremes of the early years and the new age of computers, consists of two parts: the prefix (occasionally suffix) letters indicating the series and/or price category, and the number of the recording in that series. These groups of letters and numbers have always held a fascination for the collector, and the way the various series work – never quite the same from one company to another – has exercised the imagination of the enthusiast and perplexed the mind of the tyro. Many of these systems have a kind of stern logic when they first come into use, but as they age and market forces act upon them, they tend to run out of control, becoming unwieldy within themselves and colliding with the systems of rival companies, until a newcomer examining their workings might come to the conclusion that their creators were, or should be, inhabitants of padded cells.

There is insufficient room here to go too closely into the details of many of these systems, but some examples are given below to illustrate the complicated processes of international marketing and the ingenious, or insane, ways chosen to clarify certain situations that have turned the useful record number into, in some cases, a nightmare. The system adopted by the EMI combine in the UK will serve to show how a huge organisation set about controlling their record numbering series once electrical recording had become established.

HMV's electrically recorded 78s generally had separate letter prefixes according to their country or territory of issue; where prefixes were used internationally, eg: the 12in DB and 10in DA series, the number blocks were different (7000–9999 in the UK, 4200–4399 in Spain, and so on). On the other hand, Columbia's earlier 78rpm series used different number blocks for different countries, but the letter D was a prefix common to the UK, Austria and Hungary, France and Belgium, the Netherlands, Italy and Switzerland, although other countries had their own letters. Later, Columbia allocated different letter series for each territory. Within such a closely organised company as EMI, with central control ever since 1931 over general policy of the otherwise autonomous HMV and Columbia labels, surely it was unnecessary for there to be any confusion over series prefixes; after all, there was the whole alphabet to draw on for their one- and two-letter prefixes. Yet there were on the UK market simultaneously the three following series:

DB 12in HMV
DB 10in Columbia
BD 10in HMV

One may imagine the confusion caused when dealers were passing orders to their suppliers over a crackling or faint telephone line.

Fortunately such confusing coincidences were rare: the 12in HMV Royal Series of 78s and the 12in Argo LP series are sufficiently dissimilar, as well as being from different eras, for their common prefix of RG to offer no danger of confusion. We shall soon see, though, that this relatively trouble free state was not to continue.

With the advent of LP, EMI's policy for all labels was standardised more strictly, and the UK price structure of 12in and 10in premier labels and 12in and 10in secondary labels (plus an occasional cheaper series) was adopted with unaccustomed unanimity throughout the industry, at least for a few years. Study of the Long Playing Prefixes chart will show that considerable logic was followed in the various letter prefixes even if the use of L and LP (for long playing) and S (for stereo) throughout the industry revealed a lack of imagination.

For its international activities, EMI's policy for all labels was for a simple code letter to be added to the standard prefixes, so that, for instance, British ALP equals French FALP (but usually with a different disc number). Apart from a few isolated exceptions for locally produced repertoire, these were the code letters:

E = India   L = Spain   S = Sweden
F = France   N = Norway   V = Austria
H = Holland O = Australia W = Germany
K = Denmark Q = Italy

(ALPC, BLPC, etc, sometimes encountered,

Long Playing Prefixes (UK, from the early 1950s)

	HMV		Columbia		Decca		Philips		DG[6]		Archiv[6]	
	mono	stereo	mono	stereo	mono	stereo	mono	stereo	mono	stereo	mono	stereo
Premier 12in	ALP[1]	ASD	33CX[3]	SAX	LXT	SXL	ABL	SABL	LPM 18 000	SLPM 138 000	APM 14 000	SAPM 198 000
Premier 10in	BLP[1]	BSD	33C[3]	SBO	LX	–	ABR	–	LP 16 000	SLP 133 000	AP 13 000	SAP 195 000
Secondary 12in	CLP[2]	CSD	33SX[3]	SCX	LK	SKL	BBL	SBBL	LPEM 19 000	SLPEM 136 000	–	–
Secondary 10in	DLP[2]	DSD	33S[3]	SDO	LM	–	BBR	SBR	LPE 17 000	SLPE 135 000	–	–
Premier 7in EP	7ER[1]	RES[1]	SEL[4]	ESL[4]	CEP	SEC	ABE	SABE	EPL 30 000	SEPL 121 000	EPA 37 000	SEPA 181 000
Secondary 7in EP	7EP[2]	PES[2]	SED[5]	ESD[5]	DFE	STO	BBE	SBBE	EPH 20 000	SEPH 224 000	–	–

[1] Red label.

[2] Plum label.

[3] The '33' segment was later omitted.

[4] Light blue label.

[5] Dark blue label.

[6] DG and Archiv prefix letters were entirely dropped in the mid-1960s since the number blocks carried all the necessary price and size identification.

The frequent use of 'L' for long playing, 'E' for extended play, and 'S' for stereo will be noted; furthermore, label colours were signalled in the HMV and Columbia EP prefixes, and this was carried further in the green label HMV (7EG/GES) and Columbia (SEG/ESG) EPs, and in the standard play 7in HMV red label (7R) and plum label (7P) discs.

were international special issues made in the UK. The 'C' is understood to mean 'continental', although with, for example, Indian recordings appearing on ALPC, it should perhaps be taken to signify 'cosmopolitan').

It will be noticed that the one- and two-letter prefixes of late 78rpm days had become mainly three-letter prefixes for LP, with rarer four- and even five-letter combinations. Had the industry restricted itself to three-letter combinations and omitted letters which might be mistaken for numbers (I, O) and combinations that would bring a blush to delicate cheeks, there would have been over 450 000 permutations to choose from – enough, one would have thought,

for confusing duplications to have been avoided completely. This is, however, far from being the case. The prefix groups in the Prefix Duplications chart have existed simultaneously on the UK market since the beginning of LP, and the list is far from being exhaustive.

Part of the reason for these duplications is the strange ability of record company executives sometimes to ignore totally the current market practices of their rivals, and/or to set a policy so rigid that it becomes impossible to change it when industry trends demand change. When the Nixa Record Co began to issue classical recordings from certain American labels, the basic 'LP' prefix was qualified by the initial letter

Prefix Duplications (LP era, UK)

ALP – Artia; HMV; Phoenix
ALPS – Artia; HMV (single-sided)
BLP – HMV; Nixa; Qualiton (Welsh)
C – Columbia; Island; Virgin
CAS – B & C; Word
CC – Pickwick; Rubini
CCL – Capitol (10in); Pye
CL – Alpha (10in *and* 12in); Fontana
CLP – HMV; Nixa; Pye
CS – B & C; CBS
CX – Columbia; Transatlantic
DA – Argo; Dell'Arte
DC – Acanta; Nimbus
DEL – Delta; Delysé (7in)
DL – L'Oiseau-Lyre (10in); Vox
DPS – Pye (two-disc pack); RCA (two-disc pack)
ES – Envoy; Esoteric
FT – Fantasy; Liberty
GM – Gemini; President; RCA
GRS – Grosvenor; Guild
GULP – Gull; Indigo
HLP – HMV; Nixa
HM – Harmonia Mundi; London; Pye
JB – Acanta; Decca
LBS – Beltona; Liberty
LP – DG (10in); Sound Stories (10in *and* 12in)
LPE – DG (10in); Cetra (10in)
LPM – DG; Supraphon (10in)
LPV – Cetra; Supraphon

LRM – Audio Impact; Chapter One
LSP – Liberty (two-disc set); RCA
P – Capitol; Jupiter (7in)
PR – Discocorp; Preiser
QUAD – Pye; Qualiton (Welsh)
R – Reprise; Rococo
RL – Pickwick; RCA
SB – Decca; RCA
SCM – RCA; Tower
SDD – Decca; EMI
SDL – Deram; Saydisc
SDR – Invicta; Saydisc
SE – Ember; Stateside (7in)
SER – RCA; Word
SET – CBS; Decca
SFM – Famous; Fontana
SH – London; World Record Club
SKL – Decca; DG (boxed sets)
SL – Audio Impact; Saydisc; Sonologue; Stateside
SLP – DG; Waverley
SLS – HMV (boxed sets); Sunset
SP – Capitol; Cetra (7in); St Paul (12in *and* 7in)
SPR – CBS; Rex
SRS – RCA; Starline
ST – Buena Vista; Capitol; World Record Club
STO – Decca (7in); Odeon
SW – Argo; Capitol
SXL – Decca; Muza
T – TAP; Topic (8in); World Record Club
TM – Argo (10in); Telefunken (10in)
WCS – Decca (Churchill series); Wand

From Studio to Sitting room

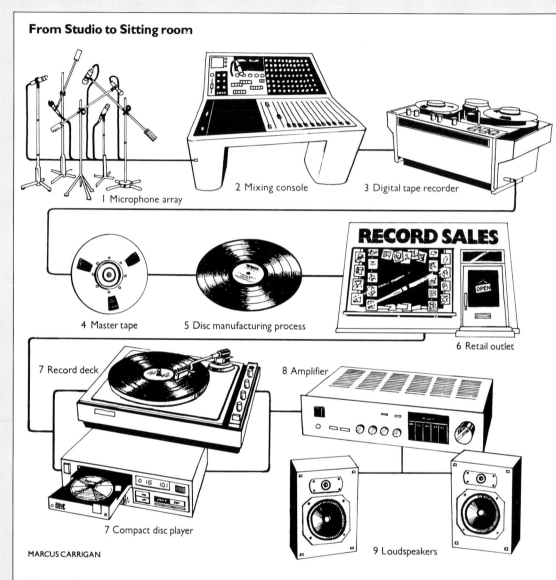

1 Microphone array

2 Mixing console

3 Digital tape recorder

RECORD SALES

OPEN

4 Master tape

5 Disc manufacturing process

6 Retail outlet

7 Record deck

8 Amplifier

7 Compact disc player

9 Loudspeakers

MARCUS CARRIGAN

How music is collected, stored and relayed to the consumer.

1 Microphone array, which collects sound in mechanical form (air pressure) and converts it to electrical energy.

2 Mixing console, with which the recording engineer balances the incoming sound.

3 Digital tape recorder, which stores the sound in the form of digits. Editing and further mixing of the many channels may also take place at this stage, before a master tape is made.

4 Master tape, containing the finished, approved, recording in digital form.

5 Disc manufacturing process (see separate diagrams), which converts the sound from digital to mechanical form.

6 Retail outlet. Once the finished pressings are sleeved, boxed, and distributed, the recording is ready to be offered to the public.

7 Record deck, which converts the mechanical signal to electrical impulses and, alternatively, a compact disc player which reads the disc optically and again provides an electrical signal. The two-channel stereo signal is fed to the amplifier.

8 Amplifier, which increases the amplitude of the electrical signal and feeds it to the loudspeakers.

9 Loudspeakers, which change the sound from electrical energy back into sound waves.

Stages in the processing of a standard LP record

The master tape is transferred to an aluminium disc coated with lacquer (a) via a cutting stylus. This lacquer is then coated with silver, placed in a plating tank and electro-plated with nickel. When the master (b) has thus been 'grown' onto the lacquer, the two surfaces are peeled apart. A separating agent is then applied to the surface of the master and a nickel mother (c) is electroformed onto it. This in turn is treated with a separating agent and a nickel stamper (d) is grown onto it. This is the final negative from which the finished pressings (e) are made.

a

original lacquer (positive)

b
master (negative)

c
mother (positive)

d
stamper (negative)

e
pressing (finished record)

How Compact Discs are made

A polished glass plate coated with photoresist (a) is inscribed by a laser with a spiral track of pits and blank spaces (b) which is then etched (c), silvered (d) and nickel plated (e) to form a negative 'master'. From this master a positive metal 'mother' is formed (f) and this in turn generates negative 'stampers' (g) which are used as moulds to make actual discs (h). A reflective coat of aluminium is 'evaporated' onto the surface (i) and a transparent protective layer is applied (j). The accompanying diagrams are not to scale. A compact disc is a product of extreme miniaturisation: its thickness is 1·2mm, of which only 30 microns comprise the actual disc; the rest is protective coating for the spiral track. The pits in this track are 0·1 micron deep – a micron is one millionth of a metre.

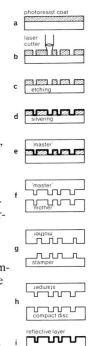

Cross-sections of record grooves

A Lateral cut. The groove depth remains constant but the playback stylus oscillates from side to side. This format is used by mono LPs and by most 78rpm discs.
B Vertical cut ('hill-and-dale'). The signal is imparted to the stylus by the varying depth of the groove, causing vertical movement of the stylus. 'Hill-and-dale' cutting was used for most cylinders and for some early 78rpm discs.
C Stereo groove. This comprises a combination of A and B, the whole turned through an angle of 45° in relation to the disc surface to give a complex stylus motion in which the floor of one groove (a) carries one signal, the floor of the other (b) carrying the other signal. The pick-up cartridge is sensitive to movement (a) for one channel only and converts it to an electrical current for subsequent amplification through the reproducing chain. Similarly, movement (b) generates a different signal through the cartridge and amplifier, the two signals being kept completely separate until they are blended in the atmosphere of the listening area to form a solid ('stereo') sound picture. By convention it is the outer groove wall which carries the right-hand channel as heard by the listener.

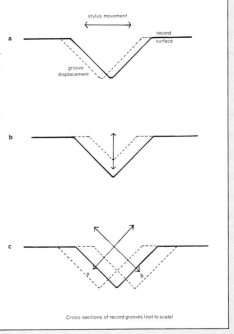

Cross-sections of record grooves (not to scale)

of the label of origin (in most cases), as follows:

BLP = Bach Guild
CLP = Concert Hall
HLP = Haydn Society
LLP = Lyrichord
NLP = Nixa's UK recordings
OLP = Oceanic
PLP = Period
QLP = Renaissance and Remington
ULP = Urania
VLP = Vanguard
WLP = Westminster

(All the above were 12in discs; the occasional 10in series was identified by a 'Y', eg: HLPY).

This meant that BLP, CLP and HLP duplicated HMV prefixes. Luckily, HMV BLP was 10in with a four-digit number while Nixa BLP was 12in with a three-digit number. However, HMV *and* Nixa CLP were 12in four-digit series and the record number CLP 1212, for example, existed on the market simultaneously for two entirely different records. HMV's History of Music in Sound series ran from HLP 1 to 27; the numbers HLP 13–18 and 22–24 were duplicated by Nixa's string quartet recordings from the Haydn Society catalogue. Therefore, once again, totally different 12in LP records bore identical catalogue numbers, thus requiring extra care of the customer, the record dealer staff and the order clerks in the factors handling both labels.

One of the most remarkable coincidences concerning record numbers occurred in two recordings of the 'Flute Concerto in D major' by Michael Haydn, hardly an over-recorded composer. Both Vox, working in America in the 1950s in their PL series, and Hungaroton working in Hungary in the 1960s in their LPX series, contrived to arrive at the number 11530 for their recordings of the work thus identified; ironically, two *different* Flute Concertos in D by Michael Haydn are involved, so confused cataloguers and record archivists are confounded still further.

While many prefix letters seem to have been chosen at random, there has recently been an effort to make some of them more memorable by relating them to the repertoire of the series. **Perhaps the first to do so** were EMI with their cleverly conceived 7FX series for sound effects records (the extended play discs generated an even more appropriate prefix: EFX). Decca have contributed HDN for their massive Haydn recording project, RING 1–22 for the complete recording of Wagner's *Der Ring des Nibelungen* conducted by Georg Solti, Solti's own SOLTI prefix, and WCS (Winston Churchill Set) for the album containing that war leader's memoirs and speeches. Argo commenced a new series with a recording of Benjamin Britten's *Noye's Fludde* and duly prefixed the whole series with NF (ZNF for stereo), and what more obvious when RCA issued a sampler record to mark a UK tour by Eugene Ormandy and the Philadelphia Orchestra, than to prefix it OPO? The same company's DPS series of two-disc packages derives its prefix from the phrase 'double-pack sleeve'.

Any group of letters, then, may be selected for a series prefix, and if it has the advantage of easy recall in the record store it might well improve its publicity. Sharp practice is suspected when Mercury launched a stereo extended-play series and, without turning a hair, coined the prefix SEX. Another company, when planning a mid-price operatic label and wishing to use 'O' in a three-letter prefix, very nearly descended to blasphemy for the mono issues and obscenity for the stereo ones until someone managed to avert the disaster with alternative prefixes that filled the bill with less bad taste.

Numbers, too, have been juggled in the interests of customer and dealer recognition: occasionally, numbers will bypass the next number to be allocated in favour of an easily remembered one higher in the series, usually a round figure which is instantly memorable. American Vox, whose four-digit system in the early 1950s was never easy for the uninitiated to fathom, nevertheless flouted their own internal rules when they wished to issue the world's first single-disc LP of Beethoven's *Choral* Symphony. This was numbered PL 10000. Some years later, when the same recording was transferred to a cheaper label in the GBY series, that system, too, was violated when the reissue retained the full-price number: GBY 10 000. For the long-awaited original cast recording of *My Fair Lady*, Philips created a new series – RBL – the first in that series, naturally enough, being 1000.

Today there is a move away from letter prefixes altogether as the dreaded computer takes over more and more aspects of our lives. This is to be welcomed if it relieves us of the letter-number mixtures apparently so loved on the continent in the 1960s (eg: BM30L1510; 60CS507; ARN 30S152) – but see below! Like telephone numbers, record numbers are going number-only. Consequently the numbering systems of PolyGram, CBS and Supraphon are nightmarish strings of characterless numbers signifying by their subtle changes all the various series and subseries in their respective catalogues. Recent Supraphon numbers are a stuttering outbreak of binary insanity, eg: 1111 2617 – even if the eye can comprehend such numbers, usually printed in minute figures on the sleeve, do they mean anything to anyone but a computer? For their international operation EMI are moving in the same direction with a system in which every digit presumably means something important. An example is OC 063o06073Q (the lower-case 'o' has now been replaced by a hyphen). The London end of EMI are to be congratulated on retaining the familiar UK numbers on their domestic sleeves (in this instance ASD 3193) while carrying the 12-digit horror for the benefit of their export market, but in June 1983 appeared the first sign that even the tradition-conscious minds at HMV were beginning to bow to pressure from the computers, for which nothing is easy unless it is complicated. That month's new issues retained the prefix letters but added two digits to the front of the number and a further digit at the rear, the latter signifying disc or cassette format (eg: ASD 143440 1 = disc; TCC-ASD 143440 4 = cassette). Furthermore, it may be inferred from the rest of the June 1983 supplement that while '1' means one stereo disc and '4' means

one cassette, '3' means a multiple disc set and '9' a multiple cassette set.

Probably the most straightforward numbering system for a continent-wide series is that used by Melodiya (formerly Mezhdunarodnaya Kniga) in Russia. The matrix number equals the issue number, which means that each issued record has two numbers (eg: 33 C 10–13685-6). Transliterated, the prefix letters are D and ND for mono, S for stereo, and the more recent 'compatible stereo-mono' records are designated SM (= CM in Cyrillic). The 33 before the prefix letter, of course, refers to the speed of rotation of the disc (and, incidentally, recalls early UK mono 10in Columbia LPs with their '33C' combination). Numbers beginning '0' are 12in; those with '000' are 7in, and a number beginning with any other figure is 10in.

Many points of censure have been raised above concerning record companies' numbering practices and perhaps it is too late for any improvement to be expected. The move to computer numbering may be an attempt to achieve a world-wide system that would avoid another prefix duplication situation, in which case its completion may be anticipated with joy. It is more probable, however, that rival companies will continue to programme their computers in their own idiosyncratic ways, and the scene will become more chaotic than anything yet experienced. Perhaps companies should reflect upon the fact that, whatever else they do, computers do not buy records.

Cataloguing a Record Collection

The seasoned record collector will already have evolved an efficient method of filing his or her records in the best way for easy selection, almost certainly in conjunction with a home-made catalogue. The following remarks are for the benefit, therefore, of the new collector who plans to expand his record library.

For any sizeable collection a personal catalogue is vital, and the larger the collection grows the more necessary it becomes; the claim once made by a famous cataloguer, that his pub-

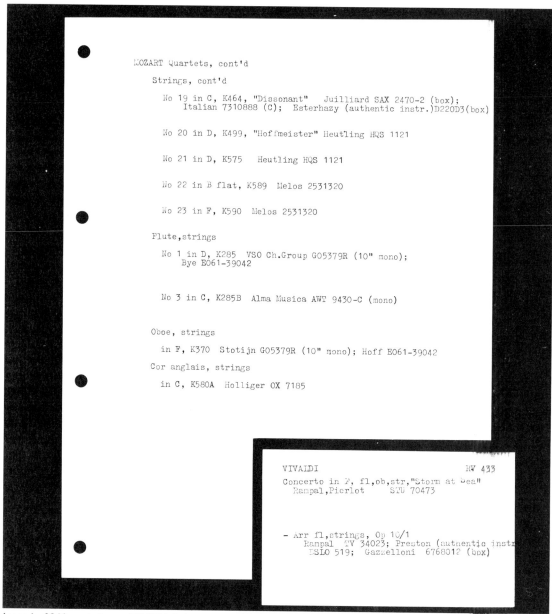

```
MOZART Quartets, cont'd
    Strings, cont'd
        No 19 in C, K464, "Dissonant"  Juilliard SAX 2470-2 (box);
            Italian 7310888 (C);  Esterhazy (authentic instr.)D220D3(box)

        No 20 in D, K499, "Hoffmeister" Heutling HQS 1121

        No 21 in D, K575   Heutling HQS 1121

        No 22 in B flat, K589  Melos 2531320

        No 23 in F, K590  Melos 2531320

    Flute,strings
        No 1 in D, K285  VSO Ch.Group G05379R (10" mono);
            Bye E061-39042

        No 3 in C, K285B  Alma Musica AWT 9430-C (mono)

    Oboe, strings
        in F, K370  Stotijn G05379R (10" mono); Hoff E061-39042
    Cor anglais, strings
        in C, K580A  Holliger OX 7185
```

```
VIVALDI                                    RV 433
Concerto in F, fl,ob,str,"Storm at Sea"
    Rampal,Pierlot     STU 70473


- Arr fl,strings, Op 10/1
    Rampal  TV 34023; Preston (authentic instr
    DSLO 519;  Gazzelloni  6768012 (box)
```

Loose-leaf folder or index cards? Which is the more suitable for your collection?

lished catalogue of all his country's LP releases would serve collectors as an index to their own private collections, was seen to be absurd the moment a record company deleted a record (which was then dropped from subsequent editions of the published catalogue), or the collector purchased a disc of other than domestic origin. That ill-advised claim does not appear in more recent issues of that catalogue.

The keyword for a personal catalogue should be simplicity, and its aims clarity, flexibility and maximum usefulness. It should be borne in mind that any personal listing will be used by an extremely small number of individuals, probably only one, as a key to a unique record collection, and it should be constructed accordingly. It follows, therefore, that the blank catalogue files occasionally offered for sale by accessory firms are unlikely to be of equal assistance to every collector; they may control a record collection efficiently enough in its early days but they tend to become quickly outgrown, and further supplies of the printed loose-leaf sheets may become difficult to locate. Furthermore, such systems often come with numbered labels, gummed, to be affixed to the record sleeves. As we shall see, these are not a good idea.

The new collector is advised to choose between a standard-sized loose-leaf binder and a card index; which choice he makes will depend entirely upon just what he requires of his catalogue. If he plans to transport it to and from fellow-collectors' abodes in order to discuss and compare its contents, or perhaps to take it under his arm when record browsing so that he may avoid undue duplication (assuming his memory to be unreliable or his collection very large), a card index tray or box will be unwieldy and may even come to grief on a rain-soaked road. On the other hand, a static card index catalogue offers the greatest possible flexibility and versatility and is maintained with the least expenditure of time: even the neatest loose-leaf catalogue will contain some sheets appearing unduly empty while others are cluttered with additions and messy crossings-out, and will eventually have to be rewritten.

What to put in your catalogue? The answer is not as obvious as it seems, and once again will differ with every collector. It is up to each individual to decide what he wants his catalogue to tell him. Is the collection artist-orientated? If so, the catalogue will be organised alphabetically by artist, or perhaps by voice or instrument, with all the tenors in one place and all the pianists in another. If the music itself is of more immediate interest than the artist(s) performing it, the catalogue will be organised either by composer or by title, depending upon the type of music in the collection and/or the readiness with which either the composer's name or the title comes to mind. It is unhelpful to catalogue in composer order if the collector can bring to mind the titles of countless operatic arias in their original language but cannot for the life of him remember who composed *Otello*.

Collections of lighter music will most usefully be catalogued by artist, or possibly by title – perhaps even by both. The artist approach would appear to be the better here because it is the artists' performances that are of prime importance, even when popular items become duplicated; the earnest collector who is likely to compare his seven different recordings of, say, *Blowin' In The Wind* will, of course, make his listing by title.

The serious music collector will also find duplications building up as his collection grows. If he uses a card index, his card of, for instance, Tchaikovsky's *1812* Overture may eventually fill up, and then may be supplemented by a second card. On the other hand, if his catalogue is in a loose-leaf file, that work may share a page with other works, so it is important to space out entries on the page to the point of extravagance if constant rewriting is to be avoided.

As for the entries themselves, the amount of detail included is a matter of taste, but simplicity is recommended. One may wish to make a grand, all-inclusive, archival heading:

TCHAIKOVSKY, Peter Ilyich (1840–93)
Russian:
1812 – Ouverture Solonelle in E flat major, Op 49 (1880, published 1882; first performed in Moscow, 20 August 1882)

Unless you want a central repository of such details, and use them frequently, pedantry of this scale is time-consuming, and anything that goes beyond the bare TCHAIKOVSKY: *1812* Overture is contained in the record sleevenotes or in reference books. Similarly, there is no need to list couplings in the catalogue itself: if that information is required, one may go to the actual record on the shelf and obtain it at first hand. Furthermore, why list the entire cast of an opera on the catalogue card or sheet? This information is printed clearly and accurately on the presentation material with which the records are supplied, and if your catalogue is doing its job well it will direct you to that package without delay. Your catalogue information need include just the principal artist(s) or the conductor, and even these names are dispensable if you have only one version of the work.

However, collectors with exhaustive representation of many works which come under one general heading (Schubert *Lieder*, Scarlatti Sonatas, Albinoni Concertos, etc) will certainly need to use the reference numbers in published thematic catalogues in order not only to locate given works in the files but also to avoid duplicating music by future purchases (or, if duplication is desired, so that some control over it may be exercised). Sadly, record companies often find it easier to record a work than to identify it, and in the case of Vivaldi, where there are half a dozen reference numbers for most works, each referring to a different method of listing his music, it is anyone's guess which numbering system (if any) will appear on a given sleeve. In a case like this, it may even be necessary to purchase the most reliable and up-to-date thematic catalogue in order to identify all the works in one's collection, and then model one's listing on that. The use of Ryom numbers in the personal catalogue will bring a consistency to the Vivaldi collection lacking on the record sleeves, and the effort is worth it if it enables a desired recording to be located quickly and its contents identified accurately.

Which brings us to the most important question of all: in which order should your records best be filed? A small collection is easily memorised, if only by sleeve design or spine colour, but as it increases in size some kind of coding becomes vital. If newly-acquired discs are simply added at the end of the rack, confusion will inevitably result as the collection grows. Filing by composer or by artist works neatly until the inevitable day when that irresistible record contains overtures by Beethoven, Berlioz, Weber, Rossini and Glinka, played by two orchestras under four conductors; and if it makes sense to file it under the only common denominator – overtures – it then becomes necessary to remember that there are many other overtures, some possibly duplicating those on the new disc, lurking in the symphonies section, where they occupy parts of sides as

fill-ups. Long-playing may be a boon in many ways but it fails to take account of the fact that most composers do not, and did not, write to LP length; but many of them obligingly provided overtures and other short works to act as makeweights.

The printed, gummed number labels mentioned above, or home-made equivalents, may be stuck to the record sleeves, and the catalogue entries need refer only to these numbers. However, if it is decided at a later date to trade in a recording against a more up-to-date version, these labels will need to be removed. Assuming the gum has been strong enough to retain its grip over months or years of shelf-life, it is unwise to assume that it will relinquish it when required to do so. When worked upon with a knife or some solution it may eventually loosen, but it is almost certain to take with it a portion of record sleeve, leaving a ragged white scar that may halve the second-hand value of the record. Why, then, apply these personal numbers in the first place, when the records come ready equipped with a number of their own? The maker's catalogue number may seem cumbersome and difficult to remember (we have remarked upon this failing above), but the collector hardly needs to remember it; he need only write it down in his catalogue, whereupon it provides the all-important clue as to the whereabouts of the disc upon which this (sometimes) unique and (sometimes) clearly printed identification appears, (usually) in the top right-hand corner of the back of the sleeve. Record dealers, wholesalers, and manufacturers, from the moment the product becomes a viable catalogue proposition, refer to the recording by this number; why should it not continue to be of use once the record has been purchased? It is fervently to be hoped, incidentally, that the American CBS sleeve recently issued with a series of black and white supermarket checkout stripes replacing the record number is an aberration that will not be copied by the rest of the industry. However, even this sleeve bows sufficiently to tradition to display the record number on its spine; perhaps the death of the manufacturer's catalogue number is not yet imminent.

Sizes, Speeds and Singularities

In the 1950s the turntables of most record players were designed to rotate at three speeds: 78, 45, and 33⅓rpm (revolutions per minute), these being considered to be the three 'standards'. 78rpm was the accepted pre-LP norm, LP records revolved at 33⅓rpm, and 45rpm was used for the 7in microgroove replacement for the then obsolescent 78. Accepted record sizes at that time were described as 10in and 12in for both 78rpm and 33⅓rpm discs, and 7in, of course, for 45rpm.

Some of these long-accepted values are quite false, and this book is as guilty as any other in quoting them as a form of instantly-understood substitute for the truth. The 'standard' speed for the '78rpm' disc was 78·26rpm or 77·92rpm, depending upon where you lived, and before standardisation the speed at which recordings were made might have been anything at all between 65 and 100rpm. Melba's earliest discs, made in March 1904, revolved variously at 70, 71, 72, 74 and 75rpm! In the matter of disc sizes, 7in, 10in and 12in have always been, and still are, very much the exception rather than the rule.

To take rotational speed first, the reason for the divergencies from 78rpm were that the early constant-speed electric motors in America ran at 3600rpm and used a reduction gearing of 46:1, giving 78·26rpm at the turntable, while in Britain, with a mains frequency of 50Hz, the standard speed dropped to 77·92rpm at the turntable.

In the matter of disc sizes, one must take into account the fact that 'Imperial' measurements are by no means in world-wide use, and the metric alternatives often given of 17cm, 25cm and 30cm are appreciably smaller than the values 7in, 10in and 12in. It is to the former, metric, measurements that most manufacturers work, or at least they do so more closely than they conform to the Imperial measurements, although variations by a millimetre or two in either direction are common even from the same manufacturer. Of a number of recent Russian LPs examined, for instance, the majority measure 30cm, a few were a millimetre smaller, and some ran to 30·2cm. Furthermore,

writers on such matters frequently 'round up' or 'round down' to the nearest inch while others are more precise. A disc referred to by one as '7in' may be described as '6¾' by another, and it has been impossible to check every example physically to ascertain which of these references is correct; if either is correct.

Sizes – Cylinders

Edison's first commercial cylinders were 4³⁄₁₆in (10·6cm) long × 2⅛in (5·4cm) in diameter, and this size was current for some years. In 1890 the 6in (15·2cm) cylinder (also of 2⅛in diameter) was introduced, a size which remained in use until as late as the 1940s in dictating machines.

American Columbia introduced the 4in (10·2cm) diameter cylinder in 1898. **Cylinders of the smallest diameter** were those of 1⁵⁄₁₆in (3·35cm), issued by the Graphophone Co from 1886.

The largest diameter cylinders measured 9in (22·9cm) and were marketed by Edison's National Phonograph Co in 1899.

The shortest cylinders in length were the earliest standard models of 4in (10·2cm) (although experimental and test cylinders were often shorter); **the longest** were the 8in (20·3cm) of the North American Phonograph Co of 1888–9 and Edison's 'Kinetophone' (designed for talking pictures) of 1912. The latter were 5½in (14·0cm) in diameter. Multiphone, in about 1907, envisaged 25in (63·5cm) long cylinders for use in juke-boxes, but fortunately this fiendish device never progressed beyond the planning stage.

Sizes – Discs

Perhaps the clearest way to present this complicated aspect of disc production is by means of a chronological chart, from which it will be seen that early confusion eventually led to the adoption industry-wide of only two sizes. Imperial sizes only are given in the text; a conversion table to metric values as will be found on p. 125, but attention is drawn to the caveat in the fourth paragraph of this Section.

c 1890 Berliner's discs made for children by Kämmerer und Reinhardt were approximately 5in in diameter (giving about 1 minute playing time), and 3in, although some $3\frac{1}{8}$in discs were made for talking dolls.

1898 On 6 December Emile Berliner founded the German branch of The Gramophone Co producing $6\frac{3}{4}$in discs, giving about 2 minutes' playing time.

1901 Victor issued 10in discs, with a playing time of 3 minutes.

1903 **The first 12in discs** were issued in the Angel 'Monarch' series, giving a maximum of $4\frac{1}{2}$ minutes. Victor abandoned 7in discs to concentrate on 10in and 12in. A later 8in series was discontinued about 1908. The International Talking Machine Co's Odeon records were single-sided 7in and $10\frac{3}{4}$in; the latter were double-sided from 1904.

1904 Fonotipia issued double-sided $10\frac{3}{4}$in discs. Later, the same company and Victor issued records of $13\frac{3}{4}$in diameter. Neophone issued 20in discs.

c 1906 Pathé centre-start record sizes were $9\frac{1}{2}$in and 11in; later, their range was $8\frac{1}{4}$in, 9in and 20in.

1906 L'Association Phonique des Grandes Artistes produced discs of $10\frac{3}{4}$in. Beka, also founded this year, issued 7in, 8in, 11in, and (from 1911) 12in discs.

1915 Italian Phonotype issued $10\frac{3}{4}$in discs.

1922–35 Woolworths marketed records on a variety of labels and in a variety of sizes: Mimosa, 5in and 6in (1922); Broadcast Junior and Little Marvel, 6in (1922); Victory, 7in (1928); Eclipse, 8in (1931); Crown, 9in (1935). From 1927, Marks and Spencer offered competition with their Marspen and Broadcast labels at 6in and 8in respectively. Because of the implied connection with radio, the playing of Broadcast records on the air was banned by the BBC in 1931, **the only instance of a whole label being thus banned**.

Victor Disc Sizes

Early in the century the Victor Company denoted their record sizes on their matrices by a letter code which also reflects the chronological order of the introduction of these sizes:

A 7in (1901–3, although they remained on sale until at least 1905)
B 10in (1901–)
C 12in (1903–)
D $13\frac{3}{4}$in (1904)
E 8in (1904–8)

Disc Diameters

Diameters of disc records offered for sale. This list also serves as a conversion chart to metric values.

inches	cm
$1\frac{3}{8}$	3·5
3	7·6
$3\frac{1}{8}$	8·0
5	12·7
6	15·2
$6\frac{3}{4}$	17·2
7	17·8
8	20·3
$8\frac{1}{4}$	21·0
9	22·9
$9\frac{1}{2}$	24·1
10	25·4
$10\frac{3}{4}$	27·3
11	28·0
12	30·5
$13\frac{3}{4}$	34·9
16	40·6
20	50·8

1924 HMV produced a $1\frac{3}{8}$in disc containing a brief version of *God Save the King*.

1926 Bell Laboratories produced the 'Vitaphone' discs for Warner Bros' film soundtracks. They were 16in and, rotating at $33\frac{1}{3}$rpm, gave a playing time of 10 minutes, equalling a 1000ft (305m) reel of film. NBC made 16in $33\frac{1}{3}$rpm plastic transcription discs for broadcasting purposes until about 1942.

1936 5in unbreakable single-sided discs of music-hall artists were issued by Aircraft Products Ltd of London. Aluminium 5in discs upon which the public might record a message for 6d

(2½p) were dispensed in kiosks on railway stations and elsewhere by automatic voice-recording machines.

1949 7in 45rpm discs introduced.

1953 The Coronation ceremony for Queen Elizabeth II on 2 June was recorded by the BBC and transferred to 16in vinylite discs for despatch by the BBC Transcription Service to radio stations all over the world.

1960 Early in this decade the 10in format had been abandoned by all the major companies, leaving 33⅓rpm 12in and 45rpm 7in discs as standards.

(Further factors concerning disc sizes and their relation to playing speeds may be found in Section IX.)

The largest records ever made were the 20in Pathé Grand series of 1906 – see above.

The smallest functional gramophone record ever made was the 1⅜in royal disc of 1924 – see above.

The smallest functional record.   EVENING ARGUS, BRIGHTON

Speeds – Cylinders

There is no means of knowing for certain the speed of revolution of the cylinder in Edison's earliest experiments. No gearing was involved, so if we assume that he cranked his device twice per second the speed would have to be **120rpm** – slower, presumably, towards the end of a long stint. The earliest commercial cylinders were made to revolve at 120rpm; this was increased to a standard of **160rpm** in 1901 (with 100 grooves to the inch) when moulded cylinders became a commercial viability.

Speeds – Discs

Today's two 'standard' speeds of 33⅓ and 45rpm were slow to evolve, and most of the experiments of earlier days closely allied speeds to the sizes of the discs.

c 1890 The hand-cranked children's disc players made by the German toy firm of Kämmerer und Reinhardt used 3in and 5in discs

rotating at **c 100rpm**. By 1898, playing time had been increased by subsequent disc makers by the dual expedient of increasing the disc size to 6¾in and reducing the playing speed to **c 78rpm.**

1906 Pathé's earliest discs were single-sided, label-less, vertical-cut, and nearly half an inch thick. They were designed to rotate variously at **90** and **120rpm**, the windings starting at the centre. Later, **80rpm** became the Pathé standard speed, with outside start and two recorded sides, and (from 1916) paper labels.

1923 Pemberton Billing 'World' Records were introduced in England. These **constant linear speed** discs, by rotating slowly at the outer winding and gradually increasing in speed as the pick-up crossed the disc, offered up to 8½ minutes' playing time per side, but they proved unsuccessful for three reasons: (1) they required a special playing deck equipped with a wheel that tracked the disc surface to control the turntable speed; (2) the increased playing time put an unacceptable strain on the needles of the time, which were designed to play only one or two standard sides (ie: they were worn out after c 3–6 minutes); and (3) at this time many homes still lacked mains electricity and the spring motors of the time were not equal to the Pemberton Billing records' extended duration. (The concept of constant linear speed discs had been covered, but not followed up, by the Tainter and Bell experiments of the 1880s. It has recently

1954 The 7in 33⅓rpm disc introduced in Europe. This format was largely ignored in America and the UK except by smaller companies. In the UK, EMI's first (and only?) 7in single playing at 33⅓rpm was issued in January 1971: Capitol CL 15668, featuring the American group Grand Funk Railroad. Playing time of the sides was 9 minutes 20 seconds and 8 minutes respectively.

1956 'Talking Books' were issued in Germany

A 45rpm 7in disc autochanger. This 1952 HMV version was identical to the American Victor model.

been revived for the CD, or Compact Disc – see Section IX.)

1926 **The first 33⅓rpm discs** were produced by Bell Laboratories for Warner Brothers film soundtrack of *Don Juan* starring John Barrymore. The system was called 'Vitaphone', but it was eventually replaced by a soundtrack on the film itself for subsequent films.

1935 Speech-only discs at **24rpm** were introduced by Talking Books for the Blind. They gave 30 minutes' playing time.

1948 Long-playing discs at 33⅓rpm introduced.

1949 The **45rpm** 7in disc introduced. Originally designed to replace the 78rpm disc by offering a maximum of c 4 minutes per side, these were later produced with double this playing time: the so-called 'extended play' (EP) discs. EP became obsolete during the early 1970s.

and America at **16⅔rpm**. Discs at this speed containing music programmes approximately double the length of 33⅓rpm LP records were offered by Vox the following year in America but did not hold the market for many months. **The first 'talking book' 16⅔rpm disc to be put on general release in the UK** was *Tales of Terror*: stories and poems by Edgar Allan Poe, read by Nelson Olmsted on Top Rank 45/001. The playing time was 1 hour and 35 minutes, and the release date was December 1959. Spoken word and drama discs at 16⅔rpm were on sale in Eastern Europe (eg: Romania) as recently as the late 1960s.

1959 Virtually all remaining EMI 78rpm discs were deleted on 31 January, signalling the demise of the coarse-groove record in the UK. This demise had occurred somewhat earlier in

America and was soon to be world-wide. (Further factors concerning disc speeds and their relation to sizes may be found in Section IX.)

The fastest coarse-groove disc was the 120rpm Pathé record of 1906 – see above.

The slowest coarse-groove '78' was Columbia's 10in single-sided *The Song of the Shirt*, recited by Sir John Tollemache-Sinclair. It was recorded at **65rpm**.

In 1978 a curious hybrid LP appeared in America, marketed by Crystal Clear. It was a 12in disc playing at 45rpm, its higher linear speed giving the advantage of improved sound quality but the disadvantage of shorter playing time. Although arousing little interest in the States (or in the UK – EMI offered a 'Dynamic Sound Series' in 1979 giving $9\frac{1}{2}$ – 20 minutes per side), this format has since been taken up more successfully by the British Nimbus Co, which developed full-length 45rpm LPs running for up to about 26 minutes per side which show a noticeable improvement in quality without the drawback of reduced playing time. So entrenched is the idea amongst collectors that 12in equals $33\frac{1}{3}$rpm, however, that even the legend '45RPM' emblazoned across both sleeve and label is not enough to prevent the records from being played by the inattentive at the wrong speed, with disturbing results.

The printing of durations of items and/or side lengths on the label or sleeve or both is now standard practice with most companies in the US and the UK (with the exception of EMI). Producers of radio programmes appreciate this facility since it saves them the chore of physically timing a recording when making up recorded concerts for broadcasting.

The first company to print timings on its labels was World Records Ltd of London in 1923 (see above). The purpose then was also commercial: World Records presented an ingenious means of increasing playing time by constantly increasing the speed of revolution from $33\frac{1}{3}$rpm at the outer edge to 78rpm at the centre. This required a novel playing deck – see above. The longer playing times were boasted about on the

labels. The invention of this variable-speed disc was the work of Noel Pemberton-Billing (c 1880–1948), an English writer, playwright, aviator and sometime Member of Parliament.

Perhaps the oddest hybrid records ever made were issued in 1949 by the Australian Record Co of Sydney. Recorded by Prof Elkin, they were a series of chants and rituals of the Australian Aborigines. The discs were double-sided, 16in dia, $33\frac{1}{3}$rpm, coarse-grooved, and the groove windings began in the centre.

The fastest microgroove discs were the Teldec experimental video disc of 1970 which revolved on a layer of air at 1500rpm, and the Philips/Sony laser-read video disc of 1975 with a signal carried in minute depressions in the surface and revolving at 1800rpm.

Singularities

A century of trial and error has produced a fair number of freaks; in the software and hardware of the record industry one will find many equivalents of the five-wheeled car, the painting done by bicycle tyres, and the two-headed pig.

Coloured Discs

The first edible discs were produced by Stollwerck in about 1905: they were of an appetising hue – and brand – of chocolate. The deep-brown-to-dirty-pink shades of the earliest discs eventually gave way to the customary black; yet various types of plastic materials were used alongside shellac, and these gave the possibility of all kinds of colours. Browns and reds continued through the 1920s with such makes as Paramount, Vocalion, Aeolian, and Gennett, while the cream-coloured celluloid Goodson discs gave an unexpected bonus to the used-needle hoarder, for they had to be played only with worn needles lest a fresh point should render to powder that Milky Bar-coloured surface.

In the late 1920s Duophone offered flexible discs, and Phonycord in Germany followed with transparent celluloid discs of the utmost pliability. In England, Filmophone brightly-coloured celluloid unbreakable discs were advertised with a text apparently designed to make the product appeal to the most awkward and vandalistic of purchasers: 'You can bend, roll, drop, sit on, walk on, even dance on a Filmophone Flexible record and it sustains no damage.' You could not, however, play them: once on a turntable their flexibility proved itself all too willingly by tending to develop a curl while playing which would effectively dislodge the pick-up.

Filmophones, together with the short-lived (spring to autumn 1931) Empire record, also made of celluloid, carried the recording information on the label-less central area – etched in, as on the early Berliners. In Section III the first labelled discs are given as those put out by Johnson in 1900 as 'Improved Gram-O-Phone Records', but a strange circumstance suggests that there may have been earlier examples. The story may even contain a hint of that modern curse: piracy.

In about 1898 a 30-page catalogue of 'Wonder' discs was issued by the makers of the Wonder Talking Machine, a conventional disc-player with two brass horns angled to spread the sound. The contents of the catalogue was virtually identical with Berliner's of 1898, so either the records were leased from Berliner or were in some way pirated. Brian Rust (*The American Record Label Book*) favours the former possibility and suggests that in order to obliterate Berliner's etching in the central area, sticky labels were applied carrying the 'Wonder' trade mark. What may have begun as a commercial necessity, therefore, led to the opportunities afforded by colourfully-designed paper labels.

But that was not enough for some manufacturers. In December 1931 Trusound Pictorial advertising discs offered pictures covering the whole surface; 11 years earlier, Talk-o-Photo in America brought out discs with music on one side and a photograph of a movie star on the other, although whether the two sides were related in any artistic way is unknown since no copies are known to have survived. **The World's first square records** (about 3in × 3in = 7·6cm × 7·6cm) did relate their two sides: the first (on a

helical groove) gave about a minute and a half of patter and song by a comedian; the second gave his picture and a sketch of his career. The 'discs' were made of celluloid-and-fibre laminate and were given away with 'Record' cigarettes from about 1934.

Returning to coloured discs, Blu-Disc was just that – a royal blue record of December 1924 containing jazz material. Apparently they met with no success, for the nine-title release was never followed up. With the return of plastic as a basic material for pressings in early LP days, several companies issued brightly-coloured discs, including Lyrichord in America and Record Society and Philharmonic in the UK. Most colours were available – red, green, blue, purple, orange – but red was the most popular. **The first picture LP** was issued in 1970: Warner WSX 3012. Titled *Airconditioning*, by Curved Air, its psychedelic-stroboscopic central design was surrounded by the titling, **the first instance of the label going round the groove** rather than *vice versa*. Pressings of the EMI Beatles' *Sgt Pepper's Lonely Heart's Club Band* LP in 1979 bore the sleeve design on the disc itself, the central drum motif having the appearance of a wildly eccentric label.

The first completely colourless LP was Steve Hillage's *Rainbow Dome Music* on the Virgin label (1977).

Short-Lived Labels

If Blu-Disc's existence was short-lived (see above), even less noteworthy were Chatauqua (one issue, recorded about 10 June, 1922, in New York: *Diddle-Diddle-Dum* by the Original Memphis Five), and Capital (*not* Capitol) (one issue: *Missouri Squabble/I Don't Believe You*, by Pete Sullivan and his King Taste Pilots, made in New York about 1928). These make Durium's existence of some 9 months from 8 April, 1932, seem quite successful by comparison. Duriums were sold through bookstalls, not record shops, and were once again of the pale-brown unbreakable celluloid-and-cardboard laminate variety, with fine and easily-damaged grooves giving some $4\frac{1}{2}$ minutes per 10in side.

The first record to carry all the names of the newly-affiliated EMI companies.

Mayfair discs did not sell at all: they were exchanged for coupons presented with Ardath cigarettes in the UK in 1931–2. One wonders whether the artists (Red Nichols, Annette Hanshaw, Joe Venuti, Benny Goodman, and Al Bowlly) ever received royalties, since all appeared on the labels of Mayfair under pseudonyms.

Puzzlers

The first puzzle record was made in 1898 by Berliner: two piano solos were recorded on parallel grooves, the needle deciding which of the two should be heard. In 1901 Berliner issued a three-groove example with a song within a monologue within a piano solo. Other trick records followed: Regal Zonophone's *Back Your Fancy* was a race commentary with six different results recorded on six different grooves at the end (1932), and HMV put out Claude Hulbert reciting limericks, alternative last lines being supplied at the end according to the whim of chance. (See also Section III.)

Oddities

The first spiritualist recording was made in 1931 at the Columbia studios, London, when Mrs Meurig Morris held a séance. In the following

year EMI in association with the *Daily Mail* issued a 10in *Mystery Record* (RO 1000) with a prize of £1950 (a strange amount) for guessing the names of the artists thereon. Its label was **the first to bear the names of all the recently-affiliated British EMI companies**: HMV, Columbia, Parlophone, and Regal Zonophone.

The first comedy record to sell a million copies cruelly exposed the errors of others. Called *Radio Bloopers*, it was an anthology of unscripted and involuntary remarks made on US radio and assembled by Kermit Schafer (Jubilee, 1947).

Noises 'Off'

A moment of recording studio procedure comes vividly to the listener at the start of the final side of Mozart's String Quintet in G minor, K516, played by the Griller Quartet with Max Gilbert, viola. Apparently, the signal to start playing for a new 78rpm side was two short rings of an electric bell – which are duly recorded on the run-in groove of Decca AX 343. Other 'noises off' are noted in Section III, but the following deserve mention:
Columbia ML 4089 (US): a dog barks quite distinctly during Ormandy's recording of Rimsky-Korsakov's *Scheherazade*. Parlophone R 20077: a guitar strums in the distance while Conchita Supervía tries to sing *Non so Più*.

With modern recording clarity, traffic and train noise is all too frequently heard; indeed, it is only possible to detect tape edits because of the sudden appearance or disappearance of unwanted background 'effects'. Birdsong is inevitably picked up by the microphones in recordings made in church and cathedral: French Eratos made in the 1950s and 1960s were particularly prone to this charming interference, and Argo ZRG 836, issued in the UK in 1976, provides the **first** (possibly fortuitous) **example of a musical obligato by a feathered friend**: in the last movement of Telemann's Overture in D, a sparrow in the roof of St Mary's Church, Rotherhithe, London, seems to echo for a bar or so the phrases of the solo oboe.

Artists are no less guilty of perpetrating unwanted contributions. The first 'artistic' noise

SAYDISC Double play length LP 33⅓rpm

KILVERT'S DIARY
'He Being Dead Yet Speaketh'
AN ANTHOLOGY OF READINGS READ BY TIMOTHY DAVIES

& Edited by Jerry Friar
from the election Edited by William Plomer

An hour and a half from one 33⅓rpm LP. BBC

to emerge from the hiss of 78rpm pressings was the 'fiddler's sniff', specially noticeable on close-miked sonata and quartet recordings and still with us today. Fingernail squeaks are also frequently heard from guitarists, and conductors and pianists (Toscanini, Barbirolli, Glenn Gould, and many others) supply an often quite loud, and rarely tuneful, vocal refrain. Sensitive modern microphones sometimes pick up a noisy page-turn, and recent digital recordings, with

their increased bass response, now faithfully relay the foot movements of conductors. There is, perhaps, a case for the solid concrete rostrum. The reader will doubtless have encountered many other examples.

As an antidote, a playing of *Auditory Memory* is recommended. Marketed in November 1974 by Jerry Cammarate of Staten Island, New York, it consists of 52 minutes, 10 seconds of total silence: the gramophone's answer to John

Cage's 4 minutes 33 seconds in which any number of musicians with any type of instruments remain perfectly silent for that length of time.

Value?

The longest playing time on a standard 12in 78rpm disc offered for sale is believed to be in the UK HMV Haydn Quartet Society Series, Volume II (DB 1927/8), issued in 1932, in which one side of a disc plays for 6 minutes, 45 seconds, and the other for 6 minutes, 15 seconds, a total of 13 minutes. Longer playing 'Variable Micrograde' 78s were issued in the late 1940s by DGG – see Section IX.

The shortest playing time for one 12in 78 side is on Columbia LX 1204 (side two of Beethoven's Symphony No 1, conducted by Bruno Walter), where the duration is a mere 1 minute, 19 seconds.

The longest playing time on a 10in 78 disc is 6 minutes each side, on Sterno 5022: Ballet Music from Rossini's *William Tell*, and Verdi's *Sicilian Vespers*, played by Joseph Lewis and his Orchestra.

The longest LP musical records run, according to the makers, 'up to 43 minutes per side' in the American release of Wagner's *Ring* cycle, recorded at La Scala, Milan, in 1950 (Mercury 940477). Experiments were made in Japan in the 1960s with side lengths of c 40 minutes, but with poor volume and bass response, and American Vox in the 1950s released half-speed ($16\frac{2}{3}$rpm) LPs offering c 45 minutes per side. Again, these met with scant success. **The longest $33\frac{1}{3}$rpm 12in spoken word sides** (with musical background) are *Kilvert's Diary – 'He Being*

Dead Yet Speaketh', read by Timothy Davies on Saydisc SDX 309, issued in 1980, the two sides of which play for precisely 45 minutes each.

The shortest 12in LP side known to the authors is side two of Nixa PLP 517 (1952), containing Schubert's *Quartettsatz* in C minor, D703, which runs for just $7\frac{1}{2}$ minutes.

Double Play

Finally, singular records may be played on singular machines. Duophone, who issued the flexible discs mentioned above, put out a gramophone in about 1925 in which two sound boxes were incorporated in the pick-up, operating in tandem, in an attempt to double the volume. The similarly-named Deuxphone was marketed early this century in England. It was a conventional spring-operated disc-playing horn gramophone. However, remove the record, stand the machine on its side, clip a mandrill onto the spindle, adjust the speed of rotation and the angle of the soundbox, and, Lo! the Deuxphone became a cylinder player. **This was the first disc/cylinder player.** In 1907 came the Devineau Biophone, an attachment for a cylinder player which would convert it to a disc player. In 1951 the Chancery Instrument appeared in the UK. It consisted of two metal plates between which was a gearing system. When placed on a 78rpm turntable, the lower plate turned at that speed but the upper one, suitably reduced by the gearing, revolved at $33\frac{1}{3}$rpm for the new LPs. With the Chancery Instrument one was expected to purchase an LP pick-up equipped with three suction pads which, if one's saliva was equal to it, would fasten the base to the motorboard of the existing player.

Section VIII

Repertoire

Part One

The first part of this Section consists of a chronological chart showing the growth and expansion of the commercially available recorded musical repertoire, from its tentative beginnings as a toy disc to sing songs to children. Step by step, the industry gained credence as an acceptable, then a useful, and finally as an indispensable disseminator of music, and, as it did so, it improved its techniques until it reached its present sophisticated stage.

It would take many volumes to chart this progress in minute detail: a more general overall view is needed, so we have included in the pages that follow only those recordings that have widened the scope of the industry, have decisively consolidated previous gains, or have an intrinsic interest and significance. Focus, therefore, is on 'firsts', best-sellers, trends, important projects, and the outstanding items that have been offered to the public in nearly a century of commercial recording. Boom times and recessions, crazes and wars, technical advances and fashions: all are reflected in this chart.

The turmoil of the years immediately after World War II as the various strands of recorded music twisted about in search of a firm direction, does not admit of clear chronological charting. Instead, a portion of text for the years 1945–54 has been inserted in an attempt to describe the evolving trends as they settled down again in the mid-1950s. The earliest recording days are also amplified in the text (see Sections II and III), as are electrical recording (Section IV) and Long Playing (Section IX).

The second part of the present Section is occupied by a series of lists that show the record industry in an enormously wide variety of non-musical roles, from stern mentor to light-hearted friend, with a thousand different moods in between.

A chronological listing of unusual, notable and pioneering musical projects, and some of the most popular records of the day.

1888 **The first recordings in the world to be offered for sale** were in *disc* form, and were intended for children (see below: p. 161, Children's records).

No further recordings were made for commercial sale until 1890, but in **1888** the young pianist Josef Hofmann recorded a cylinder in Edison's laboratory, and Edison's London agent, Colonel Gouraud, recorded parts of Handel's *Israel in Egypt* on cylinder on 29 June, at the Crystal Palace Handel Festival. **These were the first recordings of serious music.** In **1889** Brahms made a recording in Germany, while in the Metropolitan Opera House, New York, Edison recorded a concert given by Hans von Bülow. All were in the nature of test records, not made with commercial gain in mind.

1890–6 **The first cylinders offered for sale** were of Stephen Foster melodies, Sousa Marches, polkas, and popular songs ranging from *Rule, Britannia* to *Ta-Ra-Ra-Boom-De-Ay*. In **1893** American Columbia made **the first advertising cylinders**: popular tunes were interspersed with advertising text and were made to order for any company or business.

c 1896 Bettini (see Personalia) offered for sale copies of his privately recorded master cylinders made by famous artists including Sarah Bernhardt, Yvette Guilbert, Melba, Victor Maurel and Tomaso Salvini, which he had been recording since 1888.

1896 **The first operatic disc recording in the US**: Ferruccio Giannini singing *La donna è Mobile* from *Rigoletto*.

1897 **First dance discs issued in America**; discs of waltzes, marches and polkas were also popular.

1898 **First UK recordings of a comedy song** (Ted Handy), **piano solo** (*Under The Double Eagle* by 'Mr Castle'), and **cello solo** (*Simple Aveu* by Thomé, played by W H Squire). Military bands, popular in the US, spread later to the UK. **First orchestral disc**: *Washington Post March* (Hotel Cecil Orchestra).

1899 **Outbreak of the Boer War.**

Earliest pure ragtime recording. War songs. Dame Clara Butt and Kennerley Rumford record a duet for The Gramophone Co, **the first 'artistic' duet.**

1900 The Gramophone Co were offering disc recordings of all the best-known operatic arias and duets, performed by established Italian artists.

1901 **10in disc introduced**

First Red Label discs, by Chaliapin, Medea Mei-Figner, Nicola Figner, and others, made in Russia and issued there and in the UK.

1902 Caruso made his historic recordings for The Gramophone Co on the third floor of the Grand Hotel, Milan, on 11 April. American Columbia issued the 'Grand Opera Series' (issued in the UK in April 1903). Opera recordings made by Emma Calvé, Pol Plançon, Antonio Scotti and others.

1903 **12in disc introduced**

The ascendancy of the disc was driving cylinder makers to concentrate on the rural market with repertoire mainly of ballads and light songs. **First US-made Victor Red Seals** issued in April: artists included Ada Crossley. Columbia countered with their first vocal celebrity recordings to be made in the US. Joseph Joachim (violin) and Raoul Pugno (piano) recorded for The Gramophone Co. **First complete opera recording**: Verdi's *Ernani*, on 40 single-sided discs by the Italian Gramophone Co.

1904 Società Italiana di Fonotipia founded: **the first label to devote itself exclusively to serious music. First Melba releases**: 14 12in discs with special mauve 'Melba' labels. **First recordings of John McCormack. First recordings of Gregorian Chant** by the Sistine Choir.

1905 **First double-sided discs introduced**

First chamber music recordings, of isolated movements by Mendelssohn and Schumann.

1906 Best sellers were music hall songs and solos by instruments that recorded well: banjo, concertina, cornet, piccolo and xylophone. Edison announced his Grand Opera Series of cylinders, with artists from the Metropolitan Opera. This low priced series (75¢) was unsuccessful and was discontinued in 1911. G & T recorded *Il Trovatore* complete but piecemeal and by different artists at different times. Orchestral accompaniments to operatic artists now regularly replaced the piano.

1907 **First complete opera to be issued in the UK**: Leoncavallo's *I Pagliacci*, under the composer's direction. Strauss's *Die Fledermaus*

HALL OF FAME

Count John McCormack, tenor

1884 14 June: Born in Athlone, Eire.

1903 Won singing prize at the Irish Music Festival (Feis Ceoil), Dublin.

1904 Went to America to perform at the St Louis Exhibition.

1904 **Made his first recordings** for Edison, Edison Bell, and G & T, including the popular *Believe Me if all Those Endearing Young Charms* (made on 19 September, 1904 for G & T).

1905 Went to Milan to study with Vincenzo Sabatini.

1906 Signed contract with Odeon Records for 12 sides per year for 6 years. (Victor purchased this contract in 1910 for £2000.)

1907 15 October: Made his Covent Garden début in Mascagni's *Cavalleria Rusticana*. He took part in every summer season there from 1908 to 1914.

Late **1907** or early **1908 Made his first opera**tic title for Odeon (given as '*Siciliana*' on LX 2488).

1909 18 November: His first American solo concert was at Manhattan Opera House.

1910 29 November: He made his Metropolitan Opera House début in Verdi's *La Traviata*.

1919 June: Became an American citizen.

1928 Made a Papal Count by Pope Pius XI.

1929 Made his only full-length film: *Song o' my Heart*.

1942 10 September: **Made his last recording session**.

1945 16 September: Died in Dublin, aged 61.

During and after his career he sold over 200 million records. The song *I Hear You Calling Me* (recorded for Odeon twice in 1908, and for Victor in 1910, 1911, 1921, and 1927) was his best seller.

recorded complete in Germany on 21 sides. Vladimir de Pachmann recorded some Chopin piano works.

1908 Bizet's *Carmen* (36 sides) and Gounod's *Faust* (34 sides) recorded complete.

1909 Wilhelm Backhaus (piano) made his first disc: Bach's *Prelude in C sharp*. **First large-scale commercial orchestral recordings**: Tchaikovsky's *Nutcracker Suite* (four double-sided English Odeon discs) by the London Palace Orchestra conducted by Hermann Finck; **first commercial recording of a complete symphony** made in Germany: Beethoven's Fifth Symphony, by the Berlin Philharmonic Orchestra under Arthur Nikisch (eight single-sided discs; issued in the UK on HMV 040784–91 in 1914).

1910 Sentimental ballads were selling well, as were 'coon-songs': Sophie Tucker (known then as a 'coon shouter' and later as 'The Last of the Red-Hot Mamas') recorded hot ragtime numbers for Edison cylinders in the US. **First recording of a concerto**: Backhaus (with the New Symphony Orchestra under Landon Ronald) recorded the first movement of Grieg's Piano Concerto, abbreviated on two single-sided discs. Mark Hambourg recorded Beethoven's *Moonlight* Sonata.

1911 *Alexander's Ragtime Band* by Irving Berlin helped to spark off the ragtime dance craze. Schubert's *Unfinished* Symphony recorded in a drastically shortened form on one two-sided disc by the Court Symphony Orchestra under Charles Prince. **The first complete orchestral work to be issued in the UK** was Beethoven's Overture *Leonora III*. Paderewski recorded works by Chopin.

1912 The *Titanic* sinking on 14 April was commemorated in song by Robert Carr on an Edison Bell disc.

1913 *'Tis A Story That Shall Live For Ever*, sung by Stanley Kirkby, the story being that of Captain Scott's Antarctic expedition. American Columbia issued strict tempo dance records directed by the dance authority G Hepburn Wilson, who actually danced with a partner during the recording. Victor issued a rival series supervised by Vernon and Irene Castle. Hunting calls

Vernon and Irene Castle.

recorded on HMV by Master of Foxhounds, Viscount Galway, MP. Edison again tackled the operatic market with his Blue Amberol cylinders.

1914 **World War I began**
It's A Long Way To Tipperary (first recorded in 1912) and similar songs taken as marching tunes by the British Army, becoming enormously popular. *Cohen On The Telephone* recorded by Joe Haymen (comedy dialogue song). **First show songs with original casts** recorded by British Columbia, starting a popular line of development. **The oldest recording eventually to reach one million sales** was Alma Gluck's *Carry Me Back To Old Virginny* (Victor Red Seal

single-sided 12in (30·5cm): 74420). Army Cavalry Calls by Trumpeter Anderson recorded on Edison Bell Winner. Sir Edward Elgar makes his first HMV recording: *Carissima*.

1915 **The first foxtrot recording** made by the Van Eps Trio in December. The personality cult spreads from operatic to orchestral recordings when Thomas Beecham and Henry Wood were signed by British Columbia, starting a boom in orchestral recordings in the UK. Beecham recorded Mozart's *Magic Flute* Overture/ Borodin's *Prince Igor* Dances. Wood recorded Wagner's *Lohengrin* Prelude to Act III/Tchaikovsky's *Scherzo* from Symphony No 4. **First recording of a Bach orchestral work**: the 'Double' Concerto, played by Kreisler and E Zimbalist.

1916 *If You Were The Only Girl In The World* (from *The Bing Boys Are Here*), sung by George Robey and Violet Loraine. UK Columbia's Regal label offered 'War Records', the proceeds of which went to the Prince of Wales Fund in aid of the war effort.

1917 **First jazz records** (see Section III). **The first jazz cylinder** was *Canary Cottage* by the Frisco Jazz Band, recorded on 10 May and issued on Edison Blue Amberol. **First Gilbert and Sullivan recording**: *Mikado* (HMV). **First recording of music by Stravinsky**: *Dance of the Firebird* (abridged), from *The Firebird*, conducted by Beecham. **First discs of the Philadelphia Orchestra** issued by Victor. **First violin and piano duet**: two abridged movements of Grieg's Sonata in C, by Albert Sammons and William Murdoch.

1918 **Armistice**
Mary, by Joseph C Smith's Orchestra was sung by Harry Macdonough, Charles Hart and Lewis James. **This was the first dance record with vocal refrain** and was recorded in New York on 29 July. Caruso recorded *Over There!* in July.

1919 **First UK issue of a jazz disc**: the Original Dixieland Jazz Band playing *At The Jazzband Ball/Barnyard Blues*, recorded 16 April. This, Ben Sèlvin's *Dardanella* (HMV) and Art Hickman's *Sweet and Low* (Columbia) started trends that continued in popularity for 20 years. A series of Wagner orchestral pieces recorded in

Ivan Menzies as Koko in Mikado *in 1924.*
BBC HULTON PICTURE LIBRARY

Germany by Parlophone.

1920 **The first record to reach one million sales**: Paul Whiteman's *Whispering/The Japanese Sandman*. *Puck-a-Pu*, played by the Mayfair Dance Orchestra led by George W Byng, had **the first vocal refrain on a UK dance record** – sung by Eric Courtland (pseudonym of Ernest Pike). Velvet Face founded. It brought many London-based artists (eg: Dr Adrian Boult, Sir Dan Godfrey, Eugene Goossens and Hamilton Harty) to records. Its most ambitious recording was an abbreviated version of Elgar's *The Dream of Gerontius* on eight discs. The label ceased production in 1929.

1921 Popular trends: music hall acts and songs both humorous and sentimental, brass bands, light orchestral pieces, and big bands such as The Benson Orchestra's *Ain't We Got Fun?/Wabash Blues*, and the California Ramblers' *The Sheik*.

1922 *Nola* played by Vincent Lopez, and *Three O'Clock In The Morning* by the Savoy Havana Band, continued this trend. **First recording of a complete work by Stravinsky**: *Fireworks*, conducted by Leopold Stokowski.

1923 **First commercial recording of Country Music**: *The Little Old Log Cabin In The Lane/The Old Hen Cackled And The Rooster's Going To Crow*, by Fiddlin' John Carson, recorded 14 June. **First complete string quartet recording**: Brahms's Quartet Op 51/1, by the Catterall Quartet (HMV). Holst conducted his Suite *The Planets* (for UK Columbia).

1924 Best sellers: *California, Here I Come* by the California Ramblers; *What'll I Do?* by Vincent Lopez; and the best-selling pre-electric Victor recording: *The Prisoner's Song/The Wreck Of The Old 97* by Vernon Dalhart. George Gershwin recorded his *Rhapsody In Blue* (the 1927 re-make was a best-seller). Classical repertoire was widening: symphonies by Beethoven (No 8 – Weingartner), Dvořák (*New World* – Harty), Mozart (No 39 – Weingartner), and Schubert (*Unfinished* – Stokowski) all recorded complete for the first time. **The first British Symphony to be recorded** was McEwen's *Solway* Symphony. **First complete opera in English**: Puccini's *Madame Butterfly*, on 14 double-sided HMV discs. The National Gramophonic Society formed in the UK under the guidance of Sir Compton Mackenzie and others associated with *The Gramophone* magazine to record music not otherwise available. Its first issue was Beethoven's String Quartet Op 74 in October. Within a year it had released Debussy's Quartet, Schubert's Piano Trio in E flat, Brahms's Sextet Op 18, and Schoenberg's *Verklaerte Nacht*. Its last issue appeared in April 1935: Paul Juon's Chamber Symphony.

1925 **Electrical Recording introduced**
The first electrical recordings are mentioned in Section IV. Popular numbers included Frank Crumit's *Abdul Abulbul Amir* and Jack Hylton's *Feelin' Kind O' Blue* **the first UK electrical dance record**. First recordings of the new dance craze, the Charleston; tangos were also very popular. According to one English report,

popular music had 'gone American' and was 'unspeakably vulgar'.

1926 Best sellers: *The Blue Room* by the California Ramblers, *Deep Henderson* by the Coon-Sanders' Original Nighthawk Orchestra, and *Some Of These Days* by Sophie Tucker with Ted Lewis and his Band. **First commercial recording by Bing Crosby**: *I've Got The Girl*, made 18 October. A recording of 4000 children violinists with the Grenadier Guards Band was recorded at the Crystal Palace, London.

1927 First recording by Jimmie Rodgers (the 'Father of Country Music', 1905–77): *The Soldier's Sweetheart*. *Charmaine* (Guy Lombardo) and *Side By Side* (Savoy Havana Band and Paul Whiteman). *Hear My Prayer/Oh, For The Wings Of A Dove* recorded by Ernest Lough. UK Columbia celebrated Beethoven's centenary with an ambitious recording programme (see p. 82).

1928 **First million seller from a talkie**: *Sorry Bob/There's a Rainbow Round My Shoulder* by Al Jolson (from *The Singing Fool*). Paul Whiteman recorded *Ramona*. Columbia in the UK celebrated Schubert's centenary by announcing an International Composers' Contest. Atterberg's Symphony No 6 won first prize for an original composition. Prizes for completions of Schubert's *Unfinished* Symphony went to Frank Merrick and J St A Johnson (joint first), and Havergal Brian (second).

1929 **Wall Street Crash (October); Start of World Depression**
Band records maintained their hold on the popular market: Ben Selvin's and Nat Shilkret's *Broadway Melody*, and Waring's Pennsylvanian's *Jericho*.

1930 Best sellers: *Mood Indigo* by Duke Ellington; *Exactly Like You* by Sam Lanin; and *I Bring A Love Song* by Leo Reisman. **The first million seller by a vocal quartet** was *Tiger Rag/Nobody's Sweetheart* by the Mills Bros. *The Columbia History of Music*, edited by Percy Scholes, began to appear in May; there were five volumes altogether, the last appearing in January 1939.

1931 **RCA's LP discs were issued**. (See Section IX.)

Roy Fox recorded *Oh Mo'nah!*; Ray Noble recorded *Goodnight Sweetheart*. The first HMV Society issues appeared in April (Hugo Wolf *Lieder*). First issue of Parlophone's *2000 Years of Music*, directed by Curt Sachs. The recording of truncated classical works had largely ceased, yet other sins remained: songs and arias were sung in the wrong language (even Neapolitan songs were recorded in German), words were frequently added to instrumental pieces, making nonsense of, for instance, some of Mendelssohn's *Songs Without Words*, and Parlophone issued Chopin's Piano Concerto No 1 played by Moriz Rosenthal on three 10in and two 12in discs.

1932 Latin American dance music was in vogue. Roy Fox recorded *Lullaby Of The Leaves*. Jazz issues were made on RCA's 'LP' discs. The International Record Collectors' Club was formed to promote the re-issue of archive recordings: the first issue featured Geraldine Farrar.

1933 Best sellers: *Somebody Stole My Gal* by Billy Cotton; *Bugle Call Rag* and *Canadian Capers* by Harry Roy. **The first American symphony to be recorded** was Roy Harris's 'Symphony 1933', issued by American Columbia shortly after composition. Leopold Stokowski conducted, and gave a spoken introduction to, Schoenberg's *Gurrelieder*, complete on 28 sides.

1934 *Anthologie Sonore*, the French history of music series, began to appear.

1935 **Recovery from Depression**
The only noteworthy popular recording of the year was *King Porter Stomp* by Benny Goodman.

1936 Paul Whiteman recorded *Slaughter On Tenth Avenue*. *Indian Love Call* (from *Rose Marie*), recorded by Jeanette MacDonald and Nelson Eddy, was **the first show tune to sell one million copies.** *Two* versions of Beethoven's *Hammerklavier* Sonata were issued in the UK, by Schnabel and Kempff. Ormandy and the Minneapolis Symphony Orchestra recorded Bruckner's Symphony No 7 complete on 15 sides.

1937 **First million seller by a female group:** *Bei*

Mir Bist Du Schon by the Andrews Sisters. **Bing Crosby recorded the first of his million sellers**: *Sweet Leilani*, Tommy Dorsey and his Orchestra recorded *Marie*; and other best sellers were: *Doggin' Around* (Count Basie), *I Can't Get Started With You* (Bunny Berigan), and *South Rampart Street Parade* (Bob Crosby). Parlophone issued two 10in discs of hunting sounds to accompany the book *Hunting By Ear*, by Michael Berry and D W E Brock. The first complete recording of Bruckner's Symphony No 4 was made by Karl Böhm and the Saxon State Orchestra.

1938 Best sellers: *Bach Goes to Town* (Benny Goodman), *Begin the Beguine* (Artie Shaw), *Lambeth Walk* (Billy Cotton), and *Jalousie* (Boston Pops Orchestra under Arthur Fiedler). **This was the first light orchestral record to sell a million** (by 1952); it was recorded in 1935 but release was delayed for three years. A real oddity: *M'appari tutt' Amor*, the tenor aria from Flotow's *Martha*, was recorded by Connie Boswell with Bob Crosby's Bob Cats. Part of the soundtrack of Walt Disney's first full length feature cartoon *Snow White and the Seven Dwarfs*, was issued by Victor as a three-disc set. Weingartner became **the first conductor to complete a recording of all nine Beethoven symphonies**, a project which began with No 6 in 1927 and was mainly undertaken between January 1933 and March 1938. Karajan made his first recording: Mozart: Overture *Le Nozze di Figaro*. Bruno Walter's concert performance of Bruckner's Symphony No 9 with the Vienna Philharmonic Orchestra on 16 January was recorded for commercial issue. He also started a studio recording of Act II of Wagner's *Die Walküre*, but the *Anschluss* forced him to flee to France, then to America, and the recording was completed by Bruno Seidler-Winkler and issued on ten 10in discs.

1939 **World War II began**
Despite the war (which brought issues such as *Kiss Me Goodnight, Sergeant Major* and *Colonel Bogey*), this was a boom time for discs. The following million sellers were issued: *Little Brown Jug*, *Moonlight Serenade*, and *In The Mood* (all Glenn Miller); *Over The Rainbow*

Tommy Dorsey, a best-selling band leader.

PICTORIAL PRESS LTD

(Judy Garland, from the film *The Wizard Of Oz*); *Body And Soul* (Coleman Hawkins); and *Lili Marlene* (Lale Anderson), **the first German disc to sell a million** and the only one to ignore sides during the war, becoming immensely popular also with Allied forces. Stokowski's coupling of Strauss's *Tales From The Vienna Woods/Blue Danube* also sold a million. *Drummin' Man* (Gene Krupa) and *At The Woodchopper's Ball* (Woody Herman) also entered the best selling lists.

1940 The record companies reported that their presses were working 24 hours a day keeping pace with the demand for 'swing' music. Among the best sellers: *Tuxedo Junction* (Gene Krupa), *In The Mood* (Joe Loss), and *I'll Never Smile*

Again (Tommy Dorsey). This last was 'No 1' in *Billboard*'s **first chart of top sellers** (20 July, 1940). First RAF Squadronnaires Band record released in June: *The Man Who Comes Around/ With The Wind And The Rain In Your Hair*. Excerpts issued from the London show *Haw-Haw* (with Bebe Daniels, Ben Lyon and Max Miller, opened 22 December, 1939). The show was a light-hearted skit on William Joyce ('Lord Haw-Haw'), the British traitor who broadcast messages from Germany.

1941 Swing and big band jazz continued to make money: *You Made Me Love You* and *By The Sleepy Lagoon* (Harry James); *Chattanooga Choo-Choo* (Glenn Miller); *Take The 'A' Train* (Duke Ellington); *Green Eyes* and

Tangerine (Jimmy Dorsey). Country and Western was also popular, with artists such as Ernest Tubb and Roy Acuff. First recording of Schoenberg's *Pierrot Lunaire* (American Columbia).

1942 Recording Embargo in the US (from 31 July)

The largest-selling record of all time was recorded, with sales in excess of 25 million at last count: *White Christmas*, sung by Bing Crosby. Glenn Miller received his first gold disc for one million sales of *Chattanooga Choo-Choo*. Spike Jones recorded his first million seller: *Der Führer's Face*.

1943 First recording of a complete Broadway musical: *Oklahoma*, with the original cast. **Frank Sinatra's first million seller**: *All Or Nothing At All*, re-issued after its first, unsuccessful, 1939 release. *Pistol Packin' Mama* recorded by Al Dexter and Bing Crosby.

1944 First best sellers for Perry Como (*Till The End Of Time*) and The Ink Spots (*Into Each Life Some Rain Must Fall*, featuring Ella Fitzgerald). *On The Sunny Side Of The Street* recorded by Tommy Dorsey. First recording after the musicians' recording strike was *Ave Maria* by Bach, arr Gounod.

Trends 1945–54

With the end of World War II came a totally unexpected and dramatic buoyancy in the record industry, most notably in America. It was a confident and optimistic time. With the return to normal manufacturing and trading conditions, the demand for records rocketed, and with it the demand for new talent. So prolific and diverse was this talent that it changed the 'pop' scene completely, a change that calls for a different approach in our repertoire chronicle. Attention had been focussed upon the popular music scene by the *Billboard* chart of best-selling records begun in 1940; this was joined on 15 March, 1945, by the *Billboard* chart of best-selling albums, No 1 that week being the *King Cole Trio* album. Incidentally, the word 'album', meaning a collection of related 78rpm

discs contained in a stout board folder, was transferred to the LP disc in America, this also being a collection of related items; in the UK, however, 'album' used for LPs still meant a collection of discs (eg: a boxed opera set), and since few popular issues were multiple-disc sets in the UK, the word fell out of use in lighter music circles. Since the mid-1960s, due to American influence, 'album' has been used increasingly in the UK to mean 'LP record', while continuing to mean 'set of LPs' to the classical collector. Similarly the word 'band', meaning a portion of music set off from the rest of the record side by rills, has given way almost entirely to the American 'track'. These examples illustrate how dependent became the UK upon America, not only for its best sellers but also for its terminology. Many of the details which follow reflect happenings in the American 'pop' scene, but generally, unless otherwise stated, what became popular in the US also sold well in the UK. It was a time dominated by American artists.

Films and Shows

In 1946, American Decca issued *The Jolson Story*, **the first multiple-disc 78rpm album to sell a million sets**. In time for Christmas 1947 the same company produced an album titled *Merry Christmas*, starring Bing Crosby. On two of its eight numbers he is joined by the Andrews Sisters. This was transferred to LP in 1948 (10in) and 1963 (12in, with four extra numbers) and went on to sell many millions of copies. It has been claimed as **the American record industry's top selling album**.

The LP disc, introduced by American Columbia in 1948, proved to be a natural format for the 'films and shows' album. **1949** saw the release of **the first original stage cast recordings**: Rodgers and Hammerstein's *Oklahoma* (Decca, transferred from the 1943 78s) and *South Pacific* (Columbia), both of which sold millions of copies in ensuing years. The silver screen, too, generated immense sales of discs: in February **1950** the film *Jolson Sings Again* (starring Larry Parks) stimulated interest in a 7in EP issued by American Decca later that year in which Jolson sang *Songs He Made Famous* (*Swanee*, *California, Here I Come*, *April Showers*, and *Rock-a-bye Your Baby*). This sold in excess of a million copies, as did the LP of the film soundtrack of *An American In Paris* (music by George Gershwin, with pianist Oscar Levant) issued by MGM in **1952**.

Many singles releases were actual soundtracks from, or re-recordings of numbers in, popular films. **The first major post-war instrumental success of this kind** was the recording by Anton Karas, zither, of *Harry Lime Theme* from Carol Reed's film *The Third Man*, issued in **1950** and selling some four million copies. Another example of the popular power of films was seen in **1945**, when the screen portrayed the story of composer Frederick Chopin in *A Song To Remember*. José Iturbi was the pianist on the soundtrack, and his recording of Chopin's *Polonaise in A flat*, released the same year, sold one million in two years. Perry Como based *Till The End Of Time* on the same music in **1945**, and the following year his *I'm Always Chasing Rainbows* was based on Chopin's *Fantaisie Impromptu in C sharp minor*. Both became immensely popular.

Big Bands

During the period under discussion the trend was firmly away from the big band sound that had been so popular in the 1930s and 40s. Only Woody Herman's *Laura* (from the film of that name) and two numbers by Stan Kenton (*Tampico*, and *Artistry In Rhythm*) achieved outstanding sales in 1945. Thereafter, the following attracted by such music was faithful but less numerous. Kenton's popularity continued until the mid-1950s but did not bring any spectacular sellers – only healthy ones.

The Ballad

To achieve a place in the charts, artists and record producers tried countless gimmicks in their attempts to attract a share of the money that seemed to be available in ever-increasing quantity for recorded entertainment. A host of styles jostled with each other for supremacy, but by far the most popular was the sentimental ballad. Only a few of the biggest hits of the era can be mentioned – enough, perhaps, to give the atmosphere of a time when the tender love song seemed to be everybody's favourite art form.

In **1945**, Bing Crosby recorded *I Can't Begin To Tell You*, Les Brown recorded *Sentimental Journey*, and Perry Como added to the success of *Till The End Of Time* with *Temptation*. In **1946** his second Chopin-based hit, *I'm Always Chasing Rainbows* was joined by *Prisoner Of Love*. Tony Martin and The Ink Spots both made successful versions of *To Each His Own*, and Al Jolson added *Rock-a-bye Your Baby*, *You Made Me Love You*, *Sonny Boy*, and *The Anniversary Song* to his formidable list of 'greats'.

Frankie Laine with *That's My Desire*, and Art Lund with *Mam'selle*, each registered their first really big hits in **1947**, the Andrews Sisters and several other artists recorded *Near You*, and Perry Como sang *When You Were Sweet Sixteen*. That same year Bing Crosby made an unlikely hit with the Yale University's *Whiffenpoof Song*, following it in **1948** with *Now Is The Hour* based on a Maori original. It didn't seem to matter what the man sang! Other top hits of 1948 included *A Tree In The Meadow* by Margaret Whiting, *Lazy River* by the Mills Bros, *It's Magic* by Doris Day, *Because* by Perry Como, *Blue Moon* by Billy Eckstine, *Shine* and *When You're Smiling* by Frankie Laine, and *Nature Boy* by Nat 'King' Cole. At this time, the autumn of 1948, the gramophone industry's old rival, radio, with which there had been an ambivalent relationship for many years, appeared to bury the hatchet for good and all. Radio Luxembourg's Sunday night 'Top Twenty' was **the first programme based on current selling strength**, and the additional air time further boosted sales.

Vic Damone's first hits appeared in **1949**: *Again* and *You're Breaking My Heart*; but the song of the year was *Cruising Down The River*, recorded by Russ Morgan and Blue Barron, among others. Bing Crosby scored again with *Dear Hearts And Gentle People*, and yet again, in **1950**, with the first duet he recorded with his son Gary: *Sam's Song*. The same year also saw

Mona Lisa by Nat 'King' Cole, *La Vie en Rose* by Edith Piaf, the *Tennessee Waltz* and *All My Love* by Patti Page, *Goodnight, Irene* by the Gordon Jenkins Orchestra, *Cry Of The Wild Geese* by Frankie Laine, and the successful bid by Mario Lanza, a tenor of operatic ability who had made many films, to enter the pop market with *Be My Love*. He repeated his success in **1951** with *The Loveliest Night Of The Year*.

The popularity of the sentimental ballad reached its peak in 1951. Four artists each had more than one hit in the charts (Frankie Laine with *Jezebel*, *Jalousie*, and *Rose, Rose, I Love You*; The Four Aces with *Tell Me Why* and *It's No Sin*; Tony Bennett with *Because of You* and *Cold, Cold Heart*; and Patti Page with no less than four best sellers: *Mockingbird Hill*, *Would I Love You*, *Detour*, and *Mister And Mississippi*), and there were single successes by other established artists: Doris Day with *A Guy Is A Guy*; Perry Como with *If*; Nat 'King' Cole with *Too Young*; and Billy Eckstine with *I Apologise*. *Any Time* was sung by a newcomer to the charts, Eddie Fisher.

Fisher achieved three more hits in **1952**: *Tell Me Why*, *Lady Of Spain*, and *Wish You Were Here*. Mario Lanza, too, maintained his popularity with *Because You're Mine*, and Perry Como maintained *his* with *Don't Let The Stars*. *Glow Worm* by the Mills Bros, and *High Noon* by Frankie Laine were hits. *Here In My Heart*, by Al Martino was No 1 **in the first UK chart of**

HALL OF FAME

Perry Como, vocalist

1913 18 May: Born Pierino Como, Canonsburg, Pennsylvania, in a house on Third Avenue (since renamed Perry Como Avenue).

1934 Joined Freddie Carlone's Band, touring with them for some 3 years as vocalist.

1936 Joined Ted Weems's Band, staying until 1942.

1943 Signed recording contract with Victor; also that year signed film contract with 20th Century Fox (7 years), but was released in 1947, having made a number of successful films, including *Something for the Boys*.

1945 Recorded his **first million seller**: *Till The End of Time*; also in that year he recorded *If I Loved You*, *A Hubba-Hubba-Hubba*, and *Temptation*, all of which reached one million sales, the first two simultaneously in 1946.

From 1946 to 1962 he maintained a stream of top sellers, including, in addition to those mentioned above: *I'm Always Chasing Rainbows* (1946), *When You Were Sweet Sixteen* (1947), *Because* (1948), *If* (1950), *Don't Let the Stars Get In Your Eyes* (1952), *Wanted* (1954), *Hot Diggity* (1956), *Round and Round* (1957), *Catch a Falling Star* (1958), *Delaware* (1960), and *Caterina* (1962). In addition to records, he is highly successful on radio and TV ('The Perry Como Show'). His record chart presence resumed in the early 1970s with *It's Impossible* (1971), *And I Love You So* (1973), and *I Want to Give* (1974).

THE NEW MUSICAL EXPRESS

Editorial and Advertisement Offices:

5, DENMARK STREET,
LONDON, W.C.2.

PHONE: TEMPLE BAR 0962/3.

EDITOR: RAY SONIN.

Assistant-Editor: JACK BAVERSTOCK.

Advertisement Manager:
PERCY C. DICKINS.

Announcing the first
RECORD HIT PARADE

FOR the first time in the history of the British popular music business, an authentic weekly survey of the best-selling " pop " records has been devised and instituted.

We are proud to have been able to launch this Record Hit Parade, which we know will be of the greatest interest and benefit to all our readers.

It would not have been possible to organise this without the willing co-operation of the largest gramophone record retailers, in all parts of the country, who are supplying us weekly with details of their biggest selling discs.

We express our great appreciation of their assistance.

(For Week ending November 8, 1952)

1. HERE IN MY HEART.
   Al Martino (Capitol).
2. YOU BELONG TO ME.
   Jo Stafford (Columbia).
3. SOMEWHERE ALONG THE WAY.
   Nat Cole (Capitol).
4. ISLE OF INNISFREE.
   Bing Crosby (Brunswick).
5. FEET UP. Guy Mitchell (Columbia).
6. HALF AS MUCH.
   Rosemary Clooney (Columbia).
7. FORGET-ME-NOT. Vera Lynn (Decca).
7. HIGH NOON Frankie Laine (Columbia).
8. SUGAR BUSH.
   Doris Day/F. Laine (Columbia).
8. BLUE TANGO Ray Martin (Columbia).
9. HOMING WALTZ. Vera Lynn (Decca).
10. AUF WIEDERSEHN.
    Vera Lynn (Decca).
11. COWPUNCHER'S CANTATA.
    Max Bygraves (HMV).
11. BECAUSE YOU'RE MINE.
    Mario Lanza (HMV).
12. WALKIN' MY BABY BACK HOME.
    Johnnie Ray (Columbia)

Reproduction in whole or in part is strictly forbidden unless specific permission is obtained. Copyright by the " New Musical Express," 1952.

The first UK singles chart. BY PERMISSION OF THE BRITISH LIBRARY

best-selling singles, published by *New Musical Express* on 14 November, 1952. The ladies, too, were active in 1952. The ubiquitous Patti Page sang *I Went To Your Wedding*, Rosemary Clooney sang *Tenderly* and *Half As Much*, and Jo Stafford sang *You Belong To Me*, and *Early Autumn* coupled with *Jambalaya*. Kay Starr's first million seller, *Wheel Of Fortune*, also appeared in 1952, as did Vera Lynn's, a surprising fact; one would have assumed her wartime songs would have achieved million-seller status. Her *Auf Weiderseh'n Sweetheart* was the first record by a British artist to head the hit parade on both sides of the Atlantic. In the same year she recorded *Yours* (based on the Latin American song *Quierme Mucho*), later to become her theme song.

Patti Page again topped the charts in 1953 with *(How Much Is) That Doggie In The Window* and *Changing Partners*. Apart from these, most of the honours went to the gentlemen ballad singers this year. Eddie Fisher sang *I'm Walking Behind You* and *Oh Mein Papa*, Frankie Laine sang *I Believe*, and Dean Martin's first big hit was *That's Amore*. Also successful this year were Tony Bennett's *Rags To Riches* and *Stranger In Paradise* (based on a theme from Borodin's *Polovtsian Dances*), Frank Sinatra's *Young At Heart*, and *Hi-Lili, Hi-Lo*, from the film *Lili*, starring Leslie Caron and Mel Ferrer.

Optimistic Songs

Alongside the sentimental ballad there was a whole series of cheerful up-beat numbers, amongst the most popular of which were *McNamara's Band* (Bing Crosby, 1946), *I'm Looking Over A Four-Leaf Clover* (Art Mooney, with Mike Pingatore, banjo, 1947), *Buttons And Bows* (Dinah Shore; the Dunning Sisters), *My Happiness* (The Pied Pipers; John and Sandra Steele), *Woody Woodpecker* (Kay Kyser), *Ooh, Look-a There, Ain't She Pretty* (Buddy Greco) and *Mañana* (Peggy Lee), all released in 1948. In 1949 came *I've Got A Lovely Bunch of Coconuts* (Billy Cotton; Freddy Martin), *Mule Train* and *That Lucky Old Sun* (Frankie Laine), and 1950 brought *Music, Music, Music* (Teresa Brewer's first big hit), *Hot Canary* (Florian Zabach, violin), *If I Knew You Were Coming I'd Have Baked A Cake* (Eileen Barton's first hit), and *Rag Mop* (the Ames Bros).

Guy Mitchell recorded two such numbers in **1951**: *The Roving Kind* and *My Truly, Truly Fair*, and Jo Stafford's *Shrimp Boats* and Rosemary Clooney's *Come On-a My House* were also very popular. In **1952** both Frankie Laine and Doris Day made successful versions of *Sugar Bush*, Don Howard sang *O Happy Day*, and Guy Mitchell followed his earlier up-beat hits with *Pittsburg, Pennsylvania*. The trend virtually disappeared in **1953**, with the possible exception of Dean Martin's *That's Amore* mentioned earlier; and Rosemary Clooney's *This Ole House* is apparently the only up-beat hit of **1954**. Thereafter, as far as fast, rhythmic numbers were concerned, the rock trend took over.

Novelty Numbers

Back in **1944**, Linley Armstrong Jones recorded his new version of *Cocktails For Two* and put that number for the first and only time into the million-seller league. It was in fact a novelty, not to say anarchic, version, for the artist called himself 'Spike' Jones, and his band The City Slickers. His musical antics had proved a runaway success during the war with *Der Führer's Face*, and now he brought his percussive games, vocal inanities and a wet brass sound to bear on popular ballads. His *Glow Worm* in **1946** also hit the million mark. One of his resident vocalists and violinist Ernest Jansen ('Red') Ingle formed his own gang, The Natural Seven, for the extremely popular *Tim-tayshun*, with vocal by Cinderella G Stump (alias Jo Stafford), a Wild West send-up of *Temptation*, in **1947**.

There were other novelty numbers at this time, among them *Open The Door, Richard*, recorded by many artists including Louis Jordon, Count Basie, and 'Dusty' Fletcher; and the partnership of Bing Crosby and Al Jolson, the only time they sang together on disc, created a memorable coupling of *Alexander's Ragtime Band* and *The Spaniard That Blighted My Life*. 'Red' Ingle returned in **1948** with *Cigareets And Whuskey and Wild, Wild Women*, and his former colleague 'Spike' Jones greeted the festive season with *All I Want For Christmas Is My Two Front Teeth*. Twelve months later, for Christmas **1949**, Harry Stewart, calling himself Yogi Yorgesson, made a hit in America with an unlikely Swedish skit called *I Yust Go Nuts At Christmas*, coupled with *Yingle Bells*.

Thereafter, nonsense and humorous songs continued to appear but entered the best-selling lists less readily. Phil Harris had made several recordings, the most successful being *The Thing* in **1950**, part of the appeal of which was that 'the thing' was identified only by a rum-ti-tum drum rhythm that refused to be dislodged from the memory.

Possibly the longest title for a popular song was *How Could You Believe Me When I Said I Loved You When You Know I've Been A Liar All My Life?*, sung by Fred Astaire and Jane Powell in the film *Wedding Bells* (original American title: *Royal Wedding*), released in **1951**. In **1952** appeared *It's In The Book* by Johnny Standley; and the equally hilarious *St George And the Dragonet* coupled with *Little Blue Riding Hood*, with Stan Freberg, came the next year. Both exceeded one million sales, the Freberg disc selling 400 000 in America in the first 6 days.

Significantly, CBS released a disc titled *Three Minutes of Silence* in **1953**. Apparently not all customers in drug stores and other establishments boasting the benefits of juke-box entertainment were equally appreciative of the noises that spilled forth; some were willing to part with a nickel just to secure a brief period of relative peace.

Country and Western

Country and Western music had an accelerating influence on the hit charts after the war, reaching a peak in **1951** along with the sentimental ballad. The following is a list of the top sellers of the period:

1945 *Guitar Boogie* Arthur Smith
1947 *It's A Sin*; *I'll Hold You in My Heart*
   Eddy Arnold

New Jole Blon Moon Mullican
Smoke, Smoke, Smoke That Cigarette
    Tex Williams
1948 *Bouquet of Roses/Texacarna Baby*; *Any*
    Time; *Just a Little Lovin'* Eddy Arnold
Tennessee Waltz Cowboy Copas
Humpty Dumpty Heart Hank Thompson
1949 *Lovesick Blues* Hank Williams
Candy Kisses George Morgan
I Never See Maggie Alone Ken Roberts
1950 *Long Gone Lonesome Blues*; *Moanin'*
    Blues Hank Williams
Shot Gun Boogie Tennessee Ernie Ford
I'm Movin' On Hank Snow
Chatanoogie Shoe-Shine Boy; *Just a*
    Closer Walk With Thee Red Foley
1951 *Peace in the Valley* Red Foley
Slow Poke Pee Wee King
On Top of Old Smokey The Weavers
Indian Love Call Slim Whitman
I Wanna Play House With You Eddy
    Arnold
Hey Good Lookin'; *Cold, Cold Heart*;
    Gamblin' Man Hank Williams
1952 *It Wasn't God Who Made Honky Tonk*
    Angels Kitty Wells
Your Cheatin' Heart; *Honky Tonk Blues*;
    Jambalaya; *I'll Never Get Out of this*
    World Alive Hank Williams
1953 *Mexican Joe*; *Bimbo* Jim Reeves
Crying in the Chapel Rex Allen
1954 *I Don't Hurt Anymore* Hank Snow
More and More Webb Pierce

Rhythm and Blues

From **1948** Rhythm and Blues became popular, particularly in America, in the wake of 'Fats' Domino's and Sonny Thompson's first hits, respectively *The Fat Man* and *Long Gone*. Joe Liggins, with *Pink Champagne*, and *I Gotta Right To Cry/Honeydripper*, Roy Brown with *Hard Luck Blues*, and Ivory Joe Hunter with *I Almost Lost my Mind*, all became popular in this field in **1950**, and were joined by Percy Mayfield with *Please Send Me Someone To Love*, and Joe Turner with *Chains Of Love* in **1951**. Lloyd Price entered the charts with *Lawdy, Miss Clawdy* in **1952**, but 'Fats' Domino

returned with *Goin' Home*, following it in **1953** with four immensely popular discs: *Going To The River*, *You Said You Loved Me*, *Please Don't Leave Me*, and *I Lived My Life*. In **1954** The Orioles achieved a hit with *Crying In The Chapel*. Although popular in the States with *Earth Angel* in 1954, the group called The Penguins did not make much impact in the UK. Neither, at that time, did Hank Ballard, whose *Annie Had A Baby* and *Work With Me, Annie*, both issued in 1954, achieved the magic million; in **1960**, however, Ballard promoted the new dance The Twist, which invaded dance halls everywhere.

Commercial Jazz, etc

There were other popular trends during these years, among them Dixieland Jazz (eg: *Twelfth Street Rag* by Pee Wee Hunt, **1948**), ragtime (eg: several discs by pianist Winifred Atwell, including *Black And White Rag*, **1952**, her best seller), and a series of genuine jazz numbers that, because they achieved spectacular popularity, were denigrated by purists as 'commercial jazz'. Among these latter were *Tomorrow Night* (**1948**) by guitarist Lonnie Johnson, *Hurry On Down/Fine Brown Frame* (1948) by black pianist and jazz singer Nellie Lutcher, *Les Oignons* (**1949**) by Sidney Bechet (saxophone and clarinet), *September In The Rain* (1949) with the George Shearing Quintet, and *Flamingo* (**1950**) by Earl Bostic. The Modern Jazz Quartet (MJQ) made its first recording in **1952**; this group was to lead the 'cool' modern jazz movement in subsequent years. The first of Capitol's *History of Jazz* LPs appeared in the US in 1950.

'New' Sounds

Latin American influences also occurred fitfully, such as the popular *Wedding Samba* (**1949**) by Edmundo Ros, Peggy Lee's *Lover* (**1952**) in mambo rhythm, and *Mambo Italiano* by Rosemary Clooney, and *Papa Loves Mambo* by Perry Como (both **1954**).

The most significant new sound, however, was the style of the singer Johnny Ray, whose *Cry*, coupled with *Little White Cloud That Cried*, and *Here Am I, Broken Hearted* brought

HALL OF FAME

'Fats' Domino, pianist, singer, songwriter *

1928 26 February: Born Antoine Domino in New Orleans.

c 1938 Taught himself to play the piano and supplied music for local bars in return for tips.

c 1943 Worked on the production line of a factory, where he damaged his hand and had to develop a new method of playing the piano.

c 1947 Hired by bandleader David Bartholomew as pianist. This led to Domino's **first recording** with Imperial records, *The Fat Man* (1948), which became a million seller by 1953.

1956–7 Given the title 'Rhythm and Blues Personality of the Year'.

1957 Appeared in the film *The Girl Can't Help It.*

1963 Signed contract with ABC Records; his Imperial records remained available. Since then he has continued as a popular rock 'n' roll/rhythm and blues artist, touring with his own group in concerts, dances and nightclubs, including regular appearances at Las Vegas's prestigious Flamingo Hotel.

c 1972 Signed recording contract with Warner/Reprise.

Between 1952 and 1960 he recorded at least one million seller each year (a total of 22), including *Goin' Home* (1952), *Going to the River* (1953), *Love Me* (1954), *Ain't That a Shame* (1955), *Blueberry Hill* (1956), *I'm Walkin'* (1957), *Whole Lotta Lovin'* (1958), *Be My Guest* (1959), and *Walkin' to New*

PICTORIAL PRESS LTD

Orleans (1960). In all, he sold over 60 million records by 1977, and remains a steady seller. His *Blueberry Hill* was re-issued in 1976 and once again entered the charts.

* 'Fats' Domino never learnt to write music. He sings his numbers onto a tape, and they are transcribed by David Bartholomew.

---

an emphatic heavy beat to the charts in **1951**. Arguably, it was this throbbing emphasis that brought about a revolution.

1954 was a momentous year for popular music, but it was not immediately apparent that a revolution was about to occur. The expected stars continued to hit the charts: Doris Day with *Secret Love*; Jo Stafford with *Make Love To Me*; Eddie Fisher with *I Need To Know*; 'Fats' Domino with *Love Me* and *Don't Leave Me This Way*; The Four Aces with *Three Coins In The*

Fountain and *Stranger In Paradise*; and the Ames Bros with *Naughty Lady Of Shady Lane*. Two newcomers to the top end of the charts also recorded in **1954**: Kitty Kallen with *Little Things Mean A Lot* and *In the Chapel In The Moonlight*, and tenor David Whitfield with *Cara Mia*.

Other newcomers in 1954 were Rudi Maugeri, Pat Barrett, Ray Perkins and Johnny Perkins, a Canadian group who called themselves The Crew Cuts. Their record of *Sh-Boom (Life Could Be A Dream)*, originally recorded by a black group called The Chords, was **the first rock 'n' roll hit**. It heralded a phenomenal upheaval in popular music.

Post-War Classical recordings

Outside the popular repertoire the immediate post-war years saw a gradual return to normal. Sadly, the American Foundation for the Blind found a new market in returning servicemen for their series of Talking Books, issued in **1946** on long playing discs revolving at $16\frac{2}{3}$rpm, while in Europe the German industry was re-emerging with renewed vigour and an exciting new project as if to erase the bitter memories of the war years. In **1947**, Deutsche Grammophon launched an extremely ambitious programme of recordings designated 'Archiv Produktion' to examine the history of early music from Gregorian Chant to c1800 (a period later extended in both directions). Amongst the first releases on 78rpm discs, were some Bach organ works and a Bach cantata, performed respectively by artists who were to become leading figures in the catalogues: Helmut Walcha and Dietrich Fischer-Dieskau. The Archiv series had its repertoire planned out with all the precision of a military operation: the history of music was divided into a series of eras, each further divided into musical genres (see Section IX, where Archiv's presentation is discussed). The intention was to bring familiar and unfamiliar music to records in performances as authentic as modern scholarship could make them. This meant that, as the series continued and scholarship made further progress, some works had to be re-recorded in the light of more recent musicological findings and the availability of more authentic instruments and artists to perform on them. Presentation, at first severely practical and informative, has undergone several changes over the years: the latest Archiv Produktion releases are as attractively packaged as any LP production on the market. This is a reflection of recent market pressures. At first, the Archiv Produktion image was apparently designed for the extreme snob end of the market: presentation was casual-customer-proof, promotion low key, and market penetra-

tion extremely limited in consequence. With the realisation that many fine recordings were thus hidden, DG began to exploit its Archiv catalogue, firstly with reissues on the Musique Royale label (**1969**), and later by slipping in Archiv material, some of it very old, into the mid-price DG Privilege label series.

While Archiv's repertoire coverage was unlimited within its historical span, HMV's *History of Music in Sound*, planned in tandem with *The Oxford History of Music* volumes (published by the Oxford University Press) and launched in **1953** with volumes II and III, is finite: ten volumes under the general editorship of Gerald Abraham, covering *Ancient and Oriental Music* (Volume I) to *Modern Music* (Volume X), each containing excerpts – complete works are rare – and each a once-for-all programme with no provision for extension in any direction. The series was completed in **1959** and ran to 228 78rpm sides, or 48 12in LP sides on 27 discs (six of which were single-sided).

The standard classical repertoire was comparatively well represented on disc in the years immediately after World War II. Earlier solecisms had largely disappeared: inconvenient formats and inartistic releases (in which, say, Mendelssohn's Violin Concerto, written with applause-proof links between movements to ensure the greatest possible unity, might be issued by one company with different artists playing different movements) were now rare, but the main drawback was the short playing time afforded by 78rpm discs. Only the shortest instrumental and orchestral pieces (up to about 4 minutes long), and isolated songs and arias, could be presented to the serious buyer without side breaks damaging the continuity of the music. However, once the standard concert works had been covered (to be continually, and often superfluously, renewed by fresh recordings), the companies began to turn their attention to items rarely, if ever, heard in the concert hall, and subsidiary and independent companies away from the main centres (but particularly in European countries) catered for both general and more local requirements. But although the catalogues seemed buoyant and the classical record held a small but reliable share of the market (boosted by issues such as Stravinsky's *Petrushka* conducted by Ansermet in **1946** in startlingly realistic Decca ffrr sound), the industry was holding its breath for the inevitable breakthrough in playing time.

It came at last in America in 1948 (see Section IX), and it brought with it not only a feeling of immense relief at the escape from the 4-minute side, but also a dramatic revolution in the availability of serious music. In the half-decade that followed, countless new record companies sprang up, each seeking a fair share of what quickly became a booming market by digging ever deeper into music archives and publishers' lists for unknown music by both famous and obscure composers. For example, in the field of Mozart's symphonies it was possible to obtain in the days of 78s most of the later works in many recordings, but coverage became thinner as one sought the symphonies of the middle period: by diligent scouring of domestic and foreign catalogues, Nos 28, 27, 26, 25, 24, 20, and 14 could be tracked down, but of the numerous earlier works, only one movement from Symphony No 13 was to be had on 78s anywhere in the world. After five years of LP, however, all the numbered and some of the unnumbered symphonies were available on microgroove in America while today, of course, it is possible to obtain even some of the earliest works in more than one recording, and when an unremarkable early work was rediscovered late in 1980 it was recorded, twice, as soon as a printed edition was made available.

In other areas of serious repertoire, too, long playing brought an amazing expansion. Those first 5 years saw the first complete recordings (on LP *only* – they were not offered in 78rpm format) of piano concertos by Prokofiev (Nos 1 and 2) and Rimsky-Korsakov, the Violin Concerto by Goldmark, Frank Martin's Concerto for Wind, Percussion, Timpani and Strings, Martinů's *Concerto Grosso* and his *Sinfonietta la Jolla*; symphonies by Bruckner (Nos 3 and 6), Dvořák (No 3 in E flat), Haydn (many early and middle-period works), Ives (No 3), Martinů (No 3), Mendelssohn (No 1 in C minor), and

Schubert (No 1); string quartets by Arriaga (Nos 1–3), Bliss (No 2), Mozart (K173), and Schoenberg (Nos 1–4); and choral works by Boismortier (the cantata *Diane et Actéon*), Haydn (*Cecilia Mass*, the *Mass in Time of War*, and the oratorio *The Seasons*), and Mahler's *Des Knaben Wunderhorn*. The most dramatic expansion occurred in operatic repertoire: Cimarosa's *Il Matrimonio Segreto*, Donizetti's *Il Campanello* and *La Fille du Regiment*, Haydn's *Orfeo ed Euridice*, Montemezzi's *L'Amore di Tre Re*, Mozart's *Apollo et Hyacinthus*, *La Finta Giardiniera* and *Der Schauspieldirektor*, Nicolai's *The Merry Wives of Windsor*, Pepusch's *The Beggar's Opera*, Puccini's *La Fanciulla del West* and *Suor Angelica*, Rossini's *Cenerentola*, Richard Strauss's *Elektra*, *Rosenkavalier* and *Salome*, Verdi's *I Lombardi*, and *Nabucco*, and Wagner's *Tristan und Isolde* all appeared complete for the first time on LP.

MOR (Middle of the Road)

Another important branch of repertoire is the light orchestral release which, along with films and shows, forms a major part of 'MOR'. Leroy Anderson's *Syncopated Clock*, and *Charmaine* and *Wyoming* by Mantovani were amongst the best sellers of **1951**; the latter's *Greensleeves* appeared the next year. In **1953**, the cinema provided two such hits: the theme from *Limelight* (written by Charles Chaplin and played by Frank Chacksfield and his Orchestra), and the song from *Moulin Rouge* (recorded by both Mantovani and Percy Faith). Mantovani's *Swedish Rhapsody*, based on the work of that name by the Swedish composer Hugo Alfvén, was popular the same year, and Eddie Calvert ('The Man With The Golden Trumpet') recorded his enormously successful *O Mein Papa*.

Rock 'n' Roll

The amazing pop record boom from the late 1940s was destined to be vastly exceeded and almost forgotten in a series of waves of new crazes and block-busting LP albums during the next two decades starting in the mid-1950s. During this period, all previous sales records

Bill Haley and His Comets at the Dominion Theatre, London, in 1957.   PICTORIAL PRESS LTD

were broken again and again on both sides of the Atlantic. **It was the healthiest period in the history of the record industry**. At first, America continued to lead the way, but in the 1960s the UK more than restored the balance. Rock 'n' Roll was the phrase that opened the floodgates.

The first world wide Rock 'n' Roll hit was *Rock Around The Clock* by Bill Haley and His Comets. Originally recorded on 12 April, 1954, it became a hit when it was played behind the credits of the film *The Blackboard Jungle*, released in **1955**. This number firmly launched the rock era world wide. Sales of this and related records reached phenomenal heights. *Rock Around The Clock* itself has been recorded in 35 different languages and its total sales exceed 22 million. Bill Haley's *Shake, Rattle and Roll*, recorded on the same day, was the second prong of an attack on the market that changed the industry.

An affluent record industry attracted many young artists, lured by an entry in the charts and its subsequent fame and riches; a plethora of artists in turn spawned new record companies, some of which produced independent hits, and inevitably the freely-flowing dollars and pounds encouraged unsavoury factors like the payola scandal, and drug abuse. The payola scandal

was a storm in a teacup surrounding the supposedly immoral passing of money to disc jockeys by record producers who wished their discs to receive a share of air-play time. Drug abuse, an infinitely more pernicious, and often fatal, by-product of the pop scene, came about partly through the impossibly severe schedules artists had to maintain to satisfy their affluent young fans: a 'shot' would stimulate them for a further appearance, and once circulating amongst the artists themselves, the drugs inevitably spread outwards to the fans.

As the following yearly chart unfolds the reader will find many new names in the popular arena. Such was the volume of numbers issued that only those which achieved multi-million sales can be included. The films and shows and classical markets also had their remarkable successes. The attractively-packaged LP album, which held its 1950 price level in an inflating world until the late 1960s, became a fast-selling commodity. Less successful commercially but still worthy of note were the many special products which became popular in an affluent industry.

1954 Elvis Presley made his first recording: *That's All Right Mama. The Glenn Miller Story*

HALL OF FAME

Elvis Presley, 'The King of Rock 'n' Roll'

1935 8 January: Born Elvis Aron Presley, in East Tupelo, Mississippi.

1954 6 July: Made **his first commercial recording**: *That's All Right Mama/Blue Moon Over Kentucky* (Sun Records).

1956 11 January: Recorded his **first gold disc**: *Heartbreak Hotel/I Was The One* (RCA). This was number one on the Country and Western, Rhythm and Blues, and Pop charts all at the same time in April 1956: **the first record to attain this hat-trick.** *Heartbreak Hotel* was the first of seven numbers recorded in 1956 to become million sellers.

1956 Made his **first film**: *Love Me Tender*.

1957 Recorded his **first million selling LP album**: *Elvis*.

1958 24 March: Entered the US Army at the height of his career.

1960 5 March: Demobbed, returning to make films exclusively and issue songs from them. **His first post-service film** was *G I Blues* (1960), the soundtrack from which became his 30th million selling disc.

1969 26 July: Returned to live performing at Las Vegas.

1973 14 January: Recorded his **first million selling quadraphonic album**, the songs from the TV spectacular *Aloha From Hawaii*, which was sent out via satellite all round the world.

From 1973 He continued giving successful concerts and made a few recordings in 1975–6 at his home.

1977 16 August: Died in Memphis at the age of 42.

Between 1956 and 1962, 31 of RCA's 39 million sellers were by Presley. **His biggest selling disc**, *It's Now Or Never* (1960), has

sales well in excess of 20 million world wide. Between 1961 and 1970 he recorded another 35 million sellers, including *Can't Help Falling In Love* (1961), *Return to Sender* (1962), *Bossa Nova Baby* (1963), *Kissin' Cousins* (1964), *Crying in the Chapel* (1965), *Love Letters* (1966), *Indescribably Blue* (1967), *If I Can Dream* (1968), *Suspicious Minds* (1969), and *The Wonder of You* (1970).

The most awards to an individual have gone to Presley: 38, spanning 1958 to May 1981. He has made an estimated 80 singles selling one million copies world wide. He also made 31 feature and 2 documentary films.

10in LP released. (The 12in version followed in 1956.) Record of the Month Club founded in London by bandleader Lou Praeger to make outstanding American and British jazz artists' recordings available on a regular basis. First release: Frank Wess Quintet.

1955 Chuck Berry: *Maybelline*. Pat Boone: *Ain't That A Shame*. Little Richard: *Tutti Frutti*. The

Platters: *Only You*. Lonnie Donegan's *Rock Island Line*, originally released on LP in 1954, reached the top ten in both America and the UK. This single was the start of the skiffle craze. A subscription recording scheme was projected by the International Music Council with the assistance of UNESCO. The plan was to advance the recorded repertoire along three

HALL OF FAME

Andy Williams, vocalist

1928 3 December: Born Howard Andrew Williams in Wall Lake, Iowa. He first sang with his three brothers and parents in the church choir, later singing in their own radio shows.

1944 The Williams Brothers made their first recording as a backing group to Bing Crosby's *Swinging on a Star* (US Decca).

1946–52 The brothers teamed up with comedian Kay Thompson as a nightclub act.

1952 Andy Williams started out on a solo singing career; appeared in his own spot on Steve Allen's *Tonight* show until 1955.

1957 23 January: Recorded **first million seller**: *Butterfly* (Cadence Records).

1959 Won 'Personality of the Year' Award. Starred in his own TV series (CBS).

1961 Signed recording contract with US Columbia.

1963 Made **his first million selling LP**: *Moon River and Other Great Movie Themes*.

1964 Made his **first film**: *I'd Rather Be Rich*.

By 1970 he had achieved 13 golden discs. There followed many more top sellers including *Can't Help Falling in Love* (1970), *Home*

PICTORIAL PRESS LTD

Lovin' Man (1970), *Love Story* (1971), and *Solitaire* (1973). His popularity continues as a TV celebrity.

---

fronts: (1) an international anthology of contemporary music; (2) a world collection of recorded folk music; (3) contemporary musical experiments. The recordings were to be made in France by Ducretet Thompson. The organisation of this scheme was taken over by the National Music Committee in March 1956.

1956 Elvis Presley: *Heartbreak Hotel*. Chuck Berry: *Roll Over Beethoven*. Gene Vincent: *Be-Bop-a-Lula*. Tommy Steele: *Rock With The Cavemen*, and *Singing The Blues*, the latter establishing him as **Britain's No 1 rock 'n' roll star**. Tony Crombie and His Rockets: *Teach Me To Rock*. Johnny Mathis: *Wonderful, Wonderful*. Harry Belafonte: *Calypso* (LP). *My Fair Lady*, the original stage cast LP, released in April. It eventually sold over six million. *High Society* and *The King And I* film soundtrack LPs. Johnny Cash: *I Walk The Line*. A renewal of interest in the inter-war dance band style was

created by recordings of the Paul Weston and Les Elgart bands. Tchaikovsky's Overture *1812* recorded as a hi-fi spectacular by Antal Doráti and the Minneapolis Symphony Orchestra, complete with cannon and bells.

1957 Paul Anka: *Diana*. Anka sold over 40 million records by 1970. Eddie Cochran: *Sittin' In The Balcony*. The Crickets with Buddy Holly: *That'll Be The Day*. Everly Bros: *Bye Bye Love*. Andy Williams: *Butterfly*. Jimmy Rodgers: *Honeycomb*. *West Side Story* original stage cast (LP). *What Is Jazz?*, an illustrated talk by Leonard Bernstein. *The History of Jazz*, Vol 1: *N'Orleans Origins*, the first of a series of four discs. *The Play of Daniel*, a 12th-century music drama (or proto-opera), an important 'early music' release in the US (released in the UK in 1959). Beethoven's *Choral* Symphony ($64\frac{1}{2}$ minutes in this performance) **issued for the first time on one LP** by Vox (conducted by Jascha

KO-KO.
"THE MIKADO."

YUM-YUM.
"THE MIKADO."

THE MIKADO OF JAPAN.
"THE MIKADO."

KATISHA.
"THE MIKADO."

NANKI-POO.
"THE MIKADO."

POOH BAH.
"THE MIKADO."

PLATES 8–13 (Top and left) *These cigarette cards depicting characters from* The Mikado *date from before 1926, when Gilbert and Sullivan records were amongst the most popular of the pre-electric era* BBC HULTON PICTURE LIBRARY

PLATE 14 (Below right) *Multi-company catalogues from France, Germany, Italy, America and the UK. Decca's diminutive Music Guides are also represented* PHOTO: LES PRUDDEN

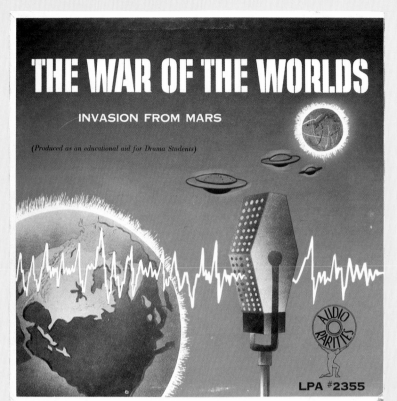

PLATE 15 *The sleeve of the LP issue of H G Wells's sci-fi novel, as adapted by Orson Welles for the radio. See page 168*

PLATE 16 *Sir Winston Churchill was the most prolific of all recording politicians*
DECCA RECORDS

PLATE 17 *Danny Kaye's charming 1940s stories for children retain their popularity on long playing records*
MUSIC FOR PLEASURE

PLATES 18–20 *The BBC's catalogue of sound effects discs is the biggest and most diverse in the world. It ranges from the eerie and futuristic (above) and homely (below) to the experimental (right)*
BBC RECORDS

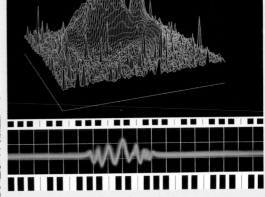

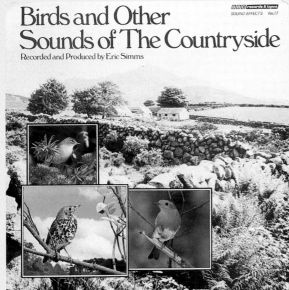

PLATE 21 *A Musical souvenir of America, issued to mark the bi-centenary of the United States*
WALT DISNEY PRODUCTIONS

PLATE 22 *Inside a small modern talks recording studio in London. Equipment in use includes a Neve mixing desk, a Studer tape recorder, and a Neumann microphone*
P THOMPSON

PLATE 23 (Below left) *A compact disc, the most perfect sound-carrier yet invented*
PHOTO: LES PRUDDEN

PLATE 24 (Below) *Elton John in the studio listening to a play-back of* Blue Moves. *Front left: Elton John; Front right: Freddie Mercury (Queen); Back left: John Reid, Elton John's manager; Back right: Gerry Collins of Marquee Studios; Background: Phil Dunn, engineer*
PICTORIAL PRESS

Horenstein).

1958 Connie Francis: *Who's Sorry Now?* Bobby Darin: *Splish Splash.* Kingston Trio: *Tom Dooley. Peter Gunn,* **the first million-selling TV soundtrack LP.** *The Music Man* original stage cast LP. *South Pacific* film soundtrack LP, which sold over five million by 1966. *My Fair Lady,* **the first LP to sell a million.** First *Sing Along With Mitch Miller* LPs. *Satchmo – A Musical Autobiography,* four LPs of mainly new recordings of his numbers from the 'Hot Five' of 1925 to date. *Dazzling Jazz:* three LPs titled 'Traditional (1926–56)', 'Big Sound (1939–56)' and 'Modern (1956)', played by many well-known names. *The Immortal Charlie Parker:* recordings made between 1944 and 1948, some issued for the first time: five LPs. Tchaikovsky's Piano Concerto No 1, played by Van Cliburn, winner of the First Prize in the First International Tchaikovsky Competition in April 1958. His studio recording made in America became **the world's top-selling classical LP,** selling two million by 1965.

1959 Chubby Checker: *The Twist.* Ray Charles: *What'd I Say?* Cliff Richard: *Living Doll. Persuasive Percussion* LP by the Enoch Light Orchestra. *60 Years Of Music America Loves Best,* two LPs of the most popular classics and pops. Chris Barber and his Jazz Band, with Monty Sunshine, clarinet: *Petite Fleur. Das Rheingold,* conducted by Solti, the first in the Decca/London complete *Ring* cycle. *Siegfried* appeared in 1963; *Götterdämmerung* in 1965, and *Die Walküre* in 1966. *Glyndebourne – Memories of the First 25 Years,* a commemorative issue featuring various artists.

1960 Rolf Harris: *Tie Me Kangaroo Down, Sport.* Roy Orbison: *Only the Lonely.* Ferrante and Teicher: Theme from *The Apartment; Exodus. Sound of Music* LP: original stage cast. *Spirituals To Swing,* two LPs of Carnegie Hall concerts by Benny Goodman, Count Basie and Big Bill Broonzy. *Paul Robeson At Carnegie Hall,* his 60th birthday appearance on 9 May, 1958.

1961 Nana Mouskouri: *The White Rose Of Athens. Judy Garland at Carnegie Hall* (double album). *West Side Story,* film soundtrack. Dave Brubeck: *Take Five.* Kenny Ball and his Jazzband: *Midnight In Moscow. Thesaurus of Classic Jazz:* four LPs (transferred from 78s) featuring Miff Mole, Joe Venuti, and the Dorsey Bros. *A Beecham Anthology,* two LPs to mark his death, selected from recordings made between 1915 and 1958. *Dame Nellie Melba:* a selection of recordings (mostly from 1904) to mark the centenary of her birth. **The first recording consisting entirely of serious music by New Zealand composers:** a mono disc (Kiwi label) of works by Heenan, Pruden and Ritchie. Electrola (Germany) commenced its *Music in Old Towns and Residences* series, mainly of 18th century music from royal courts and musical establishments. The initial six-LP release was centred on Düsseldorf, Eisenstadt, Hamburg, Mannheim, Potsdam, and Salzburg.

1962 The Tornados: *Telstar.* The Beatles: *Love Me Do,* **their first British hit parade entry** (see Hall of Fame). Herb Alpert: *The Lonely Bull. Peter, Paul and Mary* LP. *Jazz Sounds of the Twenties:* King Oliver, Clarence Williams, ODJB, etc. Subscription series started for classical sets by German DGG: large boxed sets initially issued at bargain prices, reverting to standard price after a predetermined period. HMV issued two LPs of music by Delius to commemorate his centenary: re-issued post-war Beecham recordings. Pathé (France) issued three 3-disc volumes of early vocal recordings: *L'Age d'or de La Scala de Milan; L'Age d'or de l'Opéra;* and *L'Age d'or de l'Opéra Comique.*

1963 The Beach Boys: *Surfin' USA; Be True To Your School; Surfer Girl.* The Beatles: *I Want To Hold Your Hand,* their first US million-seller. Rolling Stones: *Come On,* their first recording. *International All-Star Festival,* with profits to the United Nations Commission for Refugees: advertised as 'The greatest ever 12in LP for the Greatest ever Cause', Louis Armstrong, Bing Crosby, Doris Day, Ella Fitzgerald, Nana Mouskouri, Caterina Valente and many others were released from contract to record a song new to them, giving their services free. Pressed and distributed at cost, the LP was sold in the UK for £1. Countless records issued of the new *Bossa Nova* dance craze. Britten's

HALL OF FAME

The Beatles, singing group
George Harrison (born 1943)
John Winston (later **John Ono**) **Lennon** (1940–80)
(James) Paul McCartney (born 1942)
Ringo Starr (**Richard Starkey**) (born 1940)

1956 McCartney, Lennon and Harrison formed the skiffle group 'The Quarrymen'.
1961 **Made their first recording** as 'The Beat Brothers', for Polydor in Hamburg, with vocalist Tony Sheridan, guitarist Stuart Sutcliffe, and drummer Pete Best: *My Bonny/ When the Saints Go Marching In.* This sold over one million by 1964.
1962 Re-formed as 'The Beatles' after the death of Sutcliffe, the departure of Sheridan, and the replacement of Best by Ringo Starr.
1962 Signed exclusive contract with EMI. First disc: *Love Me Do/PS I Love You* (Parlophone).
1962 17 October: Made **TV début** on Granada TV, England.
1963 April: **First gold disc awarded** for one million sales of *She Loves You.*
1963 30 December: Capitol released their **first million selling single in America**: *I Want to Hold Your Hand*; it had sold over one million copies by mid-January 1964.
1964 February: Visited America; the release of the LP *Meet the Beatles* was made to coincide with their arrival and sold three million by the end of March. Made their **American**

TV début on the Ed Sullivan Show.
1964 Recorded *Can't Buy Me Love*, **the first record to achieve one million UK sales** (ie: firm orders) *before* release. In America the same disc achieved 2 100 000 advance sales. On 31 March that year the Beatles monopolised the American charts:

Singles:
No 1 *Twist and Shout*
No 2 *Can't Buy Me Love*
No 3 *She Loves You*
No 4 *I Want to Hold Your Hand*
No 5 *Please Please Me*

Long Playing Albums:
No 1 *Meet the Beatles*
No 2 *Introducing the Beatles*

1964 Made their **first film**: *A Hard Day's Night.*
1965 All four Beatles were individually awarded the MBE, an honour later rejected by Lennon. Made their second film: *Help!*
1966 August: Gave their last stage performance in San Francisco.
1967 June: The LP *Sergeant Pepper's Lonely Hearts Club Band* released in America and the UK. This sold seven million copies in a decade.
1968 The release *The Beatles*, a double-LP album, sold two million in the first week.
1968 The Beatles formed their own record company: Apple.
1968 Produced, directed and appeared in

War Requiem, conducted by the composer. Mozart's complete wind music – first recording. *Music From Mathematics*, performed by an IBM 7090 computer and Digital-to-Sound Transducer and produced by the Bell Telephone Laboratory scientists. The label politely acknowledged our forbearance with the legend 'Thanks for listening'.
1964 The Animals: *House Of The Rising Sun.* Rolling Stones: *It's All Over Now.* Cilla Black: *Any One Who Had A Heart.* Louis Armstrong: *Hello Dolly*, his first million seller. *Fiddler On The Roof*, original stage cast. *Goldfinger*, film soundtrack. *My Fair Lady*, film soundtrack. *Mary Poppins*, film soundtrack. *Jazz In The*

Making, Vol 2: *The Swing Era (1933–40). Jazz Odyssey*, Vol 1: *The Sound Of New Orleans (1917–47).* American Columbia's 1903 'Grand Opera Series' issued on two LPs. Mozart's Marches and Dances: first complete recording begun. DGG's Subscription series (Brahms) issued in the UK.
1965 The Beatles: *Yesterday*, the tune that became **the most recorded song**. Bob Dylan: *Like A Rolling Stone.* Tom Jones: *It's Not Unusual. Sound Of Music*, film soundtrack. *The Original Sound Of The Twenties*, a three-LP series of popular and jazz re-issues. EMI (UK) commenced its 'Music Today' series of modern serious music with the support of the Calouste

LFI

their first TV film: *Magical Mystery Tour*.
1969 Recorded their last hit single as a group: *The Ballad of John and Yoko*.
1969 Recorded their last LP, *Abbey Road*; *Let it Be*, recorded earlier, was issued in 1970.

The Beatles were **the most successful recording group of all time**, with estimated sales to 1980 of over 100 million singles and 100 million LPs.

After the Beatles disbanded in 1970, Paul McCartney went on to form the extremely successful group 'Wings' (with his wife Linda and others), being awarded by *The Guinness Book of Records* a unique rhodium disc on 24 October, 1979 as **the most successful songwriter of all time**. Wings's *Mull of Kintyre* (released November 1977) was **the first single to sell over two million copies in the UK**.

The other ex-Beatles have also pursued successful independent recording careers, that of John Lennon being terminated by an assassin's bullet on 8 December, 1980.

Gulbenkian Foundation: first issue: Gerhard's Symphony No 1/Dances from *Don Quixote*. Four LPs of music by Schoenberg. Two unusual marketing ideas: Bach's Keyboard Concertos Nos 1 and 5 and the *Italian* Concerto, played respectively by Frank Pelleg, harpsichord, and Mindru Katz, piano, issued simultaneously on two discs (Pye, UK). Beethoven's *Hammerklavier* Sonata played by Louis Kentner (issued by Saga in the UK at only 50p), pressed in an unconventional disc layout in which side one contained movements four and one, and side two movements two and three, thus accommodating the long Adagio third movement (19 minutes) without interruption. Hawaiian, Samoan and Cook Islands vocal and instrumental music introduced to the UK market for substantially the first time (Viking imports).
1966 Nancy Sinatra: *These Boots Are Made For Walkin'*. Donovan: *Sunshine Superman*, his first million seller. The Mamas and The Papas: *Monday Monday*. The Monkees: (TV group): *Last Train To Clarksville*. Decca (UK) completed the issue of **the first integral recording of Wagner's *The Ring*** (see 1959). *Westminster Abbey 1065–1965*: The 900th Anniversary Service, including the *Ceremonial Prelude* specially composed by Sir Arthur Bliss for the occasion.
1967 The Beatles: *Sergeant Pepper's Lonely*

Hearts Club Band, which sold seven million in ten years. Engelbert Humperdinck: *Release Me*. Sandie Shaw: *Puppet On A String,* Eurovision Song Contest winner. Bee Gees: *New York Mining Disaster 1941*, their first million seller. Dolly Parton: *Dumb Blonde*. Three important issues in the Jazz Music Society: *Blue Guitars* (Eddie Lang and Lonnie Johnson); *Luis Russell* (from electrically-recorded OKeh 78s); King Oliver's Jazz Band (also from OKeh originals). *Wuthering Heights*, opera by Bernard Herrmann (4 LPs). *West Meets East*, a musical collaboration between Yehudi Menuhin and Ravi Shankar.

1968 The Beatles, **the fastest-selling UK LP**, which sold two million in its first week. *Hair*, original stage cast. Tammy Wynette: *Stand By Your Man*, **the biggest-selling C & W disc by a female artist**. *Switched-On Bach*, synthesised by Walter Carlos. *Music of the Court Homes and Cities of England* (six volumes). First recording of Busoni's massive Piano Concerto, played by John Ogdon. Decca (UK) launched a complete recording of all of Mozart's Serenades.

1969 Lulu: *Boom Bang-a-Bang*, Eurovision Song Contest Winner. Jackson Five: *I Want You Back*. The Who: *Tommy* (double album). Several hit albums issued by Credence Clearwater Revival (also four singles) and Led Zeppelin. *Easy Rider*, film soundtrack. *World Star Festival* LP, to raise funds for the United Nations. Caruso's 1904–6 US recordings reissued. *Pli Selon Pli* by Boulez, conducted by the composer.

1970 Elton John: *Your Song*, his first million seller. *Jesus Christ, Superstar* (double album). *Three Decades of Jazz* (1939–69): recordings by Sidney Bechet, Earl Hines, Miles Davis, John Coltrane, Ornette Coleman and Eric Dolphy. *The Raft of the Medusa*, oratorio by Hans Werner Henze. DG issued their *Beethoven Edition 1970*: 12 multi-disc boxed sets of new and re-issued material totalling 74 12in discs, commemorating Beethoven's bicentenary. Much of this 'Edition' reappeared, repackaged, in 1977 to mark the 150th anniversary of his death.

1971 The Osmonds: *One Bad Apple*, their first

hit. Paul McCartney: *Another Day*, his first post-Beatle hit. Rod Stewart: *Every Picture Tells A Story*, LP. John Denver: *Take Me Home Country Roads*. Electrola began a series of medieval music: 50 records had been issued by 1980. In April, HMV (UK) in association with the British Institute of Recorded Sound, announced plans to issue vinyl pressings of certain 'golden age' vocals from the 78rpm shells. A minimum of 500 copies each of four 10in and 16 12in discs would be pressed if sufficient advance orders were obtained. This quantity had been comfortably exceeded on all titles by October.

1972 Donny Osmond: *Puppy Love*; *Too Young*; *Why?* Tommy (Rock Opera) LP. *Amazing Grace*, by the Scots Dragoon Guards. Two retrospective jazz issues by publishing companies: Readers' Digest: *Kings Of Swing*: six discs, 72 tracks by 32 bands. Time-Life: *The Swing Era*, stereo reconstructions of popular numbers of 1941–2 as played by Glenn Miller and others. The series was extended during 1973–4 to cover 1930–6 (numbers made famous by Benny Goodman and others), 1936–7 (Tommy Dorsey), 1939–40 (Duke Ellington), and 1942–4 (Harry James). *Twenty-Five Years at the Aldeburgh Festival*, two disc commemorative issue.

1973 Pink Floyd: *Dark Side Of The Moon* album. *American Graffiti*, film soundtrack (double album). *The Golden Years of Disney*, recorded excerpts from the films to mark Walt Disney Productions' 50th anniversary. Fats Waller: the first in a projected re-issue of all his recordings. Festival Records issued ten discs of music by modern Australian composers, **the largest project of this type to date in Australia**. *A Voice to Remember* (EMI), a package of two discs and a 64-page book marking 75 years of commercial recording. Alistair Cooke introduced 53 archive recordings including *Comin' Thro' The Rye*, The Gramophone Co's very first recording (1898). *The Grand Tradition – Seventy* (sic) *Years Of Singing* (HMV), reissues from Caruso (1902) to Flagstadt (1952).

1974 Abba: *Waterloo*, Eurovision Song Contest winner. *The Sting*, film soundtrack. The

Norwegian Cultural Council began a series of recordings of Norwegian serious music. A five-disc set of historical recordings (DG) included Nikisch's pioneering version of Beethoven's Symphony No 5. EMI issued a disc of musical boxes and Parisian street and barrel organs from the John Tagger Collection.

1975 Bay City Rollers' first million selling album. *Tommy*, film soundtrack. *Herb Alpert And His Friends*, a nine-disc Readers' Digest re-issue. The Dutch Swing College Band, a double album of 27 years' recordings by Europe's longest-lived jazz band. Dave Brubeck double album of 1956–65 re-issued. Art Tatum, a 13-disc set of 121 titles from December 1953 to January 1955, made at four marathon sessions.

1976 The Brotherhood of Man: *Save Your Kisses For Me*, Eurovision Song Contest winner. Wings: *Wings Over America*, three-album set. The Sex Pistols: *Anarchy In The UK*, **the first 'punk' hit**. *A Star Is Born*, film soundtrack. *Jaws*, film soundtrack. Classical re-issues: a two-disc set (DG) to mark the centenary of the Bayreuth Festival; Delius, a five-disc set (World Records) of Beecham's inter-war recordings with a reprint of Beecham's book *Frederick Delius*; *The Art of Maria Callas*, four-disc HMV set; *Dame Nellie Melba – The London Recordings (1904–26)*, a five-disc set (HMV).

1977 First Digital Recordings made in the US Bee Gees: *Saturday Night Fever*, film soundtrack, **the biggest-selling double album world wide**. Wings: *Mull of Kintyre*, **the first single to sell two million in the UK**. *Evita*, London stage production, double album. *Star Wars*, film soundtrack, double album. *The Golden Age Of British Dance Bands, 1925–39*, a six-disc mono set (World Records), including a further record of American bands: *Bands Across the Sea*. *50 Years Of Jazz Guitar (1921–71)*, double album. Decca's 'Vintage' Series offered four nostalgic items: Lew Stone (1932–9); Ambrose (1933–7); Maurice Winnick (1937–8); and Anne Shelton (1940–6).

1978 Home Taping Seriously Threatens the Record Industry Boney M: *Rivers Of Babylon/Brown Girl In*

The Ring. John Travolta and Olivia Newton-John: *You're The One That I Want*. *Grease*, film soundtrack, double album. *Annie*, original London cast. *The Record of Singing*, a 12-disc HMV set of pre-1914 recordings.

1979 Start of World Recession; Record Sales Dramatically Reduced, especially 'singles' Village People: *YMCA*. Blondie: *Sunday Girl* and *Heart Of Glass*. Police: *Message In A Bottle* and *Walking On The Moon*. Art Garfunkel: *Bright Eyes* (theme from film *Watership Down*). 'Classical Singles', a series of 45rpm stereo 7in discs, with fragments of popular classics against a thumping rock beat. *The Art of John McCormack, 1904–28)*, six discs (Pearl). *New Year's Day Concert*, recorded 1 January and issued in April as **the first digital recording on conventional discs** (double album).

The 1980s

The beginning of the 1980s has been a tragic time for the record industry. The bubble has burst. Several factors have combined to produce a slump in sales so damaging that shops are fighting desperately to stay in business and record companies are trimming their costs drastically and 'rationalising' their activities, which in some cases means merging with other companies.

First signs of this slump were seen in the mid-1970s. After the boom times of Elvis Presley and the Beatles, the steam went out of the singles market and companies concentrated on the LP album which, being more expensive, automatically drove away the small but numerous contributions of less pecunious buyers. Not content with extorting an LP price from the customer, companies turned to the indivisible double album, squeezing yet more money out of every purchase. For a time this worked well; several block-busting double albums appeared and faithful buyers in their millions dug deeply into well-filled pockets to purchase them.

The world recession has emptied those pockets; high unemployment figures mean less money for everyone, and luxury items like

The Guinness Book of Recorded Sound

gramophone records are amongst the first things to be crossed off pared-down shopping lists. Consequently, the sales records set up in the 1970s stand secure, and another damaging factor is ensuring that they will remain unchallenged, for no new releases will really sell while each copy sold is subjected to illicit cassette copying by perhaps as many as a dozen individuals. In Section V, the convenience of modern cassette recording is discussed. It has never been easier to indulge in undetectable flouting of copyright laws by collectors understandably intent upon saving money by copying commercial recordings for their own use, but it will lead in only one direction: to the total collapse of the recorded music industry. All branches of the industry are at risk; at the time of writing apparently no-one has the answer to this problem. Perhaps it lies in the promised technical advances offered by the laser-tracked compact disc, whose quality should be so high that no cassette tape formulation will be a match for it.

The world recession and home taping are two of the causes of the present malady. Another is that the popular market has lost its sense of direction, and until a new figure comes along who can set a new trend the industry will continue to flounder around amongst a dozen idioms that move closer to each other with every passing fad.

An unbecoming greed has led into a vicious circle. Aware of the collapsing market, artists, agents, publishers, copyright-holders, and the record industry itself all demand larger slices of the diminishing cake, anxious that their nests should be adequately feathered when the collapse is complete. This leads inevitably to higher prices in the shops, thence to lower sales, and, of course, to smaller profits for everyone.

Meanwhile, record companies insistent upon grabbing the last atom of profit from a dwindling market, are driven back onto tried and tested formulae. Nostalgia is 'in': the huge sets of dance music and jazz from earlier decades (see the late-1970s in the chart above), together with classical re-issues on an unprecedented scale, indicate that the industry, in its anguish,

has entered its second childhood.

The serious music side of the business has not escaped from the general decline; but for a stroke of good fortune it might be even worse off than it is.

The unprecedented expansion in classical recorded repertoire up to about 1960 was followed by a decade of consolidation. Public taste had widened but was still within well-defined limits; if these limits were exceeded at all it was by an infinitesimal amount as the industry sought 'new' sounds in eccentric and unconventional music, not much of which captured the imagination in the money-spinning way the industry had hoped. At the start of the 1970s there were signs of crystallisation in public taste, and the recorded repertoire narrowed, only a few of the earlier gains being substantiated. The 1960s had experienced a move towards 'complete' editions, begun in the mid-1950s when, for example, baroque concertos were recorded in dozens rather than singly. The 'subscription' series, first launched by DG with Karajan's complete recording of Brahms's symphonies, *St Anthony Variations*, Violin Concerto, and *German Requiem* (seven discs at a UK discount of 50p per record; later issued separately at full price) encouraged this habit of bulk buying, and 'integral' editions became common. Other European companies quickly copied DG's subscription idea (also called 'limited editions', the limit being upon the length of time the sets were offered at a reduced price), and a great deal of money was spent on vast recording projects. The subscription concept lost its impetus and eventually died after the abandonment of retail price maintenance in the UK in July 1969.

At the start of the 1970s, the UK and US markets together offered only one complete Wagner *Ring* cycle, no integral recording of Haydn's symphonies, and two recordings of Mahler's titanic Symphony No 8. A decade later these works were represented respectively by five, two, and six complete recordings. (The Haydn Symphonies project by Decca is reported to have taken 281 recording sessions and 350 miles of tape, making it **the largest**

complete musical recording project to date.)

In the 1970s attempts were made to widen the repertoire with carefully selected 'relations' of tried and proved repertoire: unnumbered symphonies by Schumann and Mendelssohn, for instance, piano concertos of the romantic school *not* actually by Tchaikovsky or Grieg, and works not only by Mozart's father but also by his son. These obscure items rarely offered top quality music and did not make a good showing at the tills, so yet again the 'standard classics' edifice had to be repeatedly repainted in different shades by younger artists, driving the classical market into a rut.

A new phrase entered the vocabulary of advertising copywriters and by good luck caught the classical customer's attention: 'authentic instruments'. Select groups of professors had been playing esoteric music for years on strange old instruments, apparently unnoticed by the majority of record buyers, but now there emerged a breed of young artists who had been taught how to handle period instruments and copies of them, and an active army of musicologists supported them with information about early performance practices and a widening repertoire of available music. Very often, musicologist and performer were one and the same.

Arguably the greatest populariser of early music was the Englishman David Munrow (1942–76) who, through his artistry on many instruments and his engaging way of introducing them in his TV programmes, stimulated interest in the 'new' sounds of serpent, crumhorn, Garkleinflötlein, and the like. This interest spread inevitably to the standard repertoire: the symphonies of Haydn, Mozart and Beethoven are all being subjected to the attentions of the authentic instrument promoters, and with the favourable response of buyers the trend is sure to spread. It would be ironic if early music, pioneered on authentic instruments in a minute way by Eugène Arnold Dolmetsch (1858–1940), during the 1920s (he founded the Haslemere Festival in 1925) brings about a large-scale renaissance of the classical market not only in sound but also in sales.

After its entertainment value, the most important function of the record industry is as the preserver of historically significant and interesting documentary sounds. If a sound is known to man, it is almost inevitable that some enthusiast somewhere has recorded it. From the heartbeats of an unborn child to the ultrasonic radar squeaks of a bat (the latter perceptible to man only when the tape speed is reduced) and from the sounds of actual war to the chug of an ancient railway locomotive, all have been recorded, and when the whole gamut of 'genuine' noises is inadequate to express man's delight in sound, he manufactures his own, either for sheer fun (*musique concrète* and electronic music composers have produced many sophisticated works from natural and electronically created sounds) or for use (the BBC's Radiophonic Workshop has invented many ear-tickling compositions for broadcasting, and their sound effects discs have included both extra-terrestrials and ghosts for drama groups).

None of the categorised and chronological lists which follow is intended to be exhaustive, but it is hoped that they will illustrate the extent and importance of the documentary role played by the cylinder, the disc, and tape in preserving sounds for posterity.

Achievements

Recordings made by or about heroes and heroines in the field of exploration and endurance.

Aviation

1926 (26 October) *To Australia and Back in Six Minutes* (ie: two 3-minute sides), recorded in London by Sir Alan Cobham, British aviator, for Edison Bell Winner. Sir Alan also recorded *How to Fly an Aeroplane* for Columbia in London on 12 November, 1926.

1927 (11 June) *Actual Moments in the Reception to Colonel Charles A Lindbergh at Washington, DC*, upon his return home after making the first solo trans-Atlantic flight, from Roosevelt Field, Long Island, to Le Bourget, Paris, a distance of 3610 miles (5810km) in 33½ hours in *The Spirit of St Louis* on 20–21 May, 1927. Charles Augustus Lindbergh (1902–74), the American aviator, returned to Washington, DC, on 11 June, 1927; in addition to recording and issuing his reception, Victor also recorded his *Address Before the Press Club, President Coolidge Welcomes Charles Lindbergh* (three sides) and *Colonel Lindbergh Replies to President Coolidge*, all on the same day.

1927 (18 June) *Our Transatlantic Flight*, recorded in Berlin in both English and German by Clarence Duncan Chamberlin (*b* 1893) and Charles A Levine, the American aviators who flew the Atlantic from New York to Eisleben, Germany, in the monoplane *Columbia*, a distance of 3905 miles (6285km) in 42 hours 45 minutes on 4–6 June, 1927. The talk was issued by Odeon and Parlophone.

1928 (13 March) *Hinkler's Message to Australia* and *Incidents of my Flight*, recorded by Bert Hinkler (1892–1933), the Australian aviator who set several long-distance flight records, made at Homebush, NSW, and issued by Columbia.

1928 (17 June) *The Southern Cross Trans-Pacific Flight*, recorded by Australian aviators Charles B Kingsford-Smith (1897–1935) and Charles Thomas Philippe Ulm (1897–1934). Kingsford-Smith broke several long-distance records in his aircraft *Southern Cross*. He recorded the above talk at Homebush, NSW. On 13 March, 1929, at Richmond Aerodrome, Sydney, he recorded *The Farewell Message of the Southern Cross*. Both recordings were issued by Columbia. In London in October 1930 he made an advertising record for Exide Batteries before setting off on his record-breaking England–Australia flight of 16½ days.

1930 (3 February) *A Solo Flight from England to Australia*, recorded for Columbia by Frank (from 1967 Sir Francis) Chichester (1901–72) at Homebush, NSW, to celebrate his solo flight in a *Gipsy Moth* in December 1929.

1930 (9 June) *The Story of My Flight*, recorded for Columbia by Amy Johnson (1903–41), English aviator. The flight concerned was that made in May 1930 when she became the first

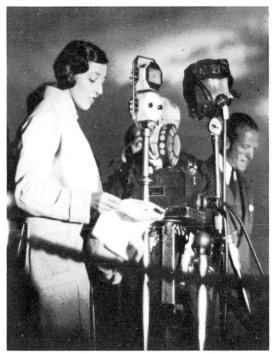

Amy Johnson, the famous aviator, at the microphone.

female to fly England–Australia solo. Jack Hylton praised her achievement in his record *Amy, Wonderful Amy* (1930).

1931 (5 March) *How I Flew Round the World*, by Mrs Victor Bruce (née Mildred Mary Petre, *b* 1895), recorded in London (Columbia). She took a Dictaphone to record her impressions, **perhaps the first time a recording machine had circumnavigated the globe.**

c 1935 A broadcast made by Amelia Earhart (1898–1937?), American aviator, the first female to fly the Atlantic, accompanied and solo, is extracted on Oriole.

1960 *The Story of Flying*, an HMV 10in LP issued in December, including the voices of Lord Brabazon of Tara, holder of the first British pilot's licence; Group Captain Sir Douglas Bader; Group Captain Leonard Cheshire, and others in a collection of information about civil and military aviation.

Exploration

1890 (13 May) Henry Morton Stanley (real name John Rowlands, 1841–1904), English explorer and leader of the Emin Pasha Relief Expedition to find Dr Livingstone, recorded a wax cylinder for Edison at a Guildhall reception, London, held in honour of the expedition.

1906 (14 January) Commander Robert Edwin Peary (1856–1920), American Arctic explorer, anticipated *The Discovery of the North Pole* (which he reached on 6 April, 1909 after several attempts) in New York. It was issued by Victor/HMV.

1907 (March) *A Gramophone on the Labrador Coast*, recorded in London for G & T by Wilfred Grenfell (1865–1940), the English Arctic explorer and author. He also recorded *A Modern Mission in the Arctic* (in the same month), and *Adrift on an Ice Floe in The Arctic Ocean* (HMV, 22 February, 1911).

1909 (23 June) *The Dash For the South Pole*, by Ernest H Shackleton (1874–1922), Scottish Antarctic explorer recorded in London (HMV/Victor). On 30 March, 1910, he recorded *My South Polar Expedition* for Edison in London. According to HMV's publicity in 1914, Sir Ernest took 'a gramophone and a bright lot of records' with him on his expeditions to the Antarctic.

1909 (2 October) *How I Reached the Pole*, recorded in New York by Frederick A Cook (1865–1940), the American Arctic explorer who claimed to have reached the North Pole on 21 April, 1908, but his claim was dismissed for lack of evidence. He was subsequently discredited, and later was jailed (1923–30) for offences connected with an oil fraud. The above recordings were issued by Victor/HMV.

1913 Captain Scott's ill-fated expedition to the South Pole was recalled in song – see above, in the Chronological Chart.

Space Exploration

A number of LP records dealing with rocketry, space travel and the scientists concerned with these subjects have been issued, among them:

1959 *The Conquest of Space*, a conversation between Dr Wernher von Braun (1912–77) and Willy Ley (1906–69) (Vox).

1959 *Rockets, Missiles and Space Travel* (Vox)

1961 *Man in Space* (US Columbia)

1962 *First American Manned Orbital Flight – John H(erschel) Glenn Jr* (b 1921) (Reprise; issued in the UK by the *Daily Express* newspaper.)

1964 *America's Men in Space* (CMS)

1967 *Man in Space* – Conversations between man in orbit and man on earth (Folkways)

1969 The Apollo 11 Moon Landing generated a number of American recordings:

Apollo 11 – Flight to the Moon (Capitol)

Eagle Has Landed, and *Man's Journey to the Moon* (Intrepid, two discs)

Footsteps on the Moon (Command)

Journey to the Moon (King)

Man on the Moon (Warner)

Original Soundtrack – Apollo 11 (Evolution)

We Came in Peace for All Mankind (Decca)

We Have Landed on the Moon (the official NASA tapes – Capitol)

Other Achievements

1911 (3 October) *How I Swam The Channel* was recorded in London for HMV by T W Burgess, who swam the English Channel north to south in 22hr 35min on 5–6 September, 1911. Apparently the record was never issued.

1931 (January) *My World's Record*, by Malcolm Campbell (1885–1948), (knighted later that year), discussing his water speed record of 141·7mph in *Bluebird* on Coniston Water, Lancashire (Furness), England, in 1930. The recording was made for Filmophone.

Children's Records

Children's records have been with us from the start. **The very first recordings ever offered for sale** were Berliner DISCS in **1888** with titles including *Simple Simon*, *Tom He Was a Piper's Son*, and *Who Killed Cock Robin*. This market was catered for fully in the 78 era, but the coming of the flexible LP and EP (see Section IX) widened the repertoire. More recent issues have included an HMV EP series performed by famous artists and pressed on highly-coloured vinyl (**1960**), *Music for School Practice* (Paxton EPs, **1960**), *The Grammarnomes – A Child's*

Guide to Grammar (HMV EP, **1966**), *Cassettes for Children*, a British series designed by Children's Heritage for children in the 3–12 year-old range, and 'Tellastory' cassettes including Beatrix Potter stories, etc (**1980**).

Composers Who Recorded Their Own Music

The magic of recording arrived too late to capture the definitive performances of such composers as Beethoven and Schubert, while other composers who did live into the recording age (Bruckner and Dvořák, for example) were never lured into the recording studio or (like Fauré, Granados, Scriabin, Mahler, Moszkowski and others) made piano rolls instead. However, some composers *did* make cylinders and discs in the early days, among them:

Brahms, Johannes (1833–97) made a cylinder for Edison's German agent in Vienna in **1889**. He was **the first famous composer to record**, although Josef Hofmann (1876–1939), who later composed under the name of Michel Dvorsky, recorded as Hofmann in **1888**.

In **1903** several composers recorded for G & T:

Chaminade, Cecile (1857–1944) in Paris;
Drdla, František (1868–1944) in Vienna;
Grieg, Edvard Hagerup (1843–1907) in Paris; and
Leoncavallo, Ruggiero (1858–1919) conducted selections from his *I Pagliacci*. His *Mattinata* was **the first work to be specially written for the gramophone**, and he accompanied Caruso in its first recording.

Pablo de **Sarasate** (1844–1908) recorded for G & T in Paris in **1904**, as did Claude **Debussy** (1862–1918), who went on to make piano rolls about 2 years later.

Edward **German** (1862–1936) and Dame Ethel **Smythe** (1858–1944) both recorded for HMV in England in 1914. The former made electrical recordings for Metropole in about 1930.

Valuable recordings have also been made by:
Bartók, Bela (1881–1945), as pianist with his wife in piano duets, and with Joseph Szigeti and Benny Goodman;

Benjamin, Arthur (1893–1960), as conductor in his own music;

Bernstein, Leonard (*b* 1918), as conductor and pianist in his own and other composers' music;

Britten, Benjamin (1913–76), as conductor and pianist; he recorded most of his compositions for Decca UK, who had first option on all his works;

Cilea, Francesco (1866–1950), who accompanied Caruso in Milan in November 1902 in an aria from his new opera *Adriana Lecouvreur*;

Copland, Aaron (*b* 1900), as conductor, including an important recent series of his own works for CBS;

Cowen, Sir Frederic Hymen (1852–1935), who recorded his orchestral suite *The Language of Flowers* for HMV;

Elgar, Sir Edward (1857–1934), conducted his own music for HMV between 21 January, 1914, and 29 August, 1933 (see p. 164);

Gershwin, George (1898–1937), as pianist for Columbia and Victor not long before his death;

Glazunov, Alexander (1865–1936) recorded for Columbia;

Hanson, Howard (1896–1981), as conductor for Mercury in his own and others' music;

Holst, Gustav (1874–1934) recorded *The Planets*, *Two Songs Without Words*, and his *St Paul's Suite* for Columbia;

Khachaturian, Aram (1903–78), as conductor, including valuable series for UK Columbia in the 1950s and for Decca in the 1960s;

Mascagni, Pietro (1863–1945) made records for Cetra, Parlophone and Polydor;

Paderewski, Ignace (1860–1941), as pianist for Victor/HMV from 1911 until the later 1930s, some of the records being made at his Swiss home;

Rakhmaninov, Sergei (1873–1943) recorded for Victor, including all his concertos and the *Paganini Rhapsody*;

Saint-Saëns, Camille (1835–1921) recorded for HMV in 1919;

Shostakovich, Dmitri (1906–75), as pianist; his son Maxim has made an international name as a conductor of his father's and other works;

Sir Edward Elgar and 'The Symphony Orchestra' recording at the HMV Hayes Laboratory in the early 1930s.   EMI

Sousa, John Philip (1854–1932), the 'March-king', conducted many of his marches for Edison cylinders, some of which were transferred to LP by Pye in 1968;

Stanford, Sir Charles Villiers (1852–1924) conducted excerpts from his *Suite of Ancient Dances*, his *Irish Rhapsody* No 1, and other works for HMV;

Strauss, Richard (1864–1949) conducted some of his own works for Polydor in 1935 and 1941, as well as the last three Mozart symphonies for the same company;

Stravinsky, Igor (1882–1971) was **the most prolific of all recording composers**. A commemorative issue of 31 LPs was released by CBS in 1982 to mark his centenary. The vast majority of the performances were by the composer himself, yet by no means all of his recordings were included since the set concentrated on those he had made only during the last few years of his life;

Tippett, Sir Michael Kemp (*b* 1905), as conductor;

Walton, Sir William (1902–83), as conductor;

Widor, Charles-Marie (1844–1937) recorded for Pathé and HMV from 1926.

Today, the value of the recording studio is recognised by many composers, and those noted below who have made authoritative recordings of their own music (and, where noted, that of others) for study and consideration not only stand a better chance of public acceptance thereby but also help to build a store of priceless documentary data for posterity.

Arnold, Malcolm (*b* 1921), as conductor;
Bennett, Richard Rodney (*b* 1936), as pianist;
Berio, Luciano (*b* 1925), as conductor;
Boisselet, Paul (*b* 1920), as performer;
Boulez, Pierre (*b* 1925), as conductor; also of other composers' works;
Crumb, George (*b* 1929), as performer;
Glass, Philip (*b* 1937), as performer;
Henze, Hans Werner (*b* 1926), as conductor;
Hovhaness, Alan (*b* 1910), as conductor of a large number of his own works;
Lutosławski, Witold (*b* 1913), as pianist;
Maxwell Davies, Peter (*b* 1934), as conductor and performer;
Messiaen, Olivier (*b* 1908), as pianist;
Panufnik, Andrzej (*b* 1914), as conductor;
Partch, Harry (1901–74), as performer;
Penderecki, Krzysztof (*b* 1933), as conductor;
Reich, Steve (*b* 1936), as performer and leader;
Stockhausen, Karlheinz (*b* 1928), as performer and electronic programmer;
Tavener, John Kenneth (*b* 1944), as performer.

The first composer fully to understand the value of the gramophone as a disseminator of his music was Sir Edward Elgar. His long series of recordings in the EMI studios at 31 City Road, London, at Hayes, and at Abbey Road, and also at the Albert, Queen's, and Kingsway Halls (plus three in September 1927 in Hereford Cathedral) are of immense historical value, showing the gramophone to be a documentary source of the first importance. **Elgar's first recording** was made at City Road in 1914 (21 January), when he conducted 'The Symphony Orchestra' in his *Carissima*. **His last** in person was at the Kingsway Hall, London, in 1933 (29 August), when he conducted the London Symphony Orchestra in his *Serenade for Strings* and *Elegy for Strings*. On 22 January, 1934, he supervised from his bed at his home in Worcester by GPO landline a recording by the London Symphony Orchestra under Lawrence Collingwood of his *Caractacus* as it took place at the Abbey Road studios, London.

The following Elgar recordings represent occasions upon which the gramophone record of a work has been made before the concert première:

	recorded	concert première	recording issued
Carissima	21.1.1914	15.2.1914	April 1914
Pomp and Circumstance March No 5	18.9.1930	20.9.1930	15.1.1931
Nursery Suite	4.6.1931	20.8.1931	mid-August 1931
Severn Suite	23.6.1932	7.9.1932	October 1932

The gramophone has been responsible for other musical premières, among them works by Shostakovich, Haydn and Vivaldi, but **the first to be recorded and issued before its concert première** was Kurt Atterberg's Symphony No 6, which formed a part of Columbia's Schubert Centenary celebrations in 1928. That recording was made by Sir Thomas Beecham and the Royal Philharmonic Orchestra; Atterberg himself recorded the work later with the Berlin Philharmonic Orchestra for Polydor.

Many well-known conductors and performers have also recorded works of their own composition. Amongst the best-known are:

Bechet, Sidney (1897–1959), black American jazz saxophonist and clarinettist. His ballet *Le Nuit est une Sorcière*, with Bechet as saxophone soloist, was recorded by London in 1954.
Dankworth, John (*b* 1927), British jazz band leader, saxophonist, clarinettist, and composer, prolific composer of film scores, orchestral and chamber works. He recorded his *Improvisations* for jazz band and orchestra (1959) for Saga in 1961.
Doráti, Antal (*b* 1906), American conductor of Hungarian birth; composer of orchestral, vocal, chamber and piano pieces. He conducted his Piano Concerto (1974) and *Bartók Variations* (1971) for Vox in 1976.
Furtwängler, Wilhelm (1886–1954), German conductor and writer, composed many works in various genres. He recorded his Symphony No 2 (1947) for DG in 1952.
Klemperer, Otto (1885–1973), German con-

ductor, composer of an opera and other works, including six symphonies. He conducted his Symphony No 2 (1969) for EMI.

Martinon, Jean (1910–76), French conductor who set aside a part of each year for composing. He recorded his Symphony No 4, 'Altitudes' (1965) for RCA.

Previn, André (*b* 1929), German-born American conductor and pianist, formerly a successful jazz musician. He has composed for musical shows, films and concerts. During the 1950s and 1960s he recorded many of his popular jazz pieces on several American labels.

Shankar, Ravi (*b* 1920), Indian sitarist. He has composed for films, and the ballet stage, and has written two Sitar Concertos. He recorded No 1 (1971) for HMV.

Disasters

1900 After the crash of Count Zeppelin's dirigible, he recorded a message asking for financial help to continue his airship activities. Three hundred copies were sent out to wealthy people throughout the world. The response is not known, but this was undoubtedly **the first begging record**.

1906 *The Destruction of San Francisco*, a recording by the Columbia Band commemorating the catastrophic earthquake of 18 April, 1906, which destroyed San Francisco, claiming some 700 lives and starting a fire that caused $400m damage.

1912 (14 April) The *Titanic* disaster was recalled in song by Robert Carr in the same year, and again much later in a duet by William and Versey Smith (for Paramount in 1927). Zonophone also issued a recording commemorating the disaster.

1925 *The Wreck of the Shenandoah*, sung by Vernon Dalhart for Victor on 9 September, but not issued. The *Shenandoah* was a 680ft (204m) US Army dirigible that broke up in the air on 3 September with the loss of 14 lives.

1937 *The Hindenburg Disaster*, a special issue by the NBC. The Hindenburg airship burst into flames at her moorings at Lakenhurst, NJ on 6

May, 1937. It was the last of the civil airships. Herb(ert) Morrison's distraught radio commentary of the occasion has become widely known.

Drama, Poetry, and Spoken Word

The advantages of the long playing record in dramatic recordings is self-evident, and companies were quick to exploit its continuity. Oddly, children were the first to benefit from this. In its earliest days in America, LP offered *Goldilocks*, *Little Red Riding Hood* and *The Pied Piper of Hamelin*, and Lewis Carroll's *Alice in Wonderland* soon followed.

The first Shakespeare play to appear on LP was *Othello*, with Paul Robeson in the title role on US Columbia in **1948**. **The first Charles Dickens LP recordings** came the same year on the same label: *A Christmas Carol*, and a compilation titled *The Adventures of Oliver Twist and Fagan* (sic), both with a cast headed by Basil Rathbone. The same artist performed Robert Louis Stevenson's *Treasure Island* in **1948**, and Errol Flynn appeared in Alexandre Dumas's *The Three Musketeers* the following year. Dumas's classic was recorded again by Douglas Fairbanks Jr in 1952.

The first dramatic recording to appear on LP in the UK was Arthur Miller's *Death of a Salesman*, narrated by the author, on Brunswick in September **1950**. (He re-recorded excerpts from this and from his *The Crucible* for Argo in 1959.) Paul Gallico's *The Snow Goose* followed, with Herbert Marshall and Joan Loring on a 10in Brunswick disc, and T S Eliot's *The Cocktail Party*, with Alec Guinness, was issued in March 1951.

The first British LP release of plays by Shakespeare came in the Autumn of **1951**: *Julius Caesar* (with Griffith Jones and Ralph Truman), and *Romeo and Juliet* (with John Gielgud and Pamela Brown). **The first UK release of an LP of Charles Dickens's work** came at the same time: *A Tale of Two Cities* (with Griffith Jones and Jack Livesey).

Claimed as the first recorded political satire on LP was *The Investigator*, made in Canada in

Tony Hancock in the BBC TV comedy The Blood Donor, *first shown in 1961 and subsequently released on disc.*   BBC

1954 and distributed in America by Dauntless International of New York (from December 1954), and in the UK by Oriole (from September 1955). It was a send-up of the witch-hunt tactics used by Senator McCarthy in his 'Unamerican Activities' investigations, and was written by Reuben Ship. Other notable recordings of this type include *Fool Britannia* (recorded by RCA in America but issued by Ember in the UK) with Anthony Newley, Joan Collins and Peter Sellers (1963), and *He's Innocent of Watergate*, performed almost entirely by Peter Sellers (Decca, 1974).

The largest recording project of any kind to date is the *Complete Works of William Shakespeare*, issued by Argo in the UK between 1957 and 1964 on 137 double-sided LP discs. HMV recorded scenes from the Old Testament (*The Living Bible*), spoken by Sir Laurence Olivier on 12 LPs in 1962. The project entailed 1023 hours of recording.

Poets and Authors

The first recording of a poet, although of considerable documentary value, was not a notable success. Robert Browning (1812–89) attempted to record his own poem *How They Brought The Good News From Ghent to Aix* for Edison in about 1888/9, but in an apparent fit of nervousness before the unfamiliar cylinder recorder, he forgot his own words and, amid apologies, compliments Mr Edison upon his 'marvellous machine'.

The following are amongst those poets and authors who have recorded their own works:

1890 (15 May) Alfred Lord **Tennyson** (1809–92) recorded *The Charge of the Light Brigade* and other of his works for Edison.

c1895 Mark **Twain** (real name: Samuel Langhorne Clemens, 1835–1910), American author of *The Adventures of Tom Sawyer* (1876) and other famous yarns, recorded a speech for Edison in New York.

1907 (October) Leo (Lev) **Tolstoy** (1828–1910), Russian author, recorded *Thoughts From the Book for Every Day* for The Gramophone Co in London. He made others in both Russian and English, but details are not available.

c1927 George Bernard **Shaw** (1856–1950), Irish novelist, playwright and music critic, made two Linguaphone records in London titled *Spoken English* and *Broken English*. He also made several recordings for HMV in 1926 and 1933, none of which was issued. In 1969 the BBC issued an LP titled: *George Bernard Shaw: Some of His Broadcasts.*

1928 (27 March) John **Drinkwater** (1882–1937), English poet and playwright, recorded *The Speaking of Verse* on two Columbia discs in London; and on 30 January, 1929, he made *John Drinkwater Reading His Own Poems*, also for Columbia.

1928 (25 September) Edgar **Wallace** (1875–1932), English novelist, playwright, war correspondent for Reuters (Boer War, 1899–1900), *Daily News* (1900), and *Daily Mail* (1901–2), recorded *The Man in the Ditch* for Columbia in London.

In June and July **1929** the London-based company Dominion made a series of important literary recordings:

William Wymark **Jacobs** (1863–1943), English author and playwright: *The Dreamer*; extracts from his *Short Cruises* (1907).

Dame Rose **Macaulay** (1881–1958), British novelist: four short stories.

Sir Edward Montagu **Compton Mackenzie** (1883–1972), author, playwright and founder of the British record magazine *The Gramophone* (1923), of which he was editor until May 1961, recorded *Rogues and Vagabonds*, written in 1928.

Alan Alexander **Milne** (1882–1956), playwright and author: *Winnie-The-Pooh*.

Alfred **Noyes** (1880–1958), English poet and novelist who spent much time in America: *The Highwayman*.

Hugh **Walpole** (1884–1941), English author

Caedmon's 1959 sleeve for a popular American poet-humorist.

and playwright: *Wintersmoon*.

Rebecca **West** (1892–1983), British author: *Harriet Hume.*

1929 (7 August) Sir Henry John **Newbolt** (1862–1938), English man of letters, recorded seven of his poems for Columbia in London.

1930 (14 May) Sir Arthur Conan **Doyle** (1859–1930), creator of Sherlock Holmes, made *Conan Doyle Speaking* for HMV in London a few weeks before his death.

1934 (18 January) Herbert George **Wells** (1866–1946), English novelist, historian and visionary, made *Whither Britain*, a broadcast issued much later by Oriole.

1934 (5 November) Aldous **Huxley** (1894–1963), critic and author, made *Causes of War* for the BBC in the HMV studios, London.

1940 John Boynton **Priestley** (b 1894), English author, made *A Tribute to the Little Ships at Dunkirk*, later issued by Oriole.

1941 (14 April) Alan Patrick **Herbert** (1890–1971), English author and playwright, made *Let's Be Gay* for HMV in London.

1942 (27 July) Ogden **Nash** (1902–71), American humorous poet, recorded 13 of his poems in New York for American Decca. He later recorded 28 poems for Caedmon (1959), and

50 more in 1968 for an RCA disc: *Everybody Knows the Trouble I've Seen*. His 15 poems to accompany Saint-Saëns's *Carnival of the Animals* were first recorded by Philips in 1957, with Noel Coward (1899–1973) reciting.

1953 Dylan **Thomas** (1914–53) played the Narrator and the Rev Eli Jenkins in the New York production of the first performance of *Under Milk Wood* on 14 May, 1953, less than 6 months before his death. This performance was recorded privately (and possibly illegally) in the theatre and issued in the UK in 1959 on the Caedmon label. Several discs of Dylan Thomas reading his own poems were issued posthumously by Caedmon in the later 1950s, and a series of eight discs, including this *Under Milk Wood*, appeared in 1970.

1954 Dame Edith **Sitwell** (1887–1964) spoke her poems for Walton's *Facade*, 'An Entertainment', for Decca, with Peter Pears and the English Opera Group. Some poems were issued in 1959 on the Jupiter and Caedmon labels in the UK.

1957 Thomas Stearns **Eliot** (1888–1965) recorded his *Four Quartets* for Argo; the same company issued his *Old Possum's Book of Practical Cats* in 1958.

1959 Walter de la **Mare** (1873–1956) and Noel **Coward** recorded for Caedmon; **J B Priestley** and William Butler **Yeats** (1865–1939) recorded for Argo.

1960 Wystan Hugh **Auden** (1907–73) made recordings for both Argo and Caedmon, and Robert Ranke **Graves** (b 1895) appeared on Argo, Jupiter and Listen.

1962 Kingsley **Amis** (b 1922) recorded his poems on Jupiter and Listen.

1965 Stevie (Florence Margaret) **Smith** (1902–71) read her poems for Argo. In December, Argo issued six LPs titled The Poet Speaks: 41 modern British poets reading their own poems, recorded between 10 October, 1960, and 26 May, 1965. Further issues came later.

1975 Robert **Graves**, on the occasion of his 80th birthday, recorded a selection of his poems on the Claddagh label, together with nine songs taught to him in his youth by his aunt.

Poets Laureate Who Recorded

Of Poets Laureate who have lived since the beginning of recording, it would appear that Alfred **Austin** (1833–1913, laureate from 1896) and Robert **Bridges** (1844–1930, laureate from 1913) were not enticed into the studios to make recordings. However, the following have left us mementoes of their voices:

Alfred, Lord **Tennyson** (1809–92, laureate from 1850), see above.

John **Masefield** (1878–1967, laureate from 1930) read his *Story of Osian* in 1959 and *A Fox's Day* in 1960, both for Argo, and selections of poems for Caedmon and Argo in 1962.

Cecil Day **Lewis** (1904–72, laureate from 1968) recorded his poems *Sheep-dog Trials*, *The Gate* and *View From an Upper Window* for Argo in 1959, and further recordings in 1965.

Sir John **Betjeman** (b 1906; laureate from 1972) recorded a large selection of his poems in 1959 for Argo and has made a number of records since, including *High and Low* for Polydor in 1970.

Some Landmarks in Drama and Poetry Recording

Perhaps the busiest recording artist of the 19th century was Russell Hunting, whose numerous monologues were extremely popular (see Personalia).

Gray's *Elegy* was recorded in 1933 by Ion Swinley in the churchyard at Stoke Poges, Buckinghamshire, England, in which it was written.

War of the Worlds: the broadcast put out as a Hallowe'en prank at 8pm EST on 30 October, 1938, by Orson Welles and his Mercury Theatre Players of the H G Wells classic, adapted to a contemporary American setting, caused widespread panic in the New York area and in New Jersey, so lifelike and convincing was the production. Listeners left their homes and took to their cars to escape the 'Martian invasion', jamming roads and causing distress amongst thousands of people, so potent was the power of radio when in the hands of an imaginative producer. The broadcast was issued on LP in the 1950s in America on the Audio Rarities label,

Sir John Betjeman.   BBC HULTON PICTURE LIBRARY

and despite the poor quality it is still possible, even now, to believe in the threat it contains.

Dylan Thomas's *Under Milk Wood* was issued by Argo in 1954 in a performance by Richard Burton and Hugh Griffith. This was from the BBC radio production; a performance of the play starring the author himself is mentioned under Poets and Authors, above.

The mid-1950s was a vintage time for recorded drama. By 1954 the French record industry had made much of its native classical drama available (Molière's *Le Bourgeois Gentilhomme*, Beaumarchais's *Le Barbier de Seville*, Cocteau's *La Voix Humaine*, etc), many of which were issued also in the US and UK in the original language; Sheridan's *The School for Scandal*, with Dame Edith Evans, Cecil Parker and Alec Guinness, was made in the UK in

1956, and Sir John Gielgud, Sir Ralph Richardson and Orson Welles recorded Sir Arthur Conan Doyle's *Dr Watson Meets Sherlock Holmes* and *The Final Problem* in 1957.

In 1961 Pye issued a two-disc set of a dramatisation titled *The Trial of Lady Chatterley*, in which D H Lawrence's *Lady Chatterley's Lover* was found not guilty of indecency.

Ethnic Recordings

In a loose sense, recordings of Latin American music or spirituals may be regarded as of ethnic interest in that they introduce to the catalogues music of cultures outside those which produce the standard western fare. This section lists some of the most notable attempts to bring home the more exotic and widely-flung musical styles, music like that sought by Percy Grainger, Béla Bartók and Zoltan Kodály when they took their portable disc recorders into the field early in the century; music that at times throws light on our own musical heritage and at others excites by its unfamiliarity and intricacy.

1889 **The first recordings of ethnic music** appeared in America. They were of music by the Passamaquoddy and Zunyi American Indians, recorded by Dr Walter Fewkes.
1900 Five records of Hebrew Temple Chants unaccompanied made in Warsaw by Cantor Kwartin.
1901 Russian folk songs and dances recorded by the Gramophone Co.
1902 Fred Gaisberg went to India, China and Japan to record music of the Orient.
1905 HMV recorded the singing and laughing of some Congolese pygmies who had been brought to London for the occasion.
1926 An expedition to the Grand Canyon recorded 12 sides of tribal songs and dances by the Walpi Tribe of the Hopi Indians.
1934 Parlophone issued *Music from the Orient*, 12 discs of music from nine countries.
1949 The Australian Record Co of Sydney issued *Chants and Rituals of the Australian Aborigines*, recorded in the Outback by Prof

Elkin. The 16in (40·6cm) centre-start discs were meant primarily for transcription by radio stations.

1951 Ceylonese songs and folk music on four 10in HMV discs by Surya Sena and his wife Nelun Devi.

1951 Zulu songs and music issued by Decca on LP.

1952 **The first substantial recording of the Llangollen International Musical Eisteddfod** was recorded by the BBC for the UNESCO International Music Council, but the recording first appeared the following year on the Westminster label in the US and was released in the UK only in October 1953 by Westminster's British outlet, Nixa.

1952 A group of Balinese dancers appeared at the Winter Garden Theatre, London, during the summer, and a highly successful two-LP issue titled *Music from Bali*, taken from these performances, was released by Argo in December.

1954 Decca's *Music of Africa* series began with eight 10in LPs.

1955 American Columbia issued 44 LPs of folk music from around the world in a series directed by Alan Lomax.

1956 HMV issued two 78s of Welsh folk dances, sponsored by the Welsh Folk Dance Society.

1965 *Sounds of Japan*: general sounds of everyday life – leisure, pastimes, at work, at school, and excerpts of music, etc, issued in the US by Elektra.

1974 BBC Records issued *English With A Dialect* and *Irish, Scottish and Welsh Accents*.

General Interest

1905 **The first monologue to sell one million copies** was Arthur Collins's *The Preacher and the Bear* for Victor. When issued in the UK it carried a printed guide explaining the American dialect.

1908 (18 December) Christabel Pankhurst (1880–1958), suffragette and fighter for women's rights, recorded *Suffrage for Women* for The Gramophone Co shortly after release from one of her periods of imprisonment.

c 1915 Mrs Raymond Brown recorded *Why Women Want The Vote* for Pathé in New York. Dr Stephen Wise (originally Stephan Weiss, 1874–1949), Rabbi of the New York Free Synagogue (which he founded) from 1907 to 1949, made a record about women's suffrage titled *Women and Democracy* for Pathé. He also made two recordings on current topics for Nation's Forum, the American label that specialised in recordings of documentary value and current affairs: *What Are We Fighting For?* (1918) and *President Wilson* (1920).

1923 Emile Coué recorded a two-disc set for Columbia in New York titled *Self-Mastery Through Conscious Auto-Suggestion*, repeating it the following day in French.

1951 To mark the opening of the Festival of Britain HMV issued two 12in 78s entitled *British Customs and Traditions*. They included the voices of King George VI and Princess Elizabeth, and traditional sounds such as the Ceremony of the Keys at the Tower of London. HMV also recorded the inaugural concert of the Royal Festival Hall (3 May, 1951) in the presence of the King and Queen.

1951 *Stories From World History*, an educational series of eight 78s by Rhoda Power, made by HMV in collaboration with the BBC.

1960 *Behind Closed Doors at a Recording Session*, issued by Warner in the US. Prof C Northcote Parkinson explained his 'Law' (Libraphone). *Big News of '59*, news stories of the year (US Columbia).

1961 *Inside a Communist Cell*, issued by Key.

1962 *Wine: A Discussion*, issued in the UK by Pye.

1963 *Handwriting Analysis* (Folkways). *BBC Scrapbook for 1940*, including the voices of Sir Winston Churchill, J B Priestley, Ed Murrow, Lord Haw-Haw (William Joyce) and others (Philips Fontana, with book). Several other *BBC Scrapbook* programmes have been issued on LP.

1964 *A Day at the Zoo*, with Dr Desmond Morris acting as guide (Oriole EP).

1965 *What Are The Gravediggers Doing Now?*

This recording, upon which the artist/presenter is given as Schafly, was issued by Key in the US in time for the Christmas season. The authors have not heard the disc and confess defeat at the significance or meaning of the title.

1966 Flying Saucers – Serious Business (Victor). Contents: Flying Saucers Around Ships and Astronauts; UFOs: From the A-bomb to the Blackout; in Ancient History; Their Size and Source of Power; Kooks who claim Saucer Contacts; Astronomers Report Flying Saucers; Flying Saucer Censorship; Mysteries on the Moon; Signals – and Creatures – From Space.

1967 Playback '66: most important events and famous voices of the year 1966 (Decca).

1968 Quotations From The 'Little Red Book of Chairman Mao Tse-Tung' (CMS).

1969 Modern History on Record. A series of EPs published by Longmans of Essex in which aspects of World War I, the Spanish Civil War, the Making of the Welfare State, etc, are brought to life by a mixture of recordings of politicians and 'ordinary folk'.

1970 Philips in the UK issued a disc of piano works by Beethoven, Schubert, Chopin, Liszt, Debussy, Brahms, Grieg, and Schumann played by Peter Katin and Rosemary Brown. Spice is added to this unremarkable information when it is revealed that not one of the pieces is listed in the standard work-lists of their respective composers. All, in fact, were written by Mrs Rosemary Brown as, she claims, dictation from the spirits of these dead composers. Included in the presentation is an Introduction dictated to Mrs Brown on 1 January, 1970, by Sir Donald Francis Tovey (1875–1940). No satisfactory rebuttal to the phenomenon has been published to date.

1970 BBC issued a recorded guide to *Britain's Cathedrals* and other notable edifices.

1972 Fifty Years of Broadcasting, a double album issued by the BBC to commemorate half a century of relaying (and preserving) sounds. The first of the 127 items is the chimes of Big Ben and John Snagge's famous voice calling the world from London. The last voice is that of Lord Reith in Westminster Abbey on 22 July, 1971.

1976 Great American Documents. Issued by US Columbia to commemorate the bi-centenary of American Independence, this record bears the appropriate catalogue number USA 1776. Contents: Declaration of Independence read by Henry Fonda; Original Seven Articles of the Constitution read by Helen Hayes; Emancipation Proclamation read by James Earl Jones; Bill of Rights read by Orson Welles; The Star-Spangled Banner, played by the New York Philharmonic conducted by Leonard Bernstein.

1982 To mark the 60th anniversary of broadcasting, the BBC issued a number of interesting recordings, among them a double album of 60 signature tunes of radio and TV programmes.

Health

Alcoholism

1909 Mrs Carrie Amelia Nation (née Moore, 1846–1911), whose first husband, Dr Charles Gloyd, was an alcoholic, campaigned militantly against drinking by entering saloons and destroying their stocks of liquor by laying about her with iron bars and hatchets, at first in Kansas in the 1890s (where the drinking of liquor was at that time illegal), and then in San Francisco, Washington and New York. Her conviction that what she was doing was right and necessary, as if by some divine guidance, is reflected in the title of her autobiography (1904), with its (deliberately?) misspelt version of her own name: *The Use and Need of the Life of Carry A Nation.* She visited London in 1908–9 and recorded two titles for HMV on 3 February, 1909: *Remarks on Drinking* and *Remarks on Smoking.*

1961 American Pathé issued an LP titled *Conquer Your Alcoholism.*

Drugs

Public concern over drug abuse in America in the 1960s prompted the following LPs:

1966 LSD: The Drug and its Effect (Capitol)

1967 Instant Insanity Drugs: Exposé of LSD, Marijuana and other 'mind-expanding' drugs; symptoms; control (Key)

1970 Drug Scene (Key – two LPs)

The BBC TV's recent keep-fit series transferred to LP.   BBC

The Heart

1955 *Heart Recordings* (American Columbia arranged by Dr Geckeler)

1958 *Stethoscopic Heart Sounds* (US Columbia)

1959 *How To Listen To the Heart* (US Columbia)

1962 *Auscultation of the Heart*: examples for students (Decca/London)

1963 *Herzauskultation*: series for students (DG)

1968 *The First Human Heart Transplant* under the direction of Dr Christiaan Barnard (Decca/London: two LPs)

Slimming and General Health

1914 Jack Johnson (1878–1946), the first American black to become World Heavyweight Boxing Champion (1908), recorded a talk called *Physical Culture* for Edison Bell Winner in London, *c* 30 June.

1927 Gene Tunney (1898–1978) recorded a *Talk on Health Exercises* for Victor in New York on 23 July.

1928 Tromp van Diggelen, 'The Man With the Perfect Chest', recorded *Breathing Made Easy* for Columbia in London on 17 September.

1957 *Exercises for Health and Figure* (Jay).

1958 *Good Housekeeping's Plan for Reducing* (Harmony).

Milady, Your Figure! (Capitol).

1959 *Slimnastics for Men and Women* (US Decca).

Good Housekeeping's Sporting Way for Reducing (Harmony).

1960 *Reducing Through Hypnosis* (issued by the little-known US label Personality Development).

Keep Fit (Warner: two volumes).

1961 *Now You Can Feel Fit All Day* (Carlton).

Reduce in Record Time (Living Language).

Yoga For Health (this title was used for recordings this year by Golden Crest, World Pacific, and a two disc Artia set).

1962 *Relaxing is Easy* (Epic).

Chinese Health Exercises (Colpix).

Physical Fitness (ERA, three discs).

1963 *Physical Fitness Formula* (Everest).

Physical Fitness – 44 Exercises (Capitol).

1965 *Physical Fitness* (Warner).

1966 *Yoga For Life*;

Yoga for Meditation (both issued on the Yoga label).

1967 *Stay Young With Eileen Fowler* (BBC).

Yoga for Americans (Mace, two discs).

Yoga – Common Sense Exercises (Argo, two discs).

Yoga (Yoga International, two discs).

1972 *Yoga Instruction* (Conversa-phone, two discs). The BBC has issued many health records in recent years, prominent amongst them being *Enjoy Your Slimming*; *Family Keep Fit*; *Dance, Keep Fit and Slim to Music*; *Slim to Rhythm*; *As Young As You Feel* and *Taking The Strain*, based on the TV series on relaxation.

1974 *Yoga For Health* (CBS), the music used in a TV series of the same title.

Smoking

The first anti-smoking recording was issued in 1909 – see **Alcoholism**, above. In the mid-1960s the Americans took seriously the fact that smoking is injurious to health. In 1964 the following recordings were issued there:

Stop Smoking via Relaxation and the Power of Suggestion (Ascot);

Stop Smoking the Record Way (Living Record Library);
End the Cigarette Habit Through Self-Hypnosis (Folkways);
Let's Try To Stop Smoking (Capitol).
For those Americans who had slipped through this dense anti-smoking net, Victor in 1970 issued *How To Stop Smoking Without Using Will Power*.

Health – Miscellaneous

1890 Florence Nightingale (1820–1910) recorded a cylinder for Edison in London on 30 July. This was transferred to a 10in disc in 1934 and sold to raise funds for the British Empire Cancer Campaign.
1929 *Care For The Teeth* (UK Columbia).
1956 *Natural Childbirth* (Argo).
1959 *Sounds of Medicine* (Folkways).
Human Fertility, by Dr Stone (Spoken Word).
1960 *First Aid* (ten lectures by Dr J A Parr; HMV, five LPs).
1961 *Physical Properties of Dental Materials* (Lectern).
1962 *Fluoridation – The Case Against* (Key).
1963 *Fearless Childbirth* (Saga, two LPs with book and anatomical chart).
1965 *Speech After the Removal of the Larynx* (Folkways).
1967 *Homosexuality in the American Male* (Capitol).
1975 *Breast Cancer – Understanding and Self-Examination* (Folkways).

Horoscope and Astrology

The first horoscope records were issued in Britain in about 1933. They were followed in 1937 by an English Decca release of 12 discs, one for each sign of the zodiac, with forecasts and character readings by Gipsy Petulengro. In 1962, Maurice Woodruff's recording *Know What Will Happen Tomorrow* was issued by Warner. American Columbia issued *Astrology* in 1967, and Camden issued *Listen To Your Stars*, an astrological guide to your horoscope, in 1970.

Instructional

For virtually every human activity or pastime an instructional record has appeared. The largest part of this market has been taken by language courses; these are mentioned separately below.

Apart from physical fitness and sporting discs (each with its own section, above and below) and records by politicians telling the public which way to vote (which do not count), **the first serious instructional recording** was Columbia's *Phono Vocal Method* of 1910 which taught singing with the help of textbooks and recorded examples. In 1928 Columbia also issued lectures by Sir Oliver Lodge, FRS (1851–1940): *Introduction to Physics* (four discs), and *Time and Space* (one disc). Two other lectures followed in 1929.

The first educational films, with synchronised sound on discs, were made by Electrical Research Products in the US in 1929. Further 78rpm instruction discs appeared rarely, but *How To Make an Omelette* was recorded by Zavier M Boulestin for Zonophone in London in 1932. Then, in 1935, **the first practice discs for musicians** were issued by Tilophane in Austria, the music being recorded with one part missing, that part to be supplied by the student. In 1938 Parlophone issued arias without the voice parts, also for practice. In 1937 the British Drama League issued a valuable series of recordings of British dialects. Readers included John Laurie representing Dumfries, and Freddy Grisewood representing the Cotswolds. Much later (1972) the BBC raided its archives for a disc entitled *Some British Accents and Dialects*.

One of the most disastrous mistakes was made by HMV in October 1939 when they issued two discs (BD 800–1) explaining what to do in an air-raid. On BD 800 the air-raid siren was demonstrated, but so frequently was the disc played all over England that neighbours were sent scurrying for their shelters. The Home Office ordered an immediate withdrawal of the issue. More useful were Columbia's Morse code training discs of 1941.

The first decade of LP in America saw many

records giving instruction on subjects as diverse as *Dictation* (on the Dictation Discs label), *Play Better Ball* (Urania), *Science in Our Lives* (Folkways), *Yodeling* (Bucher), *Tap Dance Practice and Instruction* (Somerset), an *International Morse Code Course* (Elektra), *Practical Vocabulary Improvements* (five volumes under the direction of Dr Bergen Evans on the Vocabulary label), 24 discs (10in) on the Campbell label in which Lotte Lehmann and her pupils gave instruction in Lieder and song interpretation, some 30 discs on the Rec-O-Dance label telling how to dance the Argentinian Tango, Cha-cha, Foxtrot, Jitterbug, Mambo, Merengue, Polka, Square Dance, etc, *Photography – Famous Photographers Tell How* (Candid), *How To Ski* (Skico), *Psychoanalysis Kit – Do It Yourself* (Hanover), *How to Play the Bongo Drum* (Folkways – followed by many other instruments), and *The Art of Investment* (a course of 13 LPs on the Spoken Word label). A less comprehensive three-disc set by ABC, *The Sophisticated Investor*, was issued in 1961.

Two courses in piano study appeared in 1961 from the Pianophone Tuition Co of London. Each LP came equipped with an instruction book and score.

All through the 1960s record companies continued to woo the autodidact with an orgy of instruction:

1960 Say It Right: How to pronounce musical names, titles, terms, composers and artists (Grayhill).

Radio Code By Word Method (Epsilon, three LPs).

Contract Bridge – The Stayman System (Dot).

1961 Better Speech Course (Living Language, four LPs).

How To Play The Hammond Organ (Washington, two discs).

How to Achieve Sexual Harmony in Marriage (Carlton).

Improve Your Etiquette (Carlton).

Improve Your Fishing (Carlton).

Handle Your Boat (Carlton).

Look Your Loveliest (Carlton).

Skin Dive (Carlton).

Take Better Photographs (Carlton).

Teach Your Child Ballet (based on Boris Kniaseff's System – Artia, two discs).

Tell Your Children The Facts of Life (Carlton).

Touch Type (Carlton).

Train Your Dog (Carlton). (The Carlton series was later re-issued on the Hear How label.)

Remember Names and Faces (Creative).

Learn Shorthand (Living Language).

1962 How To Sell (Concert Disc, five LPs).

How To Sing (Capitol).

How To Fly An Airplane (Aero-Progress, ten discs).

Play it Yourself: practice discs for the violinist (HMV, two EPs; the same company produced similar series for other instruments).

Typing: Tuch-Rite Kit (Folkways).

How To Play Winning Bridge (Hear How).

How To Plan a Perfect Dinner Party (Carlton).

1963 How To Write an Effective Composition (Folkways).

Speed Reading Made Easy (Kaydan).

Techniques in Reading Comprehension (Folkways).

In 1963 also was launched the Dictation Disc label, dealing with arithmetic, biology, chemistry, general science, geometry, physics, spelling, and typing.

1964 How To Be A Disc Jockey (Cameo).

A Guide to Correct Pronunciation (English) (Recordiction, UK).

How To Play The Appallachian Dulcimer (Folkways).

1965 How To Play Country Style Fiddle (Folkways).

A Guide to Correct Pronunciation: 1000 Foreign Words and Phrases used in English Speech and Literature (Recordiction, UK).

How To Type – With a special learning board (AA).

Stammering, Stuttering and Speech Fright, a course for their correction (Learn by Listening).

1966 Dog Training (Somerset).

1967 How To Avoid Probate (Philips).

Our Present Knowledge of the Universe, a lecture by Sir Bernard Lovell (BBC).

Dr Spock Talks With New Mothers (Caedmon).

What Everyone Should Know About Music, a

discussion by conductor Ernest Ansermet on the language and meaning of music (Decca).

1968 *Instant Care and Training of Your Dog* (Instant).

1969 BBC Study records: a series including readings from Bunyan's *The Pilgrim's Progress*; Schools programmes, archive material, etc.

Dog Training My Way, with Barbara Woodhouse (RCA).

Similar recordings appeared throughout the 1970s. Discourses, a firm based in Tunbridge Wells, Kent, issued a series *All About Music*, described as 'the new music encyclopaedia'. It included discs with illustrated booklets describing musical instruments, and lectures on musical works, Beethoven's sketchbooks, etc. The BBC issued *Learn To Dance at Home* (1971), and CBS issued *Music for Ballet Class – Basic Steps*: a disc and booklet by Sylvia Padovan (1972). In 1975 PolyGram introduced a series of cassettes in the UK in conjunction with Times Newspapers covering leisure and educational activities such as music appreciation, literature studies, *Improve Your Bridge*, *Improve Your Driving*, etc. This was **the first intensive use of the cassette medium as a teaching aid**. At about the same time the idea was taken a logical step further by the selling in motorway service stations of cassettes which would provide a running commentary for passengers about features visible from the motorway at a given speed. In 1982 the Victoria and Albert Museum, London, issued a cassette together with a series of 30 35mm slides and a cue card illustrating the historical stringed instruments preserved there. The tape gives a commentary and musical examples synchronised with the showing of the slides.

Language Courses, etc

Foreign languages have been big business almost from the start of recorded sound. **The earliest courses** were recorded by the Academy of Languages, New York, in 1891 under the direction of R D Cortina. In 1893 Columbia issued a course on 50 cylinders under the direction of Dr Richard Rosenthal. Blank cylinders and an instruction book were included and the student was invited to record his exercises and return them for grading and comment. The Linguaphone Institute was founded in London in 1924 and the first Linguaphone issues appeared in July 1926. Their first microgroove issues appeared in 1953 with simultaneous 45 and 78rpm pressings, but the latter were recommended by the company because of the greater ease with which words and phrases might be located. Many other British companies have issued language courses, including HMV and BBC, the latter linked to both radio and TV programmes for students.

The market has become saturated, particularly in America, with discs and tapes all claiming to teach the listener a language, usually without a great deal of effort on his part. Courses come in all types, from the multi-disc set complete with instruction books for the student who wishes to acquire a firmly grounded knowledge of his selected language, to the one-disc or one-tape 'get-you-by' courses with the bare essential words and phrases for the holidaymaker.

A check in an American catalogue of autumn 1969 (chosen at random, but representative of the state of the market for most of the time since the late 1950s) shows courses in no fewer than 38 different languages, plus English courses for students of 20 foreign countries, on 492 discs issued by 23 different companies. There is also a Folkways record issued in 1962 that advocates, according to its title, *One Language for the World*, an idea that would appear to threaten the invested capital of those 23 companies, one of which is Folkways itself.

In 1967 the American company Virtuoso issued a series designed for singers to enable them to both pronounce and understand the meanings of French and Italian songs, operatic arias and Schubert Lieder.

A 78rpm disc sponsored by the British Esperanto Association of London was issued in 1955. It contained four Esperanto songs, set to music by Frank Merrick and sung by Gloria Spinney. *Songs for Language Classes*, with three LPs and four EPs, was issued by HMV in 1965.

Modern techniques are represented by the

computer-planned language series PILL (Programmed Instruction Language Learning), released in 1970.

Recordings of Music by Masters of the King's/Queen's Musick

The honour bestowed upon selected composers by reigning monarchs has not always been reflected in their representation in gramophone catalogues, although some minor items may be tucked away on obscure labels or in 'recital' discs that have escaped notice. The first Master, Nicholas Lanier (1588–1666, appointed 1626) wrote much music for the stage and a large number of songs, yet only three songs have been recorded, and those only recently. The next two Masters have not been recorded at all: Louis Grabu (c 1638?–94, appointed 1666) was responsible for about five stage works and a number of songs, while Nicholas Staggins (?–1700, appointed 1674) was engaged as organiser and performer rather than composer, his compositions being negligible, their remains fragmentary.

The next Master, John Eccles (1668–1735, appointed 1700) was, on the other hand, a most prolific composer, providing music for over 70 stage works and continuing the tradition started by Staggins of writing an ode for each new year and each of the reigning monarchs' birthdays. There are about 50 such odes, although authorship of some of them has not been finally established and many are lacking the music and, in some cases, also the texts. He also wrote keyboard pieces, violin 'aires', songs and catches. Of this considerable output, just two songs and two catches appeared on 78s, and a few songs sung by Maurice Bevan and Alfred Deller have been contributed on LP. Maurice Green (1695–1755, appointed 1735) is noted for over 100 anthems, much other church music including three oratorios, stage works, 35 new year and birthday odes and some orchestral and instrumental pieces. The anthem *O Clap Your Hands Together* has been recorded several times; otherwise, a handful of his other works

have appeared – hardly a representative selection by which to judge the lifework of a Master of the King's Musick.

On the face of it, William Boyce (1711–79, appointed 1757) has been better represented. His '8 Symphonys' (mostly overtures from odes or operas) have been recorded many times and some of his other overtures, all four of his concerti grossi and several of his sonatas in three parts have been made available at various times, but of his nearly 70 anthems and numerous other choral pieces, only a fraction has appeared and, apart from the overtures, his 60 odes and many stage and vocal chamber works remain largely unheard. John Stanley (1713–86, appointed 1772), blind, like Boyce, wrote considerably less than he (four stage works, three oratorios, 15 odes for which the music has not survived, cantatas and some instrumental pieces) and is correspondingly less fully represented: most important are a number of recent discs including concertos and some organ voluntaries. Sir William Parsons (1746–1817, appointed 1786) was the first musician to be knighted, this honour being bestowed upon him by the Lord Lieutenant of Dublin in 1795. Yet so completely has his musical output, if any, disappeared that no recording can be traced of any of his music; furthermore, the good knight's memory has so receded into history that he ranks a separate entry in neither the 1954 nor the 1981 editions of *Grove*.

William Shield (1748–1829, appointed 1817) wrote chamber music, songs, over 40 stage works, and the last of the traditional odes to mark important court dates. Only the opera *Rosina* has been recorded (by Decca, almost complete; rapidly deleted), but the tune heard in the finale of its overture, and which may have been written by Shield, has received a number of recordings as *Auld Lang Syne*.

As far as we can trace, not a note by any of the next four Masters has ever been recorded. Christian Kramer (c 1788–1834, appointed 1829), François Cramer (1772–1848, appointed 1834), and George Frederick Anderson (c 1801–76, appointed 1848) were not noted composers in any case, but attention might usefully be paid by recording companies to the concertos, cantatas and other works of Sir William George Cusins (1833–93, appointed 1870 upon the retirement of Anderson). Of the church works of Sir Walter Parratt (1841–1924, appointed 1893), only one hymn, *Confortare*, has been recorded; his modest output of stage music is ignored.

Sir Edward Elgar (1857–1934, appointed 1924) made a most important contribution to the recorded repertoire, as did the gramophone to his reputation. This is discussed above. No other Master of the King's Musick has been so fully and continuingly represented on records, largely due to the efforts and faithful advocacy of Sir Adrian Boult.

Sir Walford Davies (1869–1941, appointed 1934) wrote the once-popular *Solemn Melody* for orchestra and organ which achieved a number of recordings on 78s and LP but is now unrepresented. His hymn *God Be In My Head*, and his *RAF March* have also been recorded. The three most recent Masters, Sir Arnold Bax (1883–1953, appointed 1941), Sir Arthur Bliss (1891–1975, appointed 1953), and Malcolm Williamson (born 1931, appointed 1975) have not been neglected of late on records, although Bax's orchestral music was inadequately represented until some years after his death.

Nature

The first recording of a bird song was of an Indian shama, recorded by Ludwig Koch (1882–1974) on a cylinder in 1889. Koch, noted for his many wildlife recordings, often secured only by the exercise of extreme patience under acutely difficult and uncomfortable conditions, introduced some of his bird song recordings on a 7in Talking Books disc in 1960, and made **his last field recording** (the song of a swallow) in Somerset, England, in June 1961.

Further nature recordings have been made, often as parts of valuable series for study.
1930 Location recordings were made of nature sounds: *Daybreak on a Surrey Farm* (HMV) and *Dawn in a Sussex Farmyard* (Broadcast).

1953 HMV issued four 10in 78s of British Bird song recorded by Ludwig Koch.

The following all appeared during the first decade of LP in America:

Recordings by Cornell University:
American Bird Songs
Songs of Insects
African Birds
Voices of the Night (frogs, toads, etc).

Recordings issued on the Ficker label:
Bird Songs of Dooryard, Field and Forest
Symphony of the Birds (compiled by Fassett)
(Another recording titled *Symphony of the Birds* was issued by MGM in 1967.)

Recordings issued by Folkways:
North American Frogs
Sounds of Sea Animals
Sounds of Animals
Sounds of the South American Rain Forest
Science of Insects

Recordings of bird calls were issued in 1966 by the Federation of Ontario Naturalists (seven discs, including the calls of animals as well as of birds), and Houghton Mifflin (three discs). In 1970 Capitol issued *Songs of the Humpbacked Whale*.

Many nature recordings have been issued from the BBC Sound Archives, including Ludwig Koch's first recording (mentioned above), *British Mammals and Amphibians* (1970), *Cats and Dogs*, a history with recordings of domestic and wild species (1969), *Sounds of the Countryside* (1970) from the 'Countryside' radio programmes, *Back Garden Birds* (1971), and *Wildlife of Wales* (1971). More recently have appeared *Sounds of the Living World*, *Sea and Island Birds*, *British Wild Birds in Stereo* and *Woodland and Garden Birds*. In 1969 Pye issued *Bird Sounds in Close Up*, a valuable guide for naturalists and schools recorded and compiled by Victor C Lewis, and in 1970 HMV issued *Guess the Birds*, a compilation by Lewis of bird song, arranged as an instructional entertainment.

Paul Smith's evocative musical scores for Walt Disney's 'True-Life Adventure' films *The*

Living Desert and *The Vanishing Prairie* were issued in the early 1970s on the Disneyland label in the US and the UK. *Sounds of My Life* by Sir Peter Scott, naturalist, was issued by the BBC in 1971.

The first use of a gramophone record in the concert hall as part of an orchestral score was when a recording of a nightingale was included by Respighi in his *Pines of Rome* (1924). Wisely, the composer provided a thin veil of lower strings, harp, and muted violins to conceal the scratch of the record surface. The work received its first performance in Rome on 14 December, 1924, under Bernardino Molinari. Its UK première occurred at the Leeds Festival the following year, and Toscanini gave the first American performance on 14 January, 1926. The score of the work calls for 'No R 6105 of the Concert Record Gramophone: The Song of the Nightingale.'

The first wildlife sound recording competition was sponsored by the BBC in 1965 and organised by the Natural History Unit of the BBC in Bristol.

The first international wildlife sound recording competition was again sponsored by the BBC, this time as a contribution of the European Broadcasting Union to European Conservation Year, 1970.

Other Personalities Who Have Recorded

1877 (December) **The first words ever spoken onto, and heard back from, a recording**: 'Mary had a little lamb', recited by Edison in his West Orange laboratory.

1890 Phineas Taylor **Barnum** (1810–91), the circus showman, recorded for Edison.

1896 Sir Henry **Irving** (1838–1905), the famous British actor, made two Shakespearian cylinders for Edison in London.

1898 Chauncey Mitchell **Depew** (1834–1928), American politician, recorded *Statue of Liberty Oration* (he had unveiled it on 28 October, 1886), and *Speech on Forefather's Day* for Berliner in New York on 7 January.

1903 Sir Hubert **Beerbohm Tree** (1853–1917) recorded several speeches for G & T.

1904 Adolf **Beck** (1841–1909), a Norwegian singer who was imprisoned for fraud in 1896 but released and pardoned in 1904 after a re-trial, recorded *Trial and Sentence* (1904) and *Prison Experiences* (1905) for G & T.

1906 General William **Booth** (1829–1912), founder of the Salvation Army, recorded talks for Columbia.

1911 Dame Ellen **Terry** (1848–1928), the famous actress, recorded a scene from *The Merchant of Venice* for HMV.

1912 Stephen **Coleridge** (1854–1936), co-founder of the National Society for the Prevention of Cruelty to Children and active protector of the rights of defenceless animals, made *Mercy To Animals* in London for HMV on 20 February.

1921 Lord Robert **Baden-Powell** (1857–1941), founder of the scout movement, recorded several addresses to scouts and parents for Edison Bell Winner this year, and recorded *Boy Scout Training* for Columbia in 1928. (Some addresses recorded by Zonophone in 1913 were not issued.)

1923 The film star Rudolph **Valentino** (real name Rodolpho Guglielmi, 1895–1926) made his only recording as a singer. The two songs were *The Kashmiri Song* and *El Relicario*. They were recorded by Brunswick in America but were never issued commercially; they appeared on a private label in 1930.

1929 Margaret **Bondfield** (1873–1953), Labour MP and the first female to reach cabinet rank in the UK, read a speech called *The Women's Opportunity* for Columbia.

1934 Reginald **Gardiner** (1903–80), the British actor who spent his last 40 years in Hollywood, recorded *Trains* for Decca, a monologue which was to sell over one million copies.

1934 Lord **Beaverbrook** (William Maxwell Aitken, 1879–1964), read *Causes of War*, a speech made by HMV for the BBC.

1951 St John **Ervine** (1883–1969), Irish author, broadcast an appreciation of the late George Bernard Shaw which was issued on two 78s by HMV.

Rudolph Valentino.

1955 Gerald **Moore** (*b* 1899), world famous accompanist, recorded his talk *The Unashamed Accompanist* for HMV.

1959 Eleanor **Roosevelt** read a speech on *Human Rights* for Folkways.

1962 Lord Bertrand **Russell** (1872–1970) *Personally Speaking* on two Pye LPs.

1963 Philips issued *Pope John XXIII – A Memorial*.

1968 Rev Dr Martin Luther **King**, Jr, black American leader, recorded *I Have A Dream* (20th Century Fox), *The Great March to Freedom* (Tamla Motown), and *In Search of Freedom* (Mercury).

1970 RCA issued *Great Personalities of Broadway*, including recordings by Ethel Mer-

man, Sir Harry Lauder, Al Jolson, Rudy Vallee and many others.

1975 Sir Edmund Percival **Hilary** (*b* 1919) recorded *Interview on Mountain Climbing* for Folkways.

Royalty

The earliest recording by a reigning monarch. It is reported that Queen Victoria recorded a message in *1896* for His Imperial Majesty King Menelek II, Emperor of Ethiopia, and sent it with instructions that it was to be destroyed after playing. No witness to its destruction has ever come forward, nor yet any trace of the cylinder itself has been found.

   The earliest surviving recording by a reigning monarch was made in *1903* for G & T in Bucharest by 'Carmen Sylva', a pseudonym of HM Queen Elisabeth of Romania (1843–1916). She read five of her own poems, including one in English: *A Friend*.

1911 Zonophone issued a patriotic disc marking the Coronation of King George V and Queen Mary.

1923 King George V (1865–1936), with Queen Mary, recorded an Empire Day Message for HMV on 28 March at Buckingham Palace. This is **the earliest surviving recording by a reigning British monarch**. It was made for 24 May (Empire Day) as a message to the children of the Empire. The message occupies one 10in side; on the reverse the Band of the Coldstream Guards plays *God Save the King* and *Home, Sweet Home*. King George V made many other speech and message recordings, the last at Sandringham on Christmas Day 1935 for HMV, when he read his final *Message to the Empire*.

1924 King Edward VIII (Edward Albert Christian George Andrew Patrick David, Prince of Wales from 1911 to 1936), recorded *Sportsmanship* for HMV at York House, London, on 1 July. Amongst his many other recordings are his *Daily Express Remembrance Festival Speech* at the Royal Albert Hall, London, on Armistice Day (11 November) 1927, issued by HMV, and *The King's Farewell*

King George V at the microphone.

Speech from Windsor Castle on 10 December, 1936, formally issued in America on Brunswick but also available from time to time on various unofficial discs.

1928 On 10 October the Tyne Bridge opening ceremony speech by King George V at Shipley Art Gallery, Gateshead, was recorded by Columbia and issued in February 1929. **This was the first time a monarch had made an electrical location recording**. Between the windings and the label appears an engraving by S L Scott of the Bridge and Coat of Arms. On the reverse is a welcoming address by W Swinburne, Town Clerk of Gateshead.

1929 King George VI (1895–1952) made many recordings: **his first**, as Duke of York: about 9 May, 1929, for HMV, at the Duke of York's Camp for Boys, New Romney: *My Camp: Its Purpose.* **His first as King**: 12 May, 1937, at Buckingham Palace: *A Message to the Empire* (HMV).

Amongst his other recordings were messages to

his peoples on the outbreak of World War II; on Victory; on his Silver Wedding; on the opening of the Festival of Britain; and his many Christmas and Empire Day messages. **His last recording**, *The King to his Peoples*, was made on Christmas Day, 1951, again issued by HMV.

1932 The Duke of Kent (1902 – killed in action 26 August, 1942) recorded the *Papworth Charity Appeal* in London for a flexible Durium 7½in disc.

1937 A recording of the Coronation of King George VI and Queen Elizabeth, together with the King's *Message to the Empire* of 12 May, 1937, was issued on 15 12in discs by HMV.

1939 Queen Elizabeth (The Queen Mother, *b* 1900) recorded *A Message to the Women of the Empire* for HMV on 11 November at Buckingham Palace. Her voice is also heard on *The Royal Silver Wedding*, made on 26 April, 1948 (HMV).

1940 Queen Elizabeth II (*b* 1926) has made many recordings: **her first**, as Princess Elizabeth, was *A Broadcast Message to Children* from Buckingham Palace on 13 October, 1940 (HMV). **Her first as Queen** was *A Christmas Day Message to the Commonwealth*, from Sandringham on 25 December, 1952 (HMV).

1948 The Duke of Edinburgh (*b* 1921) recorded a speech with his wife the then Princess Elizabeth at the Mansion House, London, in April; an extract was issued by Oriole.

1953 *The Coronation of Queen Elizabeth II* was issued on two 12in LPs by HMV; the same company also issued her *Coronation Day Speech*, recorded in Buckingham Palace on 2 June, 1953, and an LP, *Through Childhood to the Throne*, a commemorative album, included the voices of Kings George V and VI as well as the Queen herself, the Duke of Edinburgh and the Duke of Windsor.

1969 *The Investiture of the Prince of Wales* (1 July) at Caernarvon Castle, was issued by Delysé.

1981 The Wedding of Prince Charles (*b* 1948) and Lady Diana Spencer (*b* 1961) on 29 July was marked by a BBC recording of the actual St Paul's Cathedral ceremony. Other records concentrating on English, ceremonial, and royal

One of a series of striking sound effects LPs.   BBC

music were issued at the same time by CBS, Guild, Chandos, Philips, Hyperion, Pickwick and ASV.

Sound Effects

The earliest sound effects disc we have traced is on Columbia: *London Street Sounds* are the result of a microphone being set up in Leicester Square at 2.30pm on Tuesday, 11 September, 1928. Since then, many recordings have been offered for the benefit of amateur dramatic groups and, more recently, the home movie enthusiast. Some have been offered purely for their intrinsic qualities: the first railroad sound recordings were offered in America in October 1954: 44 78rpm sides, coupled according to customers' individual requirements.

The UK's first 'silent-surfaced' sound effects discs were offered by EMI in 1955, using vinyl material.

The following are amongst the many interesting effects discs offered since:

US Air Force – A Portrait in Sound. A sound history narrated by Arthur Godfrey, with sounds from the SPAD biplane of World War I to the F100 jet fighter passing through the sound barrier in 1958. The American Riverside series also offered airplane sounds during the late 1950s, and railroad sounds were big business on the Audio Fidelity, HIFI, Folkways, Cook, Link and Mobile labels at the same time.

In 1961 HMV issued their 7FX series of 7in sound effects discs for amateur and professional drama use. In waiving all copyright, EMI freed producers from the trouble and expense of procuring a reproducing licence (as well as from guilt and fear of prosecution); nevertheless, the discs themselves retained the customary warning on the labels that forbade unauthorised public performance and broadcasting.

The Isle of Man TT Races (two LPs: Stanley Schofield Productions, 1966).

Sounds of the Sea and Ships (Argo, 1966); *London's Last Trams* (Argo, 1967); *Engines on the Bundesbahn* (Argo, 1971); *Paris Express* (Argo, 1971); *The World of Motor Racing* (Decca, 1972: recorded at the Montague Motor Museum); *Steam Engines – The Last Chapter – Industrial Steam Engines* (Pye, 1972) and *Sounds of Bygone Transport*: London tram, paddle steamer, Mersey Railway, etc (Argo, 1974).

The BBC's sound effects series is **the most comprehensive in the UK**, and perhaps in the world. There are some 30 discs in the current catalogue, including: *London Locations and Country Backgrounds*; *Modern Warfare*; *Railways Remembered*; *The Orient Express: A Journey Through the Balkans*; *Traction Engines*; *Sounds of Death and Horror*; *Disasters*; *Off-Beat Effects* (with such delights as Electronic marshland, jabbering mice, 'explosion – musical', Ye Olde Car Engine, drinking rudely, duck laughter, whooshes, boings, doings and warbles); *Science Fiction* effects; *Birds and Other Sounds of the Countryside*; *Vanishing Sounds of Britain*; *Sounds of Speed*, and so on.

Special Projects

The industry has from time to time produced the unexpected; many instances will be found throughout this book. Others have been more difficult to categorise:

In 1968 the UK Abbey Co issued *The Searching Years '68*: three LPs of poetry and music written, composed and performed by children between the ages of eight and 17.

Argo recorded a series called *History Reflected* in 1969, consisting of six two-disc volumes of historical fare in drama, words and music. The volumes were titled:

I Agincourt 1415 – The Decline of Chivalry
II Elizabeth I – The Armada 1588
III Charles I 1649 – Court and Commons
IV Liberty – Equality – Fraternity
V The Great Exhibition 1851
VI World Wars – 1914 and 1939

Conifer Records in the UK offered a 54-cassette recording of *The Holy Koran* in Arabic and English, the project having taken three years to complete (1978–80).

Chivers Audio Books issued in 1980 a series of unabridged novels, each occupying four cassettes and giving up to 8 hours playing time. In the same year Caedmon issued 'Soundbooks': cassettes or LPs centred round famous authors (eg: Dylan Thomas, James Joyce, Edgar Allan Poe).

Sport

Baseball

1920 'Babe' (George Herman) Ruth (1895–1948), American baseball player, recorded *Babe Ruth's Home Run Story* in about September in New York. There is a rumour that this Pathé recording was actually spoken by Russell Hunting. About October 1927 Pathé also issued *Babe and Lou* (Gehrig) – *The Home Run Twins*, recorded in New York.

1930 *Knute Rockne Talks to his Team*. Rockne (1888–1931) was a Norwegian baseball player who appeared in the film *The Spirit of Notre Dame* in 1930. The scene with the above title was issued by Victor in 1931.

1955 *Baseball – An Action History* (US Columbia LP).

Jack Hobbs, cricketer, author and recording artist.
BBC HULTON PICTURE LIBRARY

Bowls

1962 *Bowl Your Best*, an instructional record (Epic).

Boxing

1927 The entire ten rounds of the Dempsey-Tunney fight in Soldiers Field, Chicago, on 22 September, 1927, in which the latter successfully defended his World Heavyweight title, was recorded by Paramount on five discs, one round per side. **This is the earliest live sporting event to be offered to the record buying public.**

1961 *Great Moments in Boxing* (US Coral). Boxers have also made a number of physical culture recordings – see **Health**, above.

Cricket

1925 Jack (John Berry) Hobbs (1882–1963), English cricketer and author of a number of cricketing books, recorded *My Cricket Record* in London for Columbia, and Broadcast issued his *How to Improve Your Cricket* in 1929.

1930 Tim (Thomas Welbourn) Wall (*b* 1904) and William Maldon Woodfull (1897–1965) both recorded a short speech on 17 September in the Small Queen's Hall, London, which were included on an HMV disc.

1930 Don Bradman (*b* 1908), the first cricketer to be knighted (1949), recorded talks for both HMV and Columbia during this year, the latter including a piano solo.

1933 Frank R Foster (1889–1958), English cricketer, recorded *Leg Theory as Viewed by Frank R Foster* in London on 29 May for Columbia.

1933 Lord Hawke (Martin Bladon, 1860–1938), English cricketer, recorded *International Cricket* and *Yorkshire Cricket* in London for a Parlophone disc in June.

1933 Harold Larwood (*b* 1904), English cricketer, recorded *Leg Theory – A Reply* in London on 29 May for Columbia.

1970 *Cricket*: reading by members of the Lord's Taverners during the tea intervals of the Player's County League 1970 Season (BBC Records).

Fishing

1970 *Gone Fishing*, a miscellany including a fisherman's quiz (BBC Records).

Golf

1922 Chick (Charles) Evans Jr (1890–1979), US golfer, recorded a five-disc album for Brunswick in New York in May entitled *Chick Evans' Golf Secrets*.

1961 *Par Golf in Eight Steps* (Dot).

Golf – Tommy Armour (Grand Award).

1971 *Famous Players, Personalities, and Events*, recorded in the UK (BBC Records).

Horse Racing

1931 From One Sportsman to Another, by His Highness the Aga Khan (Aga Sultan Sir Mahmoud Shah, 1877–1957), racehorse owner, recorded in London for Columbia.

Motor Racing

1955–60 Stanley Schofield Productions of London issued a series of nine LPs and nine EPs titled *Motor Racing*. They included excerpts from the London-to-Brighton 1956 Jubilee run of 'Old Crocks', and many other races of the period.

1956–62 The American Riverside label issued a motor racing series of recordings including Sebring races 1956–62, *Pit Stop!* (the story of a motor race), and conversations with Phil Hill, Stirling Moss, Carroll Shelby, etc.

1960 The Formula One Grand Prix Car (1937–60), written by Lawrence Pomeroy (Schofield).

1961 Karts in Action (Riverside).

Scrambles – Motorcycling (Riverside).

1963 Big Sounds of the Drags (Capitol).

1967 Hot Rods and Dragsters (Riverside).

Rugby

1971 Rugby Highlights 1971: Lions in New Zealand (Decca, issued in 1972).

Tennis

1925 Suzanne Lenglen (1899–1938), French champion tennis player and author of tennis books, recorded *Lawn Tennis* for HMV on 8 July at Hayes, Middlesex.

Sport – General

1957 The Thrill of Sport (US Columbia).

1969 Highlights of 21 years of BBC's Sports Reports (BBC Records).

Statesmen, Stateswomen, and Leaders

Very many politicians have recorded; so many, in fact, that our list is limited to only those who became leaders in their respective countries.

1888 William Ewart **Gladstone** (1809–98), British Prime Minister four times between 1868 and 1894, recorded a cylinder in London on 22 November. It was an appreciation message to Edison which begins: 'The request you have done me the honour to make, to receive a record of my voice, is one that I cheerfully comply with ...' This, and a recording of Bismarck made the same year, are **the first recordings of statesmen.**

1900 Theodore **Roosevelt** (1858–1919), US President 1901–9, made his first recording for Edison in New York about August 1900: *Roosevelt's Speech to Labor.* He went on to make several other recordings for both Edison and Victor in 1912.

1908 Andrew Bonar **Law** (1858–1923), British Prime Minister 1922–3, recorded *A Message from Andrew Bonar Law* in London for The Gramophone Co in January.

William Howard **Taft** (1857–1930) was extremely busy in the recording studios during the run-up to the elections that put him in the White House from 1908 to 1913. During August he made 12 cylinders for Edison, 13 discs for Victor, and ten discs and five cylinders for Columbia at Hot Springs, Virginia (some of the Columbia discs being released also as cylinders). He made a further seven discs for Victor on 1 October, 1912, at Beverly, Mass.

1909 In the summer, Herbert Henry **Asquith** (1852–1928), British Prime Minister 1908–16, introduced his 'People's Budget'. HMV issued a recording of a speech by him about this budget, and David **Lloyd George** (1863–1945), in opposition at the time but to become Prime Minister from 1916 to 1922, also made a recording (23 July) in London about the contents of the budget (Lloyd George made several other recordings in London between 1929 and 1942). That budget was also the subject of the very first recording by **the most prolific of all recording politicians:** Winston Spencer **Churchill** (1874–1965). His *Speech on the Budget*, made on 14 July, was issued by HMV. **His first recording as Prime Minister** (1940–5 and 1951–5) was *In This Solemn Hour* 19 May, 1940, issued by HMV. See also below: 1957–8.

1912 Woodrow **Wilson** (1856–1924), US President 1913–21, recorded six speeches for Victor on 24 September in New York.

1917 Eleuterios **Venizelos** (1864–1936), Prime Minister of Greece five times between 1910 and 1933, recorded for HMV in the Ritz Hotel, London, on 21 November the speech he had given five days earlier at the Mansion House.

1918 Warren Gamaliel **Harding** (1865–1923), US President 1921–3, made several recordings, the first being *The Republic Must Awaken* on 17 January (on the Nation's Forum label).

1920 Calvin **Coolidge** (1872–1933), US President 1923–9, recorded *Law and Order* on 3 and 4 March, and *Equal Rights* on 29 June, both at Northampton, Mass, and both issued on Nation's Forum. His *President Coolidge Welcomes Charles Lindbergh*, recorded on wire on 11 June, 1927, at Washington, DC, was issued on a Victor disc.

Franklin Delano **Roosevelt** (1882–1945), US President 1933–45, recorded *Americanism* on about 3 September in New York for Nation's Forum. In Washington, DC, on 30 September, 1934 he made four discs for Victor, and the same company issued his historical speech *Declaration of War on Germany and Japan*, which was broadcast on 8 December, 1941. Profits from the sale of the records went to charities nominated by the President.

1920 Eamonn de **Valera** (1882–1974), President of the Irish Republic 1959–74, made two discs for Nation's Forum in New York: in March or April he recorded *Recognition of the Republic of Ireland* and *St Patrick's Day Address*, and in November a *Memorial Address* for Mayor Terence McSwiney.

1923 William Ferguson **Massey** (1856–1925), Irish-born Prime Minister of New Zealand 1912–25, recorded *The British Empire* for HMV at Hayes on 22 November.

1925 William Lyon **Mackenzie King** (1874–1950), Prime Minister of Canada 1921–30 and 1935–48, is heard reassuring the audience and calling for calm and order when the lighting failed during his speech at The Forum, Montreal, on 19 October. This speech was issued on Apex.

?1926 James Ramsay **MacDonald** (1866–1937), British Prime Minister 1924 and 1929–35, recorded a speech in London for the New Leader label, and made several other records during his second premiership.

1927 Herbert **Hoover** (1874–1964), US President 1929–33, recorded a number of addresses for Victor between 1927 and 1932, not one of which, apparently, was issued commercially.

1928 Stanley **Baldwin** (1867–1947), British Prime Minister 1923–9 and 1935–7, recorded speeches for HMV (1928–38) and Columbia (1929 and 1937).

1929 Arthur Neville **Chamberlain** (1869–1940), British Prime Minister 1937–40, recorded *Conservatives and Social Reform* for Columbia in London on 15 April, *A Message to the Empire* at No 10 Downing Street on 27 September, 1938, a speech at Heston Airport on 30 September, 1938 (both issued by HMV), and the historical declaration of war on Germany on 3 September, 1939, a radio announcement which has appeared on various labels.

1929 William Morris **Hughes** (1864–1952), Welsh-born Prime Minister of Australia 1915–23, recorded *The Issues Before the People* at Homebush on 20 September (Columbia), and *A Message for Australia's 150th Anniversary* at Sydney in January 1938 (Process).

Earle Christmas Grafton **Page** (1880–1961), Australian acting Prime Minister four times (1923–37) and Prime Minister (1939), recorded *Abolition of Duplication of the Industrial Court* at Homebush, New South Wales, on 20 September (Columbia).

1931 Mahatma Mohandas Karamchand **Gandhi** (1869–1948), Indian leader, recorded *His Spiritual Message* for Columbia in London on 17 October.

Jan **Smuts** (1870–1950), South African Prime Minister 1919–24 and 1939–48, recorded his speech at the Central Hall, Westminster, London, on 23 September (HMV), and his Address to *Both Houses of Parliament* in the House of Lords on 21 October, 1942 (HMV).

1938 Bertram Sydney Barnsdale **Stevens** (1889–1973), Prime Minister of Australia

1923–9, recorded *A Message on the 150th Anniversary of Australia* in January (Process; see also W M Hughes, above, at 1929).

1944 Dwight D **Eisenhower** (1890–1969), US President 1953–61, recorded *Address to the People of Europe on the Normandy Landings*, a broadcast made on 6 June, 1944 ('D-Day'), and an *Address to the People of London After Being Made a Freeman of the City*, on 12 June, 1945, both later issued on Oriole.

1945 Clement Richard **Attlee** (1883–1967), British Prime Minister 1945–51. His broadcast about the General Election and the Japanese surrender was issued by Oriole; and his speech at the Opening Assembly of the United Nations Organisation in 1946 appeared on two HMV discs.

1947 Jawaharlal **Nehru** (1889–1964), Indian Prime Minister 1947–64, made a *Speech of Acceptance of the Independence of India* on 3 June, which was issued on Oriole.

1949 Harry S **Truman** (1884–1972), US President 1945–53. An extract from his speech on the North Atlantic Treaty Organisation, made on 5 April in Washington, DC, was issued on Oriole.

1957–8 HMV issued an 11-disc series of the wartime speeches of Sir Winston Churchill; in 1964 Decca produced a 12-LP set with book of Churchill's memoires and speeches from 1918 to 1945.

1960 Voices Towards Peace (Brunswick) is a compilation taken from United Nations archives of speeches by David Ben-Gurion, J F Dulles, Dwight D Eisenhower, Queen Elizabeth II, A Gromyko, Haile Selassie, Dag Hammarskjold, N Kruschev, Trygve Lie, Cabot Lodge, Golda Meir, Jawaharlal Nehru, Nkrumah, Lester Pearson, President Roosevelt and his wife, Harry S Truman, Vishinsky, and many others. The narrator was Ralph Bellamy.

1961 *The First Family*, a humorous send-up of President Kennedy's family by Vaughn Meader (London) became a best-seller; in 1963 London issued a follow-up by Marc London: *The President Strikes Back!*

1963 *John Fitzgerald Kennedy* – a Memorial Album, assembled and recorded by the Premier label on the day the President was assassinated, is **the fastest selling LP of all time**: four million were sold in six days (7–12 December) at 99¢ each.

1965 *The Kennedy Wit*, introduced by Adlai E Stevenson and narrated by David Brinkley, was issued by RCA.

War

A number of recorded statements about war have been made by politicians and statesmen – see above. Musical works inspired by war scenes have been recorded in quantities too numerous to detail here. They include major symphonic works (the most notorious being Shostakovich's *Leningrad* Symphony, written partly while the composer was living under siege in that city in 1941), marches and other short pieces marking events (eg: Eric Coates's *Dam Busters' March*) or hardware (Walton's *Spitfire Prelude and Fugue*), songs to boost morale (such as those sung by Vera Lynn during World War II) and many other pieces. Other recordings, some of them 'actuality' documents, are less well known. (See also Section III.)

c 1898 **The Spanish-American War** inspired a number of descriptive recordings made in New York studios:

Emil Cassi, chief trumpeter of Roosevelt's Rough Riders, recorded the calls he had sounded on 1 July for Berliner in November of that year, and later also for Columbia. *On Board the Oregon* and *The Capture of Santiago* were recorded for Columbia in 1899, *The Battle of Manila*, featuring Victor Herbert's Band, appeared on Zonophone about 1900, *The Battle of Santiago*, sung by the unaccompanied Haydn Quartet, appeared on Victor in 1902, and towards the end of the following year Columbia issued *Tone Pictures of the 71st Regiment Leaving for Cuba*.

1904 **The Russo-Japanese War**. In September, US Columbia recorded in New York *Capture of the Russian Forts at Port Arthur*, a studio description of events leading to the fall of Port Arthur to the Japanese on 1 January, 1905.

1913 Field Marshal Lord Frederick Sleigh Roberts (1832–1914) recorded *National Service Address* on 14 July, in London. It was issued on six single-sided and three double-sided HMV discs.

1914–18 **World War I**. Although recording techniques were in their adolescence, the gramophone became a powerful documentary aid. The following recordings were made in British studios:

With the Fleet off Heligoland (Regal, 28 August, 1914).

Arrival of the British Troops in France (Regal, September 1914).

The British Expeditionary Force Landing in France (Edison Bell Winner, 1914).

Courage, the *Daily Telegraph* Recruiting Song, sung by Miss Ruby Helder, 'lady tenor' in March (HMV).

Experiences on the Sinking of the 'Arabic' (a passenger ship sunk by German torpedoes on 18 August, 1915). Actor Kenneth Douglas, a survivor, recorded his experiences anonymously on 7 September for HMV at Hayes.

With Our Boys at the Front – On The March; In The Trenches, by Sgt Edward Dwyer, VC (Regal, November 1915).

A Message from the Trenches, by Labour MP and TUC Chairman Ben Tillett (HMV, June 1915).

Recruiting Speech, by Sir Charles Wakefield (1859–1941), Lord Mayor of London 1915–16 (HMV, 25 January, 1916).

Conditions at the Front were brought to American audiences by Gen Sir John J Pershing's (1860–1948) *From the Battlefields of France*, recorded for Nation's Forum in Paris in March 1918.

The first documentary location recording was made by W C Gaisberg (Fred's brother), who was also **the first to die to get a recording**. He went to the French front line near Lille and set up his portable recording machine in a ruined farmhouse on 9 October, 1918, in order to record an actual gas bombardment. He got his recording, but at a price. He was gassed, and in November, within days of the Armistice, he succumbed to an influenza epidemic due to his

'Monty' enjoys a break during his desert campaign.
POPPERFOTO

lowered resistance. HMV issued *An Actual Recording of the Gas Shell Bombardment by the Royal Garrison Artillery preparatory to the British Troops Entering Lille* as a 12in disc, coupled with *The Conundrum*, made in 1911, in which four separate tracks were recorded side-by-side so that the listener was unable to tell in advance which track would be selected by the needle. It seems an inappropriately flippant coupling in view of the tragic circumstances of its reverse side.

In *1920* the *Armistice Day Ceremony of the Burial of the Unknown Soldier* in Westminster Abbey was recorded by telephone landlines (see Section IV).

1939–45 World War II

1940 The Navy's Here. George King, Second Engineer of the *Doric Star*, recorded a talk about the rescue of 300 British prisoners from the German prison ship *Altmark* by HMS *Cossack* (commanded by Philip Vian) in Josing Fjord, Norway, on 16 February (Regal Zonophone, 8 March, 1940). *A Dog-Fight Over the English Channel*, an eye-witness account for the BBC on 14 July, 1940, by Charles Gardner, issued by Decca. *Instructions for Dealing with Incendiary Bombs* (Decca).

1942 Nightingales and Bombers. The BBC attempted to record the song of the nightingale in a Surrey wood on the night of 19 May, but the recording was interrupted by the sound of British bombers on their way to bomb Mannheim. Nevertheless, HMV issued the recording under the title given above. Field Marshal Bernard Montgomery (1887–1977) briefed his officers in Cairo on 13 August, 1942, before the Battle of Alamein; an extract was issued by Oriole.

1948 American Columbia issued what was up to that time **the world's best-selling spoken-word album**, a collection of pre-war recordings by the ace news broadcaster Edward R Murrow (*d* 1965) titled *I Can Hear it Now* (78s at first, then LP). The news items told of events in Europe leading up to the outbreak of war. As CBS correspondent, Murrow became popular

in America for his unflappable style, but he won British hearts, too, by enduring many nights of Blitz, calmly reporting what he could see from one of the most dangerous places in London – the roof of the conspicuous Broadcasting House. Consequently, his album of newscasts had a spectacular sale on both sides of the Atlantic and enjoyed a renewal of interest when CBS re-issued a two-LP set of his wartime broadcasts shortly after his death. On the whole, though, the documentary record is not a good seller unless it can be linked (or is linked by fate) to some momentous events, as in the case of the assassination of President Kennedy – see above. However, World War II, together with other wars, and the fear of World War III, have inspired many more recent recordings:

1950 In January UK Decca issued 16 double-sided 78s called *Prelude to Pearl Harbor*, with illustrations from contemporary recordings.

1956 Hitler's Inferno: speeches, rallies, and marches of Nazi Germany (Audio Fidelity).

1961 American Civil War – a Re-Created Skirmish (Riverside).

Sounds of the Third Reich (Sonic, two LPs).

Airman! – Air Force Basic Training; *Boot Camp! – Navy Recruit Training*; *Double Time! – Army Basic Training*; *Making of a Marine* (all on the US Sounds of Documentary label).

If The Bomb Falls (Tops).

Cybernetic Warfare, a discourse by a gentleman called Philbrick (Key).

1962 Sinking of the Bismarck (Oriole).

Nuremberg War Criminal Trials (Roulette).

Six Million Accuse: The Eichmann Trial (United Artists).

1971 Day of Infamy – Pearl Harbor, 7 December 1941 (Listening Library).

The anti-war protest movement got under way in 1965 with a record titled *Freedom Songs* (Folkways) and continued with *Read-in for Peace in Vietnam*, readings and comments (Broadside, 1967 – the same year that Documentary issued *Vietnam With the American Fighting Man*), and *We Shall Overcome* (Broadside, 1969).

Long Playing

At first, cylinders measured just over 4in (10·2cm) in length (they were called '4-inch cylinders' for convenience even though their true, if not invariable, length was nearer $4\frac{3}{16}$ – 10·6cm) and gave about 2 minutes' playing time. This was severely limiting for artists, who had hardly time to get under way before the operator was tapping his stopwatch anxiously. Before the end of the 19th century a number of attempts had been made to increase playing time (see Section VII). Edison's Amberol cylinders appeared in October 1908, their 4-minute playing time competing favourably with the 12in disc introduced in 1903. Shortly afterwards, Edison introduced his 'Gem D' model phonograph to accommodate both 2-minute and 4-minute cylinders. However, the 4-minute cylinders were made of wax and were found to be unsatisfactory after a few playings because they could not withstand the pressure of the stylus.

The improved Blue Amberols of 1912 were made of a tough blue celluloid material over a plaster of paris base and gave, for their time, outstandingly clear and ample reproduction, without the disadvantage of rapid wear. A machine capable of playing cylinders 25in (63·5cm) long was mooted by the inventor of the 'Multiphone' (a coin-operated cylinder-playing juke-box), but was apparently not made. Such cylinders would have given a playing time of about 15 minutes.

Meanwhile, although disc-users were happy with the 2½-minute 10in disc for popular songs, novelty numbers and music hall skits, and the 3½ to 4½-minute 12in disc for some operatic arias and short orchestral pieces, increasingly they felt the need for longer playing times. To attempt to meet this need, the English Neophone Co introduced **the first long playing discs** in 1904. Designed for use with a sapphire stylus, they measured 10in and played for 12 minutes at the then 'standard' speed of around 78rpm. The increased playing time was achieved by the adaptation to disc for the first time of the cylinder's 'hill-and-dale' cutting technique, but the results from the celluloid-and-cardboard laminate discs were disastrously

noisy even for those days. They were, however, 'unbreakable', but if left in a sunny place would curl up. Later that year, Neophone again showed an interest in revolutionary ideas to increase playing time and produced 20in (50·8cm) lateral-cut discs playing for between 8 and 10 minutes, offering, unbroken, popular light orchestral items.

The Neophone Co, then, reflecting the vision of their inventor Dr William Michaelis, in addition to being the first to produce long playing discs, was **the first to adapt vertical cutting to discs**, and **the first to offer 20in discs for sale**, all in 1904. Unfortunately, surface noise was a severe problem, and the price of the huge 20in disc at 10/6 (52½p), against 1/– (5p) for the standard 12in disc, was prohibitive. Neophone, together with its progressive and revolutionary endeavours, disappeared in 1908.

Further attacks on the bogey of short playing time were made by American Victor, Italian Fonotipia and French Pathé with vertical cut 13¾in (34·9cm) discs in 1904 (Pathé also produced 20in discs), by Marathon ('long runners'!) with their vertical cut 'microgroove' discs in 1914, and by the 16in (40·6cm) discs rotating at 33⅓rpm that were used in the 1930s for broadcast transcriptions. The American Vitaphone Co in 1926 introduced 16in shellac discs playing at 33⅓rpm to be synchronised with a film spool. Groove spacing was only slightly narrower than that of a standard 78rpm disc; therefore playing time did not exceed 20 minutes. **These discs were the first to revolve at 33⅓rpm.** They were not offered for sale to the public, of course, but other experiments were marketed, with success measured from slight to nil:

1923 The English World Record Ltd issued 12in discs designed to be used with a machine geared by a wheel tracking across the disc to adjust its rotational speed constantly relative to the position of the pick-up on the surface: 33⅓rpm at the outer winding and 78rpm at the centre, thus giving a constant linear tracking speed. (See Section VII.)
1927 In America, Edison made 10in and 12in discs in which the number of windings was increased from the standard 150 to 450 per

inch. Rotating at about 80rpm these discs gave a playing time respectively of 12 and 20 minutes per side, but the volume of sound was weak, and, ironically, Edison's catalogue contained – and his recording policy envisaged – no music that could take artistic advantage of the increased playing time. They were not sold outside the USA.

1929 June: The American Broadcast Recording Co Inc issued 8in and 10in 78rpm discs in which narrow grooving increased playing time by about 50 per cent.

1931 Another American experiment: RCA Victor produced 10in and 12in discs turning at $33\frac{1}{3}$rpm and with about 150 windings to the inch, designed for use with existing needles. Some were pressed in shellac; others in flexible plastic called Victrolac. The 12in discs gave 12–14 minutes per side, but the recordings, mainly dubbed from existing records, reproduced poorly and there was unacceptably high surface noise. **The first complete symphony recorded with long playing in mind** was Beethoven's Fifth: Leopold Stokowski and the Philadelphia Orchestra made the recording in 1931 for RCA's launch of these LP records in November of that year. The first two movements (each recorded without breaks) were complete on side one, the Scherzo and Finale (recorded as a continuous stretch of music) on side two.

1932 **The first LP jazz experiments** were recorded by Victor on 9 February by Duke Ellington and his Orchestra. The titles were: *East St Louis Toodle-Oo*, *Lots o' Fingers*, and *Black and Tan Fantasy*.

1932 British Homophone introduced the 'four-in-one' microgroove disc.

1935 Talking Books for the Blind were produced: 24rpm discs giving 30 minutes playing time.

Meanwhile, companies were trying to mitigate the disadvantage of short playing time by 'autocoupling' their multiple classical sets. With this system, the first record of, for example, a three-disc set would contain sides 1 and 6, the second disc sides 2 and 5, the third disc sides 3 and 4. By stacking the records in the correct

HMV radio-gramophones were also furniture in 1937. J FROST

order on an autochange gramophone, the first side uppermost at the bottom of the pile, the whole sequence of sides 1 to 3 would be played through before the listener had to move from his seat to turn over the stack for the second half of the cycle: sides 4 to 6. The gaps in the music remained, of course, while the pick-up returned to its rest, the next disc fell, and the pick-up placed itself onto it, but provided the listener was sanguine enough to believe that nothing could go wrong with the machinery, he was relieved of the necessity of jumping up every $3\frac{1}{2}$ to $4\frac{1}{2}$ minutes to change the record. Autocoupling became so popular that in November 1948 British Decca announced that all multiple classical sets would be available only in this format. On the other hand, EMI and other companies continued to give the buyer a choice between 'auto' and 'straight' coupling. Incidentally, autocoupling continued well into the LP era but was finally discarded when evidence was presented that the action of dropping one LP onto another, with the inevitable grit being crushed in between, was doing untold damage to the soft plastic surfaces.

Autochangers and close-grooving inevitably put a strain upon the needles then in use, but experiments with harder materials had been made many years earlier.

The Playback Stylus

The stylus used for playing back Edison's vertical cut cylinders needed the hardness of a diamond if the abrasive surface were not to take too great a toll of the point. In fact, diamond styli were sold for many years for both cylinder and disc reproduction: Edison's disc phonograph, made from 1912 to 1929, used a diamond-tipped needle for the thick Edison vertical cut close-grooved disc that played for some 50 per cent longer than a lateral cut disc. As records were made of progressively less abrasive materials it became possible to use the considerably cheaper steel needles. Furthermore, different grades of steel were sold: softer for 'soft tone', and harder for 'loud tone'.

Today's understandable concern for the preservation of expensive LP surfaces by the use of styli of correct size, shape, and material, and by the use of light-weight pick-ups, has not always been evident. On the contrary, during the heyday of the coarse-groove 78rpm disc, when pick-ups exerted a needle pressure upon the disc of anything between 100 and 200 grams, the rough disc surface was relied upon to grind down the tip of the needle in the first few (ie: fastest) windings, so that it would fit the more snugly into the groove. In addition, the abrasive content of shellac helped to strengthen the groove wall against the onslaught of the needle as it carried the weight of the pick-up and conveyed it across the surface.

By the end of one 78rpm side most steel needles were worn beyond further use and had to be discarded: so-called 'chromium' needles gave a somewhat better performance, and in 1935 the marketing of semi-permanent sapphire styli gave a life time some ten times that of

steel needles but wear on the records was increased, making necessary the development of 'light-weight' pick-ups (with a pressure of 'only' some 35 grams) to take advantage of the more durable tip without increasing wear. These pick-ups were introduced about 2 years after the appearance of the sapphire stylus. Some sapphire styli were fitted to a metal shank compressed back-to-front in its central part and bent into a half-moon shape. These were called 'trailer-type'. This gave some spring to the assembly and helped the pick-up to 'ride' the groove. The compressions of the shank, however, might have assisted in playing the by then obsolete hill-and-dale discs, but they did nothing whatever to lessen the strain upon lateral cut grooves.

Another attempt to reduce record wear was with the use of thorn, bamboo, cactus spine, or fibre needles, which barely retained enough point to last one side, so dealers sold small hand-operated grinding mills for resharpening them. Thorn needles gave a mellower tone than steel, chromium or sapphire, and were widely used by serious collectors intent upon preserving their records. Advertisements in hobby magazines of the time offering carefully used second-hand records might begin: 'For sale: fibred symphonies...'

The fibre needle with the longest life would appear to be an example, reported in 1930, that had been sharpened 16 times and had played 1091 sides.

The appearance of the sapphire stylus (a ruby stylus was also offered), with greatly increased durability, contributed to the feasibility of vinylite LP discs in 1948, the tip radius being reduced from 0·065mm for 78rpm to 0·025mm for LP. The appearance of stereo discs in 1958 required a reduction in tip radius to 0·0125mm, and in late 1965 the elliptical stylus was introduced with typical radii of 0·018mm wide by 0·0075mm front-to-back. This shape more readily complies with the shape of the groove, which is cut in the studio by a cutter approximately corresponding to these dimensions.

By 1970 diamond tip was commonplace, and playing weights were being progressively reduced. The owner of a modern playing deck, tracking at about 1 gram, should have his diamond stylus checked after about 100 hours' playing time.

The last attempt to increase playing time in the standard coarse-groove 78rpm format came in September 1950: Deutsche Grammophon Gesellschaft, together with their French affiliate Polydor (and, from 1952, Fonodan in Denmark), issued what were described as 'variable micrograde' 78rpm shellac discs (LVM 72000 series or 92000 series for auto-coupled sets) in which the groove spacing varied according to the amplitude of the music in the windings (this was to become standard cutting technique for LP discs but was rarely taken to its ultimate usefulness which would in favourable circumstances allow up to one hour on a 12in LP side). The increased playing time of about 8 minutes per side put too great a strain on the fibre or cheap steel needles then in common use, which wore out before the end of a side. Jewel-tipped needles were more successful.

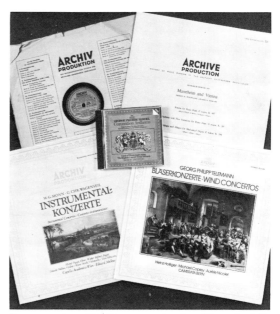

Five generations of Archiv presentation, from 78rpm 'variable micrograde' via LP to CD. COURTESY: DG

The Modern LP

A successful format for long playing records was finally developed in the laboratories of the American Columbia Co by Dr Peter Goldmark, chief of CBS Research Dept, and William Bachman, Director of Development, Columbia Records Inc, in the late 1940s, but the achievement brought with it a bitter war between rival companies that was to last for several years and spread from the US to the UK, ill-concealed from the public.

The first successful release of long playing vinylite $33\frac{1}{3}$ rpm microgroove discs was announced by American Columbia to the press at a reception at the Waldorf-Astoria Hotel, New York, on Friday 26 June, 1948. In an effort to establish a standard for the industry, Columbia had several months beforehand invited their chief competitor, RCA, to join with them in the launch. RCA, perhaps apprehensive because of their failure with long playing in 1931, appeared to hesitate. Consequently, Columbia's launch

Peter Goldmark and William Bachman, developers of the first successful long playing disc.

went ahead without them. Their discs were 10in and 12in in diameter, with 224–300gpi (grooves per inch). Machines to play them were made by the Philco Radio and Television Co of Philadelphia.

Meanwhile, RCA secretly instructed its research department to develop, and develop quickly, a long playing system totally different from, and above all incompatible with, the Columbia format. In January 1949 RCA announced the first release of 45rpm 7in discs made of vinyl, giving, at first, the same playing time as the 78rpm disc. Thus began the famous 'battle of the speeds'.

RCA Victor's 45s, although not long playing, were a modern concept, designed to replace the fragile coarse-grooved 78 by a non-breakable microgroove record. They had a centre hole $1\frac{1}{2}$in (3·8cm) in diameter which fitted over the central column of the newly-developed compact machine, with a crystal pickup tracking at 7 grams. This column incorporated an automatic change mechanism that cut the delay between the end of one record and the beginning of the next to $1\frac{1}{2}$ seconds. This is, however, a misleading figure, since the music on the first record might end several seconds before the run-out groove took the pick-up sufficiently far to the centre of the disc for the autochange mechanism to operate. Consequently, the gaps in the music were often of 5 seconds' duration or even longer, which made the format no real rival to Columbia's continuous playing time of 20 minutes or more.

When Columbia made their launch they announced that licences were available for all competitors to produce LPs, and in a year or so other companies were entering the same market.

Since Columbia's LP launch was so historical and successful (sales in the first year approached 3·5 million units), it is worth examining the first release in some detail. It was dominated by serious music, that being rightly considered the most likely to benefit from continuity. The numbering system of that first release was governed by the alphabetical list of composers represented, along the lines of the earliest Pathé cylinder catalogue of 1898. The ambitious and broadly-based catalogue of 101 discs included 12 in the 10in ML 2000 series, 55 in the 12in ML 4000 series, three complete operas (*La Bohème*, *Hansel und Gretel*, and *La Traviata*) in

the SL 100 set series, four non-operatic sets in the SL 150 series (including Shakespeare's *Othello*, starring Paul Robeson), and a number of popular items. Represented were all but two of Beethoven's Symphonies, his three most popular Piano Sonatas, the Violin Concerto, *Emperor* Piano Concerto, String Quartets and Violin Sonatas, together with Tchaikovsky's last three Symphonies, his Violin Concerto, and Overtures *Romeo and Juliet* and *1812*; Mozart's last two Symphonies, his C major String Quintet, Arias sung by Ezio Pinza, and a boxed set of Violin Sonatas; Brahms's first and last Symphonies, Violin Concerto and Piano Concerto No 2; popular works by Bach, Bizet, Chopin, Debussy, Dvořák, Franck, Gershwin, Grieg, Khachaturian, Mahler, Mendelssohn, Mussorgsky, Prokofiev, Ravel, Schubert, Schumann, Shostakovich, both Johann and Richard Strauss, Stravinsky, Wagner and Wieniawski. Artists included Bruno Walter, Rudolf Serkin, Nathan Milstein, Artur Rodzinsky, Fritz Reiner, André Kostelanetz, Eugene Ormandy, the Budapest String Quartet, George Szell, Lily Pons, and Paul Robeson. There were among the popular records (CL series) discs by Frank Sinatra, Dinah Shore, Buddy Clark, Xavier Cugat, and Harry James. Within a few months the lists had been expanded dramatically not only in the classical and popular fields but also in the areas of country music and dance (HL series), European Continental artists (FL series), and children's records (JL series). It was largely due to this wide-appealing, frankly popular and rapidly expanding catalogue that the success of Columbia's LP launch was so decisive. In addition, a large number of recordings had been made with the LP in mind, unlike the majority of those issues in RCA's abortive long playing release of 1931.

By October 1949, the cover date of **the first multi-company LP catalogue** (compiled and issued by William Schwann of Cambridge, Mass), ten companies in addition to Columbia were issuing LPs. The following chart, based upon that first *Schwann* catalogue, shows the lowest (and therefore presumably the earliest) numbers in the catalogues of these companies.

Allegro
10in   LA 1 Schubert *Trio*, Op 100
        LA 2 Beethoven *Violin Sonatas*,
          Op 12/1 and Op 96
        LA 3 Edith Weiss-Mann: Baroque
          Harpsichord Music
        LA 4 Beethoven *Trio*, Op 70/Haydn
          Trio in G
        LA 5 Bach Harpsichord Music
        LA 6 Renaissance Music for the Lute

Artist
12in   100 American Music by Copland,
        Gilbert, Cowell and Ives

Capitol
10in   L 8003 Hindemith *Mathis der Maler*
        L 8004 Bruckner *Mass in E minor*
        L 8011 Reger *Böcklin* Suite
        L 8016 Mozart *Symphony No 40*
        L 8028 Stravinsky *Jeu des Cartes*
12in   P 8000 Erna Sack: European
        Nightingale
        P 8013 Strauss *Heldenleben*
        P 8020 Sibelius *Symphony No 1*

Cetra Soria
10in   LP 40003 Respighi *Ancient Airs and*
        Dances Suite No 1/*The Birds*
12in   LP 1001 Mozart *Requiem*
12in   LP 1201 Verdi *Forza del Destino*
(sets)   (abridged)
        LP 1202 Haydn *The Seasons*
        (abridged)
        LP 1203 Mascagni *L'Amico Fritz*
        (complete)
        LP 1204 Bellini *Norma* (complete)
        LP 1205 Donizetti *Lucia di*
        Lammermoor (complete)
        LP 1206 Puccini *Turandot* (complete)
12in   50003 Verdi *Rigoletto* Arias and
        Duets
        50004 Vivaldi *Four Seasons*

Columbia – see text

Concert Hall
12in   CHC 1 Vivaldi *Four Seasons*
        CHC 2 Khachaturian *Violin Concerto*
        CHC 3 Tchaikovsky *Piano Concerto*
        No 2
        CHC 4 Brahms *Clarinet Quintet*

CHC 5 Brahms *Piano Sonata No 1*
CHC 6 Piano Recital – Layonnet

Decca
10in   DLP 5000 Bing Crosby: Hits from
        Musical Comedies
        DLP 5001 Bing Crosby Sings Jerome
        Kern
        DLP 5003 Guy Lombardo Waltzes
        DLP 5006 Jolson Sings Again
        DLP 5007 *Dancing in the Dark* –
        Cavallaro
        DLP 5008 Strauss Waltzes for
        Dancing
10in   DLP 7000 *Desert Song*
        DLP 7001 Radio City Music Hall
        Souvenir Album
        DLP 7002 *Oklahoma/Porgy and Bess*
        excerpts
        DLP 7003 Heifetz Plays Gershwin
12in   DLP 8000 *Oklahoma* – original cast
        DLP 8001 *Annie Get Your Gun* –
        original cast
        DLP 8002 *Song of Norway* – original
        cast
        DLP 8003 *Carousel* – original cast
        DLP 8004 *Merry Widow* – New York
        Production
        DLP 8005 Listening Time with Fred
        Waring

London
10in   LPS 11 Viennese Songs – Roswaenge
        LPS 13 Concert Favorites – Conley
        LPS 19 Mantovani and his Orchestra
        LPS 23 Schumann *Dichterliebe*
        LPS 24 Recorder and Harpsichord
        Recital – Dolmetsch/Saxby
        LPS 26 Operatic Recital – Conley
10in   LPB 15 Felix King
        LPB 16 On Parade – HM Irish Guards
        LPB 17 Phil Green: Rhythm on Reeds
        LPB 18 *Blue Danube* – Ronnie Munro
        LPB 20 Will Glahe Orchestra
12in   LLP 1 Brahms *Violin Concerto*
        LLP 2 Tchaikovsky *Symphony No 4*
        LLP 3 Berlioz *Romeo and Juliet*
        LLP 4 Dvořák *String Quartet No*
        6/Mozart *Adagio and Fugue*
        LLP 5 Bartók *Concerto for Orchestra*

LLP 6 Rimsky-Korsakov
Scheherazade
12in LLPA 1 Prelude to Pearl Harbor
(Pre-War Broadcasts)

Mercury
10in MG 15000 R Strauss *Don
Juan*/Tchaikovsky *1812*
MG 15001 Schumann *Symphony No 4*
MG 15004 Strauss Waltzes
MG 15005 Shostakovich *Trio in E
minor*

10in MG 25001 *Student Prince* excerpts
MG 25002 *Kiss Me Kate*/*South Pacific*
excerpts
MG 25003 Jan August, piano
MG 25004 Tony Martin, vocal
MG 25006 Old Time Favorites –
Venuta
MG 25007 Frankie Laine Favorites

10in MG 35000 Jazz at the Philharmonic,
Vol 8
MG 35002 Jazz at the Philharmonic,
Vol 10

12in MG 10000 Khachaturian *Violin
Concerto*
MG 10001 Erna Sack Sings
MG 10002 Mozart *Divertimento
K251*/Vivaldi *Concerto Grosso in D
minor*
MG 10003 Cimarosa/Vaughan
Williams *Oboe Concertos*

12in MG 20000 Alfred Newman Popular
Classics
MG 20001 Christmas Bells
MG 20002 Strauss/Waldteufel
Waltzes

MG 20003 Operatic and Musical
Favorites – Newman
MG 20004 Gypsy Music
MG 20005 *Captain from Castile* –
Newman

12in MG 30000 Songs for Little Folks
MG 30001 Kiddie Klassics
MG 30002 Kiddie Favorites
MG 30003 Alphabet Fun, etc
MG 30004 This is Christmas, etc
MG 30005 Hermine Ermine, etc

Polydor (from German Polydor[1] and
Telefunken[2] labels and from French
Classic.[3])
12in PLP 2030 Schumann *Trio in D minor*[2]
PLP 6420 Mozart *Violin Concerto No
3*/*String Quartet K171*[1]
PLP 6450 Chausson *Poeme*/Fauré
Ballade[1]
PLP 6470 'Beethoven' *Piano Concerto
in E flat*[1]
PLP 6510 Mendelssohn *Octet*[1]
PLP 6600 Pergolesi *La Serva
Padrona*[3]

Vox (from German Polydor[1] and original
recordings)
12in VLP 6240 Saint-Saëns *Violin Concerto
No 3*/Ravel *Tzigane*[1]
VLP 6340 Stravinsky *2-Piano
Concerto*/*Violin Concerto*
VLP 6490 Paganini *Violin Concerto in
B minor*
VLP 6500 Mozart *Piano Concerto
K271*[1]
VLP 6530 Tchaikovsky *Trio in A
minor*

Thus established on a broadly based repertoire, the American LP market looked set for healthy and profitable growth, but Victor's ill-advised introduction of a new size and speed of disc threw the public into doubt and certainly diverted money away from the industry. The following chronology puts the 'battle of the speeds' into perspective and also shows the spread and development of the microgroove disc.

1948 June: American Columbia issued **33⅓ rpm** LP records (**10in** and **12in**).
1949 January: RCA Victor issued **45rpm** records (**7in**).
1949 June: Columbia issued **7in 33⅓ rpm** records with a normal-sized centre hole. A notched ring was moulded into the plastic under the outer edge of the label to prevent slippage on autochangers.
1949 June: English Decca (London Records in

America) issued LPs in the US.

1950 June: **Decca issued the first LPs on the UK market**. They were made of 'Geon', this being the trade mark of British Geon Ltd. Subsequently, the words 'vinylite' and 'geon' were used interchangeably. **The first French LPs** ('microsillon') issued by L'Editions de L'Oiseau-Lyre. (This label was distributed by Decca world-wide outside France from November 1953.)

1950 September: English Decca export '45s' to the US (but their UK release was delayed until October 1954).

1950 October: EMI of London announced that they had watched the American 'battle of the speeds' with dismay and concern for the effect it was having on dealers and consumers. Therefore it had been decided that EMI would not depart from the 78rpm speed for either classical or popular repertoire without giving 6 months' public notice of its intention to do so. (This notice was duly given in April 1952, qv.)

1951 Spring: **The first Russian LPs launched**: 10in and 12in microgroove; also 10in 78rpm microgroove giving up to 9 minutes per side, and 8in (20·3cm) 78rpm microgroove giving up to 6 minutes per side.

1951 July: Nixa became the second UK company to issue LPs. The first releases were of Continental popular and light classical material.

1951 September: 45rpm discs were introduced into France from the US by the French branch of EMI.

1951 October: **French EMI issued LPs in France** (HMV, Columbia and Pathé labels).

1952 April: EMI gave notice of their intention to release LPs onto the UK market in October 1952.

1952 **DGG issued the first LPs onto the German market**.

1952 September: Dutch Philips issued 8in (20·3cm) 78rpm 'minigroove' discs with a playing time approximately equal to 12in coarsegroove discs.

1952 October: EMI issued LPs onto the UK market. 45s appeared simultaneously.

1953 April: **The first Spanish LPs** ('microsurcos') issued by the Columbia-Alhambra-Decca combine. 45s appeared in Spain shortly afterwards.

1953 July: **The first Danish LPs** released by Tono.

1953 Summer: Ducretet Thompson and others issued 24·1cm (9½in) 33⅓rpm LPs in France. **The first Extended Play (EP) 45rpm 7in discs** appeared in the US, France and elsewhere, giving about 7½ minutes per side. **First Russian LP catalogue** issued by the USSR State Music Trust.

Fidelity HF I I record player of 1956.

1953 October: 'Optional centres' appeared in 45rpm discs. An extra piece of plastic is included in the moulding to reduce the size of the central hole for use on conventional players. This extra disc could be pushed out and discarded if the record was to be used on the special Victor autochanger, which was by then also being produced in the UK under the HMV trade mark (see illustration p. 127). The large centre hole was also utilised in juke-box mechanisms. 'Spiders' (ie: plastic inserts to fit in the large centre holes) were also marketed, and some companies (eg: DGG in Germany) used these instead of incorporating the optional centre in the moulding.

1954 September: DGG entered the UK market, establishing new standards in presentation (see below). 'Gruve-gard' introduced in

A Decca advert (December 1950) and 'Johnson's' response (February 1951) to 'Dickie' Decca.

America by RCA Victor. Seen in cross section, the playing area of the disc is recessed, leaving the label area and the edge raised. This reduces scuff marks during handling and when automatic changers were used. EMI in the UK adopted this configuration from April 1955.

1954 October: Decca issued 45rpm on the UK market at last. They had been exported to the US since 1950.

Long playing had dealt a fatal blow to the so-called 'standard' 78rpm disc, despite the efforts of EMI in particular to keep it alive as a helpful aid to teaching and for the benefit of consumers in under-developed countries where the electricity supply was unreliable or non-existent. Oriole in the UK announced a brand-new series of children's records in June 1950 (an important date!) of 8in diameter and turning at 78rpm, and as late as April 1954 Decca (of all companies) marketed a new acoustic portable gramophone to play 78s only.

By this time, however, Decca had ceased pro-

duction of 78s. Demand had fallen so dramatically that EMI made massive deletions of 78s on 1 January, 1955; in this year alone EMI deleted no fewer than 7500 titles, the greater part being 78s, and the last remaining 78s in the British EMI catalogues were withdrawn on 31 March, 1962, just under 12 years after the first UK introduction of LP, and less than a decade after EMI's own entry into the LP market.

Another casualty was the 10in LP disc, especially quick to die in America. The format had been used for shorter works but was not popular because its price was uncommercial at about three-quarters that of a 12in disc for only about half the playing time. Decca (London in the US) offered cheap so-called 'Medium Play' discs ($33\frac{1}{3}$rpm) giving up to about 10 minutes per 10in side (subsequent issues were rather more generous), but by the end of 1957 most 10in LPs had been withdrawn from the American market, the UK following suit about 5 years later.

A sales ploy developed by Decca (London)

was the odd habit of numbering their monthly (or sometimes less frequent) LP releases so that, as they expanded the catalogue and newer companies mushroomed, both inside and outside the Decca organisation (but all copying the release-numbering habit), one might find in the same month one company's 24th release, another's fifth release, and yet another's 17th – an utterly meaningless confusion for the customer and the dealer.

It was this desire to show a progressive, not to say aggressive, attitude to the rest of the industry that led English Decca to produce a series of 'knocking ads' in which they implied criticism of their apparently laggardly main rival, EMI, by accusing them of failing to face the fact of LP. The two adverts reproduced opposite (by kind permission of General Gramophone Publications) illustrate this point. Decca's (left) is typical of its type, while the answer, which nowhere mentions EMI but gives the game away by announcing itself as an advertisement of the Johnson Talking Machine Co, seems to be an attempt to take public issue with constant jibes from Decca.

Index cards, which accompanied the early Archive Production LPs.   DG

Presentation

Another factor so far not mentioned that contributed to the popularity of LP was presentation. Individual sleeves had appeared as long ago as 1904 for issues of Melba records, but LP made a feature of individual sleeve designs, often of considerable artistic merit (and often not!), together with analytical notes or other texts on the reverse. Hitherto, such notes had been available in pamphlet form from record companies for some important issues; now, virtually every recording of serious music, and most of those offering lighter fare, was accompanied by reading matter.

The earliest releases of the Archive series, a division of Deutsche Grammophon Gesellschaft, set a different standard of presentation. Each recording was accompanied by an index card (sometimes two or more as necessary) giving exhaustive background information on the music, the editions used, and recording details. The accompanying illustration shows the cards supplied with APM 14004 when issued on the British market in November 1954. The reverse of each card carries the full text of its respective cantata. Later, much of this information (but by no means all, and then not unfailingly) was to be included in the standard sleeve data of most companies, but Archive was **the first company to carry out the plan so thoroughly**, making sleevenotes largely superfluous. Archive discontinued these index cards in the mid-1960s when, with a change of sleeve design, most of this data was included on the cover itself.

Early in 1981 it was announced that the International Association of Sound Archives recommended that containers of recordings should display the following information for the

COMPANY PROFILE

Deutsche Grammophon Gesellschaft (DG)

1898 Provisional arrangements were made by The Gramophone Co to assemble machines and press discs in Germany. The first sample records were received from Hanover on 11 June, 1898: E 1000, a recording of General Booth of the Salvation Army, pressed from an American Berliner matrix.

1898 August: Arrangement was made with Joseph Berliner (brother of Emile) for him to set up ten record presses in his telephone factory in Hanover.

Deutsche Grammophon's first factory, c 1900.

1898 18 September: Joseph Berliner set up a branch of The Gramophone Co at 18 Kniestrasse, Hanover, to press discs.

1898 24 November: Deutsche Grammophon Gesellschaft formed by Emile, Jacob and Joseph Berliner in Hanover. This company merged with Jacob and Joseph Berliner's Leipzig firm of Musikwerke Orpheus on 21 January, 1900 to form DG Aktien Gesellschaft. Shares of DGAG were purchased by The Gramophone Co at the start of 1901. DGAG, with headquarters in Berlin, existed as a branch of The Gramophone Co until World War I.

1914 September: Alexander Lucas appointed by the German government as supervisor of DGAG.

1914–18 DGAG operated independently in Germany, being wholly German-owned from 1917 but legally retaining the 'Dog and Trumpet' trade mark for the German market. The Gramophone Co property in Germany was liquidated by the German government on 21 November, 1916 and shares in DGAG were sold by public auction on 3 March, 1917. DGAG was sold to Polyphon Musikwerke on 21 April, 1917.

1921 A major serious music recording programme was instituted; the trade mark Polydor was used for exported goods. During

DGG's factory in 1961.

the 1920s many Polydor recordings were leased to Brunswick in the US.

1930–39 Polydor recordings were leased to Decca in the UK.

1940 Shares of DGG were bought by the electronics firm Siemens und Halske of Munich.

1941 Some recordings were issued in Germany with the 'Siemens-Spezial' label.

1950 French Polydor was sold to Philips. Polydor recordings were released in the US by Decca.

1951 DGG LPs issued in America (only!) by Decca.

1952 DGG introduced LP to the German market, establishing the DGG label for classical material, Polydor for light music, and

Archiv Produktion for a new history of music series.

1954 September: The Archiv label was introduced to the UK market by the newly-established branch named Heliodor Record Co Ltd. The DGG label followed in February 1955; Polydor (78rpm only at first) in August 1955.

1962 June: DGG and Philips merged in a 50/50 exchange of shares; the respective record labels of the two companies retained their autonomy.

1972 3 January: PolyGram formed, operat-

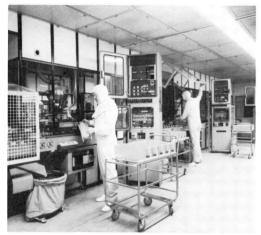

PolyGram's CD manufacturing plant in Hanover in 1982.

ing in 18 countries and compounding Polydor International (formerly DGG) and Phonogram International (formerly Philips Phonographic Industries); label and repertoire identities again to be retained.

1973 Mauricio Kagel composed *1898* for children's voices and instruments in response to a DG commission to commemorate the company's 75th birthday. The occasion was further celebrated by the presentation by DG to Oliver Berliner, grandson of Emile, of a golden Gramophone.

1980 17 January: PolyGram acquired the UK Decca Record Co.

1983 March: DG, in association with Philips and Decca, launched CD on the European market.

benefit of libraries, sound archives, and the general public:

1 The date(s) of recording;
2 The place(s) of recording (venue; town; country) also whether a 'live' recording;
3 The musical edition used, name of editor or arranger, with a note of major cuts or important changes from the score;
4 The performing forces used;
5 Duration of items, individual movements, acts, etc;
6 Names of recording producer, balance engineer, and editor.

Concerning item 3, perhaps it should be further noted whether the composer's repeats have been ignored, together with other important information concerning the repeat scheme used in the recording.

To the information called for by the IASA which, of course, should incorporate complete performer details, it is vital, especially for archivists and cataloguers as well as for the ordinary consumer, to add reference numbers for works as given in standard thematic catalogues. Furthermore, if two or more numbering systems are current (as, for instance, when one thematic catalogue is gradually giving place to a newer and more up-to-date one, as has happened recently in the cases of Domenico Scarlatti and Vivaldi), *all* available numbers should be given.

The attractive designs of many sleeve fronts contrasted sharply with the drab plain paper sleeves of 78s. LPs were becoming two-fold works of art, the colourful pictures often complementing the music within. From America came a new idea in marketing: why not turn record stores into art galleries? By displaying sleeves in 'browser-boxes', the customer was encouraged to browse through the stock. Sales increased, and the method was brought to England. **The first 'Browserie'** (a word invented by George Fenwick, manager of the HMV shop, Oxford Street, London) was opened in the lower ground floor of this establishment in the autumn of 1955. Today, most multiple stores and supermarkets have their 'browserie' section in which records are colourfully displayed in boxes or racks.

Long Playing Facts

The only major company to offer alternative LP couplings on the UK market was Decca, and then the experiment, once tried, was never repeated. On LXT 2558 Mozart's Symphonies Nos 25 and 36 (respectively Celibidache and the London Philharmonic Orchestra, and Böhm and the Vienna Philharmonic Orchestra) were coupled, while on LXT 2562 Maag's performance with the Suisse Romande Orchestra of Symphony No 29 was coupled with Böhm's No 36. (In America, Celibidache's No 25 backed Symphony No 38 played by the Suisse Romande Orchestra conducted by Ansermet, further compounding the confusion. Many other performances were recoupled for sale on the opposite side of the Atlantic.)

Cut price LPs first appeared in America in August 1950. Remington issued standard classics by little-known artists at $1.49 per 10in disc and $1.99 per 12in disc, as against the standard prices of $4.85 and $5.45 respectively. In the UK the basic price of £1.10s (£1.50) per 10in and £2 per 12in disc, which varied slightly according to market trends and the rise and fall of Purchase Tax, was well maintained on the open market for the first 18 years of LP. A number of mail order record clubs sprang up along the lines of Victor's pioneering club of 1934, offering mainly foreign recordings at about 33 per cent lower than the standard price, but the material was frequently second-rate. Then, in June 1958, Decca introduced a new label carrying reissues of earlier, now deleted, recordings that, it was announced, had recouped their initial expenditure and were to be put out to grass at £1 2s 6d (£1.12½). The name of the new label was Ace of Clubs, an implied trumping of the mail order clubs. For many customers, the significance of this clever name was lost, but the records, at virtually half price, had a profound effect upon the market, and within two years all the major manufactur-

ers had produced cheap labels of their own, mostly of earlier material but sometimes of new recordings. Decca re-issued popular mono material on the Ace of Hearts label; stereo re-issues eventually used the Ace of Diamonds logo. In America, too, the bargain label idea quickly became established, following the release of Decca Ace of Clubs material on the Richmond label in September 1958.

The first LP recording to reach one million sales was the 1949 original cast version of the Rodgers and Hammerstein show *Oklahoma* on American Decca. Sales had reached 15 million by 1958.

Long playing, despite the infamous 'battle of the speeds' and other vicissitudes, remained an enormous technical advance in both convenience and quality, but further developments were to come.

Stereophonic Sound

The word 'stereophonic' is derived from the Gk Stereos = solid + phone = voiced, and is meant to indicate a method of sound reproduction that gives the listener an illusion of spaciousness by the conducting to his ears of two or more separate sound paths. The analogy here is with stereoscopic photography, in which two views of the same scene taken from slightly different viewpoints and then viewed through a binocular instrument imitate the side-by-side disposition of the human eyes to give the illusion of depth and perspective. The picture, instead of being flat and two-dimensional, appears to have a third dimension; it seems solid.

Stereophonic sound ('stereo' in the accepted abbreviation) endeavours to give a sense of spaciousness by the lateral division of sound and the disintegration of vocal and/or instrumental timbres. In its simplest form, stereo arbitrarily channels the individual voices of a group of artists into two routes, one to the left, the other to the right, and then reproduces them in such a way that the original breadth of sound is conveyed to the listener. Given efficient recording engineers and equipment, and a reproducing chain of adequate quality, those artists to the left and right of centre will be reproduced in their correct places, while those at or near the centre will seem to come from a position between the two speakers because their sounds have been picked up more or less equally by the two spaced microphones in the studio or hall. A less appropriate word than 'solid-voiced' could scarcely be imagined. The word 'stereo' should correctly have been applied to the older system of recording, in which all the different sound sources are solidified into one path and conveyed to the listener through one outlet. For this method, though, the word 'monaural' was coined to distinguish the old system from the new, yet 'monaural' (= one-eared) is as nonsensical as 'stereophonic', and the alternative 'monophonic' (= one-voiced') is to be preferred.

The value of stereo, or, more correctly, 'two-channel', recording lies not in its ability to split up the sounds of the artists into their component parts: no composer who has laboured over fresh instrumental combinations to produce new effects would wish them to be disintegrated by recording engineers. This was a serious fault (along with 12-foot-wide piano keyboards and other idiocies) in the early days of stereo and is still to be heard even now on records produced for the high fidelity rather than the musical market. Rather, stereo's strength lies in its ability to give an added illusion of depth, atmosphere and perspective to the recorded sound.

The first demonstration of stereophonic sound was made in 1881 at the Paris Exposition by Clement Adler, using two telephones.

The world's first stereophonic records and reproducing machine were made by Pathé in France shortly before World War I (the only available dating is 'between 1910 and 1914'). The centre-start discs bore two grooves side by side, and two 'starting spots' upon which the needles of the machine's two pick-up arms were placed while the turntable was stationary. When the motor brake was released, the signals from the two grooves were fed separately to the independent front-facing sound apertures at either end of the 1m (3ft) long front panel.

The first patent covering stereophonic sound recording was taken out in December 1931 by Alan D Blumlein of The Gramophone Co in England. The British patent No 394 325 detailed equipment 'to provide a sound recording, reproducing and/or transmission system whereby there is conveyed to the listener a realistic impression that the intelligence is being communicated to him over two acoustic paths in the same manner as he experiences in listening to everyday acoustic intercourse and this object embraces also the idea of conveying to the listener a true directional impression'.

Blumlein's patent covered two possible methods of containing two sound channels in one groove. The 'VL' method ('vertical-lateral') was a combination of Edison's original vertical ('hill-and-dale') cylinder cutting system and Berliner's lateral ('side-to-side') disc cutting system, whereby the vertical movement carried one channel and the lateral movement carried the other. The 45/45 system was similar except that the whole groove was tilted at an angle of 45° to the surface of the disc. It was this latter system that was adopted as standard by the entire industry in 1958. The US patent for 45/45 stereo discs was issued to Westrex/Bell Telephone Laboratories in 1937.

In 1948 a third stereo disc method was patented by W H Livy of Edgware, England (patent No 612 163, applied for two years earlier), in which a supersonic 'carrier' frequency was modulated by two discrete frequency bands. This system, in modified form, was perfected by English Decca but was never followed up.

An interesting stereo experiment was carried out by a team led by Arthur Keller of Bell Telephone Laboratories in the Academy of Music in Philadelphia in March 1932, when Leopold Stokowski and the Philadelphia Orchestra made many recordings, some of which survive. Two microphones were used and the recordings were made on wax masters at 78rpm using two parallel vertically cut tracks. They were demonstrated at the Chicago World Fair in 1933. It was at about this time that a Stokowski concert in Philadelphia was relayed to Washington via two special cables to give the audience there the illusion of three-dimensional sound.

The first 45/45 stereo discs (ie: with both channels in one groove) were made by EMI at Hayes, England, in 1933, but were not offered for sale. Like the Bell discs of the previous year they rotated at 78rpm.

Stereophonic sound was first used commercially in the cinema: the French film *Napoleon Bonaparte* was made in 1927, but in 1935 stereophonic dialogue and sound effects were added. **The first film actually recorded with stereophonic sound** was Walt Disney's *Fantasia*, premiered in 1941 using the multiple speaker system developed for cinema use by the Altec Lansing Corporation of Beverly Hills, California, and RCA. The music was conducted by Leopold Stokowski, the conductor in the Bell experiments of 1932.

The first 'binaural' (ie: double-mono, and therefore potentially stereo) **domestic tape recorder** was developed in America in 1949 and was exhibited at the New York Audio Fair.

In 1952 the University of Illinois enlisted the help of Leopold Stokowski, with the Illinois University Student Symphony Orchestra and Oratorio Society in an educational experiment in stereo recording on tape for educational and radio use. Several microphones and two-track tapes were used. For broadcasting, one channel was relayed by FM, the other by AM, so that listeners with two receivers, each tuned appropriately, would receive stereo, though presumably with a marked quality difference. It was claimed that those with one radio, tuned to FM or AM, would hear a 'normal' broadcast.

The first stereo tapes to be marketed appeared in America early in 1955, but no major company entered this field until RCA's release in the autumn of 1956. **The first UK demonstration** was given of EMI's 'Stereosonic' tapes in London on 4 April, 1955 at the EMI recording studios, Abbey Road; they were announced for commercial sale that October, a two-tape set of the Glyndebourne Festival Opera recording of Act II of Mozart's *Le Nozze di Figaro* conducted by Vittorio Gui spearheading the release.

The first stereo discs to be marketed were made by Emory Cook of Stamford, Connecticut, in 1957. The disc surface was divided concentrically into two, the inner track carrying one channel, the surrounding outer track carrying the other. Playback was via two ganged pick-up heads attached to one arm.

The first demonstration of the Westrex 45/45 stereo disc was made at a trade reception in Los Angeles in September 1957. Shortly afterwards, Decca (London in America) demonstrated their perfected VL stereo disc in New York and London, at the same time announcing that they had two other systems ready for production (the 45/45 system, and Livy's 'carrier' system, modified), and would the industry kindly make up its mind which it wanted to become the standard method! On 25 March, 1958, the Recording Industry Association of America (RIAA) finally recommended the Westrex 45/45 system for world wide adoption, and within 2 months **the first 45/45 stereo discs were marketed** in America by Audio-Fidelity, Urania, and Counterpoint. The bigger concerns followed during the summer of 1958: RCA (following its launch announcement in May) and London in July, and Columbia a month later.

In the UK, EMI announced its intention in February 1958 to market stereo discs 'probably in about 12 months' time', and took the opportunity to point out that both (sic) methods of stereo disc cutting (ie: 45/45 and VL) are based on the Blumlein/EMI patent of 1931. EMI, together with Decca, launched stereo discs in August 1958, but both companies slipped out stereo test records, largely for dealer demonstration purposes, a month or so earlier (EMI SDD 1; Decca SKL 4001).

The first UK release of stereo discs was made by Pye in June 1958, following their press demonstration on 16 May that year. At first, Pye's stereo prices were about one-fifth higher than for mono records, but when both the EMI and Decca releases were announced as being at the same price as for mono (about £2 for a 12in premium disc), Pye reduced their prices to the same level.

Incidentally, when Decca in the UK came to market stereo, they wished to use the motto 'ffss' for 'full frequency stereophonic sound', thereby forging a link with the successful earlier 'ffrr' motto. However, 'FFSS' had been used since late 1957 in the advertising of the Long Playing Record Library of Blackpool (an organisation that sold discs in addition to operating a record library), where it stood for 'Factory Fresh Sales Service'. After representations from Decca, the Long Playing Record Library agreed to relinquish their claim to the motto.

As Blumlein had predicted in his 1931 patent, stereo discs became possible only with the use of a pressing material (vinyl) capable of carrying the high definition required by the complex stereo groove formulation.

Fake stereo first appeared in 1959. The conductor Hermann Scherchen, who, like Leopold Stokowski, was greatly interested in advanced and experimental recording techniques, and who had made a vast number of mono recordings, invented and marketed for domestic use (for about £5) a device called the 'Stereophoner', which gave fake 'stereo' from mono recordings by splitting the frequencies into layers and feeding them separately to either channel. From the early 1960s, various rechannelling systems were introduced by most record companies in attempts to make old mono catalogue material acceptable to the growing stereo market.

For many years, stereo and mono existed side by side, an unsatisfactory state of affairs that required the holding of double stocks by dealers and wholesalers, and the twin production of sleeves and labels as well as of the discs themselves. Stereo-only releases were extremely rare because makers felt obliged to continue offering mono discs to their faithful but unconverted customers. By the mid-1960s, however, pick-up manufacturers were producing reasonably cheap cartridges with high vertical (as well as lateral) compliance incorporating styli of a radius small enough to play stereo records without damage even though full stereo results would be obtained only by the much greater expenditure required by the purchase of a

stereo amplifier and twin speakers. For a modest outlay, therefore, the collector could start buying stereo records in anticipation of the time when he wished to convert completely to stereo. The need for mono pressings, therefore, evaporated, and it was time for mono to die.

'Monocide' commenced in earnest on 13 April, 1967, when EMI announced that as from July 1968 all their classical recordings were to be issued in stereo only. Decca (after issuing many stereo recordings carrying the proud legend 'also available in mono') finally converted to stereo-only in March 1969, by which time the rest of the industry on both sides of the Atlantic had taken the same step. Apart from the occasional documentary or other special issue, and for the re-issue of archive material (fake stereo having been largely discredited), the long and honourable reign of the mono disc was over by the mid-1970s.

Facts of the Stereo Era

The first classical LP to sell a million copies, and therefore the first classical 'hit' of the stereo era, was the Tchaikovsky Piano Concerto No 1 played by Van Cliburn, winner of the first Tchaikovsky International Piano Competition in Moscow in 1958. The recording, made soon after the competition, sold one million by 1961, two million by 1965, and $2\frac{1}{2}$ million by January 1970.

The first LP of any kind to reach one million sales was the original cast recording of *My Fair Lady*, issued by Philips in May 1958.

The first large-scale work ever to be specifically composed for the gramophone was Morton Subotnik's (b 1933) *Silver Apples of the Moon*, for electronic music synthesiser, a $31\frac{1}{2}$-minute work created in the composer's studio in the School of the Arts at New York University. The composition was commissioned by Nonesuch Records and was released in the US in September 1967.

The first classical recording to reach the American Top Ten is Walter (later Wendy) Carlos's *Switched on Bach* (CBS), electronically synthesised realisations. It was a best-seller in 1969.

The biggest selling double albums world wide are the Bee Gee's soundtrack for the film *Saturday Night Fever* (1977), and *Grease* (1978) with John Travolta. With these albums on the Polydor label, PolyGram had **the absolute best-selling albums in the history of the gramophone**, exceeding 25 million copies each.

The best selling album by British performers is *Dark Side Of The Moon*, recorded between June 1972 and January 1973 by The Pink Floyd, which has sold in excess of 13 million copies.

Large Recording Projects

The largest completed recording project to date is the 137-disc set of the complete works of Shakespeare made by the British Argo Co between 1957 and 1964. The price of the whole set upon completion was £260.12s 6d (£260.62½).

Possibly the most ambitious recording project ever planned was the Library of Recorded Masterpieces, of New York, begun in 1959 by the conductor Max Goberman (who conducted the score of Bernstein's *West Side Story* in the film soundtrack). His ambition was to put onto disc the complete instrumental works of Corelli and Vivaldi, and the complete symphonies and operas of Haydn, in musicologically authentic performances, the record presentation to include exhaustive documentation by noted scholars and reproductions of the full scores of all the works, thus 'establishing a permanent and authentic phonographic library of musical literature'. In addition, Goberman planned and carried out other important recorded projects, including Bach's *Brandenburg Concerti* with a facsimile of Bach's 176-page presentation copy, John Gay's *The Beggar's Opera* with all 69 original arias, and single-disc surveys of the less well-known works of Bach, Beethoven, Brahms, Debussy, Prokofiev, Schubert, Tchaikovsky and Wagner.

The Corelli series was completed in 1960 but Goberman's tragic death on 31 December,

1962, at the age of 51, occurred before the Vivaldi and Haydn projects had reached the half-way mark. Of Vivaldi's nearly 600 known concertos and sonatas, 75 were released on 17 discs. The orchestra (the New York Sinfonietta, which Goberman founded) and soloists, including Goberman himself on the violin, sometimes sound unhappy in the music, but many works appeared on disc in this series for the first time, and the albums included reduced reproductions of the then-recent Ricordi scores.

For the Haydn symphonies project, Goberman conducted the Vienna State Opera Orchestra (with the exception of Symphony No 3, played by the New York Sinfonietta) in performances that for their time (1961–2) were nearer than most others to the spirit of the composer as revealed in the recently-published authentic scores, and some of Goberman's readings remain unsurpassed. Unfortunately, although the music was played from the authentic scores, those published in miniature with the record albums were often of the older corrupt editions. Goberman actually recorded 44 symphonies and two overtures, of which 35 symphonies and both overtures were released before the demise of the Library of Recorded Masterpieces shortly after his death. The tapes passed into the hands of CBS who issued some of these and a further five symphonies, but Goberman's readings of Symphonies Nos 27, 34, 37 and the unnumbered 'Symphony A', though recorded, have to date never been issued to the public in any form. In view of the critical acclaim of those issued, this non-appearance must be **the most incomprehensible instance of waste of money in gramophone history**.

Instrumental music of the 18th century, being relatively cheap to record owing to its modest demands upon personnel, has been the subject of several large-scale complete editions. Its division into numerous masses of more or less clearly defined groups, and the modern demand for integral recordings, encourage the record companies to 'think big', but all too often there is evidence, once a series has got under way, of apathy or boredom on the part of the artists, and embarrassment in the marketing departments when faced with yet another volume of concertos or sonatas which they feel may seem to their customers indistinguishable from previous issues. The 'newness' wears off, and reduced sales inevitably bring discouragement to the artists themselves.

Domenico Scarlatti's 555 harpsichord sonatas are a good example. Fernando Valenti began his 'complete' recording for Westminster in 1952 but reached only Volume 26 (322 sonatas) before the project was finally abandoned in 1971. Those performances issued vary in quality from brilliant to routine.

Other 'complete' projects of less than uniform high quality include:

Bach Cantatas (Harnoncourt; Telefunken: 1972– in progress)
Haydn Keyboard Sonatas (McCabe; Decca/London: 1974–7, 16 records)
Haydn Keyboard Trios (Beaux Arts Trio; Philips: 1970–9, 14 records)
Haydn String Quartets (Schneider Quartet; Haydn Society/Nixa: 1950–5, 21 records, incomplete)
Haydn String Quartets (Aeolian Quartet; Decca/London: 1973–7, 36 records)
Haydn Symphonies (Doráti; Decca/London: 1970–4, 48 records)
Haydn Symphonies (Maerzendorfer; Musical Heritage Society, 1968–70, 49 records)
Mozart Symphonies (Böhm; DG: 1969–71, 30 records).

We cannot forbear to register disappointment that many exciting projects have not fulfilled their promise. The lesson would seem to be that no one performer or group can possibly have the artistic insight to record in a short period a vast corpus of music built up over many years under differing circumstances. The notably successful exceptions appear to bear out this assertion since the music lies within narrow emotional and/or instrumental ranges:

Bach Organ Music (Walcha; DG: 1950–5, 16 records, substantially complete but omitting early works, arrangements, etc)
Mozart Marches and Dances (Boskovsky; Decca/London: 1964–7, 10 records).

Unguarded Moments

Ideally, every sleeve and label should identify fully and correctly the music recorded on the accompanying disc (see the IASA recommendations, above) but unfortunately there have been moments when someone has nodded off and an error has crept past all the executives and technicians and reached the public.

By far the most common errors – too common for a list to be compilable – concern titling details. Keys, opus numbers, movement markings and even artist credits are particularly prone to error, and archival data (recording dates, timings of selections, etc) may sometimes need the proverbial pinch of salt.

More serious are major errors of fact. **The most frequent subject of misrepresentation** is the composer Haydn, to whom a large number of works have been misattributed. The *Toy Symphony*, Oboe Concerto, and String Quartet in F, Op 3/5, 'Serenade', are all frequently still given as by Haydn when it is known that all three works are spurious. Most extreme is the case of the Flute Concerto in D which was originally mistakenly listed as by 'Hayden' in an 18th century music publisher's catalogue. The same publisher corrected the error, giving the true composer as Leopold Hoffmann (1730–93), and since this correction was made as long ago as 1781 there seems no justification whatsoever for record sleeves two centuries later to carry the wrong information – unless it be a deliberate attempt to deceive the public.

A Symphony in E flat is announced as 'Symphony No 3 by Mozart' when there has never been any doubt that the correct author is Karl Friedrich Abel (1725–87). The young Mozart merely re-scored the work, replacing the original oboes with clarinets, and insomuch as all the recordings issued thus far have included the clarinet parts, the work as recorded – or at least an important aspect of its scoring – *is* by Mozart. The music, however, is by Abel. 'Mozart's Symphony No 37 in G, K444' is another example of misleading titling: the work is by Michael Haydn (1737–1806); Mozart merely added a slow introduction.

These may be intentional errors; unintentional ones can also happen. Perhaps **the two most spectacular examples** during the enlightened LP era are the cases of Heliodor 479008 (issued in the UK in 1959) and Baroque 2862 (issued by Everest Records in the late 1960s). The sleeve and labels of the Heliodor disc promised Beethoven's String Quartet in D, Op 18/3, and Haydn's String Quartet in B flat, Op 76/4. Many copies of this disc were distributed with the Beethoven duly supplied; the Haydn, however, was replaced by Smetana's String Quartet No 1 in E minor, 'From My Life', to the consternation of chamber music lovers. The Baroque record promised four works by 'Early Symphonists'. Three of the works (by Karl Stamitz, Johann Stamitz and Luigi Boccherini) were indeed as described, but the fourth, 'Sinfonia in G minor by Georg Philipp Telemann' turns out to be the Symphony in E major, Op 18/5 by Johann Christian Bach. The Heliodor error is evidently due to a simple mistake in the factory, one plate being substituted for another at pressing stage, but it is difficult to understand how Baroque's misinformation came about. For one thing, the work concerned takes only part of one side; its companion on that side is correctly identified, so no plate-switching has taken place. For another, the sleevenote writer has evidently heard what he is writing about, describing it as 'typical of the *Style Galant* cultivated by Telemann' (which he did not!) Finally, Telemann never wrote a Sinfonia in G minor unless it be a short instrumental introduction to a cantata, so whence the title?

'Pirates'

In order to circumvent contractual difficulties, or simply to avoid paying that which is due to an artist, a disgracefully large number of records have been marketed with fictitious artist credits. By the very nature of the problem, it is rarely possible to unravel the knots created in the offices of such pirate firms. An executive (who subsequently went 'legitimate') in one British

company that procured tapes from many Continental and other sources, admitted to the writer some years ago that an indispensable part of his office equipment was a recent copy of the West Berlin telephone directory from which he would select at random names behind which the true names of the artists who had performed on those tapes might be disguised. From the moment the transfer of name took place, the true and original names were vigorously suppressed and the provenance of the recordings could be discovered by outsiders only by inference.

The most recent allegation of audacious pirate operations concerns Aries Records of California, the activities of which were 'exposed' in a number of American magazines in 1981 and 1982. The label specialises in 20th century, mainly orchestral, serious music by, among others, Ben-Haim, Liebermann, Shchedrin, Bantock, Seter, Atterberg, Pauer, and Boehm, and brings to disc many works which might otherwise remain unavailable to the customer. Some of the recordings are taken from broadcasts, others from pirated tapes, and the artists' names either do not exist (eg: Versailles, Stockerau, Breslav and Coblentz Symphony Orchestras, under Claude Dupré, Charles Horton, or Walter Frimmel) or belong to real artists who have disclaimed all knowledge of the recordings (eg: Helsingborg and Jerusalem Symphony Orchestras; conductors Lennart Hedwall, Mendi Roday and Franz Freudenthal – both the latter were misspelt in Aries's labelling).

Less culpable, but just as confusing for the record historian are the use of 'house' names for orchestras, eg: RCA Victor Symphony Orchestra, and Columbia Symphony Orchestra (the Philharmonic Promenade Orchestra's true identity is revealed in Section III) which conceal the real names.

Quad

If stereo could be a success with only two channels, reasoned the record industry, four channels must offer twice the opportunity. Thus, quadraphonic (or quadrophonic – the companies failed to agree even upon the right spelling) was born in the late 1960s. For this, the customer was expected to buy a four-channel amplifier and two additional speakers. The latter were to be placed in the corners of the listening room *behind* the listener, balancing the stereo pair at the front. With this array of speakers it was supposed to be possible to imitate the ambience of the concert hall.

The first four channel recordings the authors have been able to trace were made by Acoustic Research, Boston, Mass, about 1968. These were followed by **the first British-made 'quadrasonic'** (!) **recordings** in the summer of 1970: Unicorn recorded Jascha Horenstein's interpretation of Mahler's Symphony No 3, and the American company Vanguard recorded Margaret Price, Yvonne Minton, Alexander Young and Justino Day in Handel's *Messiah*, conducted by Johannes Somary.

The first public demonstration of CBS SQ discs took place in New York in mid-1971 and in London on 6 September of the same year. EMI adopted the CBS matrix system for their first quad release in March 1972, but Pye and others opted for the rival – and incompatible – **Sansui QS system**. Confusion and doubt arose, customers waited to see which way the quad cat would jump, and, since it did not jump decisively in either direction, interest in the new wonder evaporated. In addition, the financial outlay for a suggestion of echo seemed high, and the reported ideal speaker positioning conflicted with the layout of most rooms, which have a door in one corner.

Digital

Unlike quad, digital recording did not require the consumer to invest in different or additional equipment. A digital disc was playable on any stereo playing deck with a standard stereo pick-up. However, it provided a definite advance in recorded sound, an improvement that could be appreciated even on modest equipment.

The principle behind digital recording is that the time-honoured system of recording sound onto tape is replaced by converting the sound into digits via a computer and storing the digits on tape. In theory, no degradation of the original signal is possible provided the stored digital sequence remains intact. Digital recordings are converted to an analogue signal on the standard LP disc and, as stated above, played normally.

The first UK-manufactured digital recording was Decca's two-disc set *New Year's Day Concert in Vienna*, recorded live by the Vienna Philharmonic Orchestra conducted by Willi Boskovsky on 1 January, 1979 and issued that April. **This was the first recording to receive the US Electronic and Engineering Award**.

Most record companies followed Decca's lead in digital recording, but at best this method of selling music is only semi-digital; the completely unabused sound must be subjected to some distortion in its transfer to LP and once there it is exposed to all the dust, mishandling and wear to which soft plastic is prone. What was needed to preserve that digital signal was a medium that was impervious to all these damaging factors. This would mean either a pressing material so hard and unyielding that no stylus would survive more than a few minutes of contact without serious wear, or a coating over the record grooves that would prevent scratching; it would also, however, prevent stylus contact. One solution seemed to be to make the protective coating 100 per cent transparent, and the grooves readable with some kind of light ray.

The first demonstration of 'music from a beam of light', as distinct from a soundtrack supporting a movie, was given by British Ozaphane Ltd at the Café Royal, London, on 10 February, 1937. A contemporary report states that the recording had two soundtracks on 4mm wide film, but it is not clear whether the soundtracks ran in the same direction as each other, thus giving the possibility of a stereo signal, or ran in opposite directions similar to those on mono recording tape. Neither is it clear how the Ozaphone system differed from music recordings on movie/talkie film.

Sony CDP–101 compact disc player, first marketed in 1982.
PHOTO: LES PRUDDEN

The first light-beam pick-up for disc repro-duction was the Philco model 41–629, 'Photo Electric Reproducer' of 1946. The groove was tracked by a light ray focussed from beneath the pick-up head and reflecting into a mirror in the head. The no-wear potential of this device, however, was negated by the need to track the groove with a stylus in order to keep the pick-up in position. The RCA Victrola 'Magic Brain' of about the same time apparently did away with this drawback, and in addition was advertised as being capable of playing both disc sides without the need to turn over the record. For this purpose it used a kind of double pick-up and a 'Jewel-Lite Scanner'. No further details have come to light, and it seems that the 'Magic Brain' never actually hit the market.

The first video tape recorders were made in 1957 by Ampex for professional studio use. The tapes were 2in (5cm) wide and ran at 15ips (38cm/sec).

The first video audio discs were demonstrated by Teldec at the AEG Telefunken building in Berlin on 24 June, 1970. They were single-sided thin flexible plastic foil discs of either 22·9cm (9in) diameter (giving 5 minutes' playing time) or 30·5cm (12in) (12 minutes), with a vertically cut groove some 25 times finer than that of a stereo LP, tracked at 0·02 gram with a diamond

stylus in a tangential arm. The discs revolved on a cushion of air at 1500rpm and gave a black and white picture and sound suitable for play-back through a standard TV set. A colour signal with sound was achieved in 1975. It was hoped at the time that this invention might be adapted to stereo $33\frac{1}{3}$rpm discs, but technicians elsewhere were moving towards the 'perfect' disc from different directions. The Philips/Sony laser-read TV disc appeared in 1975; the information was stored digitally in tiny pits on the surface, and the disc revolved at 1800rpm. This is the direct ancestor of the Compact Disc.

Compact Disc

The first announcement of the Compact Disc (CD) came on 17 May, 1978 from Philips Indus-tries. The product was described as follows:

Size 110mm ($4\frac{1}{2}$in) diameter (once again – see Section VII – 'convenience approximations' were being made: 110mm equals almost exactly $4\frac{5}{16}$in).
Speed 1·5m/sec (59ips) constant linear speed. Thus, the actual rotation of the disc decreases constantly from inner to outer windings.
Playing Time Up to one hour (single side).
Material Plastic, with clear protective plastic coating.
Recording Method PCM (pulse code modula-tion) encoded, using 14-bit digital code with signal-to-noise ratio of 84dB. Frequency range: 20–20 000Hz. The signal is read by a diode laser mounted in the pick-up assembly. Multiple channels are available with undetectable cross-talk.

It was clear to Philips that other systems were being developed, but up to that time no official announcements had been made by their rivals. Philips worked in close association with the Japanese firm Sony in developing a CD system but it was important to those firms that, with the vast amount of capital they were pouring into the project, it had to be their system, and not one of their rivals', that should become the

Three generations of disc, with a 78 hand-wound gramophone and a Philips CD player.   PHILIPS

eventual world standard. Either by accident or design, an announcement made at that time must have had the effect of discouraging possible competition: it was claimed that when CD was ready to be launched 'in the early 1980s', equipment upon which to play CD software would be available at about the price of good hi-fi players. Even allowing for inflation and unforeseen circumstances, Philips and Sony must have known that this was a lie. However, apparently this statement did discourage more honest developers who knew that any formulation they produced would retail at a considerably higher price. The Philips/Sony format was duly accepted as the worldwide standard.

The first launch of CD hardware and software was made in Japan in October 1982, with CBS/Sony, Toshiba/EMI, Hitachi and Sharp leading the field. The European launch was made in the UK, West Germany, France and the Netherlands in March 1983, with software by

PolyGram (ie: Philips, DG and Decca) and hardware by Philips, Sony, Hitachi and Marantz. Prices of CD playing decks in the UK ranged between £450 and £549; ie: at least twice the price of a good hi-fi record player. The discs retailed at just under £10 each. EMI, which, with its sister company Toshiba, had participated in the launch in Japan in October 1982, were not represented in the European launch. One reason was EMI's reluctance to pay the 3¢ royalty per disc demanded by Philips/Sony to help defray their immense development costs. Another was EMI's determination to avoid a software famine by building up sufficient stocks to meet a heavy demand.

Apart from the diameter of the Compact Disc, which, at 120mm ($4\frac{7}{10}$in), is 10mm larger than originally planned, its characteristics are as announced in May 1978. It shows important advantages over LP in addition to the obvious one of storage convenience. The disc is virtually indestructible, its surface being protected by a transparent plastic layer over the reflective aluminium coating which carries the digital information in tracks 1·6 micron wide (a stereo LP groove is *c* 100 microns wide). There is no physical contact between disc and 'playing head' (the microscopic pits in the tracks on the disc surface are read by a laser beam); therefore, there is no surface wear. Dust and blemishes on the disc surface are ignored by the laser beam and do not affect reproduction. Even small holes drilled in the disc's surface, or the application of thin strips of paint or opaque tape (which, of course, deprive the equipment of some of the information it needs to relay the signal), will not affect replay, and one manufacturer even suggested that the best way to deal with scuff marks might be to polish them away with an impregnated fibre metal polisher. Such abuses, however, are not recommended. It is enough that, under normal circumstances and with even fairly careless handling, a Compact Disc cannot be damaged.

The two greatest advantages of CD are the enhanced quality of sound reproduction in comparison with LP, and a playing time that allows works of one hour's duration to be accommodated without interruptions. Typical performance figures for CD (with LP figures in brackets) are: harmonic distortion 0·005% (0·2%), wow and flutter unmeasurable (0·03%), dynamic range 90dB (55dB), frequency range 20–20000Hz (30–20000Hz), and signal-to-noise ratio 90dB (60dB). The potential exists to increase the playing time by some 20 minutes (thus accommodating, say, Beethoven's *Choral* Symphony with ease on one side), and it surely will not be long before *both* sides of the disc will carry music signals, for it will doubtless be found possible to print label information onto the playing surface in such a way that it is invisible to the laser beam.

The CD surface carries much information in addition to the music signal: playing time (both 'elapsed' and 'to run') and selection numbers (ie: 'bands' or 'tracks' on LP), which are displayed on the face of the player, the start time for each item, and the title of the work, movement or number being played. This facility is ripe for development in ways unimagined at present. Meanwhile, the data now contained on the surface enables the player to perform the cueing of items or selected portions of music within items with far greater speed than is possible with tape (CD location time is a maximum of 5 seconds) and with greater accuracy and safety than is possible with LP.

The physical characteristics of the Compact Disc seem to be a summing-up of the features that have been applied, experimentally or otherwise, to the disc format ever since it first became commercially viable. Its small size and indestructibility reflect that of Berliner's first discs of the 1890s, its centre start recalls Pathé's practice of 1906, its variable speed (or, to put it another way, constant groove velocity *vis-a-vis* the sound-gathering agent) brings to mind Pemberton Billing's experimental World record of 1923, and its playing time is truly long playing, doubling that of the standard LP side. Laser tracking was anticipated by the Ozaphane tape experiments, and by the disc models of Philco and RCA (see above), and the highly reflective silver mirror-like surface occurs in the 'mother' stage of conventional LP manufacture. All these

features have been brought to a level of technical perfection in the CD record beyond which it would seem impossible to progress, but there is one physical characteristic which is unique to CD (unless some obscure development has escaped our net): the disc is played up-side-down – the laser beam reads its underside. When viewed from the top (label side), the CD revolves in the time-honoured clockwise direction, which means, of course, that from the point of view of the sound-gathering laser beam the disc revolves the 'wrong' way, ie: anti-clockwise.

Having traced the history of recorded sound with its failures, successes and excesses, perhaps we may close with a not-too-confident glance into the future. First, though, a word of warning.

Much of the energies expended by technicians in the industry has gone into the ever-more-sophisticated attempts to bring the sounds they record into the listener's room with as little distortion as possible. Today we believe that their success is virtually complete. Modern digital techniques and the compact disc bring a sound so clear and natural, with unwanted sounds reduced to inaudible proportions, that it is difficult to foresee future developments improving on them.

But it is self-evident that recording at its best can never be more than *second* best. It is a fake. The listener sitting at home in a comfortable armchair can never hear precisely what a member of the audience can hear from the seat in an opera house, a concert hall or a recital room. For one thing, recorded ambience of the studio in which the recording is made, may be naturally caught in the recording, and faithfully relayed into the listener's room, but no account can be taken of what will happen to it once it has been released from his speaker enclosures (or whatever kind of transmitting device should appear in the future). His room may be heavily furnished and draped so that high frequencies are absorbed and the liveliness of the sound deadened, or he may live in spartan surroundings in which the music will bounce from one bare wall to another, collecting spurious overtones and confusing echoes as it goes. Each individual tends to become accustomed to his listening surroundings, consciously or subconsciously making allowances for them for the sake of the music. 'Hi-finatics' often make the effort to ensure that their listening rooms are as acoustically negative as possible, but the line between over- and under-damping is a fine one, and personal taste will ensure that it varies from one listener to another. Having achieved a personal 'perfect' room acoustic, one will then begin to notice imperfections (real or imagined) in the recording venue itself, and these, furthermore, will certainly differ widely from one recording to the next and from company to company.

Satisfaction in the high fidelity world, then, is always a compromise. The 'perfect' recording does not, and cannot, exist because one man's 'perfect' is another's excruciating noise. Moreover, no person can know what another hears, or what his subjective reaction to a sound is based on.

Faced with these dead-ends, what can the future sound research technician do to justify his continued existence? By nature a restless perfectionist, we may be sure that he will find detail improvements to make in the recording and reproduction chains, but further major developments in improving recorded sound seem unlikely. His attention will doubtless turn instead to how to alter that sound again, to cater more and more minutely for listeners' personal tastes. So-called 'tone', 'presence' and 'musicality' controls have long graced the front panels of amplifiers and music centres (and even, many years ago, when music centres were called radiograms). These controls adjust the sound according to taste, but these adjustments almost always introduced distortion of some sort to a sound that was itself usually distorted. But, as we have seen, one person's bliss is another's dreadful row; many record enthusiasts have listened for a whole evening to grossly distorted sound that others would not tolerate for a moment. Why should these distortions not be put to use?

With a huge and ever-increasing range of electronic apparatus at his disposal, the sound researcher can take a recorded sound and alter it dramatically, but the time is not too distant when he will be able to reach back and alter the musician's very interpretations. Why should he be happy with, say, a singer's tempo for a song when, with the flick of one switch, he can speed it up or slow it down, and then, with the flick of another, electronically restore the result to its correct pitch? His experiments would ultimately lead to the tempo he liked best, and the pitch-rectifying circuit would then be fed into his computer for future automatic retrieval. Perhaps only parts of the song might benefit from such tempo manipulation – and the computer would be programmed to make the necessary adjustments automatically.

This would lead naturally (or unnaturally, if you prefer) to the similar adjustment of longer works so that one need no longer be satisfied with a conductor's performance of a symphony: his tempi could be altered according to taste or whim.

Studios habitually record onto multi-track tape, with sometimes as many as 32, or even 64, separate tracks being made available for individual manipulation by the recording and mixing engineers before the issue of the recording. Why should these numerous tracks not be made available direct to the customer so that he might adjust his play-back controls according to his personal taste? Perhaps a pop group's *second* guitarist's contribution may be of particular importance – boost it, then, so that not a nuance is missed, while the rest of the performance is left as a background or faded out altogether if required! Our conductor's symphonic performance, which we have already altered in the matter of tempo, may be subjected to balance changes. His apparent neglect of the tympani, for example, could be rectified, or, on a more personal note, the third trombone, who happens to be an acquaintance, may be spotlighted to solo prominence while the rest of the orchestra accompanies.

The dangers in this 'every man his own conductor and engineer' concept are obvious, yet if one chooses to abuse a recorded performance thus in the privacy of one's home, what harm is done? There might even be advantages in that a great conductor's performance of a work, fatally flawed for one listener by a momentary lapse of balance or an instant of unstable tempo, could be 'corrected' according to the taste of that listener, and the corrections consigned to the amplifier's computer for incorporation in all future playings of that recording – corrections which are furthermore cancellable at will!

The practising musician begins to seem superfluous, and so he may well become: computers can already be programmed to read the printed word, so why not printed music? This could then be synthesised into sound direct from the printed page, and an 'interpretation' formulated according to the taste of the listener. Taken to its logical conclusion, this would mean that every piece of music held in every participating library or archive throughout the world would be available, in modifiable sound, to any owner of the appropriate reproducing equipment. In addition to bypassing the musician, this would avoid all the distortions introduced by mechanical recording and reproduction, and by artists, and would obviate the need for the record industry itself. It would be a world in which hardware rules, and the private individual would be able to listen at will to *any* music from *any* period or culture, adjusting the performance precisely according to his own requirements. All he would need is a digital pad, a control panel, and an enquiring mind. A musical researcher, armed with knowledge of the performing and interpretational techniques of the period he is studying, would be able to recreate in perfect form any manuscript or published piece of music for immediate examination. The student, researching into early music hall songs, could reproduce any one of them at a moment's notice, and, with the selection of another circuit, have them performed in the style of the artist of his choice!

Whatever the development in recorded sound during the next few years, we may at least expect greater convenience in operation and greater fidelity to the original sound: goals the industry has striven for since its inception.

PERSONALIA

Some influential and important names in the history of the industry. For further references, see the Index.

Attwood, F E, joined English Decca in 1936 and retired as publicity manager on 31 October, 1958. He invented the slogans *ffrr* ('full frequency range recording') and *ffss* ('full frequency stereophonic sound') respectively in 1944 and 1958.

Barraud, Francis (1856–1924) – see Hall of Fame – Nipper.

Bell, Alexander Graham; Bell, Chichester – see Sections I and II.

Berliner, Emile – see Section III.

Bettini, Gianni, Italian inventor, born Novara, Italy, 1860. He was a lieutenant in the Italian cavalry. He moved to the USA in mid-1880s and married an American socialite. He privately recorded, on an Edison Phonograph which he himself had modified, many singers, authors, etc, from 1888, duplicating the recordings to order and selling them. He sold his business rights to Edison in 1902 and moved to Paris, where his cylinders were destroyed during World War I. From 1914 to 1917 he was war correspondent for *Le Gaulois*. He died in America in 1938.

Blumlein, Alan Dower, English inventor, born in London in 1903. He developed telephony at Standard Telephone and Cables from 1924 and joined UK Columbia on 29 March, 1929, to develop an all-British electrical recording system (since Columbia were still paying royalties to Western Electric). He designed and patented a stereophonic recording system and 78rpm disc cutter in 1931, using the vertical/lateral system. His recording of Mozart's *Jupiter* Symphony, with the London Philharmonic Orchestra conducted by Sir Thomas Beecham, recorded partly in stereo, was made on 19 January, 1934. Blumlein also developed a stereo film soundtrack in 1935, and a 405-line TV system for EMI. He died in an air crash in Warwickshire on 7 June, 1942, while testing radar equipment in a Halifax bomber.

Childs, Calvin G, American record producer with the Ohio and Columbia Phonograph companies and later recording director with Victor. He evolved a system of royalty payments and exclusive contracts with artists.

Clark, Alfred, American businessman, born in New York on 19 December, 1873. He worked in Edison's laboratory from 1889, inventing an improved hand crank and floating diaphragm soundbox in 1896. He joined Berliner that year and managed Berliner's Philadelphia retail shop during 1897. With W B Owen and the Gaisberg brothers he formed The Gramophone Co Ltd in 1897, then became head of Compagnie Française du Gramophone, Paris (founded May 1899), where he opened a studio and recorded many famous artists, offering strong competition to Pathé. He resigned on 22 January, 1908. He was chairman and managing director of The Gramophone Co from September 1930 and the first chairman of EMI in 1931; also managing director of EMI from 1931 to 1939. In April 1946 he was appointed the first President of EMI, but he retired that September and died in London on 16 June, 1950.

Culshaw, John Royds, English record producer, born 28 May, 1924. He joined Decca in 1946, first in the publicity department, then as producer, becoming manager and chief producer in 1954. He organised and carried out **the first complete recording of Wagner's *Ring* cycle** (1958–66), and about 30 other operas. In 1967 he was appointed Head of Music Programmes for BBC TV. Author of several books, including *Sergei Rachmaninoff* (1949), and *Ring Resounding* (1967), the latter being the history of his chief recording achievement. He died on 27 April, 1980, aged 55.

Easton, Edward D, the Supreme Court reporter who promoted interest in the Bell-Tainter Graphophone as a dictating machine. He was the first director of the Columbia Phonograph Co of Washington, DC, from January 1889 and president of the National Phonograph Association from 1890; later he became president of the American Graphophone Co. Died 1 May, 1915.

Edison, T A – see Section II.

Gaisberg, Fred, American musician of German extraction, born in Washington, DC, on 1 January, 1873. He made his first recording as a part-time accompanist for Columbia in 1890 with John York AtLee in *The Whistling Coon* and *The Mocking Bird*. He worked also with Tainter in 1893. On 23 July, 1898 he left New York for London to join The Gramophone Co as its first recording engineer and was thereafter responsible for many important recordings by Caruso, Tetrazini, Chaliapin, Elgar, Gigli, Schnabel, Fischer, and many others. He was EMI international artists' manager from 1931. Died in London on 2 September, 1951.

Gaisberg, William, brother of the above. He worked with Tainter in the Volta Graphophone Laboratory and gave technical assistance to Berliner in 1896. He and Fred opened the first recording studios in Philadelphia, William operating the equipment while Fred played the accompaniments. He moved with Fred to London in 1898; they worked jointly on many early recording sessions. On a mission to France in 1918 to record the sounds of war he was severely gassed. He returned to England but died on 5 November, 1918.

Goldmark, Dr Peter, Hungarian-born American electrical engineer, born 1907. He developed the $33\frac{1}{3}$ long playing disc for American Columbia in 1948 and later worked on cassette tapes and EVR (electronic video recording). He was killed in a road accident on 7 December, 1977.

Gouraud, Col Georges E, American recordist, born at Niagara Falls, New York, *c* 1842. He became Edison's chief European representative in Upper Norwood, South London, from 1878, where his house, 'Little Menlo' (named after Edison's laboratories at Menlo Park, New Jersey) became a centre of recording activities for many famous names of the 1880s and 1890s, including Gladstone, Sir Arthur Sullivan, Florence Nightingale, King Edward VII, Alfred, Lord Tennyson, etc. He was awarded the Congressional Medal of Honour in 1893. Edison severed contact with him that same year, but Gouraud continued his interest in sound recording until his death at Brighton, Sussex, in 1912.

Haddy, Arthur C, OBE, English recording engineer for Decca from 1938, responsible for developing *ffrr* for commercial use (after its military applications in World War II); he also worked on the improvement of stereophonic disc and tape quality.

Harrison, H C – see Maxfield.

Hunting, Russell, American recording artist (as 'Michael Casey') and businessman. He was editor of *Phonoscope* from 1896, and made many monologue recordings in 1898. He held a succession of important posts: Edison Bell recording director (1901), Zonophone recording supervisor (1904), head of recording department at the Sterling Record Co (1904), formed the Russell Hunting Co Ltd with Louis Sterling (1905), director general of Pathé (1908); he was then sent by Pathé to New York in 1910 to set up a laboratory and a factory.

Johnson, Eldridge R, American inventor and founder of the Victor Talking Machine Co (see Company Profile – Victor). Johnson invented the 'negative' master and the tapered pick-up arm; developed the clockwork Phonograph motor (1895), the 'Trade Mark' model sound box (with Alfred Clark, 1897), and the internal horn 'Victrola' (1906), a name which became so popular that the '-ola' suffix was adopted by many other companies to draw attention to what they considered to be technically advanced machines; the word 'Radiola' is used to this day in Russia for the combined radio/record player. Johnson, with Calvin Childs, developed the exclusive artist contract. He was appointed to the Board of The Gramophone Co in September 1920 and resigned in December 1927. He died in 1945.

Legge, Walter, English record producer, born 1 June, 1906. He joined HMV in 1927 as a classical writer, and evolved and organised HMV's and EMI's Society series of specialist music (1930–9). During World War II he was in control of the concert activities of ENSA, simultaneously filling the post of Artist and Repertoire Manager at EMI. He formed several concert-giving bodies under the name 'Philharmonia' (Orchestra, Chorus, etc), and during his years at EMI he was responsible for recording very many of the greatest artists of the time. In 1964 he left EMI and entered semi-retirement

in Switzerland and France. He died on 22 March, 1979.

Lewis, Sir Edward, English businessman, born 1900. He was chairman of Decca at his death on 29 January, 1980. (See Company Profile – Decca.)

Lindström, Carl (1867–1932), owner of a small workshop in Germany which, on 1 February, 1904, was purchased by Max Strauss and Heinrich Zunz to become Carl Lindström GmbH, with Strauss as managing director. The company was reformed as Carl Lindström AG in June 1908 and amalgamated with Beka Records AG in August 1910. He launched the 'Parlophon' label in Europe in March 1911. With the purchase that summer of Fonotipia Ltd, Lindström controlled Beka Grand, Beka Meister, Fonotipia, Jumbo, Odeon and Parlophon labels. Carl Lindström (London) Ltd was formed on 26 March, 1913. Lindström's Warsaw factory was closed by the Russians, and the British company, together with Fonotipia Ltd, was wound up by order of the Board of Trade on 8 August, 1916. In March 1920 the Transoceanic Trading Co of Holland took over Lindström's factories in France, Spain, Argentina, Chile, Italy, Switzerland and Brazil, and it formed the Parlophone Co Ltd in London on 30 August, 1923. This passed to the control of UK Columbia in 1925. The name Carl Lindström AG (GmbH from 14 October, 1969) was finally absorbed when that company and Electrola GmbH became EMI Electrola GmbH on 30 March, 1972.

Mapleson, Lionel (1865–1937), English librarian of the Metropolitan Opera Co in New York. He used an Edison improved cylinder Phonograph to record live performances at 'The Met' between 1899 and 1903. The recording horn was suspended out of sight behind the proscenium arch above the stage, so the sound was poor, and, furthermore, subject to heavy surface noise. Many of Mapleson's recordings have been destroyed by deterioration. He presented his collection of unique cylinders to W H Seltsam, founder of the International Record Collectors' Club, who issued a number in 78 and LP transcripts.

Maxfield, Joseph P, and **Harrison**, H C. They were the principal designers of the Western Electric System of electrical recording, working jointly for that company on experiments from 1919 to 1924. From their research was developed the Victrola 'Orthophonic' (the first Phonograph to use the logarithmic horn) and Columbia's 'Viva-Tonal' machine of 1925. Maxfield and Harrison's paper *Methods of High Quality Recording and Reproduction of Music and Speech Based on Telephone Research* appeared in 1926 in *Transactions of the American Institute of Electrical Engineers.*

Owen, William Barry, New York businessman, director of the National Gramophone Co from October 1896, who was sent to London by Berliner in 1897 to sell Gramophone rights. Unsuccessful, he resigned, and sought backers for his own company, The Gramophone Co, which he established in Maiden Lane, London, in 1898 to import machines and to make local recordings. He was succeeded as managing director by T Birnbaum in April 1904 and resigned from the Board in March 1906. In 1899 he purchased the picture of the dog and trumpet from Francis Barraud (see Hall of Fame – Nipper). Owen died on 19 March, 1914.

Pathé Brothers, Charles and Emile – see Company Profile – Pathé.

Poulsen, Valdemar, Danish scientist, born 1869. He invented **the world's first wire recorder** in Denmark in 1898. This machine, the Telegraphone, led ultimately to the development of the tape recorder. With some American colleagues he formed the short-lived American Telegraphone Co in 1903. Poulsen died in 1942.

Prescott, F M, born *c* 1865. American export/import merchant in Phonographic goods, dealing at first mainly with Edison's products but later with Zon-O-Phone. He was managing director of the International Zonophon Co from 1901, whose headquarters were in Berlin; then president and general manager of the International Talking Machine Co from 1904, marketing German-made machines and discs under the Odeon trade mark. These Odeon discs were **the first double-sided records.**

Seaman, Frank, American businessman, founder (in 1896) and president of the National Gramophone Co of New York, exclusive US distributors of Berliner's Gramophone. Seaman was named as treasurer when the company was reconstituted as the National Gramophone Corp in March 1899, severing its Berliner link in September that year and marketing instead the Zon-O-Phone machine. Seaman, with F M Prescott, established the International Zonophone Co in 1901.

Sterling, Sir Louis, American businessman, born 16 May, 1879. He sold newspapers in New York before becoming an exporter/importer in 1900. He joined G&T, moving to England in 1903, and became manager of British Zonophone Co from 1 January, 1904. He formed the Sterling Record Co in November 1904 (registered 17 December that year), which changed its name to Russell Hunting Co Ltd in 1905, marketing the Sterling record and acting as agents for Odeon and Fonotipia from 1906. Sterling was managing director of the Rena Mfg Co from December 1908, founder and sales manager (1909), then general manager (1914) of Columbia Graphophone Co, becoming managing director of the English company when it separated from the American Columbia companies in 1923. He secured a licence for Columbia to use the Western Electric electrical recording process and acquired control of American Columbia in 1925. Named managing director of EMI upon its formation in 1931, he was knighted in June 1931 for his services to the Empire, **the first record industry personality to be knighted**. He donated his large collection of books and manuscripts to London University, and died on 3 June, 1958, aged 79.

Tainter, Charles Sumner, English instrument-maker and professor who, with the Bell brothers (see Sections I and II), formed the Volta Laboratory Association research department in Washington, DC, in 1880. With Chichester Bell he worked on developing first the telephone, then Edison's Phonograph, building the first Graphophone and describing a method of compressed-air amplification in 1881. They made experimental vertical-cut discs in 1885.

Tainter (with the Bell brothers) organised the Volta Graphophone Co in West Virginia in 1886. Tainter joined the American Graph- ophone Co of Washington, DC (a subsidiary of the Bell Telephone Co), in 1897 as a researcher. He died in 1936.

BIBLIOGRAPHY

Appleyard, Rollo, *Charles Parsons – His Life and Work*, Constable, London, 1933

Batten, Joe, *Joe Batten's Book – The Story of Sound Recording*, Rockliffe, London, 1956

Bauer, Roberto, *The New Catalogue of Historical Records, 1898–1908/9*, Sidgwick & Jackson, London, 1947

Bawden, Liz-Anne (Ed), *The Oxford Companion to Film*, OUP, London, 1976

Bescoby-Chambers, J, *The Archives of Sound*, Oakwood Press, Surrey, 1965

Burkitt, Alan, and **Williams**, Elaine, *The Silicon Civilisation*, W H Allen, London, 1980

Caruso, Dorothy, *Enrico Caruso – his Life and Death*, T Werner Laurie, London, 1955

Cross, Nigel, *A Survey of Fanzines, Brio*, vol 18/2, Autumn/Winter 1981 (International Association of Music Libraries, London)

Foreman, Lewis, *Systematic Discography*, Clive Bingley, London, 1974

Gammond, Peter, and **Horricks**, Raymond (Eds), *The Music Goes Round and Round*, Quartet, London, 1980

Gelatt, Roland, *The Fabulous Phonograph, 1877–1977* (2nd edition), Cassell, London, 1977

Goldman, Albert, *Elvis*, Allen Lane, London, 1981

Hurst, P G, *The Golden Age Recorded* (2nd edition), Oakwood Press, London, 1963

Josephson, Matthew, *Edison – A biography*, Eyre & Spottiswoode, London, 1961

Kennedy, Michael, *Portrait of Elgar*, OUP, London, 1968

Ledbetter, Gordon T, *The Great Irish Tenor (John McCormack)*, Duckworth, London, 1977

Moore, Jerrold Northrop, *A Voice in Time*, Hamish Hamilton, London, 1976

Moore, Jerrold Northrop, *Elgar on Record*, EMI/OUP, London, 1974

Moseley, Sydney A, and **Baiton Chapple** H J, *Television To-Day and Tomorrow*, Sir Isaac Pitman & Sons Ltd, London, 1930

Murrells, Joseph, *The Book of Golden Discs*, Barrie & Jenkins, London, 1974; (2nd edition) 1978

Phonographs & Gramophones, Royal Scottish Museum, Edinburgh, 1977

Robertson, Patrick, *The Guinness Book of Film Facts and Feats*, Guinness Superlatives, Enfield, 1980

Rust, Brian, *The American Record Label Book from the 19th century through 1942*, Arlington House, New York, 1978

Rust, Brian, *Discography of Historical Records on Cylinders and 78s*, Greenwood Press, Westport, Connecticut, and London, 1979

Rust, Brian, *Gramophone Records of the First World War*: a reprint of the HMV Catalogue and supplements of 1914–18, David & Charles, Newton Abbot; London; Vermont; Vancouver, 1974

Scholes, Percy A, *The First Book of the Gramophone Record* (2nd edition), OUP, London, 1927

Young, Percy M, *Elgar OM*, White Lion, London, 1973

INDEX

Illustrations are identified by *italics*; important references are given in **bold** type. Where the names of record companies and prominent personalities occur repeatedly in the text, only major references are given.